Building Custom Tasks for SQL Server Integration Services

The Power of .NET for ETL for SQL Server 2019 and Beyond

Second Edition

Andy Leonard

Apress®

Building Custom Tasks for SQL Server Integration Services: The Power of .NET for ETL for SQL Server 2019 and Beyond

Andy Leonard
Farmville, VA, USA

ISBN-13 (pbk): 978-1-4842-6481-2
https://doi.org/10.1007/978-1-4842-6482-9

ISBN-13 (electronic): 978-1-4842-6482-9

Managing Director, Apress Media LLC: Welmoed Spahr
Acquisitions Editor: Jonathan Gennick
Development Editor: Laura Berendson
Coordinating Editor: Jill Balzano

Cover image designed by Freepik (www.freepik.com)

Distributed to the book trade worldwide by Springer Science+Business Media LLC, 1 New York Plaza, Suite 4600, New York, NY 10004. Phone 1-800-SPRINGER, fax (201) 348-4505, e-mail orders-ny@springer-sbm. com, or visit www.springeronline.com. Apress Media, LLC is a California LLC and the sole member (owner) is Springer Science + Business Media Finance Inc (SSBM Finance Inc). SSBM Finance Inc is a **Delaware** corporation.

For information on translations, please e-mail booktranslations@springernature.com; for reprint, paperback, or audio rights, please e-mail bookpermissions@springernature.com.

Apress titles may be purchased in bulk for academic, corporate, or promotional use. eBook versions and licenses are also available for most titles. For more information, reference our Print and eBook Bulk Sales web page at http://www.apress.com/bulk-sales.

Any source code or other supplementary material referenced by the author in this book is available to readers on GitHub via the book's product page, located at www.apress.com/9781484264812. For more detailed information, please visit http://www.apress.com/source-code.

Printed on acid-free paper

Table of Contents

About the Author

Andy Leonard is Chief Data Engineer at Enterprise Data & Analytics, an SSIS trainer, consultant, developer of the Data Integration Lifecycle Management (DILM) Suite, a Business Intelligence Markup Language (Biml) developer, and BimlHero. He is also a SQL Server database and data warehouse developer, community mentor, engineer, and occasional farmer. Andy is co-author of *SQL Server Integration Services Design Patterns* and *The Biml Book* and author of *Data Integration Life Cycle Management with SSIS* and the *Stairway to Integration Services* series at SQLServerCentral.com.

Acknowledgments

This small book would not have been possible without the help of others. Kirk Haselden, author of Microsoft SQL Server 2005 Integration Services (Sams, 2006, amazon.com/ Microsoft-Server-2005-Integration-Services/dp/0672327813), wrote extensively in this book about developing custom tasks for SQL Server Integration Services (SSIS). Matt Masson's blog (mattmasson.com) includes several posts tagged "extensions" which cover the topic of custom SSIS task development.

Thank you, Luther Atkinson, for proofreading and providing feedback on the manuscript, and for your encouragement.

I owe my coworkers at Enterprise Data & Analytics (entdna.com) a debt of gratitude for their encouragement and for covering for me when I stayed up too late trying to figure out how to make this revised code work. We have an awesome team!

Donald Farmer inspires me every time we interact. As Principal Program Manager at Microsoft, Donald worked extensively with SSIS and helped shape the product. Donald continues to shape software by providing vendors unique strategic guidance at TreeHive Strategy (treehivestrategy.com).

I am certain there are many excellent editors in this business. Jonathan Gennick is the best with whom I have had the privilege to work.

Finally, I thank my family for their understanding. My children Stevie Ray, Emma, and Riley who live at home at the time of this writing, and Manda and Penny who have children of their own.

Thanks especially to Christy, to whom this book is dedicated, my wife, my love. Thank you.

Foreword

Reading this book in preparation to write this foreword was a blast from the past for me. Some of the function names for custom tasks, the code, the GAC, the various steps to getting the custom task into the designer. All that brings back a rich memory of what it was like when we first built Integration Services. The year 2020 marks the 20-year anniversary of when we started coding SSIS.

SSIS started as a small team with the purpose of replacing Data Transformation Services (DTS) with something more. What exactly, it was not clear. But we all knew that the new product needed a more robust data processing engine, better control flow, and a richer design and runtime experience, and notably, we needed to address some of the design flaws with DTS. Without reminiscing too much here, it is fair to say that we set out to create a lasting, flexible, extensible, and feature-rich product that would sufficiently address enterprise data processing needs.

We ended up scrapping DTS completely until we realized that DTS actually did some pretty cool stuff that we did not support and that because we had made some design decisions to address the DTS shortcomings, we had severely limited the ability for our DTS customers to upgrade their existing packages. The answer? Embed DTS into SSIS. This was the first time, of many, that the intentional and deliberate extensibility design in SSIS to support creating custom tasks was not only important, but essential. We were able to programmatically embed the entire DTS product in a custom task within a few days in what became known as the Execute DTS Package Task!

Andy makes mention here of my contribution to the annals of SSIS documentation. I wanted to share a few things about that before moving on to highly recommending Andy's book.

First, my contributions to the SSIS project have often been overstated. I have noticed that because my name is associated with that book, I am sometimes primarily associated with the product's successes. There were many on the team who did amazing things: Ashvini Sharma, Matt David (Technical Editor for my books), Mike Blaszczak, Kamal Hathi, Donald Farmer, Slobodan Bojanic (code reviewer for my books), James Howey, Michael Entin, Runying Mao, Silviu Guea, Nick Berezansky, Sergei Ivanov, Mark Durley, Euan Garden, Anjan Das, Bill Baker, Jeff Bernhardt, Bryan Hartman, Craig Guyer,

Ranjeeta Nanda, Ovidiu Burlacu, and a few others whom I'm sure I've missed! SSIS was truly a team effort that resulted in a product that continues to evolve, improve, far outgrow, and outperform our initial vision. It was an honor to be a part of that team.

When I started writing that book, I had severe misgivings; the kind of self-doubt that I've since learned is quite common among authors. From the very beginning, I asked myself these kinds of questions: "Is this worth the time?" "Will anybody even buy the book?" "Is there any value in me doing this thing?" "Will people just see the errors and faults, or will they appreciate the effort and passion that I'm pouring into this?"

Early in the process, a group of people that wanted to also write an SSIS book reached out to me and asked if they could have my table of contents for my book as a starting point for their book. I said, of course. My reasoning was that the more people writing about SSIS, the better adoption it would have.

As I was preparing to publish, the SSIS user education team approached me. For various reasons, they were behind in documenting SSIS and needed a jumpstart. They asked if they could have my manuscript as a starting point for the SSIS books online documentation. I said yes, of course. I was honored. Much of what I had written became Books Online content before I even published my book.

Why do people write technical books? There are many reasons. Some more valid than others. It is certainly *not* to make a lot of money. For me, personally, I had a passion for SSIS, and I wanted the community to have as much help absorbing the product as possible. And so, it was ironic to receive comments about my book on Amazon such as "You can get everything in this book from books online" and "This is not a tutorial."

So, what's your point Kirk? Of the technical authors I know and with whom I have had the pleasure of associating, they are genuinely passionate about the products they document. It was not fame, notoriety, career advancement, or money that truly drove them, or me, to write. It was love of the product and the desire to help people adopt and be successful with it.

Andy is no different. There is nobody who knows, uses, teaches, and understands SSIS better than Andy Leonard. And I know that he personally writes these books out of the passion he has around helping people be successful at what they do using SSIS.

So, as you read, use, and learn from this book, keep all this in mind. If you find what you believe is a fault or a shortcoming here, remember, this is a labor of love. It is a product of passion combined with kindness with the intent of helping you be successful. Writing a technical reference is just plain hard work! It is not just words, it is code; it has to pass not just the critical eye of you the reader, but the tyranny of the demo code compiler as well.

And, when you find that this book has been essential in your SSIS pursuits, remember to reach out to thank Andy for all the hard work. That is the best reward a technical author can experience.

I cannot remember the first time I met Andy. I am fairly sure we have never met in person. However, over the years, we have conversed through various channels and come to know each other virtually. I have watched Andy's training, read some of his books, and watched as he has firmly established himself as one of the most knowledgeable experts on enterprise data and analytics generally and SSIS specifically.

This book is a deep dive into a subject that requires such a treatment.

In several places in this book, Andy makes the disclaimer that he is no C# programmer. Do not let him fool you, and do not let that dissuade you from using this reference. The guidance given here is both functional and unique. Building a custom component to plug into any complex system is hard. Building an SSIS custom task can be confusing, and it is not uncommon to hit roadblocks that have no immediately obvious solution. I know. Even though I was part of the team that designed custom task architecture, I still ran into problems implementing them. Andy walks you through each step in meticulous detail while calling out the gotchas that are easy to overlook.

Andy is an SSIS expert. If you want to extend SSIS to do something that it currently does not support, building a custom task is one powerful and highly flexible way to do that. This book does not just capture the books online details. It documents the things that you cannot learn there or anywhere else for that matter about how to build an SSIS custom task.

Best of luck in your Custom Task adventures!

—Kirk Haselden

Author's First Edition Thoughts

This small book was originally written as a series of blog posts hosted on the Linchpin People website in 2012.

I have delivered SQL Server Integration Services (SSIS) solutions for over ten years at the time of this writing. Before SSIS, I worked with Data Transformation Services (DTS) for a couple years. Although SSIS has supported custom tasks and components since its 2005 release, I initially recommended that my consulting clients *not* develop custom SSIS tasks and components. Why?

1. The source code needs to be maintained and supported throughout the lifecycle of SSIS solutions that use the custom tasks and components.

2. One needs to invest in Visual Studio Professional (roughly $1,000USD) to build the code.

3. One needs fairly serious .Net developer skills to understand the intricacies of building a Visual Studio toolbox component.

My first concern stands but with a much lower barrier to entry – at least cost-wise. When Microsoft® released free versions of Visual Studio (Visual Studio Express and, more recently, Visual Studio Community Edition), my second concern lapsed once I learned I could use the free tools to build a custom SSIS task (the topic of this book).

This book addresses my third concern.

Writing the blog series and revisiting the series to produce this book was fun for me. I pray you enjoy reading it as much as I enjoyed writing it.

—AndyFarmville, VirginiaApril 2017

Author's Second Edition Thoughts

I was pleasantly surprised by the response to the first edition of this book. Initially intended to be a self-published work, Jonathan Gennick, my (excellent) editor at Apress, talked me into sending him the manuscript just as I was ready to click the Publish button at Amazon.

Many readers communicated that they liked the length of the manuscript. They shared, "I can read this in an afternoon." I envy their reading speed.

I type these thoughts on the last day of the last November in the 20-teens. After a (book-) writing hiatus that has lasted over two years, I realize

1. It's time to update the content.

2. It's time to update the example.

As my friend and brother Chris Yates is apt to say, "Let's roll!"

—AndyFarmville, VirginiaDecember 2020

CHAPTER 1

The Story of This Book

Occasionally, my engineering curiosity gets the better of me, and I ask myself questions like, "Self, do I think such-and-such is possible?" Most of the time, these questions lead to some brain exercise and little else of use. Sometimes, some good comes from the effort.

One day in late summer 2012, I asked myself, "Do you think it is possible to create a custom SSIS task using Visual Basic Express?" Crazy question, right?

The short answer is: Yes.

Why is this significant? Because the Visual Studio IDE (Integrated Development Environment) is now free. This means if you have a license for SQL Server, you do not need to spend more money to extend SSIS with custom tasks and components. You may *want* to spend money to obtain some of the tools and features of other versions of Visual Studio, though.

I revised the blog series to produce this book. Experienced developers will notice I used Visual Studio 2019 Community Edition and targeted the SQL Server 2019 Integration Services (SSIS 2019) versions of .Net Framework.

Tribal Knowledge

I ran into some issues along the way. Initially, I didn't know if the issues were related to the free Express Edition. It is difficult to work through issues when you do not know something is possible. It took time and determination, but I worked through enough issues to write a series of blog posts, which became the inspiration for this book.

In 2012, I was admittedly an out-of-practice software developer. Before the .Net era, I was a Microsoft Certified Solutions Developer (MCSD). For you, young whipper-snappers, I achieved that certification back in the good ol' days when the years began with "1" and we had to carve our own chips out of wood. #GetOffMyLawn ☺

© Andy Leonard 2021
A. Leonard, *Building Custom Tasks for SQL Server Integration Services*,
https://doi.org/10.1007/978-1-4842-6482-9_1

Some things I encountered are dreadfully obvious to experienced software developers. After years of developing software, those experienced developers possess tribal knowledge – they don't remember all the stuff they know. So, when a relative .Net n00b (like me) asks a question, they assume I've done all the things they would have done by the intellectual equivalent of rote muscle memory.

I had not done all those things (did I mention I was a .Net n00b?).

One result was the things that tripped me up were relatively minor. It was all well and good once I knew the tricks, but the tricks are considered so basic that people rarely share them when answering forum questions. It is assumed that if you build Visual Studio plugins and assemblies aimed for the Global Assembly Cache (GAC), you must know the essentials.

If you are not a .Net n00b, you probably know these essentials. But that did not apply to me at the outset.

Now, I am no slouch when it comes to coding. But I was also no longer a professional software developer in 2012. Before .Net arrived on the scene, I developed software. I already mentioned the MCSD certification. I learned BASIC in 1975 and began writing Visual Basic when version 2.0 was released in 1992. Many VB programmers never made the leap to Object-Oriented Programming (OOP) first supported by VB 4 (if memory serves), but I did. Modeling objects via classes made sense to me and has served me well in the years since. It even led me to the concept of design patterns which have some application in data integration development with SSIS.

I've since made the leap to C#, developing the tools and utilities found in the DILM Suite using C#.

One difference between this edition and the previous edition is I've switched the source code to C#.

A Starting Point

My goal in this book is to produce a template that anyone can use as a starting point for creating a custom SSIS task using the free version of the Visual Studio IDE. In the chapters that follow, I will demonstrate one way to achieve this.

For development, I am using a virtual machine running Windows Server 2019 Datacenter. The VM is configured with four CPUs (although you do not need four CPUs) and 32GB RAM (in the first edition of this book, the VM had 8GB RAM; I recommend a minimum of 4GB RAM). SQL Server 2019 Developer Edition is installed along with the Visual Studio 2019 Community.

The Problem We Are Trying to Solve

What is the problem we are trying to solve? This is always an important question. We're trying to solve *two* problems at once:

1. Document the steps necessary to build a relatively simple custom SSIS task.

2. Build a useful custom SSIS task.

The SSIS Catalog is an awesome piece of software engineering. However, there are gaps in the functionality provided by the SSIS Catalog – especially for enterprises practicing Data Integration Lifecycle Management (DILM) and/or DevOps. One of the gaps is a limitation of the SSIS Execute Package Task. Developers cannot select an SSIS Package in another project.

The Execute Catalog Package Task that we will build in this exercise will allow us to do just that: start an SSIS Package that resides in an SSIS Catalog. Is this a complete, production-ready implementation of SSIS Catalog Package execution functionality? Goodness no! This is a basic example of a custom SSIS task. But since you are building the functionality, you can extend it at will. I *want* you to extend it!

Updates to the 2019 Edition

There are differences between the 2019 and previous editions. For one, the the sample code is written in C# instead of Visual Basic. For another, in this edition, Azure DevOps supplants source control. What that means is that

- Git replaces Team Foundation Server.

- Using Git impacts chapter order and flow; the local Git repository (repo) is created *first*.

Read on then, to learn about creating custom tasks in C# using modern version control with Git.

CHAPTER 2

Preparing the Environment

One of the first things martial arts students are taught is how to fall. Why? So they don't hurt themselves. Before we begin developing this task, I want you to know: you are going to experience failures. Tests will fail, code will not behave as anticipated, and things will go wrong. When they do, I want you to accept a couple universal truths of software development:

1. Failure is normal.

2. How to recover.

I cannot overemphasize the need for lifecycle management, of which source control is central. I use Microsoft Azure DevOps, but feel free to use any of the excellent source control solutions available. At the time of this writing, Azure DevOps is free for teams of five or less. Source control is your number one method for code recovery. Do it. (You have been warned.)

Creating an Azure DevOps Account

Before you can create an Azure DevOps project, you need an Azure DevOps account. You may create an Azure DevOps account by visiting dev.azure.com. At the time of this writing, basic Azure DevOps Services for individuals are free – with some limitations – for up to five users, as shown in Figure 2-1:

5

© Andy Leonard 2021
A. Leonard, *Building Custom Tasks for SQL Server Integration Services*,
https://doi.org/10.1007/978-1-4842-6482-9_2

Azure DevOps Services	Azure DevOps Server

INDIVIDUAL SERVICES

Azure Pipelines

1 Free Microsoft-hosted CI/CD
1 Free Self-Hosted CI/CD

Start free >

- 1 hosted job with 1,800 minutes per month for CI/CD and 1 self-hosted job with unlimited minutes per month

- Then $40 per extra Microsoft-hosted CI/CD parallel job and $15 per extra self-hosted CI/CD parallel job with unlimited minutes

Azure Artifacts

2 GB free,
then starting at $2 per GB

Start free >

- Industry-leading NuGet Server

- Support for Maven, npm, and Python packages

- Upstream sources to help protect open-source dependancies

- Integrated with Azure Pipelines

- Sophisticated access controls

Basic Plan

First 5 users free,
then $6 per user per month

Start free >

- **Azure Pipelines:** Includes the free offer from INDIVIDUAL SERVICES

- **Azure Boards:** Work item tracking and Kanban boards

- **Azure Repos:** Unlimited private Git repos

- **Azure Artifacts:** 2 GB free

- Load testing (20,000 VUMs/month)

Figure 2-1. *Azure DevOps pricing for individual services (at the time of this writing)*

Once you have created an Azure DevOps account and configure an organization, you may create an Azure DevOps project.

Creating an Azure DevOps Project

There are a number of locations in Azure DevOps from which you may begin creating an Azure DevOps project. At the time of this writing, each displays a "+ New project" button, as shown in Figure 2-2:

Figure 2-2. *The New project button*

Clicking the New project button opens the "Create new project" blade, shown in Figure 2-3:

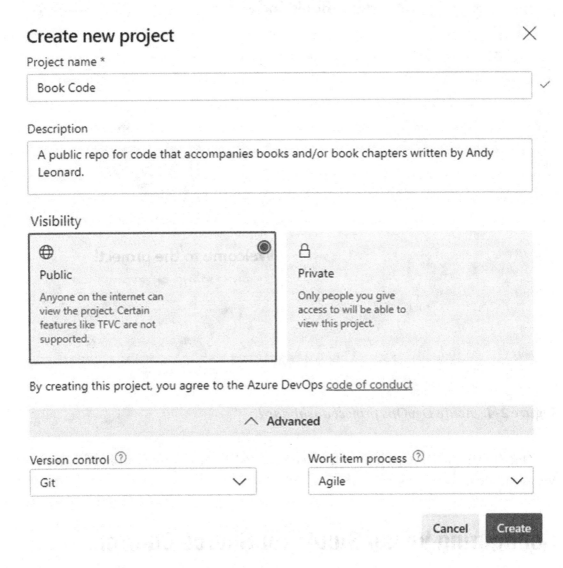

Figure 2-3. *The Create new project blade*

In this example, I created a public project named "Book Code" using Git Version Control and the Agile Work item process. Once the project is created, a dashboard is available as shown in Figure 2-4:

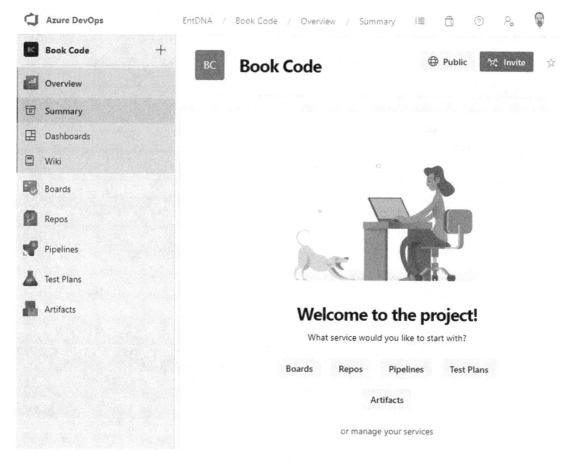

Figure 2-4. *Azure DevOps project dashboard*

Once the Azure DevOps project has been created, we may configure and connect Visual Studio to use the new project.

Configuring Visual Studio for Source Control

Open Configure Visual Studio Source Control options by clicking Tools ➤ Options as shown in Figure 2-5:

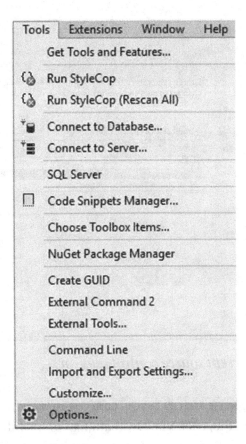

Figure 2-5. *Opening Tools ➤ Options*

When the Options window displays, expand the Source Control node, and select Plug-in Selection. Select your source control plug-in from the "Current source control plug-in" dropdown as shown in Figure 2-6:

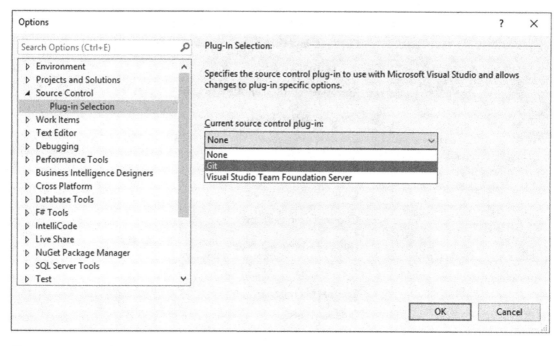

Figure 2-6. *Selecting current source control plug-in*

If you are new to Git, please visit `git-scm.com/doc` to learn more.

If you are using Git like me, click View ➤ Team Explorer as shown in Figure 2-7:

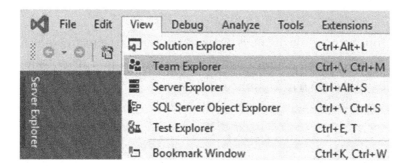

Figure 2-7. *Opening Team Explorer*

When Team Explorer displays, click the Manage Connections link and then click the "Connect to a Project..." button as shown in Figure 2-8:

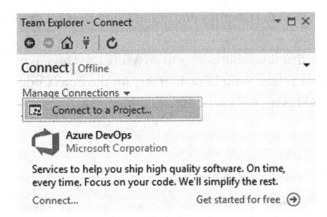

Figure 2-8. *Connecting to an Azure DevOps Project*

You may need to configure a new server and new connection to a Team Project during this step. Once configured, use Team Explorer to select the Team Project. My team project is named "Book Code," as seen in Figure 2-9:

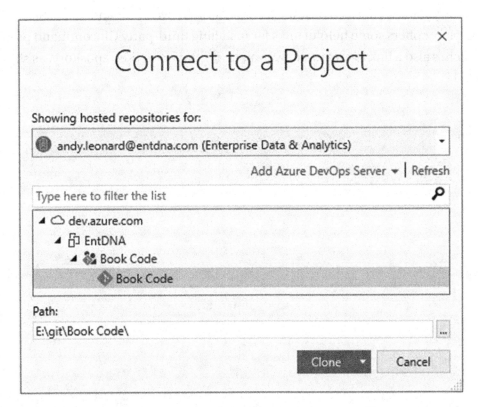

Figure 2-9. *Connecting to an Azure DevOps Project named Book Code*

Click the Clone button to copy the code in the Azure DevOps project into the Path listed in the dialog.

If this is your very first time connecting to an Azure DevOps Git repository (or "repo"), you may be surprised to find the directory for the Book Code Git repo almost empty at this time, as shown in Figure 2-10:

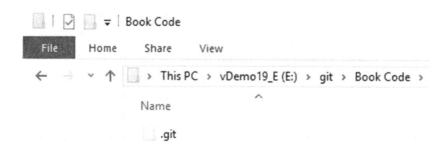

Figure 2-10. *Viewing local repo contents*

If this is your first time establishing a connection between Git and Visual Studio, Team Explorer offers some helpful links for installing third-party Git command prompt tools. There's also a link to create a new project or solution in this repository, as shown in Figure 2-11:

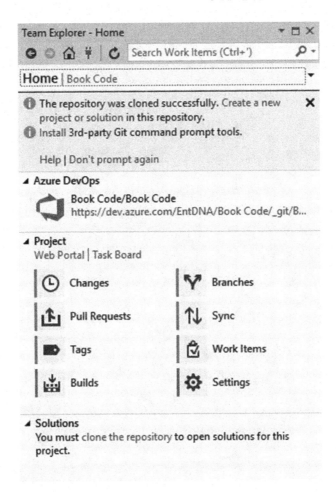

Figure 2-11. *Team Explorer*

Note the message in Team Explorer: "The repository was cloned successfully." The next message reads, "Create a new project or solution in this repository."

Conclusion

At this point in development, we have

- Created and configured an Azure DevOps project

- Connected Visual Studio to the Azure DevOps project

- Cloned the Azure DevOps Git repo locally

Visual Studio is now configured and connected to the new Git repo and ready for a new Visual Studio project.

CHAPTER 3

Creating the Assembly Project

If you followed the previous chapter and set up Azure DevOps or some other source control for your project, good! If not, you may add the assembly we build in this section to source control later, *but* if you plan to use Git, you may regret skipping the previous chapter.

Creating a custom SSIS task begins with creating a .Net assembly. We engage in practices that differ from many .Net development projects because we are creating a control that will be used in other Visual Studio projects, specifically, SSIS projects.

In this chapter, we take steps to establish the foundation of our project while considering the following steps. The very first step is how we open the Visual Studio IDE. If Visual Studio is open, please close it before continuing.

Opening Visual Studio IDE

I can hear you thinking, "Hold on a minute, Andy. Do you propose to start by telling us *how to open Visual Studio?*" Yes. Yes, I do. "Why?" I'm glad you asked. If you are new to .Net development and seeking answers to questions about developing a custom SSIS task (or similar code), this is one of the tricky things that real software developers do not remember to tell you. They are not intentionally leaving stuff out to trip you up, nor are they bad people; they simply do not remember making changes to their development environments to support this kind of development.

When you open Visual Studio, right-click Visual Studio in the Windows Start menu, hover over "More," and then click "Run as Administrator" as shown in Figure 3-1:

© Andy Leonard 2021
A. Leonard, *Building Custom Tasks for SQL Server Integration Services*,
https://doi.org/10.1007/978-1-4842-6482-9_3

Figure 3-1. *Run Visual Studio as Administrator*

You do not *have* to take this step. But taking this step will save you time and effort later. Why? Later we will configure Build operations to copy output files to the Global Assembly Cache (GAC), which will require elevated permissions.

When you click Run Visual Studio as Administrator, you will be prompted to confirm that you wish to run Visual Studio as shown in Figure 3-2:

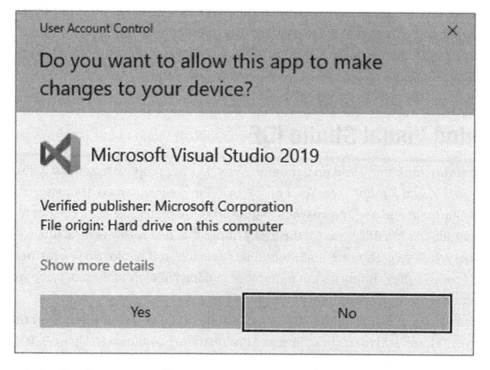

Figure 3-2. *Confirm you really want to run Visual Studio as administrator*

Once the Visual Studio startup screen displays, click the "Create a new project" tile to begin a new project as shown in Figure 3-3:

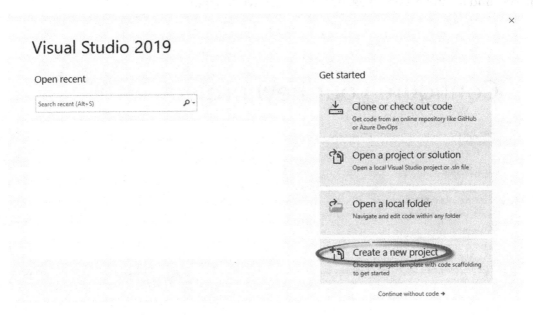

Figure 3-3. *Start a new project*

When the "Create a new project" window displays, search for, and then select, a C# Class Library (.Net Framework) project type, or in the .Net language of your choosing. I chose C# for the language and named the project ExecuteCatalogPackageTask as shown in Figure 3-4:

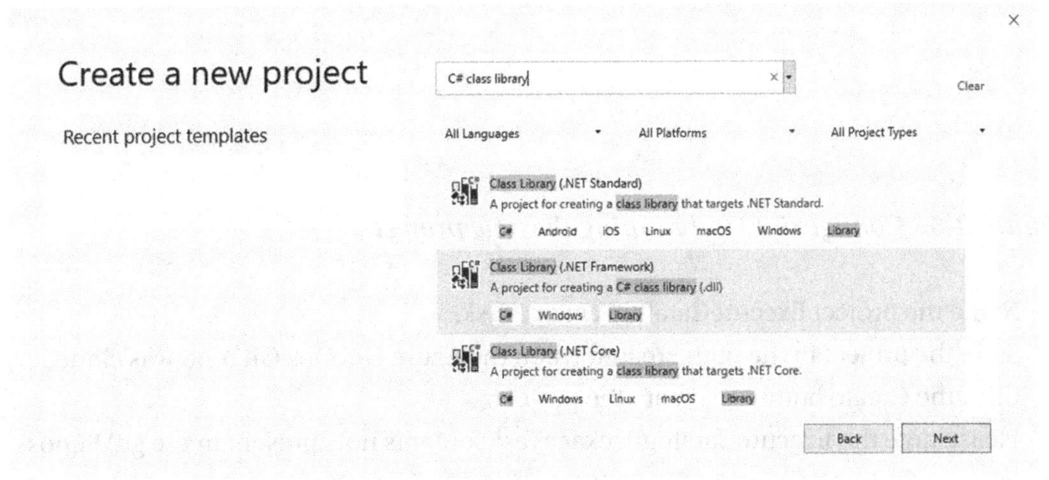

Figure 3-4. *Selecting a project type*

Select "Class Library (.NET Framework)" and click the Next button.

When the "Configure your new project" window displays, enter a name for the project and set the project files location as shown in Figure 3-5:

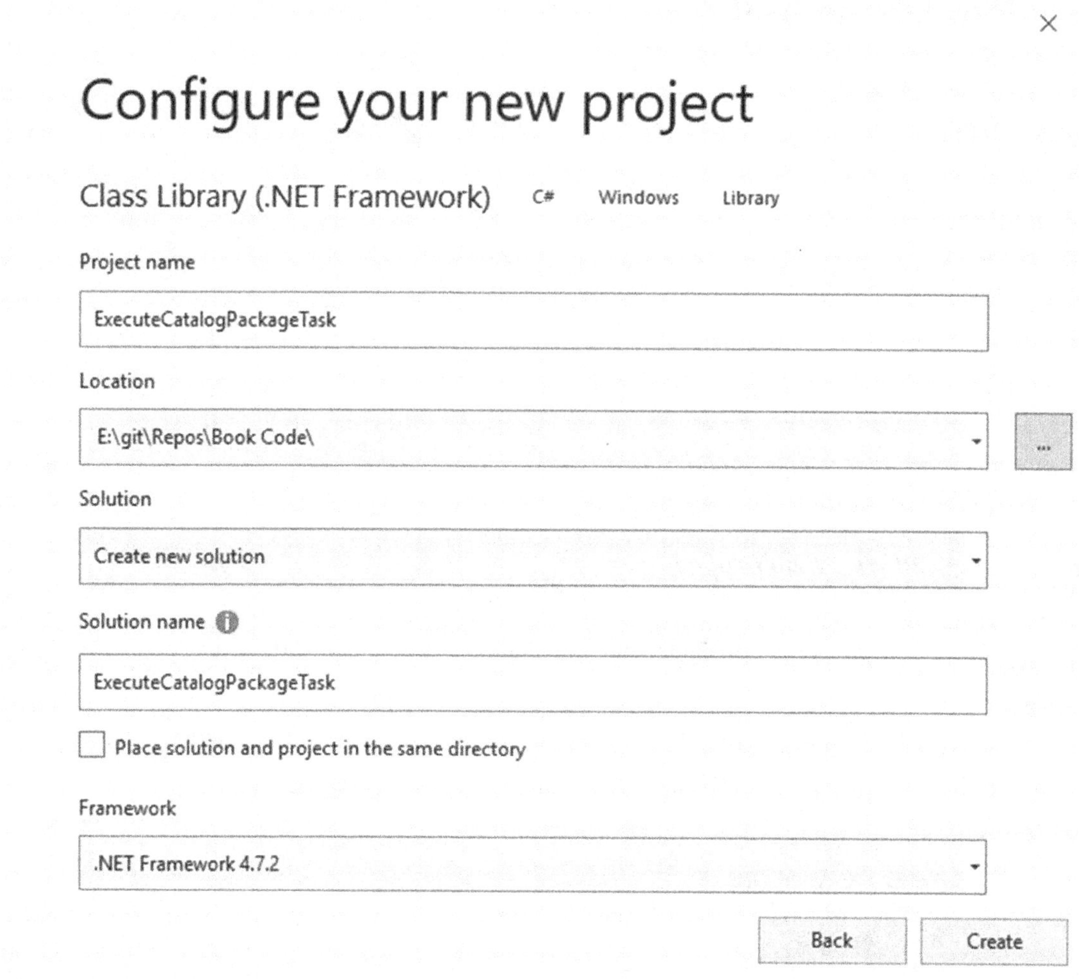

×

Configure your new project

Class Library (.NET Framework)   C#   Windows   Library

Project name

```
ExecuteCatalogPackageTask
```

Location

```
E:\git\Repos\Book Code\
```
▾   ...

Solution

```
Create new solution
```
▾

Solution name ⓘ

```
ExecuteCatalogPackageTask
```

☐ Place solution and project in the same directory

Framework

```
.NET Framework 4.7.2
```
▾

Back   Create

Figure 3-5. *Configuring and naming the new project*

Name the project ExecuteCatalogPackageTask.

Store the project in the path created when the Azure DevOps Git repo was cloned.

Click the Create button to create the project.

Please note the ExecuteCatalogPackageTask folder is now present in the git\Repos\ Book Code\ folder as shown in Figure 3-6:

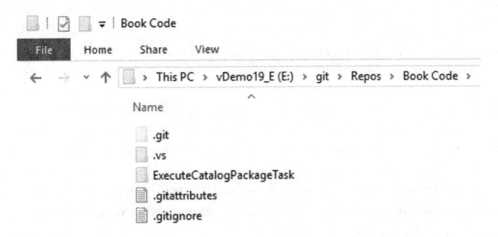

Figure 3-6. *The new Visual Studio project in the local repo*

The next step is renaming the default class that was created as Class1 in the Visual Studio project. In Solution Explorer, click on the Class1.cs class twice (slowly), and Class1 will enter rename-edit mode. Change the name to ExecuteCatalogPackageTask as shown in Figure 3-7:

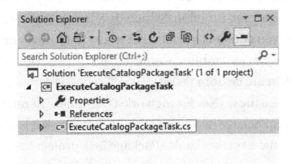

Figure 3-7. *Renaming Class1 to ExecuteCatalogPackageTask*

When you hit the Enter key, you will be prompted to change all references to Class1 to ExecuteCatalogPackageTask. Click the Yes button as shown in Figure 3-8:

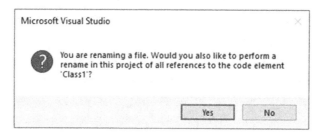

Figure 3-8. *Renaming all references*

These are the first steps to creating a custom SSIS task using Visual Studio 2019. Experienced developers will likely find this information trivial – this book is not written for experienced developers.

A key takeaway from this section: Remember to start Visual Studio as an Administrator.

Adding a Reference

The .Net Framework was invented so developers could get a few hours of sleep. It encapsulates a host of common functions which developers may use in applications. That's pretty cool, but even cooler is the fact that many platforms and applications expose functionality via .Net assemblies. Coolest of all (for our purposes), SSIS assemblies allow us to create custom tasks!

We must first *reference* these .Net Framework assemblies. To reference an assembly, open the ExecuteCatalogPackageTask Visual Studio solution if it is not already open. In Solution Explorer, click the ExecuteCatalogPackageTask project in Solution Explorer, and then expand the References virtual folder as shown in Figure 3-9:

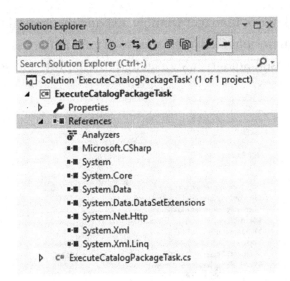

Figure 3-9. *Project References in Solution Explorer*

Let's add a reference to an SSIS assembly. Right-click the References virtual folder, and then click Add Reference as shown in Figure 3-10:

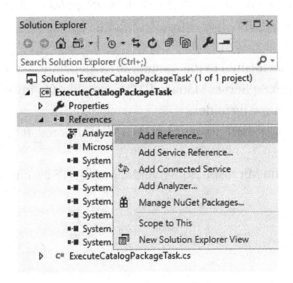

Figure 3-10. *Preparing to add a reference*

This opens the Reference Manager window. Expand the Assemblies item in the Reference Types list on the left. Click the Extensions item in the Assemblies list. Scroll until you find the Microsoft.SqlServer.ManagedDTS assembly, and select its checkbox as shown in Figure 3-11:

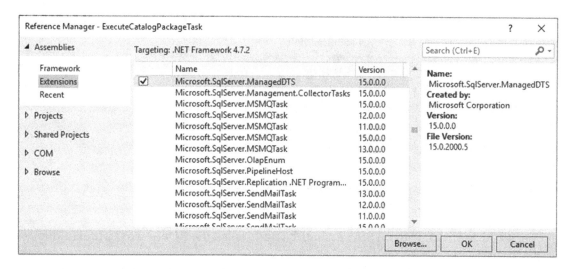

Figure 3-11. *Adding the Microsoft.SqlServer.ManagedDTS Assembly Reference from Assemblies\Extensions*

If the assembly is *not* located in the Assemblies\Extensions list, you will have to browse for the Microsoft.SqlServer.ManagedDTS assembly. On my virtual machine, I located the file in the following folder:

C:\Windows\Microsoft.NET\assembly\GAC_MSIL\Microsoft.SqlServer.ManagedDTS\v4.0_15.0.0.0__89845dcd8080cc91\

Add a reference to the Microsoft.SqlServer.ManagedDTS assembly as shown in Figure 3-12:

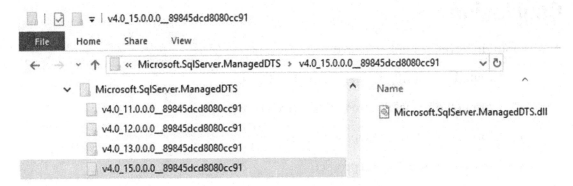

Figure 3-12. *Adding the Microsoft.SqlServer.ManagedDTS Assembly Reference from the file system*

When you click the OK button, the References virtual folder appears as shown in Figure 3-13:

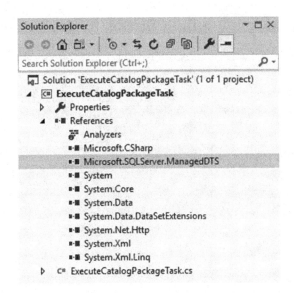

Figure 3-13. *Reference successfully added*

Conclusion

At this point in development, we have

- Created and configured an Azure DevOps project

- Connected Visual Studio to the Azure DevOps project

- Cloned the Azure DevOps Git repo locally

- Created a Visual Studio project

- Added a reference to the Visual Studio project

It's time to check in our code.

CHAPTER 4

Check in the Project Code

I just checked my watch and… yep… it's 2020. It is past time for all developers to use some form of source control (or version control). In my experience, there are two types of developers:

1. Developers who use source control

2. Developers who *will* use source control

Why? You will lose code if you do not use source control. Losing code will break your heart, and you will then start using source control.

Initialize Source Control in Azure DevOps

Let's examine the current state of our project in Azure DevOps. Click the Repos item on the left menu, as shown in Figure 4-1:

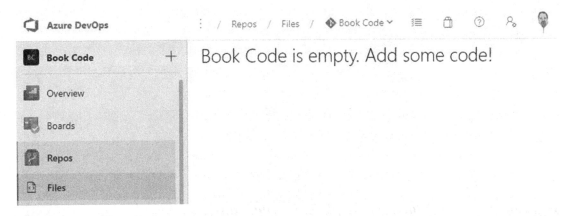

Figure 4-1. *Azure DevOps currently has no code*

© Andy Leonard 2021
A. Leonard, *Building Custom Tasks for SQL Server Integration Services*,
https://doi.org/10.1007/978-1-4842-6482-9_4

Let's examine our local Git repo as shown in Figure 4-2:

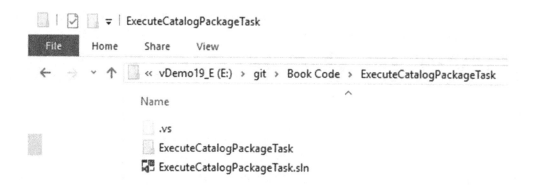

Figure 4-2. *The ExecuteCatalogPackageTask in the local repo*

Next comes the question that is the reason for this chapter: How do we get our latest Visual Studio project code into Azure DevOps? Read on to find out.

Begin by opening Visual Studio Team Explorer (if it is closed, click View ➤ Team Explorer). Click the Team Explorer Home button, and then click the Changes tile as shown in Figure 4-3:

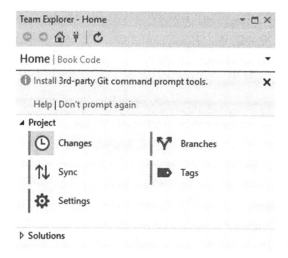

Figure 4-3. *Clicking the Team Explorer Changes tile*

When you click the Changes button, the dialog named *Team Explorer – Changes* will display as shown in Figure 4-4:

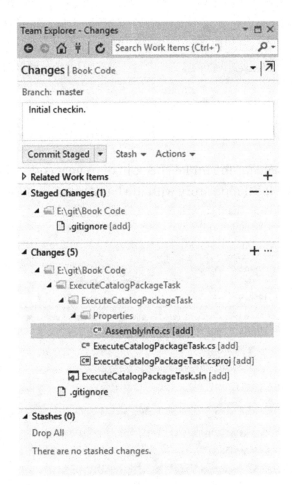

Figure 4-4. *Team Explorer – Changes*

Add a commit message. Why? Commit comments are for "future you" and/or for other team members who may view your code in the future. "Future you" will appreciate the reminder if you review this code several months – or years – later. New or other team members reviewing your code in the future will benefit from helpful commit messages.

If the button beneath the Commit Message textbox is labeled "Commit Staged," then click the Commit Staged button. Team Explorer shares a result message as shown in Figure 4-5:

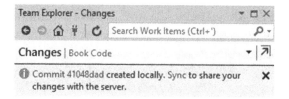

Figure 4-5. *Viewing the staged changes locally committed message*

Add a commit message for the initial check-in of project code, and click the Commit All button to update the local repository with the latest version of the project code, as shown in Figure 4-6:

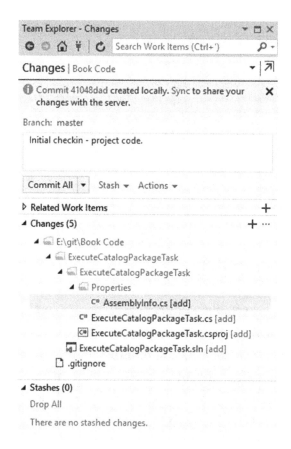

Figure 4-6. *Ready to commit all project code*

Team Explorer shares a result message as shown in Figure 4-7:

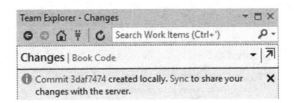

Figure 4-7. *Project code locally committed message*

This example is valid for a single developer. This example does not exhaust the capabilities of either Git or Azure DevOps.

The Azure DevOps Book Code project remains empty at this time. Click the Sync link in the locally committed message to update project code in the local Git repo. After the sync, Team Explorer is poised to push the local repo changes to the Azure DevOps Book Code project, as shown in Figure 4-8:

Figure 4-8. *Team Explorer ready to push*

In the Outgoing Commits section, click the Push link to copy project code from the local repo to the Azure DevOps Book Code repo. If the push is successful, Team Explorer provides a notification similar to that shown in Figure 4-9:

Figure 4-9. *Team Explorer displaying a successful push message*

The Azure DevOps Book Code repo now contains a copy of our latest project code as shown in Figure 4-10:

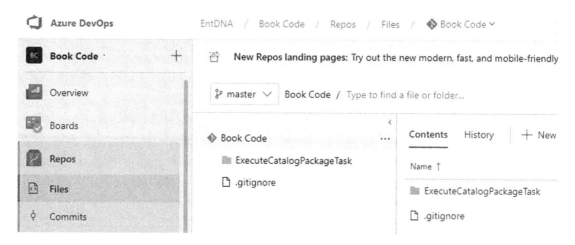

Figure 4-10. *Azure DevOps Book Code repo*

At this point in our single-developer scenario, we are using the Azure DevOps Book Code repo for source control *only*.

Blue lock icons mark items that have been checked into source control as shown in Figure 4-11:

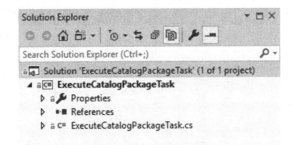

Figure 4-11. *Observing checked-in project code*

Conclusion

At this point in development, we have

- Created and configured an Azure DevOps project
- Connected Visual Studio to the Azure DevOps project
- Cloned the Azure DevOps Git repo locally
- Created a Visual Studio project
- Added a reference to the Visual Studio project
- Performed an initial check-in of the project code

We next sign the assembly.

CHAPTER 5

Signing the Assembly

In order to be used by Visual Studio in SSIS projects, an SSIS custom task assembly *must* be signed. The .Net Framework includes tools for creating and managing "key" files which are used for signing assemblies.

Preparing to Add a Key

I recommend opening a command window as an Administrator to begin. Open the Windows Start menu and locate Command Prompt. Right-click Command Prompt, hover over "More," and then click "Run as Administrator" as shown in Figure 5-1:

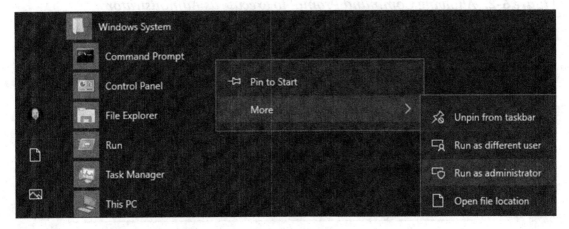

Figure 5-1. Opening an Administrator command window

© Andy Leonard 2021
A. Leonard, *Building Custom Tasks for SQL Server Integration Services*,
https://doi.org/10.1007/978-1-4842-6482-9_5

When prompted, click the Yes button as shown in Figure 5-2:

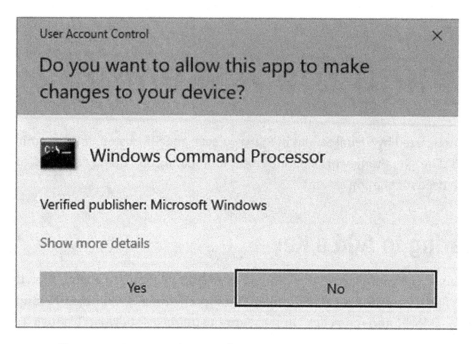

Figure 5-2. *Allowing Command Prompt to execute as Administrator*

When open, the Administrator command window appears as shown in Figure 5-3:

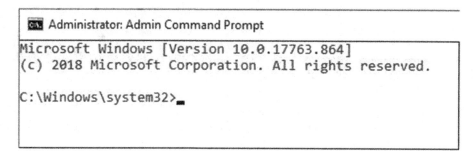

Figure 5-3. *Administrator command window*

We are creating an assembly (actually, a couple of assemblies) that will reside in the Global Assembly Cache, or GAC. In order to live in the GAC, assemblies must be *signed*. We sign assemblies using *strong name key files*. At this point in our project configuration, we need to generate a key suitable to sign our assemblies. To that end, there is good and bad news:

- The good news: Microsoft provides a Strong Name utility (sn.exe) for creating keys.

- The bad news: The Strong Name utility moves around with new releases of the .Net Framework.

If you are developing on Windows Server 2019, you can find the strong name utility in the C:\Program Files (x86)\Microsoft SDKs\Windows\v10.0A\bin\NETFX 4.8 Tools\ folder. The strong name utility is named "sn.exe," so the full path is "C:\ Program Files (x86)\Microsoft SDKs\Windows\v10.0A\bin\NETFX 4.8 Tools\sn.exe". If you are reading this verbiage in the distant future and snickering about how archaic Windows Server 2019 was, search for "sn.exe" and use the latest version you find (smarty-pants).

Tip   You can manage this process in any manner you prefer. I recommend you create a text file to preserve key-related command lines. I firmly believe Future You will thank you later.

I begin by adding a New Item to the project as shown in Figure 5-4:

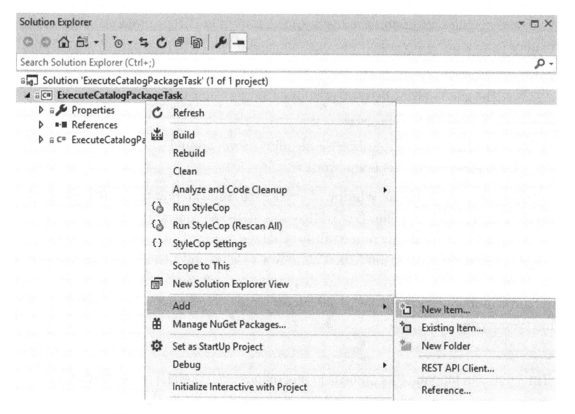

Figure 5-4. *Adding a new item to the project*

I select a Text File and name my notes file "Notes.txt" (because I am feeling especially creative) as shown in Figure 5-5:

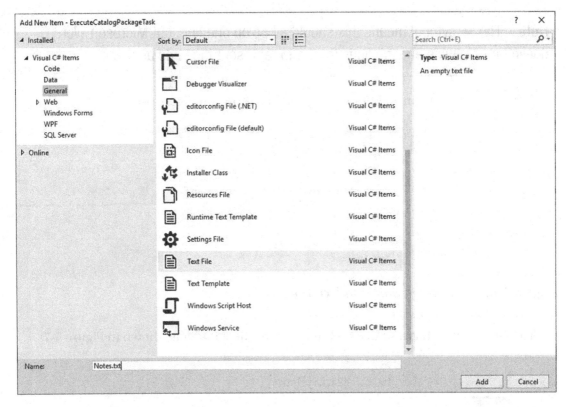

Figure 5-5. *Naming the notes file*

I next paste the following lines:

```
-- key generation
"C:\Program Files (x86)\Microsoft SDKs\Windows\v10.0A\bin\NETFX 4.8 ➥
Tools\sn.exe" -k key.snk
"C:\Program Files (x86)\Microsoft SDKs\Windows\v10.0A\bin\NETFX 4.8 ➥
Tools\sn.exe" -p key.snk public.out
"C:\Program Files (x86)\Microsoft SDKs\Windows\v10.0A\bin\NETFX 4.8 ➥
Tools\sn.exe" -t public.out
```

The first line creates the public/private key pair and puts them in a file named key.snk. The second line extracts the public part of the key pair to a file named public.out. The third line reads the public key from the public.out file.

Note   The ➡ symbol means this should all be on one line, but Microsoft Word doesn't create wide enough lines for me to represent the code as such.

Notes.txt now appears in Solution Explorer as shown in Figure 5-6:

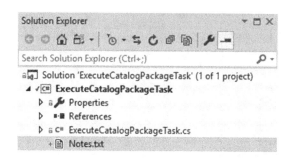

Figure 5-6. *Notes.txt in Solution Explorer*

The Notes.txt file has also been added to the project folder as shown in Figure 5-7:

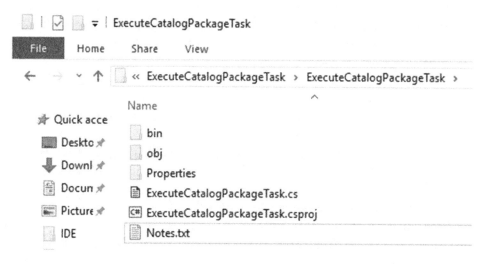

Figure 5-7. *Notes.txt in the project folder*

Creating the Key

In the command window, navigate to the ExecuteCatalogPackageTask project directory. The project directory will contain ExecuteCatalogPackageTask.cs, ExecuteCatalogPackageTask.csproj, as well as the Notes.txt file as shown in Figure 5-8:

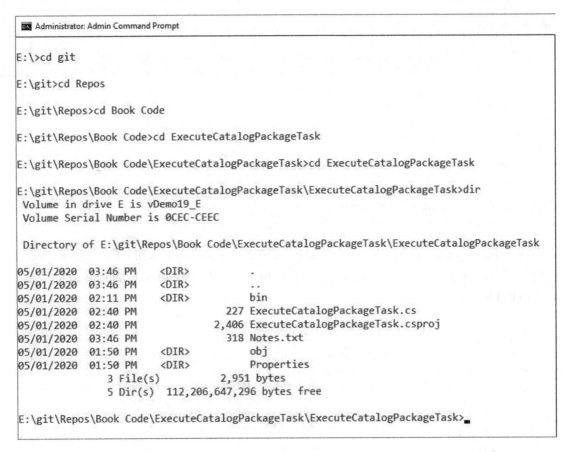

Figure 5-8. *Navigating to the ExecuteCatalogPackageTask project directory*

If it is not already open, open the Notes.txt in Visual Studio from Solution Explorer. Select the first line, copy it, and paste it into the command window as shown in Figure 5-9:

```
Administrator: Admin Command Prompt                                    —   □   ×

E:\git\Repos\Book Code\ExecuteCatalogPackageTask\ExecuteCatalogPackageTask>"C:\Program
 Files (x86)\Microsoft SDKs\Windows\v10.0A\bin\NETFX 4.8 Tools\sn.exe" -k key.snk
```

Figure 5-9. *Pasting into the command window*

Press the Enter key to execute the sn.exe command, creating the key file in the ExecuteCatalogPackageTask project directory as shown in Figure 5-10:

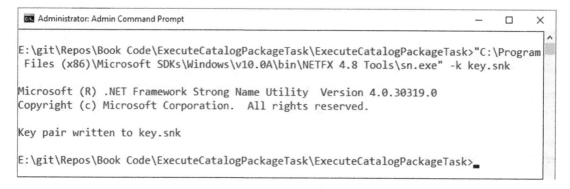

Figure 5-10. *Key.snk file created*

We need to get the public key's public/private pair from key.snk file. First, we extract the public key to a file named public.out using the second line stored in Notes.txt as shown in Figure 5-11:

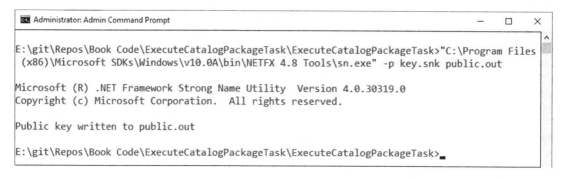

Figure 5-11. *Public key extraction*

Finally, we need to read the public key value out of the file to which we extracted it as shown in Figure 5-12:

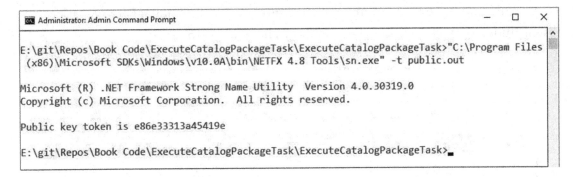

Figure 5-12. *Reading the public key*

Using the left mouse button, highlight the public key value as shown in Figure 5-13:

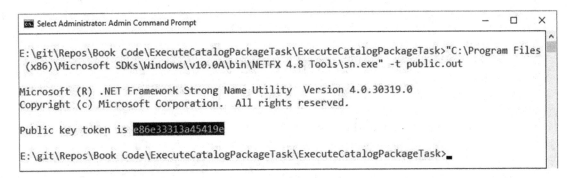

Figure 5-13. *Selecting the public key in the command window*

Right-click the highlighted text. Note that no context menu will appear. Your indication the text has been copied to the clipboard is the highlighting and "Select" text in the title bar disappears as shown in Figure 5-14:

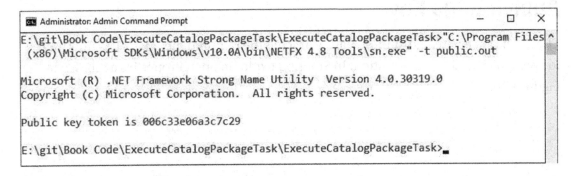

Figure 5-14. *Text selected to the clipboard*

Store the public key in a comment inside the class ExecuteCatalogPackageTask.cs in Visual Studio. We will use it here later as shown in Figure 5-15:

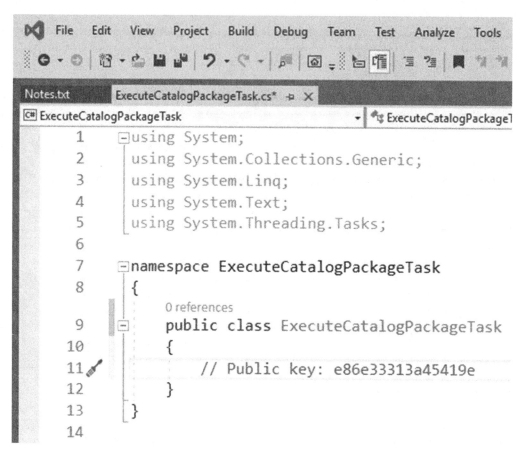

Figure 5-15. *Public key stored*

Applying the Key

The key has been created, and we have extracted the required metadata. It is now time to apply the key file to the solution. In Solution Explorer, open Properties as shown in Figure 5-16:

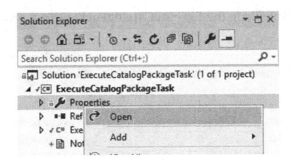

Figure 5-16. *Opening Properties*

Once Properties opens, navigate to the Signing page. Check the "Sign the assembly" checkbox. Click the "Choose a strong name key file" dropdown and select "<Browse...>" as shown in Figure 5-17:

Application

Build

Build Events

Debug

Resources

Services

Settings

Reference Paths

Signing*

Code Analysis

Configuration: N/A

☐ Sign the ClickOnce manifests

Certificate:

Issued To	(none)
Issued By	(none)
Intended Purpose	(none)
Expiration Date	(none)
Signature Algorithm	(none)

Timestamp server URL:

☑ Sign the assembly

Choose a strong name key file:

<New...>
<Browse...>

When delay signed, the project will not run or be debuggable.

Figure 5-17. *Signing the assembly*

43

Browse to the key.snk file in the ExecuteCatalogPackageTask project folder as shown in Figure 5-18:

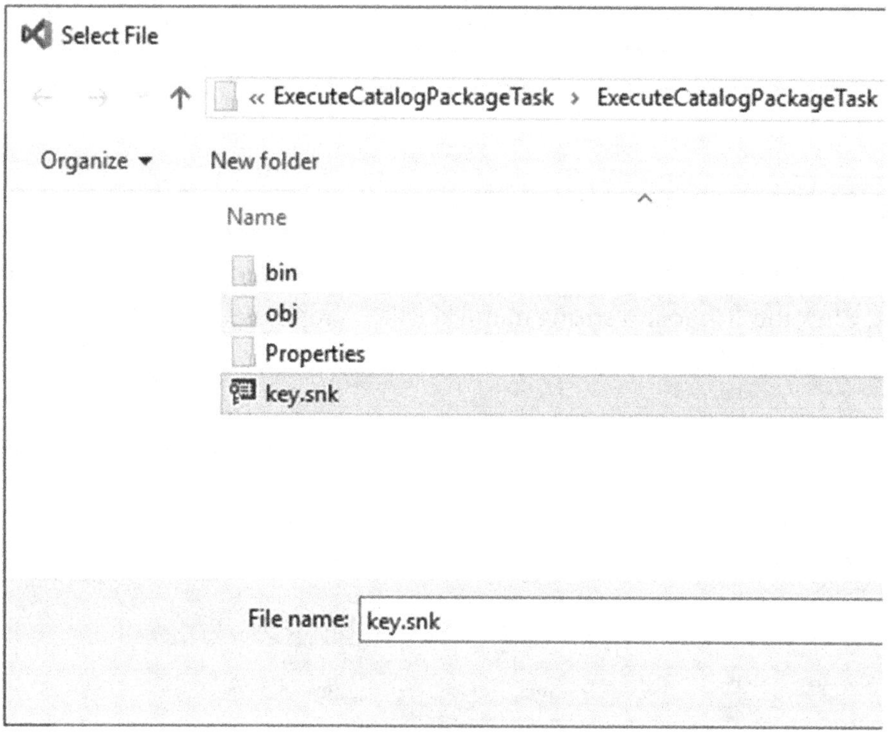

Figure 5-18. *Navigating to the key.snk file*

Click the Open button to use the key.snk file to sign the assembly as shown in Figure 5-19:

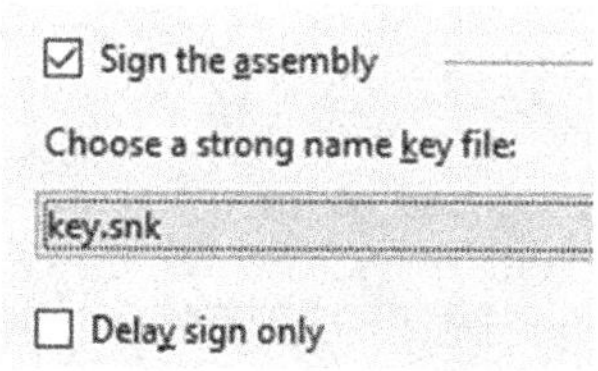

Figure 5-19. *Signed assembly*

Click the Save All button (or File ➤ Save All) to save your Visual Studio solution.

Checking In Changes

Before we check in the latest changes, please note this is a single-developer project. Git supports a number of version control scenarios, particularly for distributed developer teams. Issuing a pull request at this time serves no purpose because I am the sole reviewer of code. The next step is therefore identical to our initial check-in step.

Open Team Explorer, as shown in Figure 5-20:

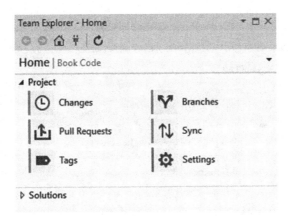

Figure 5-20. *Viewing Team Explorer*

Click the Changes tile and add a commit message, as shown in Figure 5-21:

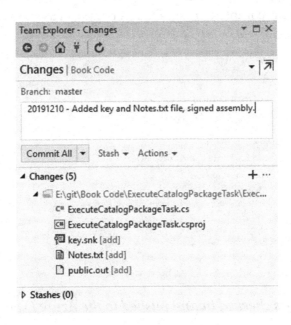

Figure 5-21. *Adding a commit message*

I have the option to save a step here by clicking the dropdown on the Commit All button. Clicking Commit All and Push accomplishes both steps in order as shown in Figure 5-22:

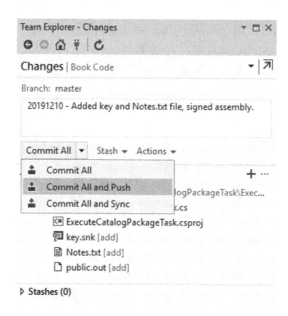

Figure 5-22. *Preparing to Commit All and Push*

When the operations complete, Team Explorer appears as shown in Figure 5-23:

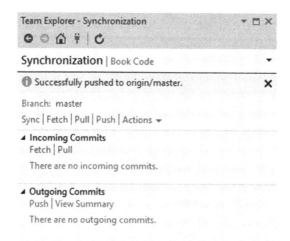

Figure 5-23. *Changes checked in and pushed to the Azure DevOps repo*

Solution Explorer reflects the new artifacts have been checked in, as shown in Figure 5-24:

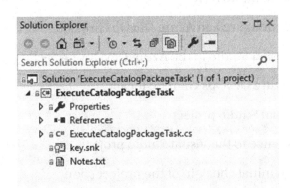

Figure 5-24. *Solution Explorer after check-in*

New project artifacts, key.snk and Notes.txt, are now found in the Azure DevOps repo, as shown in Figure 5-25:

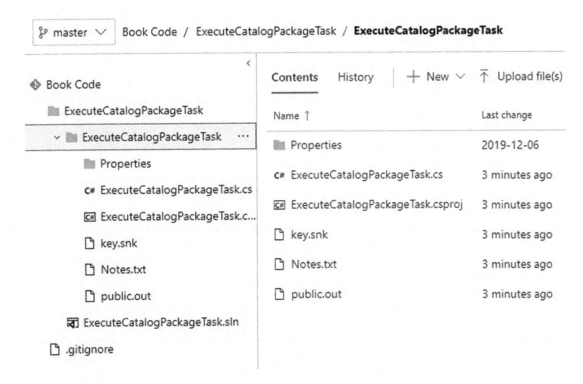

Figure 5-25. *New project artifacts in the Azure DevOps repo*

Conclusion

At this point in development, we have

- Created and configured an Azure DevOps project

- Connected Visual Studio to the Azure DevOps project

- Cloned the Azure DevOps Git repo locally

- Created a Visual Studio project

- Added a reference to the Visual Studio project

- Performed an initial check-in of the project code

- Signed the assembly

- Checked in an update

We next sign the assembly.

CHAPTER 6

Preparing to Build

Building custom SSIS tasks is neither trivial nor easy. You are building components that will be used to construct software. Perhaps you have done this before. Many have not.

Building the assembly is straightforward, consisting of two steps:

1. Build the assembly.

2. Register the assembly in the Global Assembly Cache (GAC).

Recovering gracefully when the code does not perform as expected is key. When the build/register procedure fails to achieve the desired results, a developer can take the following steps to recover:

- Unregister the assembly from the GAC.

- Clean the Visual Studio solution.

- Build the assembly in the Visual Studio solution.

- Register the assembly in the GAC.

The aforementioned steps get developers out of trouble almost as fast as we get into it, and that is a good thing.

Using Build Events to Register/Unregister

Gacutil is the utility used to *register* and *unregister* assemblies in the Global Assembly Cache (GAC). If you are following along and building the sample code as described, there is good news: C# supports *build events* – which allow developers to automate registering and unregistering assemblies in the GAC.

© Andy Leonard 2021
A. Leonard, *Building Custom Tasks for SQL Server Integration Services*,
https://doi.org/10.1007/978-1-4842-6482-9_6

Finding gacutil.exe

Like the sn.exe (Strong Name) utility mentioned in Chapter 5, gacutil.exe moves around with each release of the .Net Framework. At the time of this writing, the version is located in the C:\Program Files (x86)\Microsoft SDKs\Windows\v10.0A\bin\NETFX 4.8 Tools\ folder.

Adding Build Events

One reason Visual Studio must be started as an administrator is to support unregistering and registering the build output file in the Global Assembly Cache, or GAC. Most non-administrator accounts lack permission to unregister and register assemblies in the GAC.

Open the ExecuteCatalogPackageTask solution, and then open the Properties, as shown in Figure 6-1:

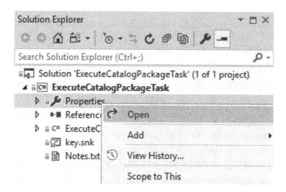

Figure 6-1. *Opening the project properties*

When the properties window displays, click the Build Events page as shown in Figure 6-2:

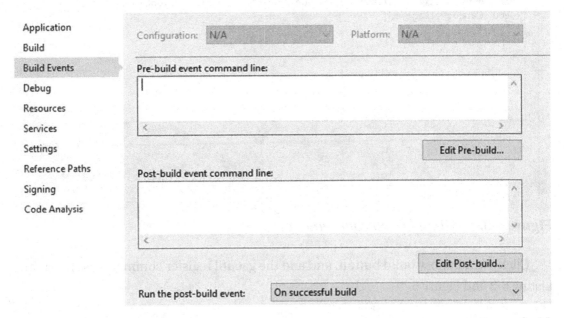

Figure 6-2. *The Build Events page*

Click the Edit Pre-build button and add the gacutil unregister command as shown in Listing 6-1 and Figure 6-3:

Listing 6-1. Unregister gacutil command syntax

```
"C:\Program Files (x86)\Microsoft SDKs\Windows\v10.0A\bin\NETFX 4.8 ➡
Tools\gacutil.exe" -u ExecuteCatalogPackageTask
```

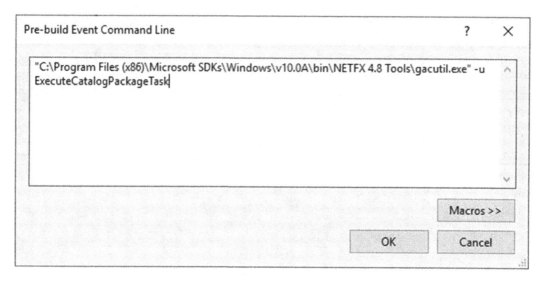

Figure 6-3. *Pre-build event command line*

Click the Edit Post-build button, and add the gacutil register command as shown in Listing 6-2 and Figure 6-4:

Listing 6-2. Register gacutil command syntax

```
"C:\Program Files (x86)\Microsoft SDKs\Windows\v10.0A\bin\NETFX 4.8 ➡
Tools\gacutil.exe" -if "E:\Program Files (x86)\Microsoft SQL ➡
Server\150\DTS\Tasks\ExecuteCatalogPackageTask.dll"
```

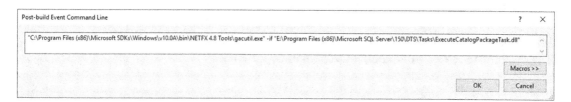

Figure 6-4. *Post-build event command line*

The gacutil "register" command registers the ExecuteCatalogPackageTask dynamic-link library (DLL) file with the Global Assembly Cache (GAC). The gacutil "unregister" command unregisters the same assembly – effectively removing it from the GAC.

Note ➥ characters in the listings above are line continuation characters. Please do *not* represent CRLF (Carriage Return Line Feed) line breaks. Please do not press the Enter key until the entire command string has been entered.

Once configured, the Build Events page will appear as shown in Figure 6-5:

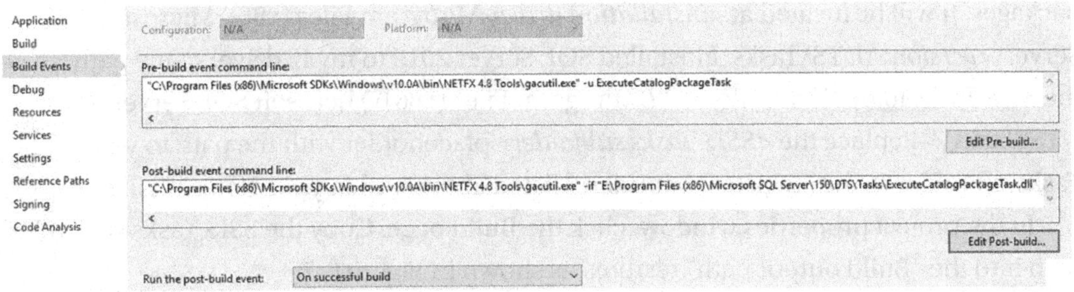

Figure 6-5. *Build events, configured*

The gacutil unregister and register commands listed above are the first and last steps, respectively, for recovery from failure. In addition to configuring the Pre- and Post-build Events, developers *may* execute the gacutil unregister and register commands in a command window opened with "Run as Administrator" permissions – similar to the key-generation process discussed and demonstrated in Chapter 5. For this reason, add the gacutil unresgister and register commands to Notes.txt, as shown in Figure 6-6:

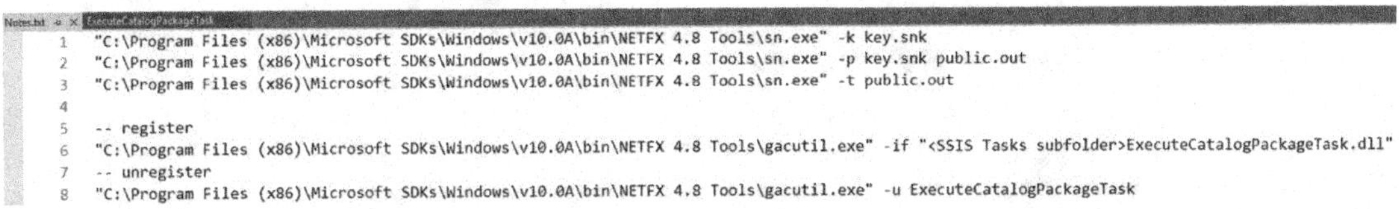

Figure 6-6. *Adding gacutil unregister and register commands to Notes.txt*

Developers may add pre- and post-build events to execute gacutil unregister and register commands automatically.

Performing this step – executing gacutil to unregister and register the assembly – is one reason for starting Visual Studio Community Edition as an administrator.

Setting the Output Path

Another reason Visual Studio must be started as an administrator is to support a system directory path – Program Files (x86) – as the Build output target. As with build events, most non-administrator accounts lack permission to configure the build output to a system directory.

Locate the SSIS Tasks subfolder used by SQL Server Data Tools to build SSIS packages. It will be located at *<installation drive>*:\Program Files (x86)\Microsoft SQL Server*<version>*\DTS\Tasks. I installed SQL Server 2019 to my E: drive, so my path to the SSIS Tasks folder is as follows: "*E*:\Program Files (x86)\Microsoft SQL Server*150*\ DTS\Tasks\." Replace the *<SSIS Tasks subfolder>* placeholder with the path to your SSIS Tasks subfolder in the "register" command listed above and in your Notes.txt file.

In the project properties window, click the Build page. Copy the SSIS Tasks subfolder path into the "Build output path" textbox, as shown in Figure 6-7:

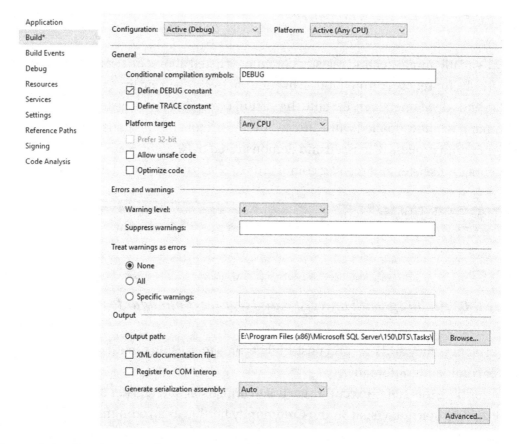

Figure 6-7. *Configuring the project Build Output*

Aiming the project build output path to the DTS\Tasks folder means the assembly will be built and delivered to the folder SSDT uses to populate the SSIS Toolbox. Note: This is *not* the location of tasks that are executed at runtime. The runtime executables must be registered in the GAC because SSIS executables are executed from the GAC at runtime.

For good measure, add the build output path to Notes.txt as shown in Figure 6-8:

```
ExecuteCatalogPackageTask        Notes.txt  ⊃  ×  ExecuteCatalogPackageTask.cs
     1    -- key generation
     2    "C:\Program Files (x86)\Microsoft SDKs\Windows\v10.0A\bin\NET
     3    "C:\Program Files (x86)\Microsoft SDKs\Windows\v10.0A\bin\NET
     4    "C:\Program Files (x86)\Microsoft SDKs\Windows\v10.0A\bin\NET
     5
     6    -- register
     7    "C:\Program Files (x86)\Microsoft SDKs\Windows\v10.0A\bin\NE
     8    -- unregister
     9    "C:\Program Files (x86)\Microsoft SDKs\Windows\v10.0A\bin\NET
    10
    11    -- build output path
    12    E:\Program Files (x86)\Microsoft SQL Server\150\DTS\Tasks\
    13
```

Figure 6-8. *Adding the project Build Output path to Notes.txt*

Conclusion

The project now sports a solid foundation and is protected via source control. We now have all the required pieces in place to begin coding our custom task functionality.

Now would be a good time to execute a commit and push to Azure DevOps.

At this point in development, we have

- Created and configured an Azure DevOps project

- Connected Visual Studio to the Azure DevOps project

- Cloned the Azure DevOps Git repo locally

- Created a Visual Studio project

- Added a reference to the Visual Studio project

- Performed an initial check-in of the project code

- Signed the assembly

- Checked in an update

- Configured the build output path and build events

We are now ready to begin coding the task.

CHAPTER 7

Coding the Task

We've worked through several chapters in preparation for this chapter, but we are finally ready to begin coding the custom task in earnest. We begin by adding references to the project, decorating the class, inheriting from a base class, and adding a property.

Using a Reference

Open the Visual Studio solution ExecuteCatalogPackageTask. In Solution Explorer, open the class ExecuteCatalogPackageTask.cs. In the top section of the class, add the line using `Microsoft.SqlServer.Dts.Runtime;`

© Andy Leonard 2021
A. Leonard, *Building Custom Tasks for SQL Server Integration Services*,
https://doi.org/10.1007/978-1-4842-6482-9_7

Your class now appears as shown in Figure 7-1:

```
ExecuteCatalogPackageTask.cs*  ↔ ×
[C#] ExecuteCatalogPackageTask                              ▼  ⚙ ExecuteCatalogPackage
    1       using System;
    2       using System.Collections.Generic;
    3       using System.Linq;
    4       using System.Text;
    5       using System.Threading.Tasks;
    6       using Microsoft.SqlServer.Dts.Runtime;
    7
    8       namespace ExecuteCatalogPackageTask
    9       {
                    0 references
   10           public class ExecuteCatalogPackageTask
   11           {
   12               // Public key: e86e33313a45419e
   13           }
   14       }
```

Figure 7-1. *Using a reference*

This line of code allows you to use objects, methods, and properties contained in the assembly Microsoft.SqlServer.ManagedDTS – a reference added to this assembly in Chapter 3.

Decorating the Class

If you are reading this near the holidays, I know what you're thinking: "Andy, the holidays are almost over. Why are we decorating now?" It's not that kind of decorating.

We decorate to inform Visual Studio this class is *different*. In this case, the class is different because it is part of an SSIS task. Our decoration code goes just prior to the class definition and is composed of the code in Listing 7-1. We add this code to tell Visual Studio more about what we're building, as displayed in Figure 7-2:

Listing 7-1. Decorating the class

```
[DtsTask(
        TaskType = "DTS<version>"
    , DisplayName = "Execute Catalog Package Task"
    , Description = "A task to execute packages stored in the SSIS
      Catalog."
      )]
```

```
ExecuteCatalogPackageTask.cs*  ₊ ×
ExecuteCatalogPackageTask                          ExecuteCatalogPackageTask.ExecuteCatalogPackageTa ▼
    2        using System.Collections.Generic;
    3        using System.Linq;
    4        using System.Text;
    5        using System.Threading.Tasks;
    6        using Microsoft.SqlServer.Dts.Runtime;
    7
    8        namespace ExecuteCatalogPackageTask
    9        {
   10        [DtsTask(
   11                TaskType = "DTS150"
   12            , DisplayName = "ExecuteCatalogPackageTask"
   13            , Description = "A task to execute packages stored in the SSIS Catalog."
   14              )]
             0 references
   15              public class ExecuteCatalogPackageTask
   16        {
   17              // Public key: 006c33e06a3c7c29
   18        }
   19        }
```

Figure 7-2. Decorating the class

The TaskType attribute is optional. SSIS 2019 is version 150. One could argue
for permitting SSIS 2012, version 110, for the TaskType attribute in the DtsTask
decoration since the SSIS Catalog was introduced with SSIS 2012. Since this project
is built using Visual Studio 2019 using the default .Net Framework – 4.7.2 at the time
of this writing – the author opted to code the task for SSIS 2019 and later.

Inheriting from Microsoft.SqlServer.Dts.Runtime.Task

Once the reference and decoration are in place, the next step is to configure inheritance from the Microsoft.SqlServer.Dts.Runtime.Task object. Inheriting Microsoft.SqlServer. Dts.Runtime.Task provides a framework for a lot of the work to come, including methods the code will override.

Modify the class definition to inherit from the Task object as shown in Listing 7-2:

Listing 7-2. Inheriting from Task

```
public class ExecuteCatalogPackageTask :
Microsoft.SqlServer.Dts.Runtime.Task
```

Your class should now appear as shown in Figure 7-3:

```
ExecuteCatalogPackageTask.cs*  ⊅ X
C# ExecuteCatalogPackageTask                                    ▼  ⚭ ExecuteCatalogPackageTask.ExecuteCatalogPackageTask        ▼
      1      ⊟using System;
      2       │using System.Collections.Generic;
      3       │using System.Linq;
      4       │using System.Text;
      5       │using System.Threading.Tasks;
      6       └using Microsoft.SqlServer.Dts.Runtime;
      7
      8      ⊟namespace ExecuteCatalogPackageTask
      9       │{
     10            [DtsTask(
     11                TaskType = "DTS150"
     12              , DisplayName = "Execute Catalog Package Task"
     13              , Description = "A task to execute packages stored in the SSIS Catalog.")]
                   0 references
     14      ⊟      public class ExecuteCatalogPackageTask : Microsoft.SqlServer.Dts.Runtime.Task
     15            {
     16                // Public key: e86e33313a45419e
     17            }
     18       └}
```

Figure 7-3. *Inheriting Task*

The actions taken so far combine to create a relationship between our code and the *base code* included in the ManagedDTS assembly we referenced and *using* statement earlier. Now it's time to build on that relationship by adding the things we want our task to do.

What do we want our task to do? We want to start an SSIS Package that's been deployed to an SSIS Catalog. To accomplish this, we need to provide the name of a SQL Server Instance that hosts an SSIS Catalog, the name of the SSIS Catalog Folder that contains the SSIS Project, the name of the SSIS Project that contains the SSIS Package, and the name of the SSIS Package.

Adding a Property

Properties provide a mechanism to expose values of internal variables to objects outside the class. In a class, a property may be coded using an internal private variable and publicly accessible property. Properties may also be coded using a get/set at declaration.

Create properties by adding the lines of code after the class declaration:

Listing 7-3. Declaring task properties

```
public string ServerName { get; set; } = String.Empty;
public string PackageCatalog { get; set; } = "SSISDB ";
public string PackageFolder { get; set; } = String.Empty;
public string PackageProject { get; set; } = String.Empty;
public string PackageName { get; set; } = String.Empty;
```

The class should now appear as shown in Figure 7-4:

```
namespace ExecuteCatalogPackageTask
{
    [DtsTask(
        TaskType = "DTS150"
      , DisplayName = "Execute Catalog Package Task"
      , Description = "A task to execute packages stored in the SSIS Catalog.")]
    0 references
    public class ExecuteCatalogPackageTask : Microsoft.SqlServer.Dts.Runtime.Task
    {
        // Public key: e86e33313a45419e

        0 references
        public string ServerName { get; set; } = String.Empty;
        0 references
        public string PackageCatalog { get; set; } = "SSISDB";
        0 references
        public string PackageFolder { get; set; } = String.Empty;
        0 references
        public string PackageProject { get; set; } = String.Empty;
        0 references
        public string PackageName { get; set; } = String.Empty;

    }
}
```

Figure 7-4. *Adding properties*

Task properties will contain string values, and we will use the string values internally in the task. For example, the property named ServerName will surface name of an instance of SQL Server that hosts an SSIS Catalog. The Execute Catalog Package Task will connect to this SQL Server instance to execute an SSIS package stored in the SSIS Catalog hosted on the instance named in the ServerName property.

Note the PackageCatalog property defaults to "SSISDB" and the other properties default the String.Empty. At the time of this writing, Microsoft limits the number of SSIS Catalogs to one catalog per SQL Server instance and defaults the name of this catalog to "SSISDB." Although the PackageCatalog defaults to "SSISDB," the value may be overridden if desired. Coding the task in this manner is an example of *future-proofing*, which means allowing for things to change in the future.

Non-defaulted property values are null. Null property values cannot be written (set) or read (get). Failure to initialize property values may present a troubleshooting challenge.

Properties can be read-only, write-only, and subject to many other conditions. Most properties are read-write, like the properties we constructed. If, for example, we desired to make the PackageCatalog property read-only, we would alter the declaration code as shown in Listing 7-4:

Listing 7-4. Declaring task properties

```
public string PackageCatalog { get; } = "SSISDB";
```

I prefer to leave the property read-write and recommend not removing the "set;" code from the declaration.

Investigating Task Methods

Earlier, we added inheritance to the ExecuteCatalogPackageTask class – `public class ExecuteCatalogPackageTask : Microsoft.SqlServer.Dts.Runtime.Task` – remember? When you inherit one class in another, the inherited class is identified as the base class. In Visual Basic, the base class may be directly addressed using the keyword `MyBase`; in C#, it's `base`.

You can observe a bunch of information about a base class by clicking View ➤ Object Browser as shown in Figure 7-5:

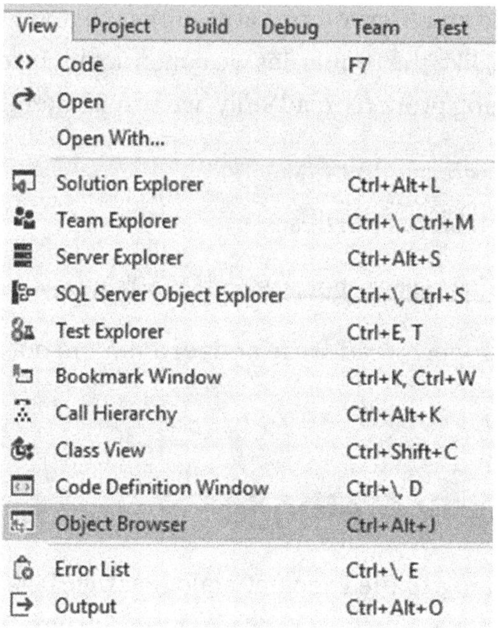

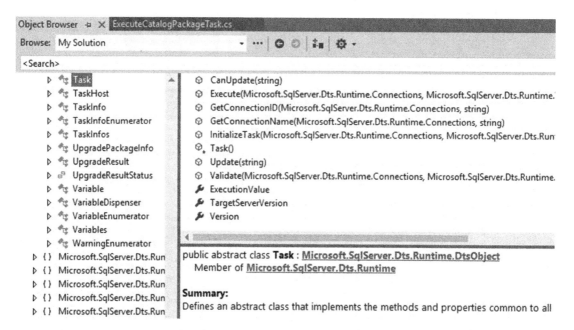

Figure 7-5. *Opening Object Browser*

Once open, navigate in Object Browser to the Microsoft.SqlServer.ManagedDTS\
Microsoft.SqlServer.ManagedDTS.Runtime\Task base class, as shown in Figure 7-6:

Figure 7-6. *Viewing the Task class in Object Browser*

Methods contained in this class are listed on the right. If we select a method, we may view details in the description pane as shown in Figure 7-7:

```
⊕   CanUpdate(string)
⊕   Execute(Microsoft.SqlServer.Dts.Runtime.Connections, Microsoft.SqlServer.Dts.Runtime.VariableDispense
⊕   GetConnectionID(Microsoft.SqlServer.Dts.Runtime.Connections, string)
⊕   GetConnectionName(Microsoft.SqlServer.Dts.Runtime.Connections, string)
⊕   InitializeTask(Microsoft.SqlServer.Dts.Runtime.Connections, Microsoft.SqlServer.Dts.Runtime.VariableDis
⊕▾  Task()
⊕   Update(string)
⊕   Validate(Microsoft.SqlServer.Dts.Runtime.Connections, Microsoft.SqlServer.Dts.Runtime.VariableDispense
🔧  ExecutionValue
🔧  TargetServerVersion
🔧  Version
```

public virtual **void InitializeTask**(Microsoft.SqlServer.Dts.Runtime.Connections *connections*,
Microsoft.SqlServer.Dts.Runtime.VariableDispenser *variableDispenser*,
Microsoft.SqlServer.Dts.Runtime.IDTSInfoEvents *events*,
Microsoft.SqlServer.Dts.Runtime.IDTSLogging *log*, Microsoft.SqlServer.Dts.Runtime.EventInfos
eventInfos, Microsoft.SqlServer.Dts.Runtime.LogEntryInfos *logEntryInfos*,
Microsoft.SqlServer.Dts.Runtime.ObjectReferenceTracker *refTracker*)
    Member of Microsoft.SqlServer.Dts.Runtime.Task

Summary:
Initializes the properties associated with the task. This method is called by the runtime and is not used in code.

Parameters:
connections: A collection of connections used by the task.
variableDispenser: A Microsoft.SqlServer.Dts.Runtime.VariableDispenser object for locking variables.
events: An object that implements the Microsoft.SqlServer.Dts.Runtime.IDTSInfoEvents interface.
log: An object that implements the Microsoft.SqlServer.Dts.Runtime.IDTSLogging interface.
eventInfos: A collection that contains events to be raised during execution of the task.
logEntryInfos: A collection of log entries.
refTracker: An object reference tracker.

***Figure 7-7.** Viewing the description of the InitializeTask method in Object Explorer*

The InitializeTask method is declared "virtual." Virtual, abstract, and override methods may be overridden. Since we inherit the Task class, we will override the InitializeTask method in our inheriting class. We will also override two other methods declared virtual: Validate and Execute. Override the InitializeTask method with the code in Listing 7-5:

Listing 7-5. Overriding the InitializeTask method

```
public override void InitializeTask(
Connections connections,
VariableDispenser variableDispenser,
IDTSInfoEvents events,
IDTSLogging log,
EventInfos eventInfos,
LogEntryInfos logEntryInfos,
ObjectReferenceTracker refTracker)
{ }
```

When you add this method to the ExecuteCatalogPackageTask class, your code should appear as shown in Figure 7-8:

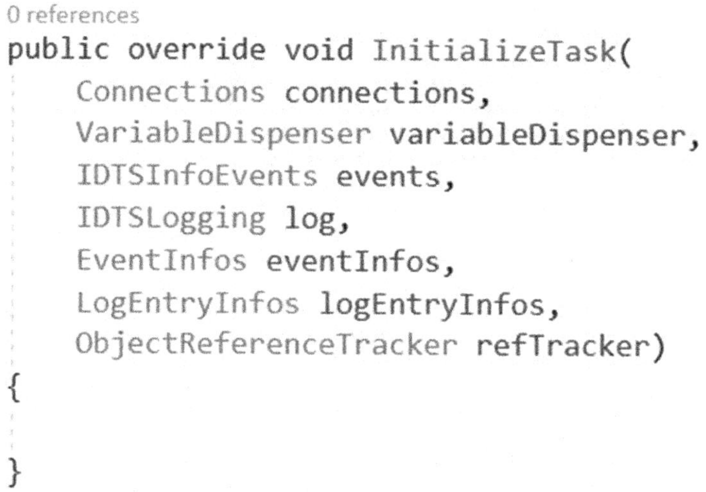

```
0 references
public override void InitializeTask(
    Connections connections,
    VariableDispenser variableDispenser,
    IDTSInfoEvents events,
    IDTSLogging log,
    EventInfos eventInfos,
    LogEntryInfos logEntryInfos,
    ObjectReferenceTracker refTracker)
{

}
```

Figure 7-8. *Overriding InitializeTask*

The InitializeTask method executes when the task is added to an SSIS Control Flow.

Overriding the Validate Method

The Validate method should be overridden in our class. Later in this book, we will implement validation code in this method. At this juncture, the custom task is not production-ready. A production-ready custom SSIS task *should always* implement validation. For now, stub this method with a DTSExecResult.Success return value.

Override the Validate method by adding the following function to our class:

```
public override DTSExecResult Validate(
Connections connections,
VariableDispenser variableDispenser,
IDTSComponentEvents componentEvents,
IDTSLogging log)
{
        return DTSExecResult.Success;
}
```

After adding this code, your class should appear similar to that shown in Figure 7-9:

```
0 references
public override DTSExecResult Validate(
    Connections connections,
    VariableDispenser variableDispenser,
    IDTSComponentEvents componentEvents,
    IDTSLogging log)
{
    return DTSExecResult.Success;
}
```

Figure 7-9. *Overriding the Validate function*

The Validate method is called when the task is added to the SSIS Control Flow, when a property changes, and when a task is executed. The line return DTSExecResult. Success tells the method to return Success – which translates to "I think I am ready to run" in *Task-Speak* – to the Control Flow when the method is invoked.

Overriding the Execute Method

As with the Validate method, we override the inherited Execute method with a bare minimum of functionality. Again, this is not *yet* production-ready code.

Add the Execute method override by adding the following code to the ExecuteCatalogPackageTask class:

```
public override DTSExecResult Execute(
Connections connections,
VariableDispenser variableDispenser,
IDTSComponentEvents componentEvents,
IDTSLogging log,
object transaction)
{
    return DTSExecResult.Success
}
```

Altogether, your class should now contain three methods and resemble that shown in Figure 7-10:

```
0 references
public override void InitializeTask(
    Connections connections,
    VariableDispenser variableDispenser,
    IDTSInfoEvents events,
    IDTSLogging log,
    EventInfos eventInfos,
    LogEntryInfos logEntryInfos,
    ObjectReferenceTracker refTracker)
{

}


0 references
public override DTSExecResult Validate(
    Connections connections,
    VariableDispenser variableDispenser,
    IDTSComponentEvents componentEvents,
    IDTSLogging log)
{
    return DTSExecResult.Success;
}


0 references
public override DTSExecResult Execute(
    Connections connections,
    VariableDispenser variableDispenser,
    IDTSComponentEvents componentEvents,
    IDTSLogging log,
    object transaction)
{
    return DTSExecResult.Success;
}
```

Figure 7-10. *Overriding Execute*

That is all we are going to code in this task at this time. We will add more code to these methods later in this book. The additional code will make this custom SSIS task more production-ready.

Conclusion

The project now contains the beginnings of custom task functionality.

Now would be a good time to execute a commit and push to Azure DevOps. At this point in development, we have

- Created and configured an Azure DevOps project

- Connected Visual Studio to the Azure DevOps project

- Cloned the Azure DevOps Git repo locally

- Created a Visual Studio project

- Added a reference to the Visual Studio project

- Performed an initial check-in of the project code

- Signed the assembly

- Checked in an update

- Configured the build output path and build events

- Overridden three methods from the Task base class

We are now ready to begin coding the task interface.

CHAPTER 8

Coding a Simple Task Editor

An SSIS task needs an editor. We begin creating a simple editor for ExecuteCatalog PackageTask by adding a project to the ExecuteCatalogPackageTask solution.

Adding a Task Editor

Open the Visual Studio solution ExecuteCatalogPackageTask.sln. In Solution Explorer, right-click the solution, hover over Add, and click New Project as shown in Figure 8-1:

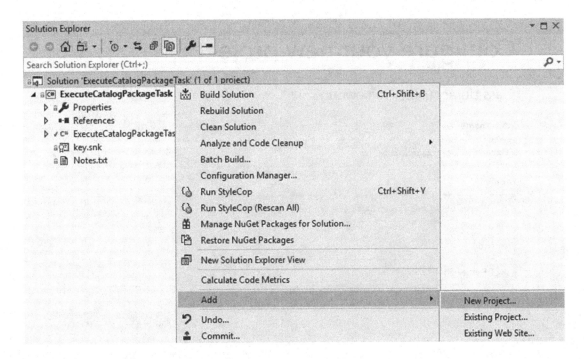

Figure 8-1. *Adding a new project*

71

© Andy Leonard 2021
A. Leonard, *Building Custom Tasks for SQL Server Integration Services*,
https://doi.org/10.1007/978-1-4842-6482-9_8

Select a C# Class Library (.NET Framework) as shown in Figure 8-2:

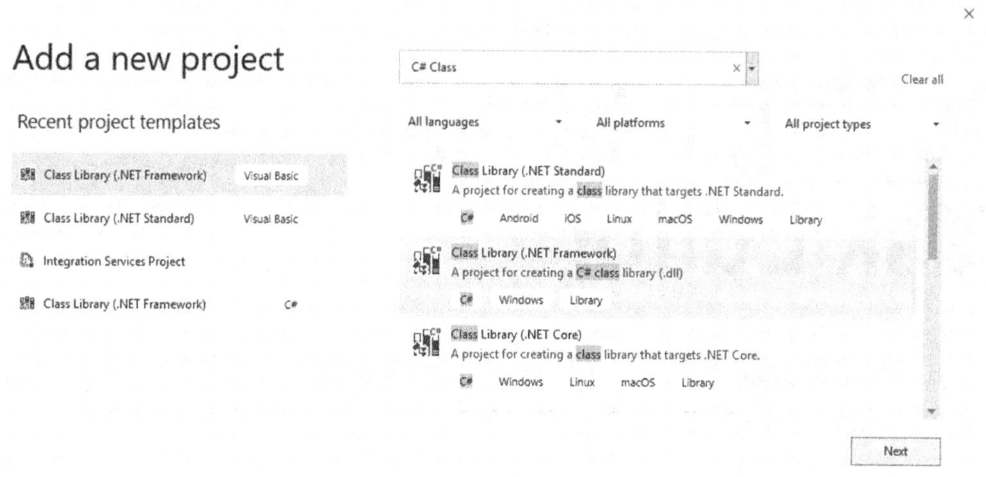

Figure 8-2. *Selecting the project template*

Name the project ExecuteCatalogPackageTaskUI as shown in Figure 8-3:

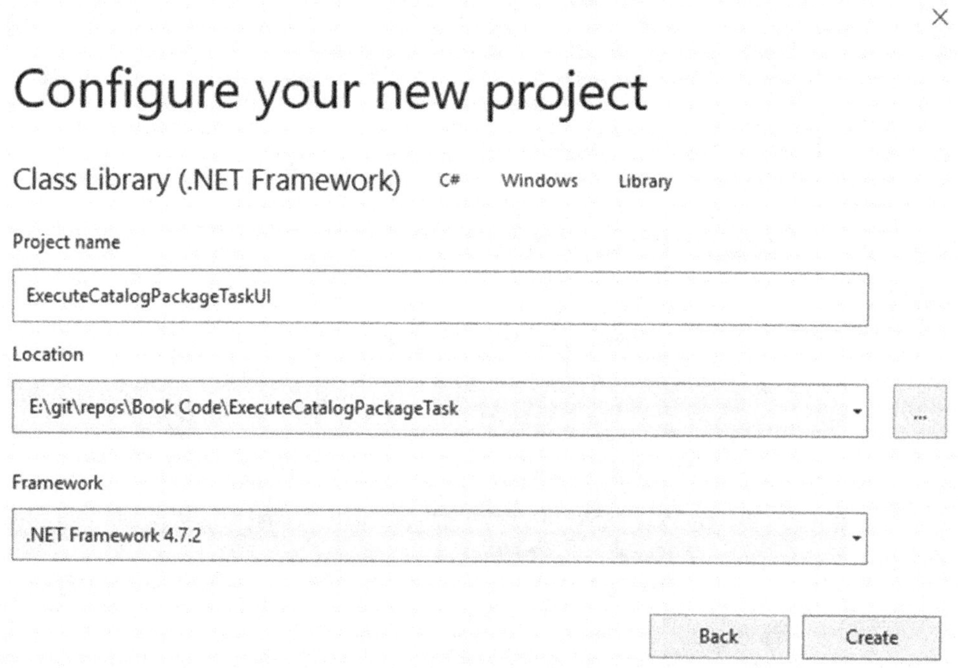

Figure 8-3. *Naming the project*

Click the Create button, and rename Class1.cs to ExecuteCatalogPackageTaskUI.cs as shown in Figure 8-4:

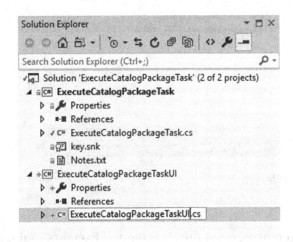

Figure 8-4. *Renaming Class1 to ExecuteCatalogPackageTaskUI*

When prompted, click Yes to rename all Class1 references to ExecuteCatalog PackageTaskUI references as shown in Figure 8-5:

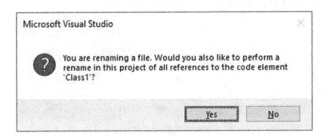

Figure 8-5. *Confirming the Class1 rename operation*

Adding References

As with the task project, we need to add references to the task UI project. In Solution Explorer, right-click the ExecuteCatalogPackageTaskUI project's References folder, and click Add Reference. When the Reference Manager displays, expand Assemblies and click Extensions. Scroll until you find Microsoft.SqlServer.Dts.Design and Microsoft. SqlServer.ManagedDTS, and select them as shown in Figure 8-6:

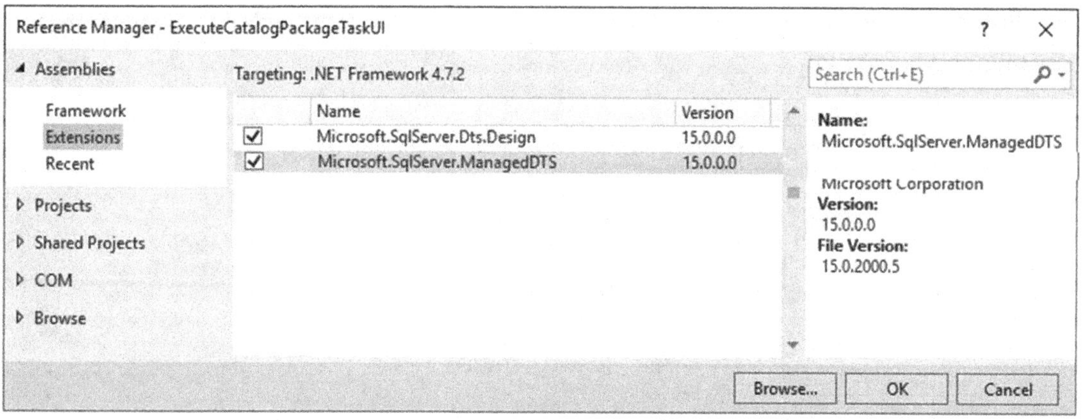

Figure 8-6. *Adding references*

To use the new references, open the class named ExecuteCatalogPackageTaskUI.cs. At the very top of this class, add the using statements shown in Listing 8-1:

Listing 8-1. Using references

```
using Microsoft.SqlServer.Dts.Runtime;
using Microsoft.SqlServer.Dts.Runtime.Design;
```

ExecuteCatalogPackageTaskUI.cs should now appear as shown in Figure 8-7:

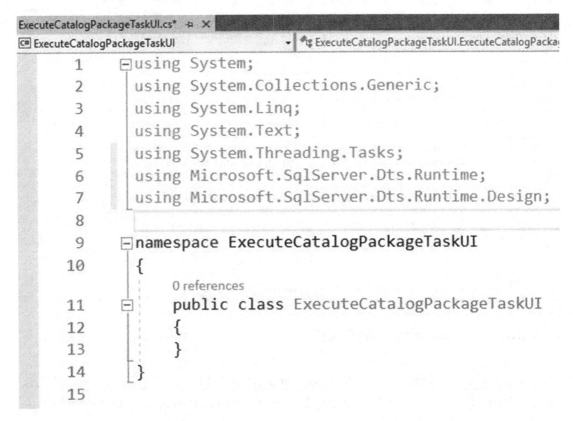

Figure 8-7. Using referenced assemblies

Some Implementation

Next, we implement the IDtsTaskUI interface by modifying the class declaration statement public class ExecuteCatalogPackageTaskUI as shown in Listing 8-2:

Listing 8-2. Implementing IDtsTaskUI

```
public class ExecuteCatalogPackageTaskUI : IDtsTaskUI
```

Your class will appear as shown in Figure 8-8:

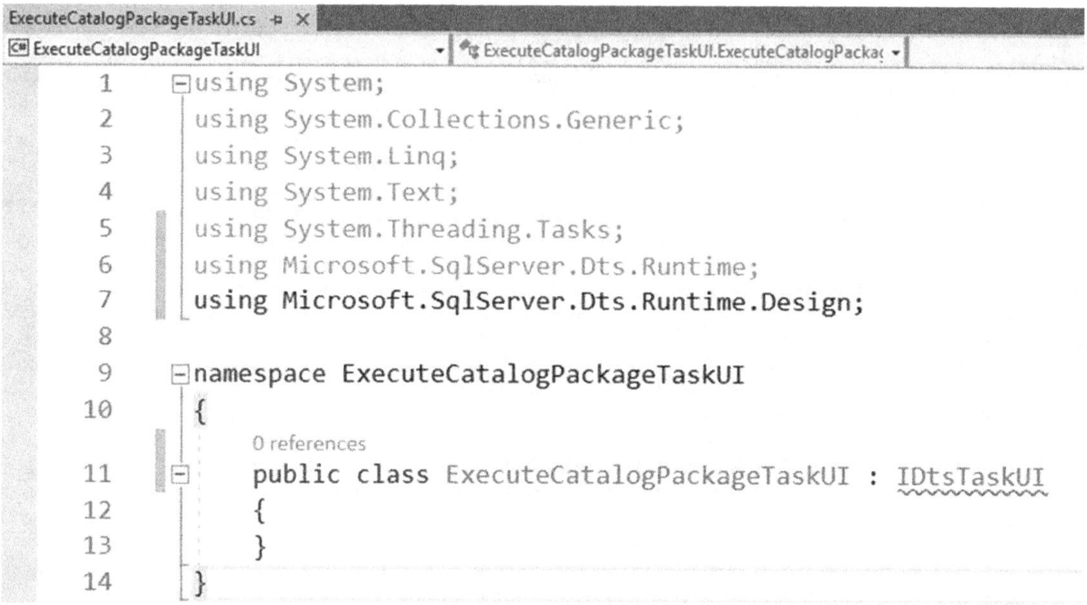

Figure 8-8. *Implementing IDtsTaskUI*

The squiggly line beneath the interface name (IDtsTaskUI is a .Net interface) informs us of an issue. Hovering over the squiggly line causes a tooltip to display as shown in Figure 8-9:

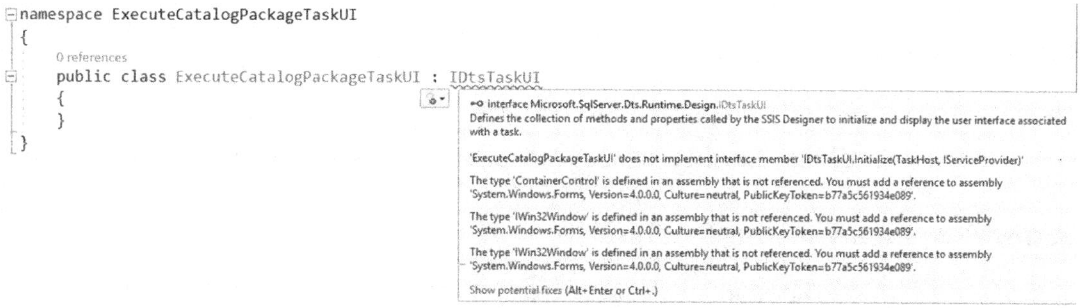

Figure 8-9. *Interface implementation requirements*

The IDtsTaskUI interface we are implementing requires we implement an Initialize "interface member." The message supplies messages for other requirements to achieve compliance with the IDtsTaskUI interface.

The first message informs us we need to implement an Initialize interface member to make ExecuteCatalogPackageTaskUI compliant to the IDtsTaskUI interface we are implementing. The Error List (View–>Error List) displays information regarding additional interface members required for implementing the IDtsTaskUI interface, shown in Figure 8-10:

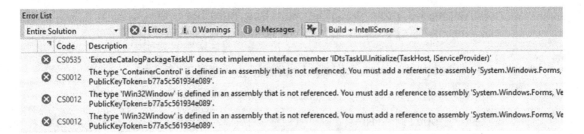

Figure 8-10. *Error List showing required methods for IDtsTaskUI implementation*

A TaskHost object variable is needed to implement some of this functionality, so let's add a new TaskHost variable just after the Implements statement as shown in Listing 8-3 and Figure 8-11:

Listing 8-3. Declaring the taskHostValue variable

```
private TaskHost taskHostValue;
```

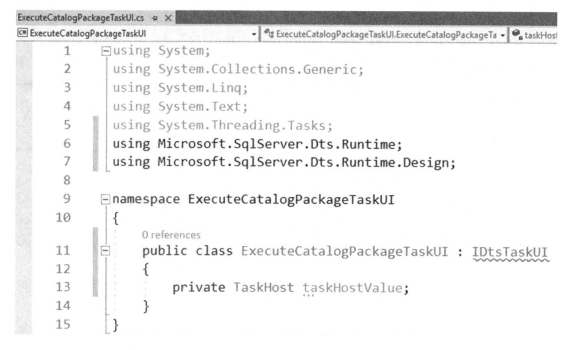

Figure 8-11. *Declaring the taskHostValue variable*

To prepare to add a Windows form, which will serve as the Task editor, we must first add a reference to the .Net Framework assembly named System.Windows.Forms in the ExecuteCatalogPackageTaskUI.cs class, as shown in in Figure 8-12:

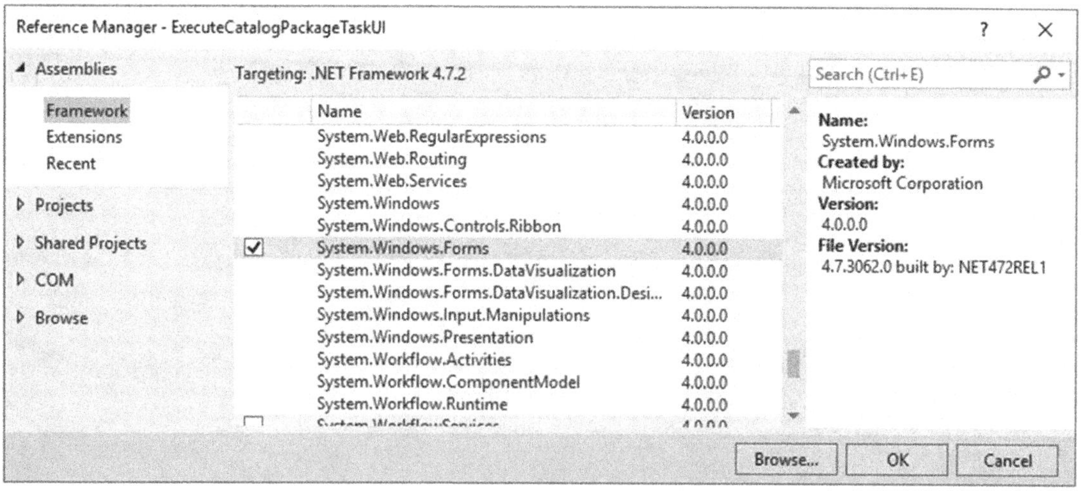

Figure 8-12. *Adding a reference to System.Windows.Forms*

In Listing 8-4 and Figure 8-13, we use the new reference by adding a using statement to the ExecuteCatalogPackageTaskUI.cs class:

Listing 8-4. Using System.Windows.Forms

```
using System.Windows.Forms;
```

ExecuteCatalogPackageTaskUI.cs ⊕ ✕	
C# ExecuteCatalogPackageTaskUI	▾ | ⁑ ExecuteCatalogPackageTaskUI.ExecuteCatalogPacka

```
1    ⊟using System;
2     using System.Collections.Generic;
3     using System.Linq;
4     using System.Text;
5     using System.Threading.Tasks;
6     using Microsoft.SqlServer.Dts.Runtime;
7     using Microsoft.SqlServer.Dts.Runtime.Design;
8     using System.Windows.Forms;
```

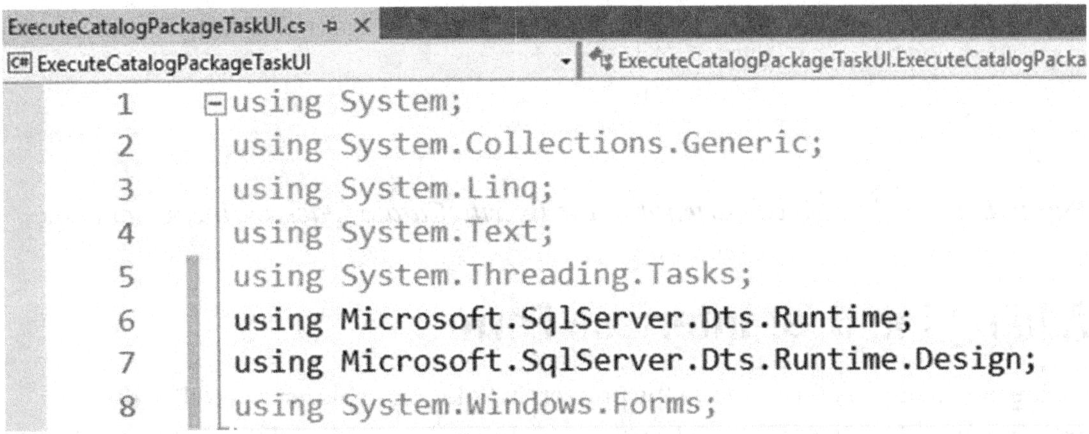

Figure 8-13. Using System.Windows.Forms in the
ExecuteCatalogPackageTaskUI.cs class

Add a generic constructor (public void New) for the ExecuteCatalogPackageTaskUI.cs class by adding the code shown in Listing 8-5:

Listing 8-5. Adding a constructor

```
public void New(System.Windows.Forms.IWin32Window form) { }
```

The ExecuteCatalogPackageTaskUI.cs class should now appear as shown in Figure 8-14:

```
0 references
public class ExecuteCatalogPackageTaskUI : IDtsTaskUI
{
    private TaskHost taskHostValue;

    0 references
    public void New(System.Windows.Forms.IWin32Window form)
    {

    }
}
```

Figure 8-14. *Adding a constructor to the ExecuteCatalogPackageTaskUI.cs class*

Adding the User Interface Form

We are now ready to add a form to the project. In Solution Explorer, right-click the project name (ExecuteCatalogPackageTaskUI), hover over Add, and then click Windows Form as shown in Figure 8-15:

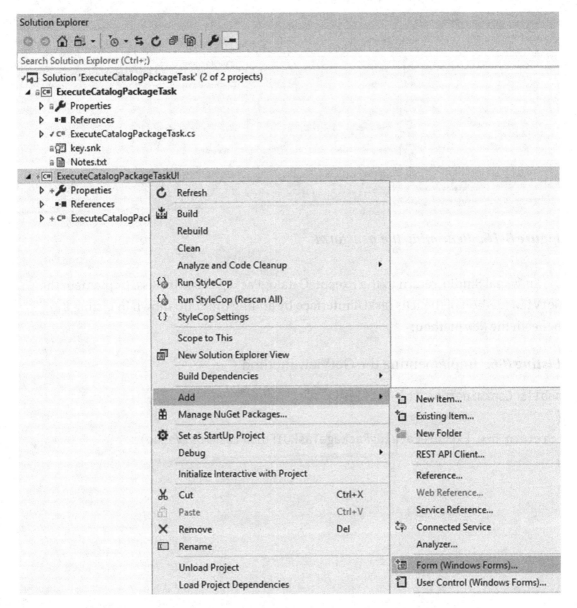

Figure 8-15. *Adding a new form*

Name the new form "ExecuteCatalogPackageTaskUIForm.cs" as shown in Figure 8-16:

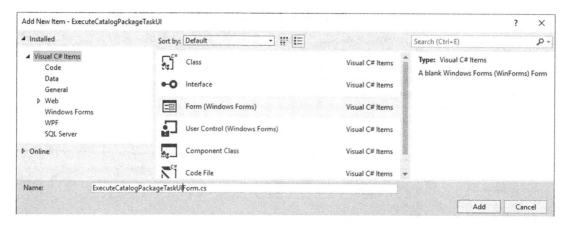

Figure 8-16. *Renaming the new form*

In Visual Studio, return to the ExecuteCatalogPackageTaskUI class. Implement the GetView method of the IDtsTaskUI interface by adding the code shown in Listing 8-6 beneath the New method:

Listing 8-6. Implementing the GetView method

```
public ContainerControl GetView()
{
  return new ExecuteCatalogPackageTaskUIForm(taskHostValue);
}
```

Your class should now appear as shown in Figure 8-17:

```
public class ExecuteCatalogPackageTaskUI : IDtsTaskUI
{
    private TaskHost taskHostValue;

    0 references
    public void New(System.Windows.Forms.IWin32Window form)
    {

    }

    0 references
    public ContainerControl GetView()
    {
        return new ExecuteCatalogPackageTaskUIForm(taskHostValue);
    }
}
```

Figure 8-17. *Implementing GetView*

The squiggly lines indicate there are no constructors (New methods) for the ExecuteCatalogPackageTaskUIForm that accept one argument of the TaskHost type. We will add a New method with a TaskHost argument in the near future.

Let's next add code to implement the IDtsTaskUI Initialize method by adding the code in Listing 8-7 to the ExecuteCatalogPackageTaskUI class:

Listing 8-7. Adding the Initialize method

```
public void Initialize(Microsoft.SqlServer.Dts.Runtime.TaskHost taskHost
                  , System.IServiceProvider serviceProvider)
{
    taskHostValue = taskHost;
}
```

The ExecuteCatalogPackageTaskUI class should now appear as shown in Figure 8-18:

```
public class ExecuteCatalogPackageTaskUI : IDtsTaskUI
{
    private TaskHost taskHostValue;

    0 references
    public void New(System.Windows.Forms.IWin32Window form)
    {

    }

    0 references
    public ContainerControl GetView()
    {
        return new ExecuteCatalogPackageTaskUIForm(taskHostValue);
    }

    0 references
    public void Initialize(Microsoft.SqlServer.Dts.Runtime.TaskHost taskHost
                    , System.IServiceProvider serviceProvider)
    {
        taskHostValue = taskHost;
    }
}
```

Figure 8-18. *Adding the Initialize method*

Finally, implement the IDtsTaskUI Delete method by adding the code shown in Listing 8-8 to the ExecuteCatalogPackageTaskUI class:

Listing 8-8. Adding the Delete method

```
public void Delete(System.Windows.Forms.IWin32Window form) { }
```

Your class should now appear as shown in Figure 8-19:

```
public class ExecuteCatalogPackageTaskUI : IDtsTaskUI
{
    private TaskHost taskHostValue;

    0 references
    public void New(System.Windows.Forms.IWin32Window form)
    {

    }

    0 references
    public ContainerControl GetView()
    {
        return new ExecuteCatalogPackageTaskUIForm(taskHostValue);
    }

    0 references
    public void Initialize(Microsoft.SqlServer.Dts.Runtime.TaskHost taskHost
                        , System.IServiceProvider serviceProvider)
    {
        taskHostValue = taskHost;
    }

    0 references
    public void Delete(System.Windows.Forms.IWin32Window form)
    {

    }
}
```

Figure 8-19. *Implementing IDtsTaskUI.Delete*

Note the squiggly lines under the IDtsTaskUI part of the class declaration public class ExecuteCatalogPackageTaskUI : IDtsTaskUI have vanished because we have completed implementing the required interface members.

The GetView() method contains squiggly lines. We will resolve this error as we begin coding the ExecuteCatalogPackageTaskUI.ExecuteCatalogPackageTaskUIForm.

We have completed building the ExecuteCatalogPackageTaskUI class. Save the class before proceeding, and remember to regularly check your code into Source Control.

Coding the Form

Open the ExecuteCatalogPackageTaskUIForm form. Add a label and a textbox to the form. Change the text of the label to "Instance:" and name the textbox "txtInstance" as shown in Figure 8-20:

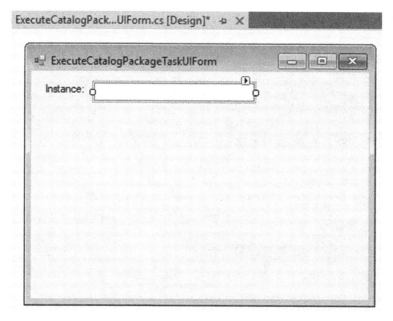

Figure 8-20. *Adding a label and textbox*

Add label and textbox controls for the Folder, Project, and Package properties as shown in Figure 8-21:

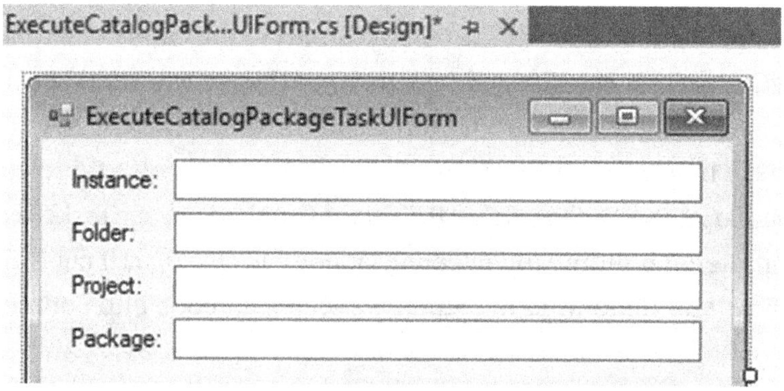

Figure 8-21. *Adding controls for Folder, Project, and Package properties*

Name the new textboxes txtFolder, txtProject, and txtPackage, respectively.

Next, add a button named btnDone and set the Text property to "Done" as shown in Figure 8-22:

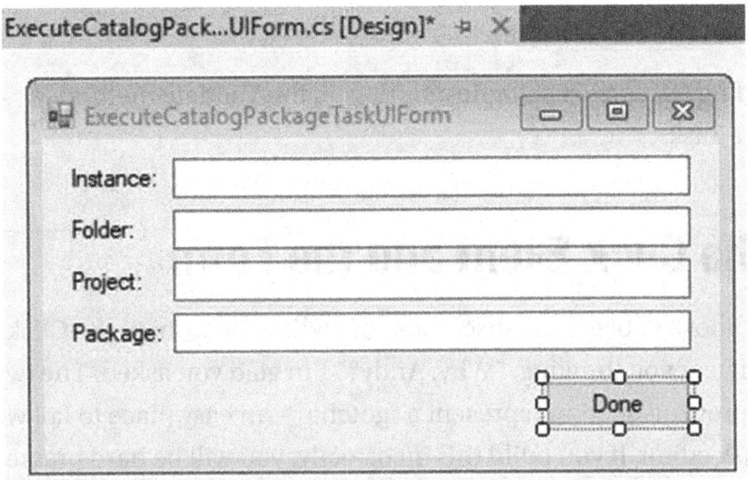

Figure 8-22. *Adding the Done button*

Finally, change the DialogResult property of btnDone to "OK" as shown in Figure 8-23:

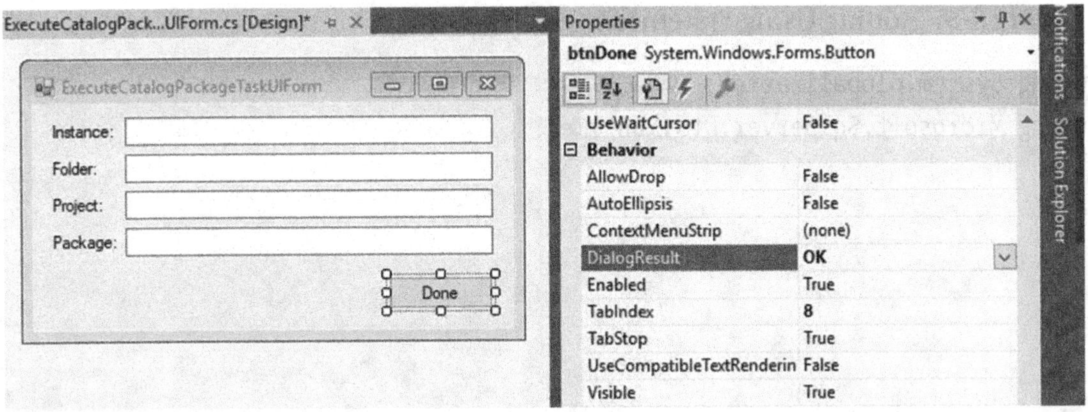

Figure 8-23. *Changing the DialogResult property for the Done button*

We will use the button's Click event to set the Catalog Package Path properties (Instance, Folder, Project, and Package) of the ExecuteCatalogPackageTask. Setting the DialogResult property to OK for the Done button is important because it accomplishes a couple of automatic functions:

- It closes the editor form.

- Sending OK as the DialogResult triggers the Validate method of the Task.

Coding the Click Event and the Form

I deliberately choose to begin the discussion of coding the form in the Click event of btnDone. I can hear you thinking, "Why, Andy?" I'm glad you asked. The two bullets at the end of the previous section represent a "gotcha" – an easy place to fail when coding a custom SSIS task editor. If you build this incorrectly, you will be hard pressed to find the answer by searching for "Validate method doesn't fire" for custom SSIS task.

We'll get to the actual code for the Click event in a bit. First, let's build out the ExecuteCatalogPackageTaskUIForm class. Begin by double-clicking btnDone to open the editor at the Click event. Before we add code directly to the Click event of btnDone, add the following using statements to the very top of the Form class, as shown in Listing 8-9:

Listing 8-9. Adding Using Statements

```
using System.Globalization;
using Microsoft.SqlServer.Dts.Runtime;
```

Your form code should now appear as shown in Figure 8-24:

```
ExecuteCatalogPackageTaskUIForm.cs  + X  ExecuteCatalogPack...UIForm.cs [Design]
[C#] ExecuteCatalogPackageTaskUI            ▼  ExecuteCatalogPackageTaskUI.ExecuteCatalogPac ▼  txtProject
    1        using System;
    2        using System.Collections.Generic;
    3        using System.ComponentModel;
    4        using System.Data;
    5        using System.Drawing;
    6        using System.Linq;
    7        using System.Text;
    8        using System.Threading.Tasks;
    9        using System.Windows.Forms;
   10        using System.Globalization;
   11        using Microsoft.SqlServer.Dts.Runtime;
   12
   13
   14        namespace ExecuteCatalogPackageTaskUI
   15        {
                 3 references
   16            public partial class ExecuteCatalogPackageTaskUIForm : Form
   17            {
                     1 reference
   18                public ExecuteCatalogPackageTaskUIForm()
   19                {
   20                    InitializeComponent();
   21                }
   22
                     1 reference
   23                private void btnDone_Click(object sender, EventArgs e)
   24                {
   25
   26                }
   27            }
   28        }
```

Figure 8-24. *Adding the Imports Statements to the ExecuteCatalogPackageTaskUIForm class*

Declare a new TaskHost variable named TaskHostValue by adding the code in Listing 8-10:

Listing 8-10. Declaring the TaskHost

```
private TaskHost taskHost;
```

Your form class should now appear as shown in Figure 8-25:

```
public partial class ExecuteCatalogPackageTaskUIForm : Form
{
    private TaskHost taskHost;

    1 reference
    private void btnDone_Click(object sender, EventArgs e)
    {

    }
```

Figure 8-25. *Declaring the TaskHost variable*

To begin coding the Click event, we need to address the task class *via* a class hosting the SSIS custom task class by adding the code found in Listing 8-11:

Listing 8-11. Adding the value of the ServerName property

```
taskHost.Properties["ServerName"].SetValue(taskHost,  txtInstance.Text);
```

Your form class should now appear as shown in Figure 8-26:

```
private void btnDone_Click(object sender, EventArgs e)
{
    taskHost.Properties["ServerName"].SetValue(taskHost, txtInstance.Text);
}
```

Figure 8-26. *Adding the value of the ServerName property*

In this method – which fires when a data integration developer clicks the Done button on the ExecuteCatalogPackageTask editor – the ServerName property of the TaskHost that is coupled to this form is set to the text property value of the form textbox named txtInstance. We built a lot of code to get here, but this is why we did it, so that we could edit a property from a task editor form.

Before proceeding, add control-to-property mappings shown in Listing 8-12 for the PackageFolder, PackageProject, and PackageName properties:

Listing 8-12. Adding property mappings

```
taskHost.Properties["PackageFolder"].SetValue(taskHost, txtFolder.Text);
taskHost.Properties["PackageProject"].SetValue(taskHost, txtProject.Text);
taskHost.Properties["PackageName"].SetValue(taskHost, txtPackage.Text);
```

Once you've added code for additional properties to the Click event method, the ExecuteCatalogPackageTaskUIForm class should appear as shown in Figure 8-27:

```
private void btnDone_Click(object sender, EventArgs e)
{
    taskHost.Properties["ServerName"].SetValue(taskHost, txtInstance.Text);
    taskHost.Properties["PackageFolder"].SetValue(taskHost, txtFolder.Text);
    taskHost.Properties["PackageProject"].SetValue(taskHost, txtProject.Text);
    taskHost.Properties["PackageName"].SetValue(taskHost, txtPackage.Text);
}
```

Figure 8-27. *Completing the Click event property coding*

The next step is the complement of the previous coding. When the form displays, we want to retrieve the values of the task object's properties (ServerName, PackageFolder, PackageProject, and PackageName) and display them in the txtInstance, txtFolder, txtProject, and txtPackage textboxes on the editor (form). To accomplish this functionality, edit the existing ExecuteCatalogPackageTaskUIForm constructor to match Listing 8-13:

Listing 8-13. ExecuteCatalogPackageTaskUIForm constructor

```
public ExecuteCatalogPackageTaskUIForm (TaskHost taskHostValue)
{
  InitializeComponent();
  taskHost = taskHostValue;
  txtInstance.Text = ➡
  taskHost.Properties["ServerName"].GetValue(taskHost).ToString();
  txtFolder.Text = ➡
  taskHost.Properties["PackageFolder"].GetValue(taskHost).ToString();
```

```
txtProject.Text = ➥
taskHost.Properties["PackageProject"].GetValue(taskHost).ToString();
txtPackage.Text = ➥
taskHost.Properties["PackageName"].GetValue(taskHost).ToString();
}
```

When done, the ExecuteCatalogPackageTaskUIForm class should appear as shown here as shown in Figure 8-28:

```
public ExecuteCatalogPackageTaskUIForm(TaskHost taskHostValue)
{
    InitializeComponent();

    taskHost = taskHostValue;
    txtInstance.Text = taskHost.Properties["ServerName"].GetValue(taskHost).ToString();
    txtFolder.Text = taskHost.Properties["PackageFolder"].GetValue(taskHost).ToString();
    txtProject.Text = taskHost.Properties["PackageProject"].GetValue(taskHost).ToString();
    txtPackage.Text = taskHost.Properties["PackageName"].GetValue(taskHost).ToString();
}
```

Figure 8-28. *Adding the form constructor*

The form constructor takes a TaskHost argument named taskHost, and this clears the error in the code in the ExecuteCatalogPackageTaskUI class's GetView function as shown in Figure 8-29:

```
0 references
public ContainerControl GetView()
{
    return new ExecuteCatalogPackageTaskUIForm(taskHostValue);
}
```

Figure 8-29. *No more squiggly line in ExecuteCatalogPackageTaskUI.GetView()*

Conclusion

In this chapter, we developed a simple editor for the custom SSIS task. We added multiple controls to a form and prepared the form for binding the editor to the custom SSIS task object. The project now contains most of the custom task functionality.

Now would be a good time to execute a commit and push to Azure DevOps. At this point in development, we have

- Created and configured an Azure DevOps project

- Connected Visual Studio to the Azure DevOps project

- Cloned the Azure DevOps Git repo locally

- Created a Visual Studio project

- Added a reference to the Visual Studio project

- Performed an initial check-in of the project code

- Signed the assembly

- Checked in an update

- Configured the build output path and build events

- Overridden three methods from the Task base class

- Added and coded most of a project for the Task editor

Next, we put together the task and editor!

CHAPTER 9

Signing and Binding

We began this book with a rambling introduction that disclosed some of how my brain works. I asked a question: "Do you think it is possible to create a custom SSIS task using Visual Studio Community Edition?"

Next, we configured our development machine and Visual Studio, and then we created a new project. We signed the project so that it would be accepted in the Global Assembly Cache (GAC) and prepared the Visual Studio environment with all the accouterments and references necessary to build a custom SSIS task. We coded the task and its editor. All that brings us here.

In this chapter, we will sign the task editor project and bind the task to the editor. Then we'll code our task's functionality, add an icon, and build and test the task.

Creating a New Public Key Token Value

The first edition of this book was written in 2017. Consider this chapter a "reboot" of the task editor design. Just to be sure, let's regenerate a key and re-extract the public key.

Before we bind the task editor to the task, let's make a new key.

© Andy Leonard 2021
A. Leonard, *Building Custom Tasks for SQL Server Integration Services*,
https://doi.org/10.1007/978-1-4842-6482-9_9

Open a command prompt as an administrator as shown in Figure 9-1:

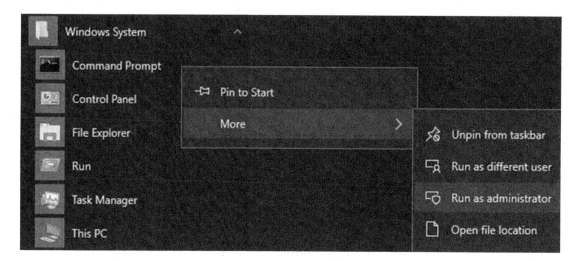

Figure 9-1. *Opening an Administrator command prompt*

In the command prompt window, navigate to the ExecuteCatalogPackageTaskUI folder as shown in Figure 9-2:

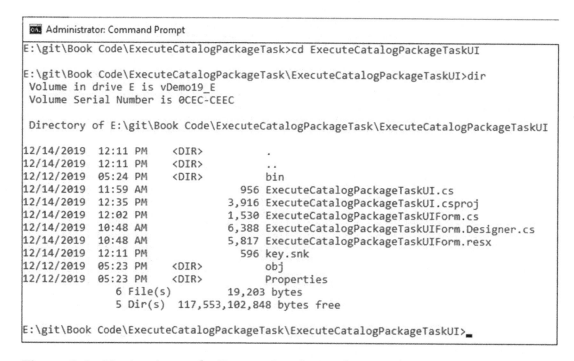

Figure 9-2. *Navigating to the ExecuteCatalogPackageTaskUI folder*

Open the Notes.txt file saved earlier in the ExecuteCatalogPackageTask project, and copy the key retrieval creation and retrieval commands as shown in Listing 9-1 and Figure 9-7:

Listing 9-1. Strong name commands

```
"C:\Program Files (x86)\Microsoft SDKs\Windows\v10.0A\bin\NETFX 4.8 ➥
Tools\sn.exe" -k key.snk
"C:\Program Files (x86)\Microsoft SDKs\Windows\v10.0A\bin\NETFX 4.8 ➥
Tools\sn.exe" -p key.snk public.out
"C:\Program Files (x86)\Microsoft SDKs\Windows\v10.0A\bin\NETFX 4.8 ➥
Tools\sn.exe" -t public.out
```

Figure 9-3. *Copying the public key creation and retrieval commands*

Paste the public key creation and retrieval commands into the Administrator command prompt window as shown in Figure 9-4:

Figure 9-4. *Creating and retrieving the public key token*

Highlight the public key token value as shown in Figure 9-5:

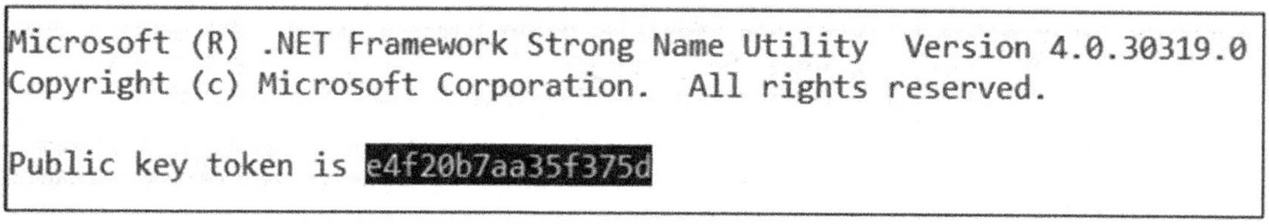

```
Microsoft (R) .NET Framework Strong Name Utility  Version 4.0.30319.0
Copyright (c) Microsoft Corporation.  All rights reserved.

Public key token is e4f20b7aa35f375d
```

Figure 9-5. *Highlighting the public key token value*

Right-click the selection to copy it to the clipboard. Paste the clipboard contents in the ExecuteCatalogPackageTask.cs file near the original Public key value for comparison as shown in Figure 9-6:

```
public class ExecuteCatalogPackageTask : Microsoft.SqlServer.Dts.Runtime.Task
{
    // Public key: e86e33313a45419e
    //             e4f20b7aa35f375d -- new key for simple UI
```

Figure 9-6. Comparing the original and new public key values

Note   A new public key is required for signing the UI assembly.

Signing the Task Editor Project

We haven't yet signed the Task Editor project. Let's do that now.

In Solution Explorer, double-click Properties under the ExecuteCatalogPackageTaskUI project to open the project properties.

Click on the Signing page, check the "Sign the assembly" checkbox, click the "Choose a strong key name file" dropdown, click Browse, browse to key.snk in the ExecuteCatalogPackageTaskUI project folder – the key.snk file we just created – and select that file as shown in Figure 9-7:

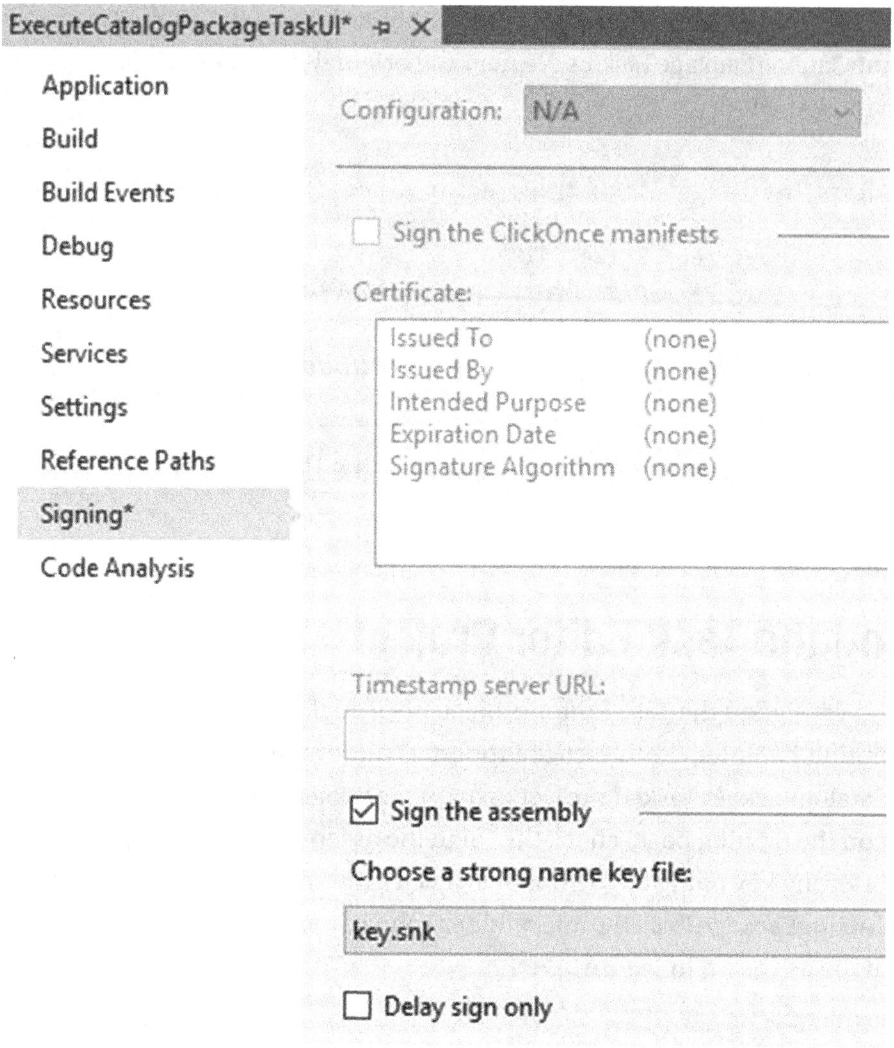

Figure 9-7. *Signing the UI project*

As with the Task project properties, click on the Build page and set the Build output path to <*drive*>:\Program Files (x86)\Microsoft SQL Server\<*version*>\DTS\Tasks where <*drive*> represents the installation drive for SQL Server and version represents the numeric version value of the SQL Server for which you are building this task, as seen in Figure 9-8:

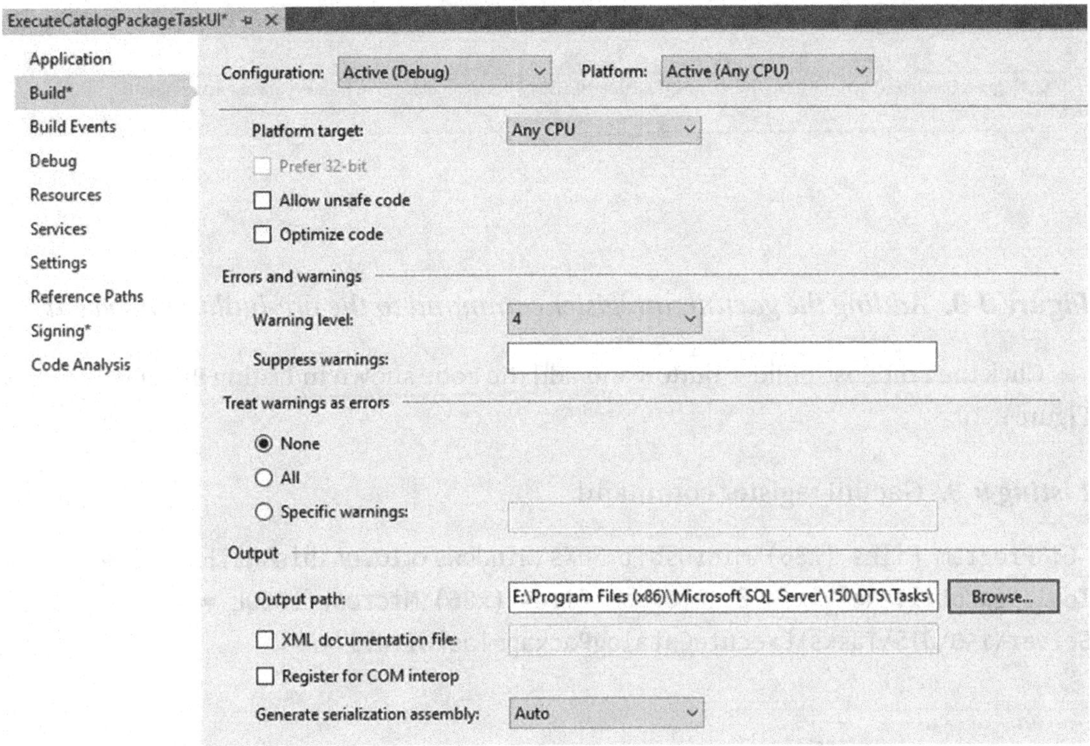

Figure 9-8. *Setting the Build output path for the ExecuteCatalogPackageTaskUI project*

As with the Task project, we may automate the gacutil unregister and register functions. Click the Build Events page, click the Edit Pre-build... button, and then add the code shown in Listing 9-2 and Figure 9-9:

Listing 9-2. Gacutil unregister command

```
"C:\Program Files (x86)\Microsoft SDKs\Windows\v10.0A\bin\NETFX 4.8 ➥
Tools\gacutil.exe" -u ExecuteCatalogPackageTask
```

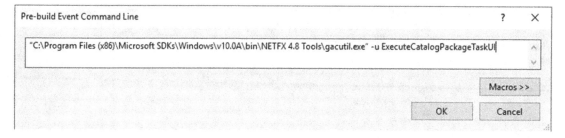

Figure 9-9. *Adding the gacutil unregister command to the pre-build build event*

Click the Edit Post-build... button and add the code shown in Listing 9-3 and Figure 9-10:

Listing 9-3. Gacutil register command

```
"C:\Program Files (x86)\Microsoft SDKs\Windows\v10.0A\bin\NETFX 4.8 ➥
Tools\gacutil.exe" -if "E:\Program Files (x86)\Microsoft SQL ➥
Server\150\DTS\Tasks\ExecuteCatalogPackageTaskUI.dll"
```

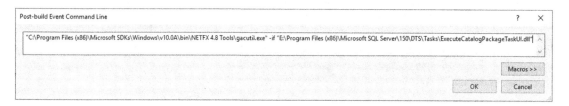

Figure 9-10. *Adding the gacutil register command to the post-build build event*

Once complete, save and close the project properties.

Binding the Task Editor to the Task

We next need to inform the task that it has an editor. Open the ExecuteCatalogPackageTask solution and the ExecuteCatalogPackageTask project in Visual Studio. Open the ExecuteCatalogPackageTask class as shown in Figure 9-11:

```
namespace ExecuteCatalogPackageTask
{
    [DtsTask(
            TaskType = "DTS150"
          , DisplayName = "ExecuteCatalogPackageTask"
          , Description = "A task to execute packages stored in the SSIS Catalog."
            )]
```

Figure 9-11. *ExecuteCatalogPackageTask, before changes*

The DtsTask attribute (decoration) is shown and documented here. In its current state, our task decoration has three values defined: TaskType, DisplayName, and Description. To couple the editor (UI) to the task, we add the multipart attribute UITypeName by adding the code in Listing 9-4 to the existing decoration:

Listing 9-4. Updating the DtsTask decoration

```
, UITypeName= "ExecuteCatalogPackageTaskUI.ExecuteCatalogPackageTaskUI ➥
",ExecuteCatalogPackageTaskUI,Version=1.0.0.0,Culture=Neutral ➥
,PublicKeyToken=<Your public key>"
, TaskContact = "ExecuteCatalogPackageTask; Building Custom Tasks for ➥
 SQL Server Integration Services, 2019 Edition; © 2020 Andy Leonard; ➥
https://dilmsuite.com/ExecuteCatalogPackageTaskBookCode"
```

Once added to the DtsTask attribute decoration, the decoration will appear similar to Figure 9-12:

```
[DtsTask(
     TaskType = "DTS150"
   , DisplayName = "Execute Catalog Package Task"
   , Description = "A task to execute packages stored in the SSIS Catalog."
   , UITypeName= "ExecuteCatalogPackageTaskUI.ExecuteCatalogPackageTaskUI, ExecuteCatalogPackageTaskUI, Version=1.0.0.0, Culture=Neutral, PublicKeyToken= e4f20b7aa35f375d"
   , TaskContact = "ExecuteCatalogPackageTask; Building Custom Tasks for SQL Server Integration Services, 2019 Edition; © 2020 Andy Leonard; https://dilmsuite.com/ExecuteCatalogPackageTaskBookCode")]
```

Figure 9-12. *Adding the UITypeName and TaskContact attributes to the DtsTask decoration*

You can find (some) documentation for the UITypeName attribute at docs.microsoft.com/en-us/dotnet/api/microsoft.sqlserver.dts.runtime.dtstaskattribute.uitypename?view=sqlserver-2017. The property/value pairs are

- Type Name: ExecuteCatalogPackageTaskUI.
  ExecuteCatalogPackageTaskUI

- Assembly Name: ExecuteCatalogPackageTaskUI

- Version: 1.0.0.0

- Culture: Neutral

- Public Key: *<Your public key>*

Coding the Task Functionality

Our task is *almost* ready to build and test. What's left? SSIS Catalog Package execution functionality. Look in the Execute method shown in Figure 9-13:

```
0 references
public override DTSExecResult Execute(
    Connections connections,
    VariableDispenser variableDispenser,
    IDTSComponentEvents componentEvents,
    IDTSLogging log,
    object transaction)
{
    return DTSExecResult.Success;
}
```

Figure 9-13. *The Execute method*

We are going to add SSIS Catalog Package execution functionality here. There are several good articles available that walk one through executing SSIS Catalog Packages via .Net. A good summary of the process of executing SSIS 2019 package programmatically is found at docs.microsoft.com/en-us/sql/integration-services/run-manage-packages-programmatically/running-and-managing-packages-programmatically?view=sql-server-ver15.

Caution   Before we proceed, I want to remind you that we are not building a production-ready Execute Catalog Package Task. We are building a minimum amount of functionality to demonstrate the steps required to code a custom SSIS task. A production-ready custom SSIS task would include more functionality that we will cover here.

We first need more .Net Framework References. Add the following references to the ExecuteCatalogPackageTask project:

- Microsoft.SqlServer.ConnectionInfo

- Microsoft.SqlServer.Management.IntegrationServices

- Microsoft.SqlServer.Management.Sdk.Sfc

- Microsoft.SqlServer.Smo

I found Microsoft.SqlServer.ConnectionInfo in the C:\Windows\Microsoft.NET\ assembly\GAC_MSIL\Microsoft.SqlServer.ConnectionInfo\v4.0_15.0.0.0__89845dcd808 0cc91\ folder on my development VM, as shown in Figure 9-14:

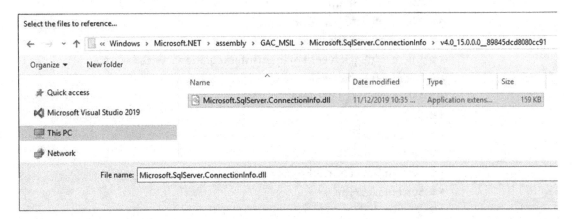

Figure 9-14. *Adding a reference for Microsoft.SqlServer.ConnectionInfo*

I found Microsoft.SqlServer.Management.IntegrationServices, Microsoft.SqlServer. Management.Sdk.Sfc, and Microsoft.SqlServer.Smo in the C:\Windows\Microsoft.NET\ assembly\GAC_MSIL\ path, as well, as shown in Figure 9-15:

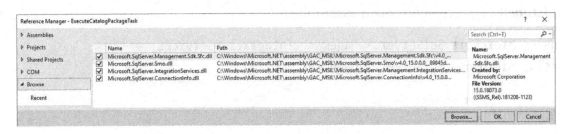

Figure 9-15. *Browsing to reference additional assemblies*

The Solution Explorer References virtual folder for the ExecuteCatalogPackageTask project should now appear as shown in Figure 9-16:

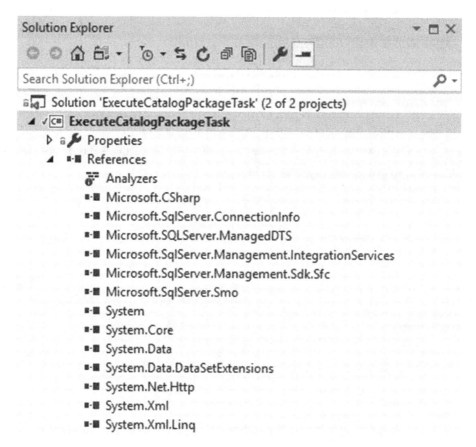

Figure 9-16. *Viewing the ExecuteCatalogPackageTask project References*

We next need to declare reference assemblies in ExecuteCatalogPackageTask.cs for use in our project, as shown in Listing 9-5:

Listing 9-5. Using referenced assemblies

```
using Microsoft.SqlServer.Management.IntegrationServices;
using Microsoft.SqlServer.Management.Smo;
```

```
using Microsoft.SqlServer.Management.IntegrationServices;
using Microsoft.SqlServer.Management.Smo;
```

Figure 9-17. *Importing Referenced Assemblies*

We're now ready to add functionality to the Execute function. Declare and initialize some variables using the code shown in Listing 9-6:

Listing 9-6. Coding the Execute method, part 1

```
Server catalogServer = new Server(ServerName);
IntegrationServices integrationServices = new ➡
IntegrationServices(catalogServer);
Catalog catalog = integrationServices.Catalogs[PackageCatalog];
CatalogFolder catalogFolder = catalog.Folders[PackageFolder];
ProjectInfo catalogProject = catalogFolder.Projects[PackageProject];
Microsoft.SqlServer.Management.IntegrationServices.PackageInfo ➡
catalogPackage = catalogProject.Packages[PackageName];
```

Your Execute method should appear similar to that shown in Figure 9-18:

```
0 references
public override DTSExecResult Execute(
    Connections connections,
    VariableDispenser variableDispenser,
    IDTSComponentEvents componentEvents,
    IDTSLogging log,
    object transaction)
{
    Server catalogServer = new Server(ServerName);
    IntegrationServices integrationServices = new IntegrationServices(catalogServer);
    Catalog catalog = integrationServices.Catalogs[PackageCatalog];
    CatalogFolder catalogFolder = catalog.Folders[PackageFolder];
    ProjectInfo catalogProject = catalogFolder.Projects[PackageProject];
    Microsoft.SqlServer.Management.IntegrationServices.PackageInfo catalogPackage = catalogProject.Packages[PackageName];

    return DTSExecResult.Success;
}
```

Figure 9-18. *Execute SSIS Catalog Package method partially coded*

Finally, add the call to execute the SSIS Package object (catalogPackage) as shown in Listing 9-7 and Figure 9-19:

Listing 9-7. Adding package execution code

```
catalogPackage.Execute(False, Nothing)
```

107

```
0 references
public override DTSExecResult Execute(
    Connections connections,
    VariableDispenser variableDispenser,
    IDTSComponentEvents componentEvents,
    IDTSLogging log,
    object transaction)
{
    Server catalogServer = new Server(ServerName);
    IntegrationServices integrationServices = new IntegrationServices(catalogServer);
    Catalog catalog = integrationServices.Catalogs[PackageCatalog];
    CatalogFolder catalogFolder = catalog.Folders[PackageFolder];
    ProjectInfo catalogProject = catalogFolder.Projects[PackageProject];
    Microsoft.SqlServer.Management.IntegrationServices.PackageInfo catalogPackage = catalogProject.Packages[PackageName];

    catalogPackage.Execute(false, null);

    return DTSExecResult.Success;
}
```

Figure 9-19. *Calling the CatalogPackage.Execute Method*

I don't want to make too big a deal over this, but we did *all this work* to add that one line of code…

Add an Icon

Before you can use an icon, you must import it into your project. Right-click the ExecuteCatalogPackageTask project in Solution Explorer, hover over Add, and then click Existing Item as shown in Figure 9-20:

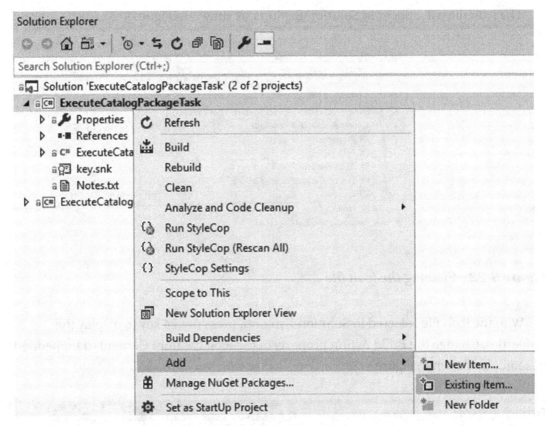

Figure 9-20. *Adding an Existing Item to the ExecuteCatalogPackageTask Project*

Navigate to the icon file you wish to use as shown in Figure 9-21:

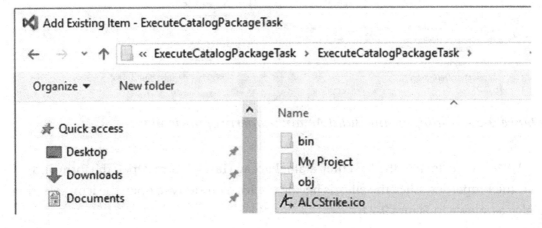

Figure 9-21. *Selecting the icon*

The icon file will appear in Solution Explorer as shown in Figure 9-22:

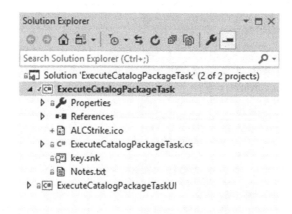

Figure 9-22. *Viewing the icon file*

With the icon file selected in Solution Explorer, press the F4 key to display the Properties. Change the Build Action property of the icon file from Content to Embedded Resource as shown in Figure 9-23:

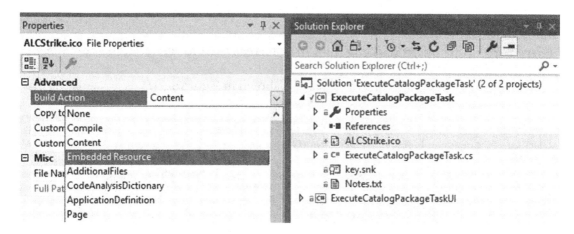

Figure 9-23. *Changing the Build Action property of the icon file*

Let's add the icon to the ExecuteCatalogPackageTaskUI form. Open the form and view the Properties. Click the ellipsis beside the Icon property to open the icon selection dialog as shown in Figure 9-24:

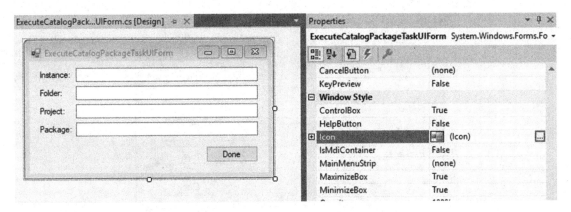

Figure 9-24. *Opening the form icon selection dialog*

Select the icon as shown in Figure 9-25:

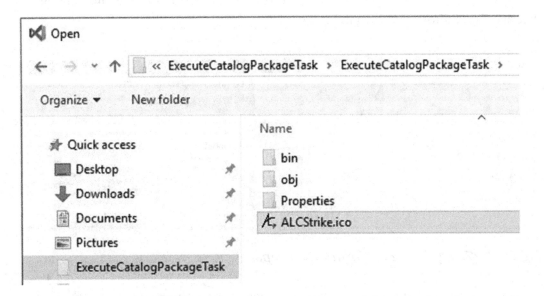

Figure 9-25. *Selecting the form icon*

The selected icon now appears as the icon for the ExecuteCatalogPackageTaskForm form as shown in Figure 9-26:

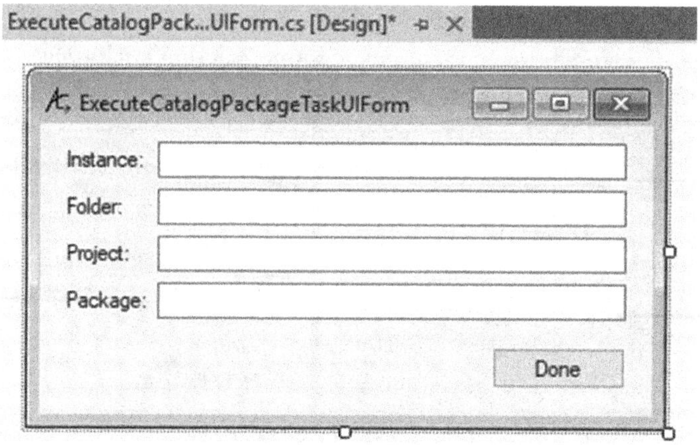

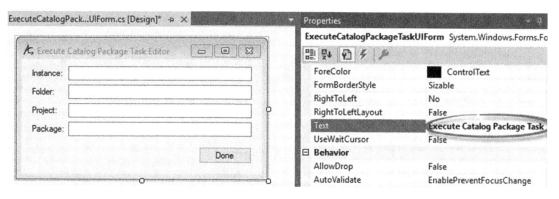

Figure 9-26. *Viewing the form icon*

While we're here, let's update the Text property of the form to "Execute Catalog Package Task Editor" as shown in Figure 9-27:

Figure 9-27. *Updating the form's text property*

SSIS won't know which icon to display until we update the DtsTask decoration for ExecuteCatalogPackageTask. Open ExecuteCatalogPackageTask.cs and add the line shown in Listing 9-8 to the decoration:

Listing 9-8. Adding the icon to the DtsTask decoration

```
, IconResource = "ExecuteCatalogPackageTask.ALCStrike.ico"
```

Your decoration should now appear similar to that shown in Figure 9-28:

```
[DtsTask(
        TaskType = "DTS150"
      , DisplayName = "ExecuteCatalogPackageTask"
      , IconResource = "ExecuteCatalogPackageTask.ALCStrike.ico"
      , Description = "A task to execute packages stored in the SSIS Catalog."
      , UITypeName= "ExecuteCatalogPackageTask.ExecuteCatalogPackageTaskUI,ExecuteCatalogP
      , TaskContact = "ExecuteCatalogPackageTask; Building Custom Tasks for SQL Server Int
0 references
public class ExecuteCatalogPackageTask : Microsoft.SqlServer.Dts.Runtime.Task
```

Figure 9-28. *Viewing updated DtsTask decoration*

Now would be an excellent time to check your code into source control.

Building the Task

We are now code-complete! It is time to build our solution, which will compile the code into an executable. From the Build dropdown menu, click Build Solution as shown in Figure 9-29:

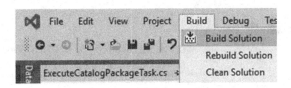

Figure 9-29. *Building the solution*

If all goes well, you should see verbiage in the Output window similar to that shown in Figure 9-30:

```
Output
Show output from:  Build                              ▼ | 全 | 全 全 | 全 | 全
1>------ Build started: Project: ExecuteCatalogPackageTask, Configuration: Debug Any CPU ------
1>  Microsoft (R) .NET Global Assembly Cache Utility.  Version 4.0.30319.0
1>  Copyright (c) Microsoft Corporation.  All rights reserved.
1>
1>  No assemblies found matching: ExecuteCatalogPackageTask
1>  Number of assemblies uninstalled = 0
1>  Number of failures = 0
1>  ExecuteCatalogPackageTask -> E:\Program Files (x86)\Microsoft SQL Server\150\DTS\Tasks\ExecuteCatalogPackageTask.dll
1>  Microsoft (R) .NET Global Assembly Cache Utility.  Version 4.0.30319.0
1>  Copyright (c) Microsoft Corporation.  All rights reserved.
1>  |
1>  Assembly successfully added to the cache
2>------ Build started: Project: ExecuteCatalogPackageTaskUI, Configuration: Debug Any CPU ------
2>  Microsoft (R) .NET Global Assembly Cache Utility.  Version 4.0.30319.0
2>  Copyright (c) Microsoft Corporation.  All rights reserved.
2>
2>  No assemblies found matching: ExecuteCatalogPackageTaskUI
2>  Number of assemblies uninstalled = 0
2>  Number of failures = 0
2>  ExecuteCatalogPackageTaskUI -> E:\Program Files (x86)\Microsoft SQL Server\150\DTS\Tasks\ExecuteCatalogPackageTaskUI.dll
2>  Microsoft (R) .NET Global Assembly Cache Utility.  Version 4.0.30319.0
2>  Copyright (c) Microsoft Corporation.  All rights reserved.
2>
2>  Assembly successfully added to the cache
========== Build: 2 succeeded, 0 failed, 0 up-to-date, 0 skipped ==========
```

Figure 9-30. *Build output*

If all goes as expected, you should have two assemblies successfully built to the DTS\
Tasks\ folder as shown in Figure 9-31:

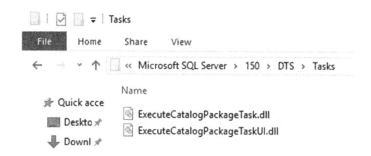

Figure 9-31. *ExecuteCatalogPackageTask and ExecuteCatalogPackageTaskUI
assemblies in the DTS\Tasks\ folder*

You should also find the assemblies in the GAC as shown in Figure 9-32:

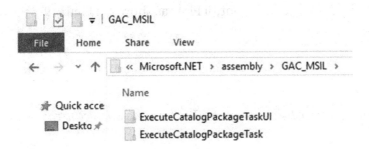

Figure 9-32. *ExecuteCatalogPackageTask and ExecuteCatalogPackageTaskUI assemblies in the GAC*

Testing the Task

The moment of truth has arrived. Will the task work? Will it even show up in the SSIS Toolbox? Let's open SQL Server Data Tools (SSDT) and find out! If all has gone according to plan, you will be able to open a test SSIS project and see the following on the SSIS Toolbox as shown in Figure 9-33:

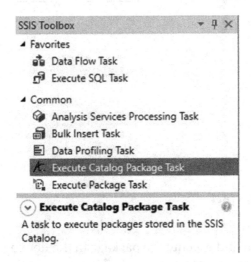

Figure 9-33. *Execute Catalog Package Task in the SSIS Toolbox*

Drag it onto the surface of the Control Flow as shown in Figure 9-34:

Figure 9-34. *Execute Catalog Package Task on the SSIS control flow*

Double-click the task to open the editor and configure the task as shown in Figure 9-35:

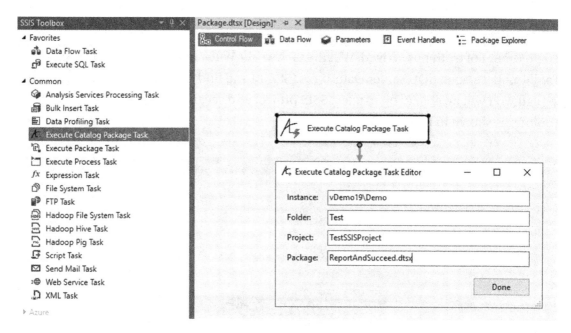

Figure 9-35. *Editing the task*

Click the Done button and execute the package in the debugger. If all goes well, our Execute Catalog Package Task will succeed as shown in Figure 9-36:

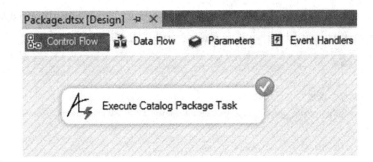

Figure 9-36. *Task execution*

Did the task *really* succeed or did it just report success? We can check by examining the SSIS Catalog Reports which are built into SQL Server Management Studio (SSMS). Open SSMS and connect to the instance that hosts your SSIS Catalog. Expand the Integration Services Catalogs node, right-click on SSISDB, hover over Reports, hover over Standard Reports, and then click All Executions as shown in Figure 9-37:

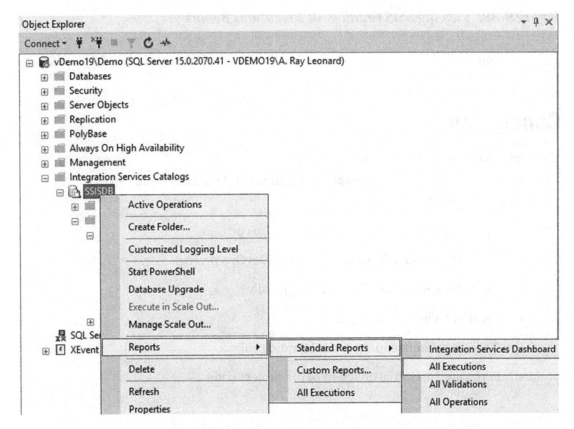

Figure 9-37. *Opening the SSIS Catalog All Executions Report in SSMS*

The All Executions Report displays SSIS Package executions in the past 7 days (by default). I confess. I executed it twice as shown in Figure 9-38:

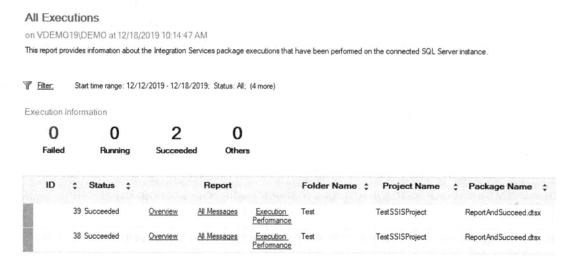

Figure 9-38. Viewing SSIS Catalog All Executions Report

Excellent!

Conclusion

The code and editor now function as a unit.

Now would be a good time to execute a commit and push to Azure DevOps.

At this point in development, we have

- Created and configured an Azure DevOps project

- Connected Visual Studio to the Azure DevOps project

- Cloned the Azure DevOps Git repo locally

- Created a Visual Studio project

- Added a reference to the Visual Studio project

- Performed an initial check-in of the project code

- Signed the assembly

- Checked in an update

- Configured the build output path and build events

- Overridden three methods from the Task base class

- Added and coded most of a project for the Task editor.

- Knit the Task Editor to the Task.

But what if things *don't* happen like this? What if there's an error? We next extend editor functionality.

Expanding Editor Functionality

The first edition of Building Custom Tasks for SQL Server Integration Services was published in 2017. Chapter 10 covered troubleshooting tips. Chapter 11 contained notes from my experience. This edition will include those chapters... only later.

This section of the book is new to the second edition. The goal of this chapter and subsequent chapters is to expand the functionality of the Execute Catalog Package Task, specifically

- Surface a more "SSIS-y" experience for users of the task including a "pretty" editor with General and Settings pages "views"

- Enable the use of SSIS Expressions

- Add design-time validation of task settings

- Surface more SSIS Catalog execution properties in the editor

We begin these efforts in this chapter, in which we refactor existing ExecuteCatalog PackageTask code and replace the existing task editor project with a new version.

Refactoring

Developers are sometimes given the opportunity to rewrite or update older versions of their code. The longer said code has been in use, the more experience a developer has with the code. *Refactoring* is defined in a few ways, including cleaning, simplifying, and restructuring existing code.

In this chapter, we begin with some refactoring of the ExecuteCatalogPackageTask code, starting with managing the scope of variables.

© Andy Leonard 2021
A. Leonard, *Building Custom Tasks for SQL Server Integration Services*,
https://doi.org/10.1007/978-1-4842-6482-9_10

Adding and Updating Task Properties

One change will directly address one of the bullets above and move us closer to solving a few others: adding SSIS Catalog, Server, and other SSIS package related objects as private properties in the ExecuteCatalogPackageTask object.

Examining the ExecuteCatalogPackageTask class in the ExecuteCatalogPackageTask project, we find the *beginning* of an SSIS Catalog object in the PackageCatalog property as shown in Figure 10-1:

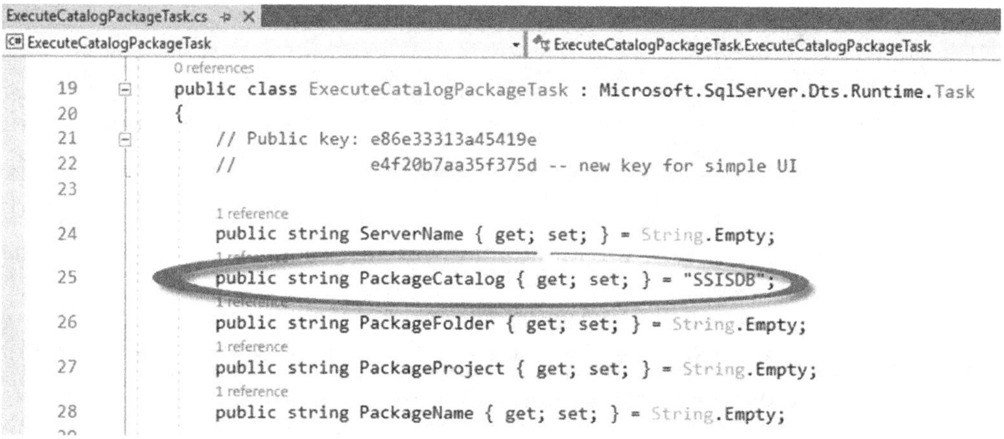

Figure 10-1. *The PackageCatalog property*

The PackageCatalog property is a string and contains the name of the SSIS Catalog. At the time of this writing, SSIS Catalog names have remained consistent and unchanged, "SSISDB." The property is included as an example of future-proofing the Execute Catalog Package Task in case future versions of the SSIS Catalog permit editing the SSIS Catalog name, but I do not like the name of the Execute Catalog Package Task's PackageCatalog property.

Rename the Execute Catalog Package Task PackageCatalog property to "PackageCatalogName," click the "Quick Actions" screwdriver icon in the left margin, and then click "Rename 'PackageCatalog' to 'PackageCatalogName,'" as shown in Figure 10-2:

Figure 10-2. *Renaming the PackageCatalog property to "PackageCatalogName"*

PackageCatalogName is a more accurate name for the property formerly known as
PackageCatalog.

The current version of the Execute Catalog Package Task includes a variable of type
Microsoft.SqlServer.Management.IntegrationServices.Catalog in the Execute method, as
shown in Figure 10-3:

```
public override DTSExecResult Execute(
    Connections connections,
    VariableDispenser variableDispenser,
    IDTSComponentEvents componentEvents,
    IDTSLogging log,
    object transaction)
{
    Server catalogServer = new Server(ServerName);
    IntegrationServices integrationServices = new IntegrationServices(catalogServer);
    Catalog catalog = integrationServices.Catalogs[PackageCatalog];
    CatalogFolder catalogFolder = catalog.Folders[PackageFolder];
    ProjectInfo catalogProject = catalogFolder.Projects[PackageProject];
    Microsoft.SqlServer.Management.IntegrationServices.PackageInfo catalogPackage = catalogProject.Packages[PackageName];

    catalogPackage.Execute(false, null);

    return DTSExecResult.Success;
}
```

Figure 10-3. *A variable of type Microsoft.SqlServer.Management.*
IntegrationServices.Catalog

How difficult is it to cut this property from the Execute method and use a new private
property for the task of the Microsoft.SqlServer.Management.IntegrationServices.Catalog
type at the class scope? We may assign a value to the catalog property once we have
enough information available during task configuration. After all, the Execute Catalog
Package Task will connect to one and only one SSIS catalog.

Begin this process by adding a new property named `catalog` of the Microsoft.
SqlServer.Management.IntegrationServices type to the ExecuteCatalogPackageTask
properties list as shown in Listing 10-1 and Figure 10-4:

Listing 10-1. Code to add the Catalog property

```
public Catalog catalog { get; set; } = null;
```

```
public class ExecuteCatalogPackageTask : Microsoft.SqlServer.Dts.Runtime.Task
{
    // Public key: e86e33313a45419e
    //             e4f20b7aa35f375d -- new key for simple UI

    3 references
    public string ServerName { get; set; } = String.Empty;
    1 reference
    public string PackageCatalogName { get; set; } = "SSISDB";
    0 references
    private Catalog catalog { get; set; } = null;
    1 reference
    public string PackageFolder { get; set; } = String.Empty;
    1 reference
    public string PackageProject { get; set; } = String.Empty;
    1 reference
    public string PackageName { get; set; } = String.Empty;
```

Figure 10-4. *Declaring a Catalog property*

Note   The name of this property is not a capital letter. That's intentional. This
property will be internal to the task. Also, the object type does not need to include
"*Microsoft.SqlServer.Management.IntegrationServices*" because the
code includes *using Microsoft.SqlServer.Management.IntegrationServices*
at the top of the class code.

Because the `catalog` property is internal to the ExecuteCatalogPackageTask class, it
is declared as `private`.

While we're at it, let's migrate other variables from the `Execute` method to
private properties, such as `catalogServer` (`Microsoft.SqlServer.Management.`
`Smo.Server` type), `integrationServices` (`Microsoft.SqlServer.Management.`
`IntegrationServices` type), `catalogFolder` (`Microsoft.SqlServer.Management.`

IntegrationServices.CatalogFolder type), catalogProject (Microsoft.SqlServer.
Management.IntegrationServices.ProjectInfo type), catalogPackage (Microsoft.
SqlServer.Management.IntegrationServices.PackageInfo type), as shown in
Listing 10-2 and Figure 10-5:

Listing 10-2. Adding additional properties

```
private Server catalogServer { get; set; } = null;
private IntegrationServices integrationServices { get; set; } = null;
private CatalogFolder catalogFolder { get; set; } = null;
private ProjectInfo catalogProject { get; set; } = null;
private Microsoft.SqlServer.Management.IntegrationServices.PackageInfo
catalogPackage { get; set; } = null;
```

Please note the full data type specification for the catalogPackage private property.
The full name of the variable type must be declared because there is a different
PackageInfo type in the Microsoft.SqlServer.Dts.Runtime assembly. Visual Studio
complains if it is not specific because Visual Studio has no way to determine which
PackageInfo type we wish to use.

```
public class ExecuteCatalogPackageTask : Microsoft.SqlServer.Dts.Runtime.Task
{
    // Public key: e86e33313a45419e
    //              e4f20b7aa35f375d -- new key for simple UI

    1 reference
    public string ServerName { get; set; } = String.Empty;
    2 references
    private Server catalogServer { get; set; } = null;
    2 references
    private IntegrationServices integrationServices { get; set; } = null;
    1 reference
    public string PackageCatalogName { get; set; } = "SSISDB";
    2 references
    private Catalog catalog { get; set; } = null;
    1 reference
    public string PackageFolder { get; set; } = String.Empty;
    2 references
    private CatalogFolder catalogFolder { get; set; } = null;
    1 reference
    public string PackageProject { get; set; } = String.Empty;
    2 references
    private ProjectInfo catalogProject { get; set; } = null;
    1 reference
    public string PackageName { get; set; } = String.Empty;
    2 references
    private Microsoft.SqlServer.Management.IntegrationServices.PackageInfo catalogPackage { get; set; } = null;
```

Figure 10-5. *Additional properties added*

Let's next update the Execute method to initialize the class-scoped variables we just added.

Updating the Execute Method

To continue our refactoring effort, update the variables declared in the Execute method to use and initialize the new internal task properties.

The current state of the Execute method is listed in Listing 10-3 and shown in Figure 10-6:

Listing 10-3. The Execute method, currently

```
public override DTSExecResult Execute(
        Connections connections,
        VariableDispenser variableDispenser,
        IDTSComponentEvents componentEvents,
        IDTSLogging log,
        object transaction)
    {
        Server catalogServer = new Server(ServerName);
        IntegrationServices integrationServices = new Integration
        Services(catalogServer);
        Catalog catalog = integrationServices.Catalogs
        [PackageCatalogName];
        CatalogFolder catalogFolder = catalog.Folders[PackageFolder];
        ProjectInfo catalogProject = catalogFolder.Projects
        [PackageProject];
        Microsoft.SqlServer.Management.IntegrationServices.Package
        Info catalogPackage = catalogProject.Packages[PackageName];

        catalogPackage.Execute(false, null);

        return DTSExecResult.Success;
    }
```

```
public override DTSExecResult Execute(
    Connections connections,
    VariableDispenser variableDispenser,
    IDTSComponentEvents componentEvents,
    IDTSLogging log,
    object transaction)
{
    Server catalogServer = new Server(ServerName);
    IntegrationServices integrationServices = new IntegrationServices(catalogServer);
    Catalog catalog = integrationServices.Catalogs[PackageCatalogName];
    CatalogFolder catalogFolder = catalog.Folders[PackageFolder];
    ProjectInfo catalogProject = catalogFolder.Projects[PackageProject];
    Microsoft.SqlServer.Management.IntegrationServices.PackageInfo catalogPackage = catalogProject.Packages[PackageName];

    catalogPackage.Execute(false, null);

    return DTSExecResult.Success;
}
```

Figure 10-6. *The current version of the Execute method*

We want to initialize the new class-scoped variables in the Execute method, so we need to remove the type declarations. Update the type declaration and initialization code to *remove* type declarations, as shown in Listing 10-4:

Listing 10-4. Removing Execute method variable type declarations

```
catalogServer = new Server(ServerName);
integrationServices = new IntegrationServices(catalogServer);
catalog = integrationServices.Catalogs[PackageCatalogName];
catalogFolder = catalog.Folders[PackageFolder];
catalogProject = catalogFolder.Projects[PackageProject];
catalogPackage = catalogProject.Packages[PackageName];
```

At this point in our efforts to expand the functionality of the Execute Catalog Package Task, we may test by building the solution and testing the task (see Chapter 9, sections "Building the Task" and "Testing the Task"). This is a good test of our changes to the Execution method.

Adding a New Editor

Two bullets from the introduction of this chapter are

- Surface a more "SSIS-y" experience for users of the task including a "pretty" editor with General and Settings pages "views."

- Enable the use of SSIS Expressions.

Before moving forward in this section, the author owes a debt of gratitude to Kirk Haselden for his outstanding early SSIS book titled *Microsoft SQL Server 2005 Integration Services* (amazon.com/Microsoft-Server-2005-Integration-Services-dp-0672327813/dp/0672327813), Sams Publishing, 2006.

I know lots of people who learned about custom SSIS tasks from Kirk's book.

Thank you, Kirk!

Complex UI Overview

This section of the book is difficult and advanced. At the heart of the complex UI is the Microsoft.DataTransformationServices.Controls assembly. Inheriting from the Microsoft.DataTransformationServices.Controls assembly is challenging and can be nonintuitive. That said, the functionality surfaced in the Microsoft.DataTransformationServices.Controls assembly is more than worth the time required to overcome any challenges and manage its nonintuitive-ness.

The Microsoft.DataTransformationServices.Controls assembly requires development of *views*, which SSIS developers encounter when we open a task editor. Each view represents a high-level collection of task properties. Views are listed on the left side of the editor and outlined by the green box in Figure 10-7:

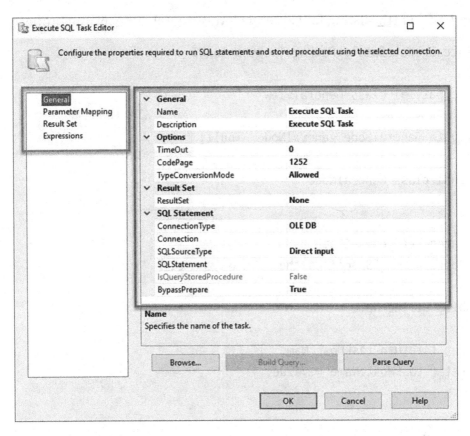

Figure 10-7. *The Execute SQL Task's General page*

Under the hood of each view is a *node,* defined as an internal C# class instantiated for each view. Each node surfaces a PropertyGrid control, which is shown in Figure 10-7 inside the blue box.

A node manages a collection of task properties organized by property category. Each task property is a C# property in the node class. An example we will build out later is the Name property in the General node of the General view. The code represents a View ➤ Node ➤ Property Category ➤ Property hierarchy. The code flows as shown in Listing 10-5:

Listing 10-5. Partial listing for General view, General node, Name property

```
namespace ExecuteCatalogPackageTaskComplexUI
{
  public partial class GeneralView
  {
    private GeneralNode generalNode = null;
  }
  internal class GeneralNode
  {
    [
      Category("General"),
      Description("Specifies the name of the task.")
    ]
    public string Name
    {
      get { return taskHost.Name; }
      set { taskHost.Name = value; }
    }
  }
}
```

The View ➤ Node ➤ Property Category ➤ Property hierarchy shown in the partial listing in Listing 10-5 begins with the view named GeneralView. GeneralView declares a private member of the GeneralNode type named generalNode. The GeneralNode class contains a string type property named Name. The Name property is decorated with Category and Description decorations, and the Category decoration contains the name for the property category ("General").

Figure 10-8 visualizes the hierarchy for the Execute SQL Task Editor. As mentioned earlier, the General view (in the green box on the left) displays the General node – represented by the propertygrid control (in the blue box on the right). The property category named "General" is shown in the red box. The Name property is shown enclosed in the yellow box, as shown in Figure 10-8:

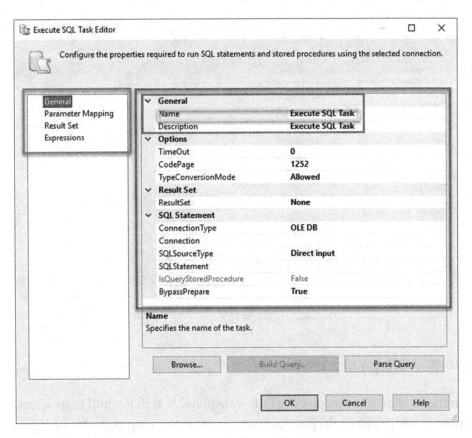

Figure 10-8. *Visualizing View ➤ Node ➤ Property Category ➤ Property*

Applied to the View ➤ Node ➤ Property Category ➤ Property hierarchy, the names of the entities for the Execute SQL Task Editor – shown in Figure 10-8 – are as follows: General (View) ➤ General (Node) ➤ General (Property Category) ➤ Name (Property). That's a lot of General's, and one – the General node – is hiding beneath the propertygrid control.

Adding the Editor Project

To begin adding a new editor, add a new project to the ExecuteCatalogPackageTask Visual Studio solution by right-clicking the solution in Solution Explorer, hovering over "Add," and then clicking "New project...," as shown in Figure 10-9:

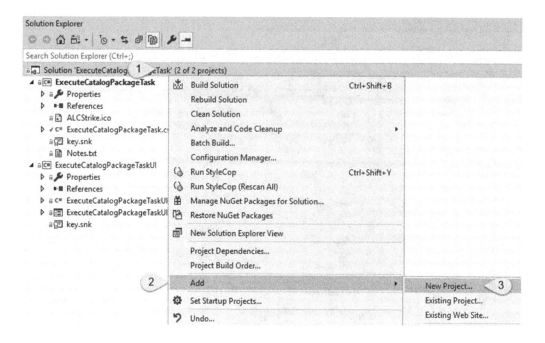

Figure 10-9. *Adding a new project*

When the "Create a new project" window displays, search for, and then select, a C# Class Library (.Net Framework) project type, or in the .Net language of your choosing. I chose C# for the language and named the project ExecuteCatalogPackageTask as shown in Figure 10-10:

Figure 10-10. *Selecting a project type*

Select "Class Library (.NET Framework)" and click the Next button.

When the "Configure your new project" window displays, enter "ExecuteCatalogPackageTaskComplexUI "as the name for the new project, and set the project files location as shown in Figure 10-11:

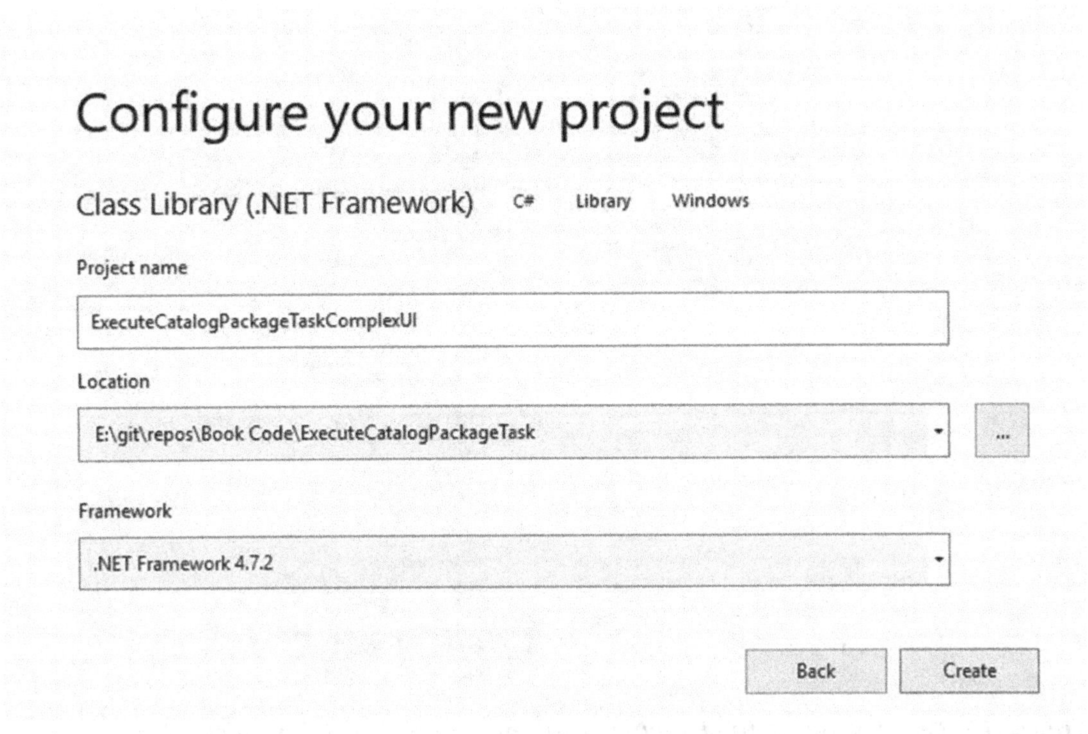

Configure your new project

Class Library (.NET Framework)   C#   Library   Windows

Project name

ExecuteCatalogPackageTaskComplexUI

Location

E:\git\repos\Book Code\ExecuteCatalogPackageTask

Framework

.NET Framework 4.7.2

Back   Create

Figure 10-11. Configuring and naming the new project

Click the Create button to add the new ExecuteCatalogPackageTaskComplexUI project.

To remove the existing ExecuteCatalogPackageTaskUI project, right-click the ExecuteCatalogPackageTaskUI project in Solution Explorer, and then click "Remove," as shown in Figure 10-12:

Figure 10-12. *Removing the ExecuteCatalogPackageTaskUI project*

In Solution Explorer, rename the ExecuteCatalogPackageTaskComplexUI project's Class1.cs file "ExecuteCatalogPackageTaskComplexUI," as shown in Figure 10-13:

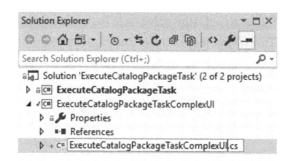

Figure 10-13. *Renaming Class1.cs to ExecuteCatalogPackageTaskComplexUI.cs*

Visual Studio will prompt, asking if you would also like to rename all references to "Class1" in the project, as shown in Figure 10-14:

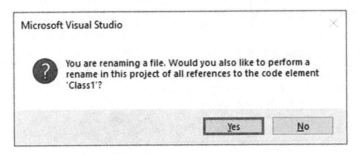

Figure 10-14. *Prompting to rename all Class1 references to ExecuteCatalogPackageTaskComplexUI*

Click the Yes button. Note the "`public class Class1`" declaration in the ExecuteCatalogPackageTaskComplexUI.cs file now reads "`public class ExecuteCatalogPackageTaskComplexUI`," as shown in Figure 10-15:

```
using System;
using System.Collections.Generic;
using System.Linq;
using System.Text;
using System.Threading.Tasks;

namespace ExecuteCatalogPackageTaskComplexUI
{
    0 references
    public class ExecuteCatalogPackageTaskComplexUI
    {
    }
}
```

Figure 10-15. *Class1 is now ExecuteCatalogPackageTaskComplexUI*

The ExecuteCatalogPackageTaskComplexUI class is now ready for references and additional coding.

Adding References

To add references to the new ExecuteCatalogPackageTaskComplexUI project, right-click References and click Add reference, as shown in Figure 10-16:

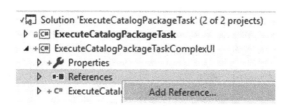

Figure 10-16. *Preparing to add references*

When Reference Manager displays, navigate to Assemblies ➤ Extensions and check the checkboxes beside Microsoft.SqlServer.Dts.Design and Microsoft.SqlServer. ManagedDTS, as shown in Figure 10-17:

Reference Manager - ExecuteCatalogPackageTaskComplexUI			
▲ Assemblies	Targeting: .NET Framework 4.7.2		
		Name	Version
Framework			
Extensions	☑	Microsoft.SqlServer.Dts.Design	15.0.0.0
Recent		Microsoft.SqlServer.DTSPipelineWrap	15.0.0.0
▷ Projects		.	
▷ Shared Projects		.	
▷ COM	☑	Microsoft.SqlServer.ManagedDTS	15.0.0.0

Figure 10-17. *Adding Microsoft.SqlServer.Dts.Design and Microsoft.SqlServer. ManagedDTS references*

Click Assemblies ➤ Framework and select Systems.Windows.Forms, as shown in Figure 10-18:

Reference Manager - ExecuteCatalogPackageTaskComplexUI

⊿ Assemblies   Targeting: .NET Framework 4.7.2

Framework		Name	Version
Extensions	✔	System.Windows.Forms	4.0.0.0
Recent		System.Windows.Forms.DataVisualization	4.0.0.0

Figure 10-18. *Referencing System.Windows.Forms*

Click the Browse button and search for the latest version of the Microsoft.SqlServer.
Management.IntegrationServices assembly folder in the *<installation drive>*:\Windows\
Microsoft.NET\assembly\GAC_MSIL\ folder. On my development virtual machine,
the full path is C:\Windows\Microsoft.NET\assembly\GAC_MSIL\Microsoft.SqlServer.
Management.IntegrationServices\v4.0_15.0.0.0__89845dcd8080cc91\Microsoft.
SqlServer.Management.IntegrationServices.dll.

Click the Browse button again and search for the latest version of the Microsoft.
SqlServer.Management.Sdk.Sfc assembly folder in the *<installation drive>*:\Windows\
Microsoft.NET\assembly\GAC_MSIL\ folder. On my development virtual machine,
the full path is C:\Windows\Microsoft.NET\assembly\GAC_MSIL\Microsoft.SqlServer.
Management.Sdk.Sfc\v4.0_15.0.0.0__89845dcd8080cc91\Microsoft.SqlServer.
Management.Sdk.Sfc.dll.

Click the Browse button again and search for the latest version of the Microsoft.
DataTransformationServices.Controls assembly folder in the *<installation drive>*:\
Windows\Microsoft.NET\assembly\GAC_MSIL\ folder. On my development virtual
machine, the full path is C:\Windows\Microsoft.NET\assembly\GAC_MSIL\Microsoft.
DataTransformationServices.Controls\v4.0_15.0.0.0__89845dcd8080cc91\Microsoft.
DataTransformationServices.Controls.DLL.

The Microsoft.DataTransformationServices.Controls assembly is the source of both
the "SSIS-y" experience and the ability to use Expressions in the custom task.

Once the assemblies are referenced, The References virtual folder in the
ExecuteCatalogPackageTaskComplexUI project should appear similar to Figure 10-19:

```
⊿  ▪▫ References
    ⅀  Analyzers
    ▪▫ Microsoft.CSharp
    ▪▫ Microsoft.DataTransformationServices.Controls
    ▪▫ Microsoft.SqlServer.Dts.Design
    ▪▫ Microsoft.SQLServer.ManagedDTS
    ▪▫ Microsoft.SqlServer.Management.IntegrationServices
    ▪▫ Microsoft.SqlServer.Management.Sdk.Sfc
    ▪▫ System
    ▪▫ System.Core
    ▪▫ System.Data
    ▪▫ System.Data.DataSetExtensions
    ▪▫ System.Net.Http
    ▪▫ System.Windows.Forms
    ▪▫ System.Xml
    ▪▫ System.Xml.Linq
```

Figure 10-19. *ExecuteCatalogPackageTaskComplexUI References*

Now that the assemblies we need are referenced, let's prepare to use them in .Net code.

Using Referenced Assemblies

To access the assemblies referenced in the previous section, add the using statements shown in Listing 10-6 near the existing using statements in the ExecuteCatalogPackageTaskComplexUI class:

Listing 10-6. Use the referenced assemblies

```
using Microsoft.SqlServer.Dts.Runtime;
using Microsoft.SqlServer.Dts.Runtime.Design;
using System.Windows.Forms;
```

Once added, the ExecuteCatalogPackageTaskComplexUI class should appear as shown in Figure 10-20:

```
using System;
using System.Collections.Generic;
using System.Linq;
using System.Text;
using System.Threading.Tasks;
using Microsoft.SqlServer.Dts.Runtime;
using Microsoft.SqlServer.Dts.Runtime.Design;
using System.Windows.Forms;


namespace ExecuteCatalogPackageTaskComplexUI
{
        0 references
        public class ExecuteCatalogPackageTaskComplexUI
        {
        }
}
```

Figure 10-20. *ExecuteCatalogPackageTaskComplexUI class after adding additional using statements*

Next, inherit the IDtsTaskUI interface by editing the ExecuteCatalogPackage TaskComplexUI class declaration so it appears as shown in Listing 10-7 and Figure 10-21:

Listing 10-7. ExecuteCatalogPackageTaskComplexUI inheriting IDtsTaskUI

```
public class ExecuteCatalogPackageTaskComplexUI : IDtsTaskUI
```

When implemented, the class should appear as shown in Figure 10-21:

```
using System;
using System.Collections.Generic;
using System.Linq;
using System.Text;
using System.Threading.Tasks;
using Microsoft.SqlServer.Dts.Runtime;
using Microsoft.SqlServer.Dts.Runtime.Design;
using System.Windows.Forms;

namespace ExecuteCatalogPackageTaskComplexUI
{
    0 references
    public class ExecuteCatalogPackageTaskComplexUI : IDtsTaskUI
    {
    }
}
```

Figure 10-21. *ExecuteCatalogPackageTaskComplexUI inheriting IDtsTaskUI*

The red squiggly line beneath "IDtsTaskUI" in Figure 10-21 indicates the inherited interface is not correctly – or *completely*, in this case – implemented. Click the line and then expand Quick Actions to view the issues, as shown in Figure 10-22:

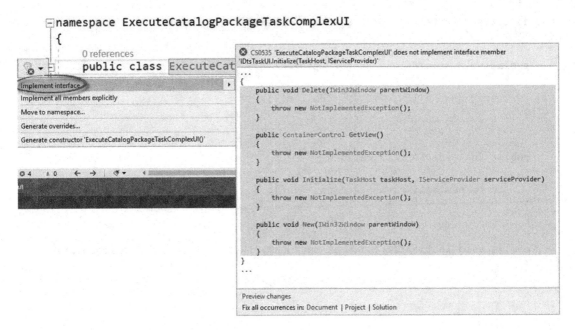

Figure 10-22. *IDtsTaskUI implementation issues*

Clicking the "Implement interface" option will implement a barebones version of the required interface members, as shown in Figure 10-23:

```
public class ExecuteCatalogPackageTaskComplexUI : IDtsTaskUI
{
    0 references
    public void Delete(IWin32Window parentWindow)
    {
        throw new NotImplementedException();
    }

    0 references
    public ContainerControl GetView()
    {
        throw new NotImplementedException();
    }

    0 references
    public void Initialize(TaskHost taskHost, IServiceProvider serviceProvider)
    {
        throw new NotImplementedException();
    }

    0 references
    public void New(IWin32Window parentWindow)
    {
        throw new NotImplementedException();
    }
}
```

Figure 10-23. *The IDtsTaskUI interface with members implemented*

Each member is implemented to throw an exception by default. Please note the red squiggly line is no longer present beneath IDtsTaskUI.

Conclusion

In this chapter, we started the process of developing a new task editor. We started by refactoring existing ExecuteCatalogPackageTask code and replacing the existing task editor project with a new version.

Now would be an excellent time to check in this solution.

CHAPTER 11

Minimal Coding for the Complex Editor

This chapter continues the goals of this section of the book, which are

- Surface a more "SSIS-y" experience for users of the task including a "pretty" editor with General and Settings pages "views"

- Enable the use of SSIS Expressions

- Add design-time validation of task settings

- Surface more SSIS Catalog execution properties in the editor

In Chapter 10, we started the process of developing a new task editor by refactoring existing ExecuteCatalogPackageTask code and replacing the existing task editor project with a new version.

In this chapter, we begin minimally coding the ExecuteCatalogPackageTaskComplexUI by creating the editor form and adding General and Settings views to the View ➤ Node ➤ Property Category ➤ Property hierarchy for SSIS tasks.

© Andy Leonard 2021
A. Leonard, *Building Custom Tasks for SQL Server Integration Services*,
https://doi.org/10.1007/978-1-4842-6482-9_11

Updating DtsTask Interface Members

The current code in the ExecuteCatalogPackageTaskComplexUI class, reordered, is shown in Listing 11-1:

Listing 11-1. ExecuteCatalogPackageTaskComplexUI current code, reordered

```
public class ExecuteCatalogPackageTaskComplexUI : IDtsTaskUI
{
  public void Initialize(TaskHost taskHost, IServiceProvider
  serviceProvider)
  {
    throw new NotImplementedException();
  }
  public ContainerControl GetView()
  {
    throw new NotImplementedException();
  }
  public void New(IWin32Window parentWindow)
  {
    throw new NotImplementedException();
  }
  public void Delete(IWin32Window parentWindow)
  {
    throw new NotImplementedException();
  }
}
```

The new order sorts well with my CDO (that's "OCD" with the letters in the proper order).

In the sections that follow, we build out the "SSIS-y" editor by adding members (internal variables), interface member methods, and views (which will translate to "pages" in the editor).

Adding Internal Variables

Begin coding by adding two variables just after the declaration of the
ExecuteCatalogPackageTaskComplexUI class, listed in Listing 11-2:

Listing 11-2. Declare the taskHost and connectionService internal variables

```
private TaskHost taskHost = null;
private IDtsConnectionService connectionService = null;
```

Once added, your code should appear as shown in Figure 11-1:

```
public class ExecuteCatalogPackageTaskComplexUI : IDtsTaskUI
{
    private TaskHost taskHost = null;
    private IDtsConnectionService connectionService = null;
```

Figure 11-1. *Adding the internal variables: taskHost and connectionService*

The taskHost and connectionService variables are used to pass values
between the ExecuteCatalogPackageTaskComplexUI editor class and the
ExecuteCatalogPackageTask class.

Coding Interface Member Methods

In the Initialize method, replace the line of code auto-generated in the previous chapter –
`throw new NotImplementedException();` – with the code listed in Listing 11-3:

Listing 11-3. Initializing taskHost and connectionService

```
this.taskHost = taskHost;
this.connectionService =
 serviceProvider.GetService(typeof(IDtsConnectionService))
  as IDtsConnectionService;
```

When finished, your code should appear as shown in Figure 11-2:

```
public void Initialize(TaskHost taskHost, IServiceProvider serviceProvider)
{
    this.taskHost = taskHost;
    this.connectionService = serviceProvider.GetService(typeof(IDtsConnectionService)) as IDtsConnectionService;
}
```

Figure 11-2. *The taskHost and connectionService variables, initialized*

In the GetView method, replace the line of code auto-generated in the previous chapter – throw new NotImplementedException(); – with the code that instantiates a new instance of the editor form listed in Listing 11-4:

Listing 11-4. Code to instantiate a new instance of the editor form

```
return new ExecuteCatalogPackageTaskComplexUIForm(taskHost,
connectionService);
```

When finished, your code should appear as shown in Figure 11-3:

```
public ContainerControl GetView()
{
    return new ExecuteCatalogPackageTaskComplexUIForm(taskHost, connectionService);
}
```

Figure 11-3. *Instantiate a new instance of the editor form*

The red squiggly line beneath ExecuteCatalogPackageTaskComplexUIForm informs us there's an issue with this line of code. Click Quick Actions gives more information, as shown in Figure 11-4:

```
public ContainerControl GetView()
{
    return new ExecuteCatalogPackageTaskComplexUIForm(taskHost, connectionService);
```
Generate class 'ExecuteCatalogPackageTaskComplexUIForm' in new file ▶   ⊗ CS0246 The type or namespace name 'ExecuteCatalogPackageTaskComplexUIForm' could not be found (are
Generate class 'ExecuteCatalogPackageTaskComplexUIForm'   you missing a using directive or an assembly reference?)

Figure 11-4. *ExecuteCatalogPackageTaskComplexUIForm does not yet exist*

Comment out the throw statements in the New and Delete interface member methods, editing the code in each method to match Listing 11-5:

Listing 11-5. Throw statements, commented out

```
// throw new NotImplementedException();
```

The New and Delete interface member methods should appear as shown in Figure 11-5:

```
0 references
public void New(IWin32Window parentWindow)
{
    // throw new NotImplementedException();
}

0 references
public void Delete(IWin32Window parentWindow)
{
    // throw new NotImplementedException();
}
```

Figure 11-5. *New and Delete member methods*

The next step is to create a form for the editor.

Creating the Editor Form

The editor form provides an interface for developers to view and configure task properties. Earlier in this book, we built a custom editor. In this section, we add a more "SSIS-y" editor.

Begin adding the editor form by adding a new class. To add a new class, right-click the ExecuteCatalogPackageTaskComplexUI project in Solution Explorer, hover over the Add menu item, and then click Class, as shown in Figure 11-6:

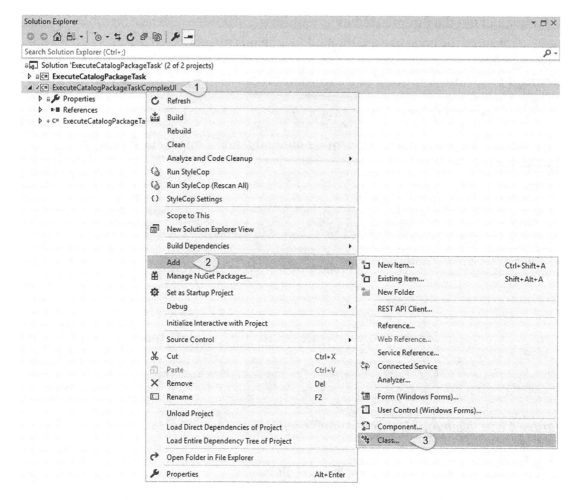

Figure 11-6. *Adding a new class*

When the Add New Item dialog displays, name the new class
"ExecuteCatalogPackageTaskComplexUIForm," as shown in Figure 11-7:

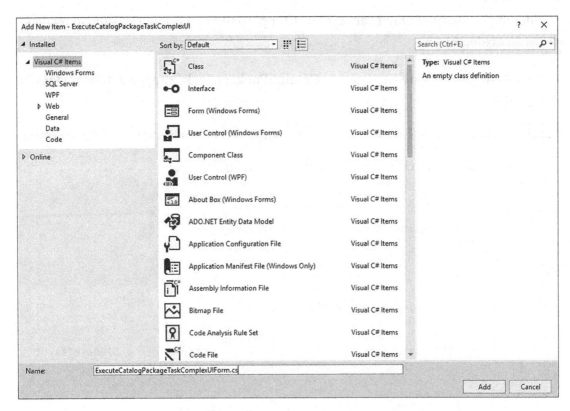

Figure 11-7. *Add the ExecuteCatalogPackageTaskComplexUIForm class*

The ExecuteCatalogPackageTaskComplexUIForm class will appear as shown in Figure 11-8:

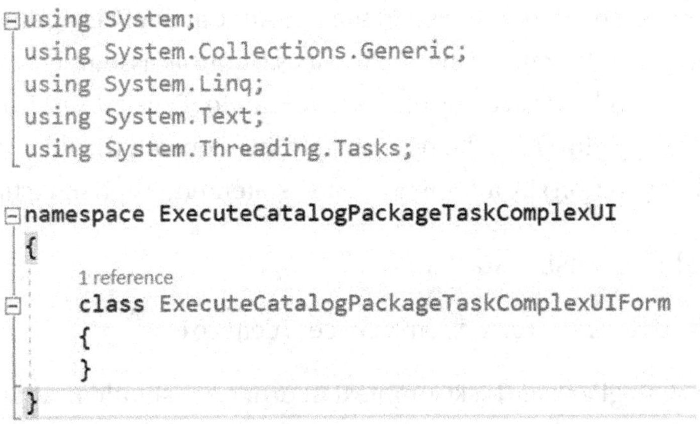

```csharp
using System;
using System.Collections.Generic;
using System.Linq;
using System.Text;
using System.Threading.Tasks;

namespace ExecuteCatalogPackageTaskComplexUI
{
    1 reference
    class ExecuteCatalogPackageTaskComplexUIForm
    {
    }
}
```

Figure 11-8. *The ExecuteCatalogPackageTaskComplexUIForm class*

Modify the ExecuteCatalogPackageTaskComplexUIForm class declaration to read as shown in Listing 11-6:

Listing 11-6. Modifying the ExecuteCatalogPackageTaskComplexUIForm class declaration

```
public partial class ExecuteCatalogPackageTaskComplexUIForm : DTSBaseTaskUI
```

The class declaration should appear as shown in Figure 11-9:

```
using System;
using System.Collections.Generic;
using System.Linq;
using System.Text;
using System.Threading.Tasks;

namespace ExecuteCatalogPackageTaskComplexUI
{
    1 reference
    public partial class ExecuteCatalogPackageTaskComplexUIForm : DTSBaseTaskUI
    {
    }
}
```

Figure 11-9. *ExecuteCatalogPackageTaskComplexUIForm declaration, modified*

The ExecuteCatalogPackageTaskComplexUIForm class inherits from DTSBaseTaskUI, an interface defined in the Microsoft.DataTransformationServices. Controls assembly. Although referenced in the ExecuteCatalogPackageTaskComplexUI project, the Microsoft.DataTransformationServices.Controls assembly is not listed in the collection of assemblies being *used* by the ExecuteCatalogPackageTaskComplexUIForm class. Remedy this (and eliminate the red squiggly line beneath the DTSBaseTaskUI inheritance implementation) by adding the using statement listed in Listing 11-7:

Listing 11-7. Adding a using statement

```
using Microsoft.DataTransformationServices.Controls;
```

The ExecuteCatalogPackageTaskComplexUIForm class should now appear as shown in Figure 11-10:

```
using System;
using System.Collections.Generic;
using System.Linq;
using System.Text;
using System.Threading.Tasks;
using Microsoft.DataTransformationServices.Controls;

namespace ExecuteCatalogPackageTaskComplexUI
{
    1 reference
    public partial class ExecuteCatalogPackageTaskComplexUIForm : DTSBaseTaskUI
    {
    }
}
```

Figure 11-10. *Microsoft.DataTransformationServices.Controls added*

The next step is adding private members for Title and Description as string constants and a public static taskIcon. Title, Description, and taskIcon will be used to configure the base class in the next step.

Inheritance, *encapsulation*, and *polymorphism* make up the foundation of Object-Oriented Programming, or OOP. Inheritance allows developers to design a *base class* that is more generic and then *inherit* members in a more-specified class called a *derived class*. See docs.microsoft.com/en-us/dotnet/csharp/ programming-guide/classes-and-structs/inheritance for more information.

Add private members for Title and Description, and a public static taskIcon declaration, by adding the code in Listing 11-8 just after the partial class declaration:

Listing 11-8. Adding Title, Description, and Icon

```
private const string Title = "Execute Catalog Package Complex Task Editor";
private const string Description = "This task executes an SSIS package in
an SSIS Catalog.";
public static Icon taskIcon = new Icon(typeof(ExecuteCatalogPackageTask.
ExecuteCatalogPackageTask), "ALCStrike.ico");
```

Members (or properties) in the base class can be set from the derived class if the base class allows.

Adding References

The next step is to add missing references. In Solution Explorer, right-click the References virtual folder and click "Add Reference...." Expand the Projects node and check the checkbox beside ExecuteCatalogPackageTask to add a reference to the ExecuteCatalogPackageTask project. Expand Assemblies, select Framework, and then add the System.Drawing assembly. Click the OK button to close the Reference Manager dialog. The added references should now appear in the References virtual folder as shown in Figure 11-11:

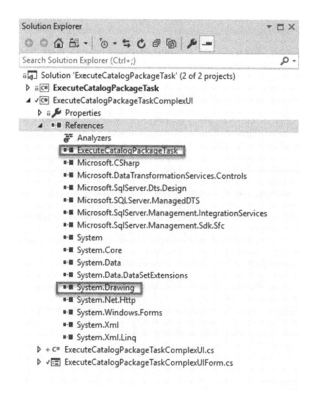

Figure 11-11. *ExecuteCatalogPackageTask and System.Drawing references added*

The next step is coding the form constructor.

Coding the Form Constructor

When an object is loaded into memory – or *instantiated* – a *constructor* initializes the state of the object by loading and initializing object members (properties). The screenshot recorded in Figure 11-12 (originally shown in Figure 11-3) contains a call to the ExecuteCatalogPackageTaskComplexUIForm class, which calls the constructor for the ExecuteCatalogPackageTaskComplexUIForm class. The call displays an error, as shown in Figure 11-12:

```
public ContainerControl GetView()
{
    return new ExecuteCatalogPackageTaskComplexUIForm(taskHost, connectionService);
}
```

***Figure 11-12.** Calling ExecuteCatalogPackageTaskComplexUIForm*

The error remains because there is no constructor for the ExecuteCatalogPackageTaskComplexUIForm class that accepts two arguments. Add the code in Listing 11-9 to create a constructor for the ExecuteCatalogPackageTaskComplexUIForm class that accepts two arguments:

***Listing 11-9.** Coding the ExecuteCatalogPackageTaskComplexUIForm constructor*

```
public ExecuteCatalogPackageTaskComplexUIForm(TaskHost taskHost, object
connections) :
        base(Title, taskIcon, Description, taskHost, connections)
    { }
```

Once added, the ExecuteCatalogPackageTaskComplexUIForm constructor should appear as shown in Figure 11-13:

```
1 reference
public ExecuteCatalogPackageTaskComplexUIForm(TaskHost taskHost, object connections) :
 base(Title, taskIcon, Description, taskHost, connections)
{ }
```

***Figure 11-13.** Adding the ExecuteCatalogPackageTaskComplexUIForm constructor code*

153

The TaskHost object is not initialized because the class header is missing a using statement for the Microsoft.SqlServer.Dts.Runtime assembly. Add the using statement shown in Listing 11-10:

Listing 11-10. Adding using Microsoft.SqlServer.Dts.Runtime

```
using Microsoft.SqlServer.Dts.Runtime;
```

TaskHost is no longer in error

Add two constants to initialize the task Title and Description properties and a static Icon to use with the editor form using the code in Listing 11-11:

Listing 11-11. Adding Title, Description, and taskIcon

```
private const string Title = "Execute Catalog Package Task Editor";
private const string Description = "This task executes an SSIS package in
an SSIS Catalog.";
public static Icon taskIcon = new Icon(typeof(ExecuteCatalogPackageTask.
ExecuteCatalogPackageTask), "ALCStrike.ico");
```

Once added, the code appears as shown in Figure 11-14:

```
using Microsoft.DataTransformationServices.Controls;
using System.Drawing;
using Microsoft.SqlServer.Dts.Runtime;|

namespace ExecuteCatalogPackageTaskComplexUI
{
    2 references
    public partial class ExecuteCatalogPackageTaskComplexUIForm : DTSBaseTaskUI
    {
        private const string Title = "Execute Catalog Package Task Editor";
        private const string Description = "This task executes an SSIS package in an SSIS Catalog.";
        public static Icon taskIcon = new Icon(typeof(ExecuteCatalogPackageTask.ExecuteCatalogPackageTask), "ALCStrike.ico");

        1 reference
        public ExecuteCatalogPackageTaskComplexUIForm(TaskHost taskHost, object connections) :
        base(Title, taskIcon, Description, taskHost, connections)
        { }
    }
}
```

Figure 11-14. *TaskHost no longer in error*

Also, the call to the ExecuteCatalogPackageTaskComplexUIForm constructor found in the ExecuteCatalogPackageTaskComplexUI GetView method is no longer in error, as shown in Figure 11-15:

```
public ContainerControl GetView()
{
    return new ExecuteCatalogPackageTaskComplexUIForm(taskHost, connectionService);
}
```

Figure 11-15. *No error in the ExecuteCatalogPackageTaskComplexUI GetView method*

The next step is to add views to the ExecuteCatalogPackageTaskComplexUIForm class.

Calling the Views

An SSIS task editor surfaces properties in a hierarchy: View ➤ Node ➤ Property Category ➤ Property. *Views* are "pages" on an SSIS task editor. The following section appeared in Chapter 10. We present it here as a review.

Figure 11-16 visualizes the hierarchy for the Execute SQL Task Editor. As mentioned earlier, the General view (in the green box on the left) displays the General node – represented by the propertygrid control (in the blue box on the right). The property category named "General" is shown in the red box. The Name property is shown enclosed in the yellow box, as shown in Figure 11-16:

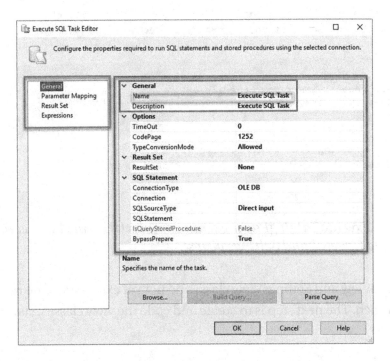

Figure 11-16. *Visualizing View ➤ Node ➤ Property Category ➤ Property*

Applied to the View ➤ Node ➤ Property Category ➤ Property hierarchy, the names of the entities for the Execute SQL Task Editor – shown in Figure 11-16 – are as follows: General (View) ➤ General (Node) ➤ General (Property Category) ➤ Name (Property). That's a lot of General's, and one – the General node – is hiding beneath the propertygrid control.

Add the code in Listing 11-12 to the ExecuteCatalogPackageTaskComplexUIForm class's constructor to call the General and Settings views:

Listing 11-12. Adding calls to the General and Settings views

```
// Add General view
GeneralView generalView = new GeneralView();
this.DTSTaskUIHost.AddView("General", generalView, null);

// Add Settings view
SettingsView settingsView = new SettingsView();
this.DTSTaskUIHost.AddView("Settings", settingsView, null);
```

Once added, the code should appear as shown in Figure 11-17:

```
public ExecuteCatalogPackageTaskComplexUIForm(TaskHost taskHost, object connections) :
 base(Title, taskIcon, Description, taskHost, connections)
{

    // Add General view
    GeneralView generalView = new GeneralView();
    this.DTSTaskUIHost.AddView("General", generalView, null);

    // Add Settings view
    SettingsView settingsView = new SettingsView();
    this.DTSTaskUIHost.AddView("Settings", settingsView, null);

}
```

Figure 11-17. *ExecuteCatalogPackageTaskComplexUIForm class's constructor with calls to the General and Settings views*

The GeneralView and SettingsView classes do not yet exist, hence the red squiggly lines beneath each. The next step is to create and code the view classes, starting with the GeneralView.

Coding the GeneralView Class

The code in this section builds part of the *View* portion of the View ➤ Node ➤ Property Category ➤ Property hierarchy. It is important to note the GeneralView class is actually a `System.Windows.Form` object, and this is why the implementation automatically added the statement `using System.Windows.Forms`. Later in this chapter, we will add standard and typical `Form` methods manually. Why not simply add GeneralView as a form? This book is written for people who are not professional software developers. Adding a class instead of adding a form is one way to emphasize the fact that forms *are* classes.

In Solution Explorer, right-click the ExecuteCatalogPackageTaskComplexUI project, hover over Add, and then click "Class…." When the Add New Item dialog displays, change "Class1.cs" to "GeneralView.cs," as shown in Figure 11-18:

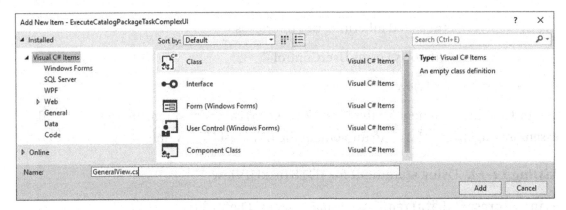

Figure 11-18. *Adding the GeneralView class*

Click the Add button to add the new GeneralView class.

Edit the class declaration using the code in Listing 11-13:

Listing 11-13. GeneralView class declaration

```
public partial class GeneralView : System.Windows.Forms.UserControl,
IDTSTaskUIView
```

Once edited, the code should appear as shown in Figure 11-19:

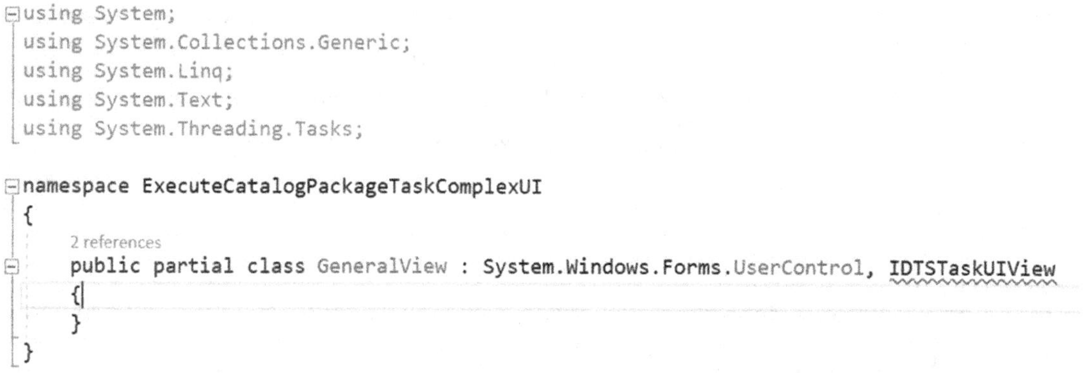

```
using System;
using System.Collections.Generic;
using System.Linq;
using System.Text;
using System.Threading.Tasks;

namespace ExecuteCatalogPackageTaskComplexUI
{
    2 references
    public partial class GeneralView : System.Windows.Forms.UserControl, IDTSTaskUIView
    {
    }
}
```

Figure 11-19. *GeneralView class declaration, edited*

GeneralView is declared inheriting two interfaces:

- System.Windows.Forms.UserControl

- IDTSTaskUIView

Add a using statement for the Microsoft.DataTransformationServices.Controls assembly – in Listing 11-14 – to implement the IDTSTaskUIView interface:

Listing 11-14. Using statement for IDTSTaskUIView

```
using Microsoft.DataTransformationServices.Controls;
```

Adding the using statement clears the immediate error in the GeneralView class, but another error exists. Hovering over the red squiggly underlined IDTSTaskUIView text, the potential fixes "helper" icon displays, as shown in Figure 11-20:

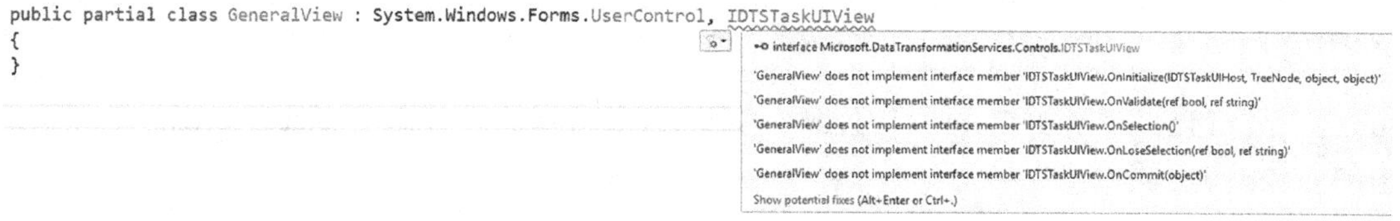

```
public partial class GeneralView : System.Windows.Forms.UserControl, IDTSTaskUIView
{
}
```

→ interface Microsoft.DataTransformationServices.Controls.IDTSTaskUIView

'GeneralView' does not implement interface member 'IDTSTaskUIView.OnInitialize(IDTSTaskUIHost, TreeNode, object, object)'

'GeneralView' does not implement interface member 'IDTSTaskUIView.OnValidate(ref bool, ref string)'

'GeneralView' does not implement interface member 'IDTSTaskUIView.OnSelection()'

'GeneralView' does not implement interface member 'IDTSTaskUIView.OnLoseSelection(ref bool, ref string)'

'GeneralView' does not implement interface member 'IDTSTaskUIView.OnCommit(object)'

Show potential fixes (Alt+Enter or Ctrl+.)

Figure 11-20. *IDTSTaskUIView interface is recognized but not yet implemented*

Click the dropdown and then click "Implement interface" as shown in Figure 11-21:

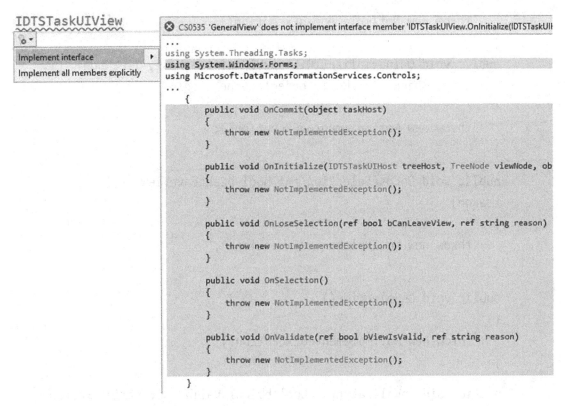

Figure 11-21. *Displaying potential fixes*

Implementing the interface adds the code in Listing 11-15, and shown in Figure 11-22:

Listing 11-15. IDTSTaskUIView implementation code

```
using System.Windows.Forms;
.
.
.

namespace ExecuteCatalogPackageTaskComplexUI
{
    public partial class GeneralView : System.Windows.Forms.UserControl,
    IDTSTaskUIView
    {
```

```csharp
    public void OnCommit(object taskHost)
    {
        throw new NotImplementedException();
    }
    public void OnInitialize(IDTSTaskUIHost treeHost, TreeNode
    viewNode, object taskHost, object connections)
    {
        throw new NotImplementedException();
    }

    public void OnLoseSelection(ref bool bCanLeaveView, ref string
    reason)
    {
        throw new NotImplementedException();
    }

    public void OnSelection()
    {
        throw new NotImplementedException();
    }

    public void OnValidate(ref bool bViewIsValid, ref string reason)
    {
        throw new NotImplementedException();
    }
}
```

```csharp
using System;
using System.Collections.Generic;
using System.Linq;
using System.Text;
using System.Threading.Tasks;
using System.Windows.Forms;
using Microsoft.DataTransformationServices.Controls;


namespace ExecuteCatalogPackageTaskComplexUI
{
    2 references
    public partial class GeneralView : System.Windows.Forms.UserControl, IDTSTaskUIView
    {
        0 references
        public void OnCommit(object taskHost)
        {
            throw new NotImplementedException();
        }

        0 references
        public void OnInitialize(IDTSTaskUIHost treeHost, TreeNode viewNode, object taskHost, object connections)
        {
            throw new NotImplementedException();
        }

        0 references
        public void OnLoseSelection(ref bool bCanLeaveView, ref string reason)
        {
            throw new NotImplementedException();
        }

        0 references
        public void OnSelection()
        {
            throw new NotImplementedException();
        }

        0 references
        public void OnValidate(ref bool bViewIsValid, ref string reason)
        {
            throw new NotImplementedException();
        }
    }
}
```

Figure 11-22. *IDTSTaskUIView interface, implemented for GeneralView*

The next step is to build out a GeneralView *Node*, the first of a few internal members (properties), a constructor, and to override the default interface implementation code.

You have options when designing the GeneralNode class. You can implement the class in a separate ".cs" file, or you may declare the class within the GeneralView.cs file. For the purposes of this example, we add the GeneralNode class to the GeneralView.cs file by adding the code in Listing 11-16:

Listing 11-16. Declaring the GeneralNode class

```csharp
internal class GeneralNode { }
```

Once added, the code should appear as shown in Figure 11-23:

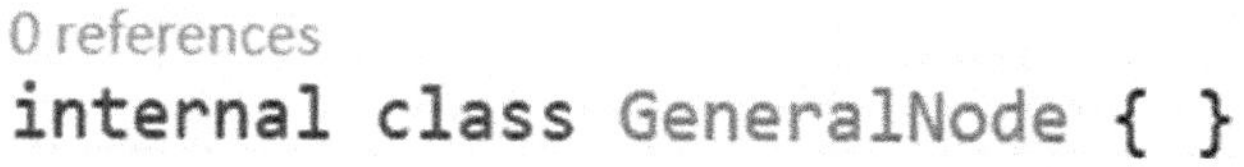

```
0 references
internal class GeneralNode { }
```

Figure 11-23. *Declaring the GeneralNode class*

Once the GeneralNode class is declared, add an initialize a private member to the GeneralView class using the code in Listing 11-17:

Listing 11-17. Declaring a private GeneralNode member in GeneralView

```
private GeneralNode generalNode = null;
```

Once added, the code should appear as shown in Figure 11-24:

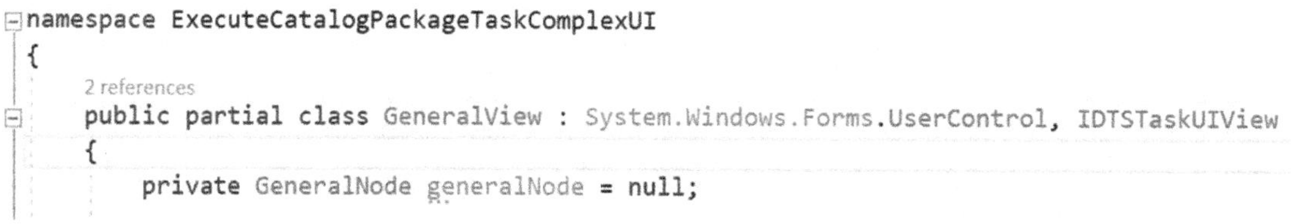

```
namespace ExecuteCatalogPackageTaskComplexUI
{
    2 references
    public partial class GeneralView : System.Windows.Forms.UserControl, IDTSTaskUIView
    {
        private GeneralNode generalNode = null;
```

Figure 11-24. *Declare and initialize a GeneralNode member*

Declare three additional members in GeneralView using the code in Listing 11-18:

Listing 11-18. Declaring the PropertyGrid, ExecuteCatalogPackageTask, and Container members

```
private System.Windows.Forms.PropertyGrid generalPropertyGrid;
private ExecuteCatalogPackageTask.ExecuteCatalogPackageTask theTask = null;
private System.ComponentModel.Container components = null;
```

GeneralView should appear as shown in Figure 11-25:

```
public partial class GeneralView : System.Windows.Forms.UserControl, IDTSTaskUIView
{
    private GeneralNode generalNode = null;
    private System.Windows.Forms.PropertyGrid generalPropertyGrid;
    private ExecuteCatalogPackageTask.ExecuteCatalogPackageTask theTask = null;
    private System.ComponentModel.Container components = null;
```

Figure 11-25. *PropertyGrid, ExecuteCatalogPackageTask, and Container members*

The next step is to add a constructor and a `Dispose` method to the GeneralView class using the code in Listing 11-19:

Listing 11-19. GeneralView Constructor and Dispose

```
public GeneralView()
  {
    InitializeComponent();
  }

  protected override void Dispose(bool disposing)
  {
    if (disposing)
    {
      if (components != null)
      {
        components.Dispose();
      }
    }
    base.Dispose(disposing);
  }
```

Once added, the code should appear as shown in Figure 11-26:

```csharp
public GeneralView()
{
    InitializeComponent();
}

1 reference
protected override void Dispose(bool disposing)
{
    if (disposing)
    {
        if (components != null)
        {
            components.Dispose();
        }
    }
    base.Dispose(disposing);
}
```

Figure 11-26. *Adding the constructor and Dispose methods to the GeneralView*

The constructor – named the same as the class (GeneralView) – calls InitializeComponent, which is not yet implemented. The Dispose method overrides the base.Dispose method, cleaning up any lingering components objects before disposing of the base object.

The InitializeComponent method contains information about controls and objects implemented on a form. If a new form is added to a .Net Framework solution, an InitializeComponent method is automatically included.

The next step is to implement the InitializeComponent method using the code in Listing 11-20:

Listing 11-20. InitializeComponent code

```
private void InitializeComponent()
  {
    // generalPropertyGrid
    this.generalPropertyGrid = new System.Windows.Forms.PropertyGrid();
    this.SuspendLayout();
    this.generalPropertyGrid.Anchor = ((System.Windows.Forms.AnchorStyles)
    ((((System.Windows.Forms.AnchorStyles.Top
      | System.Windows.Forms.AnchorStyles.Bottom)
      | System.Windows.Forms.AnchorStyles.Left)
      | System.Windows.Forms.AnchorStyles.Right)));
    this.generalPropertyGrid.Location = new System.Drawing.Point(3, 0);
    this.generalPropertyGrid.Name = "generalPropertyGrid";
    this.generalPropertyGrid.PropertySort = System.Windows.Forms.
    PropertySort.Categorized;
    this.generalPropertyGrid.Size = new System.Drawing.Size(387, 360);
    this.generalPropertyGrid.TabIndex = 0;
    this.generalPropertyGrid.ToolbarVisible = false;

    // GeneralView
    this.Controls.Add(this.generalPropertyGrid);
    this.Name = "GeneralView";
    this.Size = new System.Drawing.Size(390, 360);
    this.ResumeLayout(false);
  }
```

Once added, the `InitializeComponent` method appears as shown in Figure 11-27:

```
private void InitializeComponent()
{
    // generalPropertyGrid
    this.generalPropertyGrid = new System.Windows.Forms.PropertyGrid();
    this.SuspendLayout();
    this.generalPropertyGrid.Anchor = ((System.Windows.Forms.AnchorStyles)((((System.Windows.Forms.AnchorStyles.Top
                | System.Windows.Forms.AnchorStyles.Bottom)
                | System.Windows.Forms.AnchorStyles.Left)
                | System.Windows.Forms.AnchorStyles.Right)));
    this.generalPropertyGrid.Location = new System.Drawing.Point(3, 0);
    this.generalPropertyGrid.Name = "generalPropertyGrid";
    this.generalPropertyGrid.PropertySort = System.Windows.Forms.PropertySort.Categorized;
    this.generalPropertyGrid.Size = new System.Drawing.Size(387, 360);
    this.generalPropertyGrid.TabIndex = 0;
    this.generalPropertyGrid.ToolbarVisible = false;

    // GeneralView
    this.Controls.Add(this.generalPropertyGrid);
    this.Name = "GeneralView";
    this.Size = new System.Drawing.Size(390, 360);
    this.ResumeLayout(false);
}
```

Figure 11-27. *Adding the InitializeComponent method to the GeneralView*

In the `InitializeComponent` method, our code initializes and configures the GeneralView's `generalPropertyGrid` member and then adds the `generalPropertyGrid` member – which is a PropertyGrid control – to the GeneralView class (form).

The next step is to begin coding the SettingsView.

Coding the SettingsView

In Solution Explorer, right-click the ExecuteCatalogPackageTaskComplexUI project, hover over Add, and then click "Class…." When the Add New Item dialog displays, change "Class1.cs" to "SettingsView.cs," as shown in Figure 11-28:

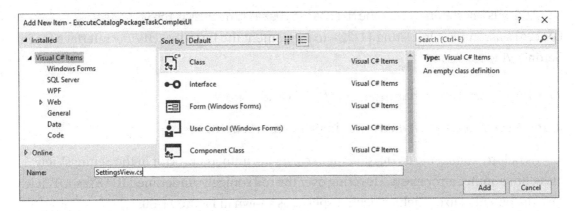

Figure 11-28. *Adding the SettingsView class*

Click the Add button to add the new SettingsView class.

Edit the class declaration using the code in Listing 11-21:

Listing 11-21. SettingsView class declaration

```
public partial class SettingsView: System.Windows.Forms.UserControl,
IDTSTaskUIView
```

Once edited, the code should appear as shown in Figure 11-29:

```
using System;
using System.Collections.Generic;
using System.Linq;
using System.Text;
using System.Threading.Tasks;

namespace ExecuteCatalogPackageTaskComplexUI
{
    2 references
    public partial class SettingsView : System.Windows.Forms.UserControl, IDTSTaskUIView
    {
    }
}
```

Figure 11-29. *GeneralView class declaration, edited*

As with GeneralView, SettingsView is declared inheriting two interfaces:

- System.Windows.Forms.UserControl

- IDTSTaskUIView

Add a using statement for the Microsoft.DataTransformationServices.
Controls assembly – in Listing 11-22 – to implement the IDTSTaskUIView interface for
SettingsView:

Listing 11-22. Using statement for IDTSTaskUIView

```
using Microsoft.DataTransformationServices.Controls;
```

As before, adding the using statement clears the immediate error in the SettingsView
class, but another error exists. Hovering over the red squiggly-underlined IDTSTaskUIView
text, the potential fixes "helper" icon displays, as shown in Figure 11-30:

Figure 11-30. *IDTSTaskUIView interface is recognized but not yet implemented*

Click the dropdown and then click "Implement interface" as shown in Figure 11-31:
Implementing the interface adds the code in Listing 11-23, and shown in Figure 11-32:

```
IDTSTaskUIView

Implement interface              ►
Implement all members explicitly

using System.Threading.Tasks;
using System.Windows.Forms;
using Microsoft.DataTransformationServices.Controls;
...
        {
            public void OnCommit(object taskHost)
            {
                throw new NotImplementedException();
            }

            public void OnInitialize(IDTSTaskUIHost treeHost, TreeNode viewNode, object taskHost, object conn
            {
                throw new NotImplementedException();
            }

            public void OnLoseSelection(ref bool bCanLeaveView, ref string reason)
            {
                throw new NotImplementedException();
            }

            public void OnSelection()
            {
                throw new NotImplementedException();
            }

            public void OnValidate(ref bool bViewIsValid, ref string reason)
            {
                throw new NotImplementedException();
            }
        }
...
```

Error: CS0535 'SettingsView' does not implement interface member 'IDTSTaskUIView.OnInitialize(IDTSTaskUIHost, TreeNode, object, object)'

Figure 11-31. *Displaying potential fixes*

Listing 11-23. IDTSTaskUIView implementation code

```
using System.Windows.Forms;

.

.

.

namespace ExecuteCatalogPackageTaskComplexUI
{
    public partial class SettingsView : System.Windows.Forms.UserControl,
    IDTSTaskUIView
    {
        public void OnCommit(object taskHost)
        {
            throw new NotImplementedException();
        }

        public void OnInitialize(IDTSTaskUIHost treeHost, TreeNode
        viewNode, object taskHost, object connections)
        {
            throw new NotImplementedException();
        }
        public void OnLoseSelection(ref bool bCanLeaveView, ref string
        reason)
        {
            throw new NotImplementedException();
        }

        public void OnSelection()
        {
            throw new NotImplementedException();
        }

        public void OnValidate(ref bool bViewIsValid, ref string reason)
        {
```

```
            throw new NotImplementedException();
        }
    }
}
```

```csharp
public partial class SettingsView : System.Windows.Forms.UserControl, IDTSTaskUIView
{
    1 reference
    public void OnCommit(object taskHost)
    {
        throw new NotImplementedException();
    }

    1 reference
    public void OnInitialize(IDTSTaskUIHost treeHost, TreeNode viewNode, object taskHost, object connections)
    {
        throw new NotImplementedException();
    }

    1 reference
    public void OnLoseSelection(ref bool bCanLeaveView, ref string reason)
    {
        throw new NotImplementedException();
    }

    1 reference
    public void OnSelection()
    {
        throw new NotImplementedException();
    }

    1 reference
    public void OnValidate(ref bool bViewIsValid, ref string reason)
    {
        throw new NotImplementedException();
    }
}
```

Figure 11-32. *IDTSTaskUIView interface, implemented for SettingsView*

The next step is to build out a SettingsView *Node,* the first of a few internal members (properties), a constructor, and to override the default interface implementation code.

As with the GeneralNode class, you have options when designing the SettingsNode class. You can implement the class in a separate ".cs" file, or you may declare the class within the SettingsView.cs file. For the purposes of this example, we add the SettingsNode class to the SettingsView.cs file by adding the code in Listing 11-24:

Listing 11-24. Declaring the GeneralNode class

```csharp
internal class SettingsNode { }
```

Once added, the code should appear as shown in Figure 11-33:

```
0 references
internal class SettingsNode { }
```

Figure 11-33. *Declaring the SettingsNode class*

Once the SettingsNode class is declared, add an initialize a private member to the SettingsView class using the code in Listing 11-25:

Listing 11-25. Declaring a private SettingsNode member in SettingsView

```
private SettingsNode settingsNode = null;
```

Once added, the code should appear as shown in Figure 11-34:

```
namespace ExecuteCatalogPackageTaskComplexUI
{
    2 references
    public partial class SettingsView : System.Windows
    {
        private SettingsNode settingsNode = null;
```

Figure 11-34. *Declare and initialize a SettingsNode member*

Declare three additional members in SettingsView using the code in Listing 11-26:

Listing 11-26. Declaring the PropertyGrid, ExecuteCatalogPackageTask, and Container members

```
private System.Windows.Forms.PropertyGrid settingsPropertyGrid;
private ExecuteCatalogPackageTask.ExecuteCatalogPackageTask theTask = null;
private System.ComponentModel.Container components = null;
```

GeneralView should appear as shown in Figure 11-35:

```
public partial class SettingsView : System.Windows.Forms.UserControl, IDTSTaskUIView
{
    private SettingsNode settingsNode = null;
    private System.Windows.Forms.PropertyGrid settingsPropertyGrid;
    private ExecuteCatalogPackageTask.ExecuteCatalogPackageTask theTask = null;
    private System.ComponentModel.Container components = null;
```

Figure 11-35. *PropertyGrid, ExecuteCatalogPackageTask, and Container members*

The next step is to add a constructor and a `Dispose` method to the SettingsView class using the code in Listing 11-27:

Listing 11-27. SettingsView Constructor and Dispose

```
public SettingsView()
  {
    InitializeComponent();
  }

  protected override void Dispose(bool disposing)
  {
    if (disposing)
    {
      if (components != null)
      {
        components.Dispose();
      }
    }
    base.Dispose(disposing);
  }
```

Once added, the code should appear as shown in Figure 11-36:

```
public SettingsView()
{
    InitializeComponent();
}

1 reference
protected override void Dispose(bool disposing)
{
    if (disposing)
    {
        if (components != null)
        {
            components.Dispose();
        }
    }
    base.Dispose(disposing);
}
```

Figure 11-36. *Adding the constructor and Dispose methods to the SettingsView*

As with GeneralView earlier, the constructor – named the same as the class (SettingsView)– calls InitializeComponent, which is not yet implemented in SettingsView. The Dispose method overrides the base.Dispose method, cleaning up any lingering components objects before disposing of the base object.

The next step is to implement the InitializeComponent method using the code in Listing 11-28:

Listing 11-28. InitializeComponent code

```
private void InitializeComponent()
  {
    this.settingsPropertyGrid = new System.Windows.Forms.PropertyGrid();
    this.SuspendLayout();
    // settingsPropertyGrid
    this.settingsPropertyGrid.Anchor = ((System.Windows.Forms.AnchorStyles)
    ((((System.Windows.Forms.AnchorStyles.Top
                    | System.Windows.Forms.AnchorStyles.Bottom)
                    | System.Windows.Forms.AnchorStyles.Left)
                    | System.Windows.Forms.AnchorStyles.Right)));
```

```
this.settingsPropertyGrid.Location = new System.Drawing.Point(3, 0);
this.settingsPropertyGrid.Name = "settingsPropertyGrid";
this.settingsPropertyGrid.PropertySort = System.Windows.Forms.
PropertySort.Categorized;
this.settingsPropertyGrid.Size = new System.Drawing.Size(387, 400);
this.settingsPropertyGrid.TabIndex = 0;
this.settingsPropertyGrid.ToolbarVisible = false;
// SettingsView
this.Controls.Add(this.settingsPropertyGrid);
this.Name = "SettingsView";
this.Size = new System.Drawing.Size(390, 400);
this.ResumeLayout(false);
}
```

Once added, the InitializeComponent method appears as shown in Figure 11-37:

```
private void InitializeComponent()
{
    this.settingsPropertyGrid = new System.Windows.Forms.PropertyGrid();
    this.SuspendLayout();
    // settingsPropertyGrid
    this.settingsPropertyGrid.Anchor = ((System.Windows.Forms.AnchorStyles)((((System.Windows.Forms.AnchorStyles.Top
                | System.Windows.Forms.AnchorStyles.Bottom)
                | System.Windows.Forms.AnchorStyles.Left)
                | System.Windows.Forms.AnchorStyles.Right)));
    this.settingsPropertyGrid.Location = new System.Drawing.Point(3, 0);
    this.settingsPropertyGrid.Name = "settingsPropertyGrid";
    this.settingsPropertyGrid.PropertySort = System.Windows.Forms.PropertySort.Categorized;
    this.settingsPropertyGrid.Size = new System.Drawing.Size(387, 400);
    this.settingsPropertyGrid.TabIndex = 0;
    this.settingsPropertyGrid.ToolbarVisible = false;
    // SettingsView
    this.Controls.Add(this.settingsPropertyGrid);
    this.Name = "SettingsView";
    this.Size = new System.Drawing.Size(390, 400);
    this.ResumeLayout(false);
}
```

Figure 11-37. *Adding the InitializeComponent method to the SettingsView*

In the InitializeComponent method, our code initializes and configures
the SettingsView's settingsPropertyGrid member and then adds the
settingsPropertyGrid member – which is a PropertyGrid control – to the SettingsView
class (form).

Commenting Out Exceptions

Prepare the minimally coded editor for a build operation by commenting out the throw statements in the views – GeneralView and SettingsView as shown in Figure 11-38:

```
1 reference
public void OnCommit(object taskHost)
{
    // throw new NotImplementedException();
}

1 reference
public void OnInitialize(IDTSTaskUIHost treeHost, TreeNode viewNode, object taskHost, object connections)
{
    // throw new NotImplementedException();
}

1 reference
public void OnLoseSelection(ref bool bCanLeaveView, ref string reason)
{
    // throw new NotImplementedException();
}

1 reference
public void OnSelection()
{
    // throw new NotImplementedException();
}

1 reference
public void OnValidate(ref bool bViewIsValid, ref string reason)
{
    // throw new NotImplementedException();
}
```

Figure 11-38. *Commented throw statements in view methods*

Conclusion

In this chapter, we began minimally coding the ExecuteCatalogPackageTaskComplexUI by creating the editor form and adding (minimally coded) General and Settings views to the View ➤ Node ➤ Property Category ➤ Property hierarchy for the ExecuteCatalogPackageTask.

Now would be an excellent time to check in your code.

The next step is preparing the assembly for build.

CHAPTER 12

Editor Integration

In Chapter 11, we minimally coded the ExecuteCatalogPackageTaskComplexUI. This chapter focuses on the operations required to couple the new complex editor (ExecuteCatalogPackageTaskComplexUI) with the ExecuteCatalogPackageTask, similar to the coupling we achieved with the previous editor in Chapters 5 and 6. Once coupled, we will test the minimally coded ExecuteCatalogPackageTask in a test SSIS package.

Signing the Assembly

Chapter 5 walks through the process of signing an assembly. In order to use the assembly in the Global Assembly Cache (GAC), the assembly must be signed. The process described in this section is nearly identical to the process described in Chapter 5.

Begin by adding a new text file named Notes.txt to the ExecuteCatalogPackageTaskComplexUI project. Right-click the ExecuteCatalogPackageTaskComplexUI project in Solution Explorer, hover over Add, and then click "New Item...." When the Add New Item dialog displays, click the General category and then click "Text File." Rename "TextFile1.txt" to "Notes.txt," as shown in Figure 12-1:

© Andy Leonard 2021
A. Leonard, *Building Custom Tasks for SQL Server Integration Services*,
https://doi.org/10.1007/978-1-4842-6482-9_12

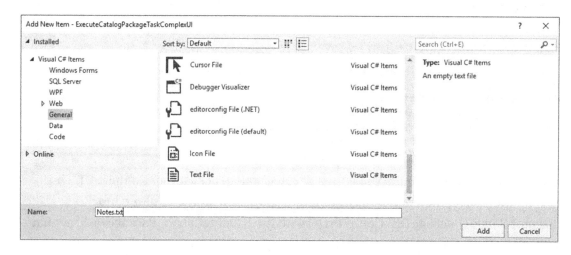

Figure 12-1. *Adding the Notes.txt file*

Click the Add button to add the Notes.txt file to the ExecuteCatalogPackageTask ComplexUI project. In my solution, I expanded the ExecuteCatalogPackageTask project in Solution Explorer, opened the Notes.txt file contained therein, selected all contents, copied the contents, and then pasted the clipboard to the new Notes.txt file in the ExecuteCatalogPackageTaskComplexUI project. I then edited the pasted contents, replacing "ExecuteCatalogPackageTask" with "ExecuteCatalogPackageTaskComplexUI," as shown in Figure 12-2:

Figure 12-2. *Copy, paste, edit Notes.txt from the ExecuteCatalogPackageTask project*

Creating the Key

You will need to locate sn.exe on your server to complete the next three steps.

Open a command prompt window and enter the code in Listing 12-1 (which should appear near the top of your Notes.txt file):

Listing 12-1. Creating the key.snk file

```
"C:\Program Files (x86)\Microsoft SDKs\Windows\v10.0A\bin\NETFX 4.8 Tools\
sn.exe" -k key.snk
```

Once executed, the results should appear similar to those shown in Figure 12-3:

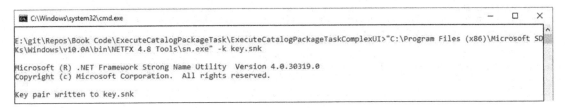

Figure 12-3. *Creating the key.snk file*

To write the public key to a file named "public.out," paste the next line of code from the Notes.txt file, which is Listing 12-2:

Listing 12-2. Writing the public key to public.out

```
"C:\Program Files (x86)\Microsoft SDKs\Windows\v10.0A\bin\NETFX 4.8 Tools\
sn.exe" -p key.snk public.out
```

The output should appear as shown in Figure 12-4:

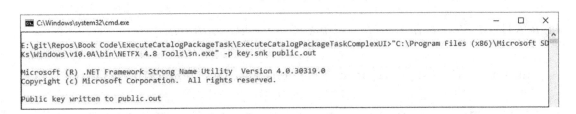

Figure 12-4. *Writing the public key to public.out*

Extract the public key token from the public.out file by executing the code in Listing 12-3:

Listing 12-3. Extracting the public key token

```
"C:\Program Files (x86)\Microsoft SDKs\Windows\v10.0A\bin\NETFX 4.8 Tools\
sn.exe" -t public.out
```

The output should appear similar to Figure 12-5:

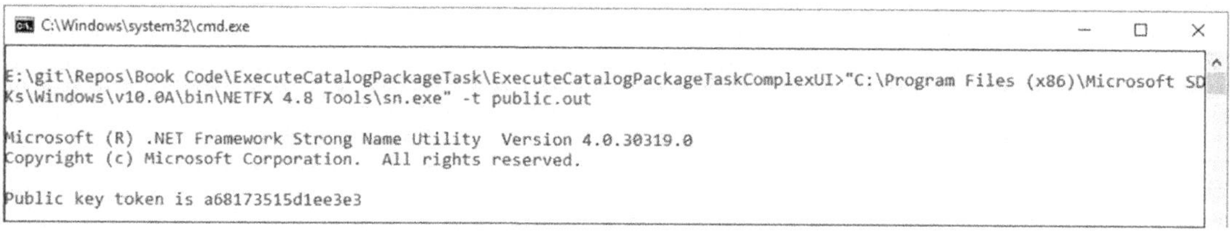

Figure 12-5. *Public key token, extracted*

Select the public key token and copy the selection to the clipboard. Paste the clipboard results – along with some text to help identify the public key token – in the ExecuteCatalogPackageTaskComplexUI class, as shown in Figure 12-6:

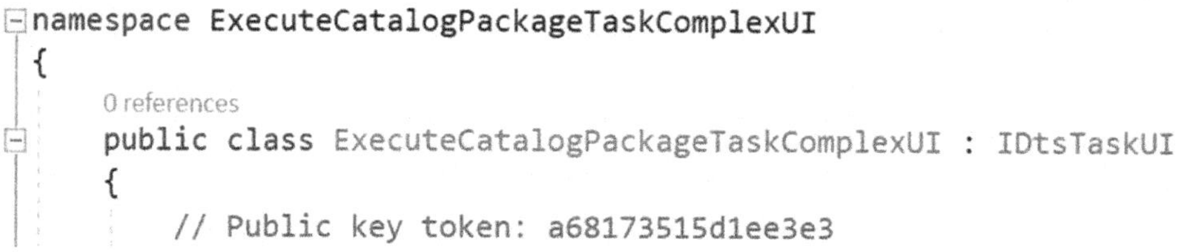

Figure 12-6. *Storing the public key token in a code comment*

The next step is to sign the ExecuteCatalogPackageTaskComplexUI assembly.

Sign the ExecuteCatalogPackageTaskComplexUI Assembly

In Solution Explorer, double-click the ExecuteCatalogPackageTaskComplexUI Properties folder. Click on the Signing page, check the "Sign the assembly" checkbox, and then browse for the key.snk file, as shown in Figure 12-7:

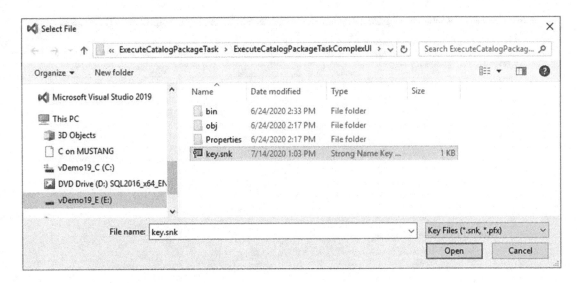

Figure 12-7. *Browsing for the key.snk file*

Click the Open button to use the key.snk file to sign the ExecuteCatalogPackage TaskComplexUI assembly.

The next step is to configure the Build output path location.

Configure the Build Output Path

Return to the Notes.txt file and copy the "build output path" location to the clipboard. Click the Build page on the ExecuteCatalogPackageTaskComplexUI properties page, and then paste the clipboard contents into the Output path textbox, as shown in Figure 12-8:

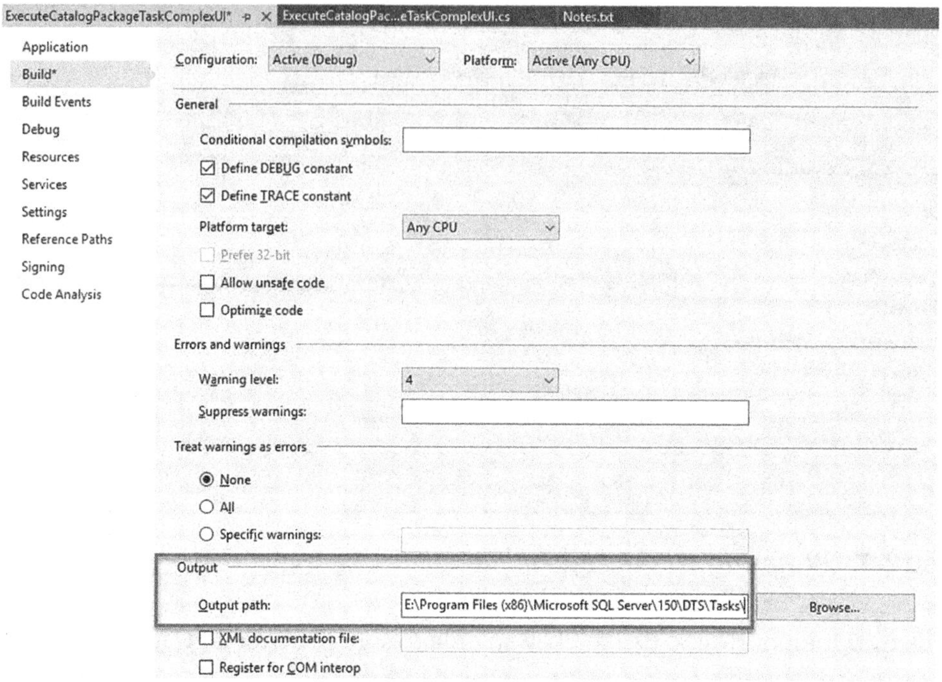

Figure 12-8. *Configuring the Build Output path property*

The next step is to configure build events for the ExecuteCatalogPackage TaskComplexUI assembly.

Configure Build Events

You will need to locate gacutil.exe on your server to complete the next two steps.

Return to the Notes.txt file and copy the "unregister" command to the clipboard. Click the Build Events page on the ExecuteCatalogPackageTaskComplexUI properties page, and then click the "Edit Pre-build..." button to open the Pre-build Event Command Line dialog. Paste the clipboard contents into the Pre-build Event Command Line textbox, as shown in Figure 12-9:

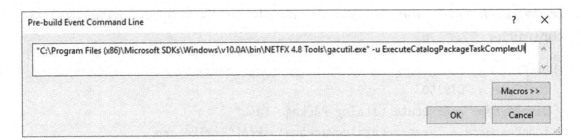

Figure 12-9. Pre-build event command line

Click the OK button to close the Pre-build Event Command Line dialog. Return to the Notes.txt file and copy the "register" command to the clipboard. Click the Build Events page on the ExecuteCatalogPackageTaskComplexUI properties page, and then click the "Edit Post-build…" button to open the Post-build Event Command Line dialog. Paste the clipboard contents into the Post-build Event Command Line textbox, as shown in Figure 12-10:

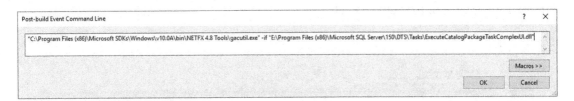

Figure 12-10. Post-build event command line

The next step is to edit the ExecuteCatalogPackageTask to use the newly signed assembly.

Editing the ExecuteCatalogPackageTask

Copy the public key token for the ExecuteCatalogPackageTaskComplexUI assembly onto the clipboard. In Solution Explorer, expand ExecuteCatalogPackageTask and open the ExecuteCatalogPackageTask.cs assembly file. Edit the DtsTask decoration for the ExecuteCatalogPackageTask constructor, replacing *your* public key token with the public key token I show in Listing 12-4:

Listing 12-4. Editing the DtsTask decoration for the ExecuteCatalogPackageTask constructor

```
[DtsTask(
  TaskType = "DTS150"
, DisplayName = "Execute Catalog Package Task"
, IconResource = "ExecuteCatalogPackageTask.ALCStrike.ico"
, Description = "A task to execute packages stored in the SSIS Catalog."
, UITypeName = "ExecuteCatalogPackageTaskComplexUI.
  ExecuteCatalogPackageTaskComplexUI, ExecuteCatalogPackageTaskComplexUI,
  Version=1.0.0.0, Culture=Neutral, PublicKeyToken=a68173515d1ee3e3"
, TaskContact = "ExecuteCatalogPackageTask; Building Custom Tasks for SQL
  Server Integration Services, 2019 Edition; © 2020 Andy Leonard;
  https://dilmsuite.com/ExecuteCatalogPackageTaskBookCode")]
```

Once edited, the DtsTask decoration for the ExecuteCatalogPackageTask constructor should appear similar to Figure 12-11:

Figure 12-11. *Editing the DtsTask decoration for the ExecuteCatalogPackageTask constructor*

The next step is to build and test the custom task solution

Build the Solution

Click the Build menu in Visual Studio, and then click "Build Solution," as shown in Figure 12-12:

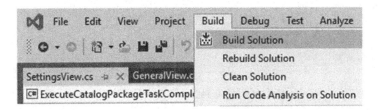

Figure 12-12. *Building the ExecuteCatalogPackageTask solution*

If all goes as planned, the Visual Studio Output window should display similar to Figure 12-13:

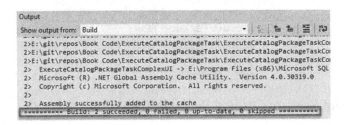

Figure 12-13. *Build succeeded*

The very first test of a .Net solution is: Does it build? This solution builds.

Test the Custom SSIS Task

Test the solution by creating (or opening) a test SSIS project. The tests are

1. Does the custom SSIS task show up in the SSIS Toolbox?

2. Can an SSIS developer add the custom task to a package without error?

When an SSIS package is open in the Visual Studio IDE (Integrated Development Environment), the SSIS Toolbox may be opened to check for condition 1, as shown in Figure 12-14:

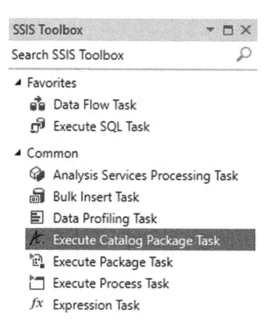

Figure 12-14. *The Execute Catalog Package Task shows up in the SSIS Toolbox*

Drag the Execute Catalog Package Task onto the SSIS package's Control Flow to see if the Execute Catalog Package Task may be added to an SSIS package without error, as shown in Figure 12-15:

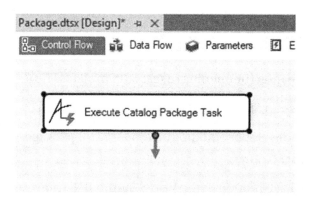

Figure 12-15. *The Execute Catalog Package Task may be added to an SSIS package without error*

Finally, double-click the Execute Catalog Package Task to see if it is possible to open the editor without error, as shown in Figure 12-16:

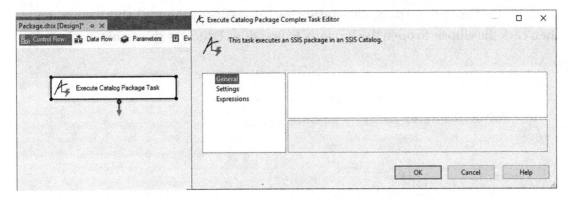

Figure 12-16. *The Execute Catalog Package Task Editor may be opened without error*

The tests pass! We now have a minimally coded Execute Catalog Package Task with a shiny, new editor.

The GeneralView and SettingsView are empty, as seen in Figure 12-16 and Figure 12-17:

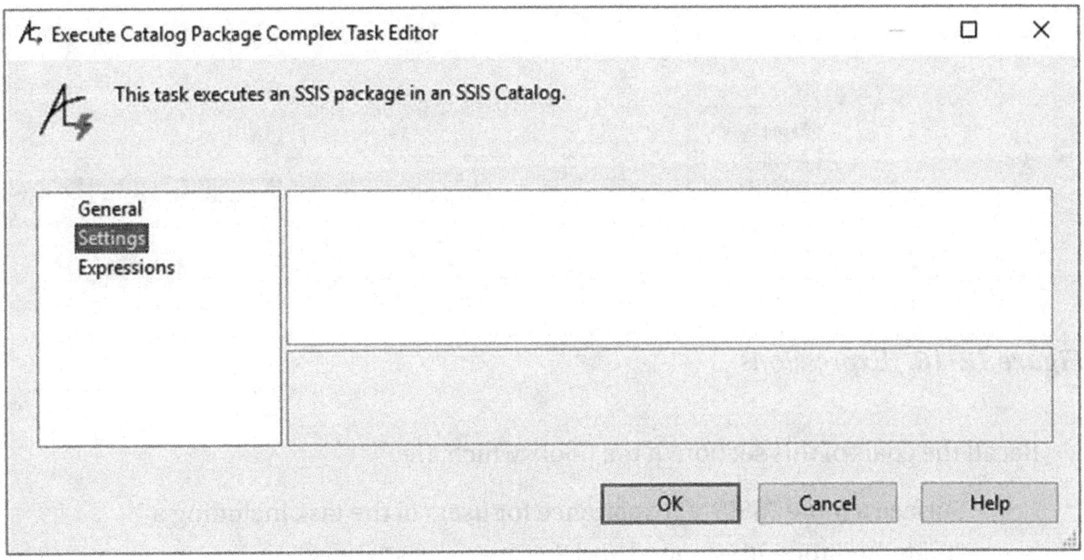

Figure 12-17. *SettingsView is empty*

Click the Expressions page, click inside the Expressions property value textbox, and then click the ellipsis to open the Property Expressions Editor, as shown in Figure 12-18:

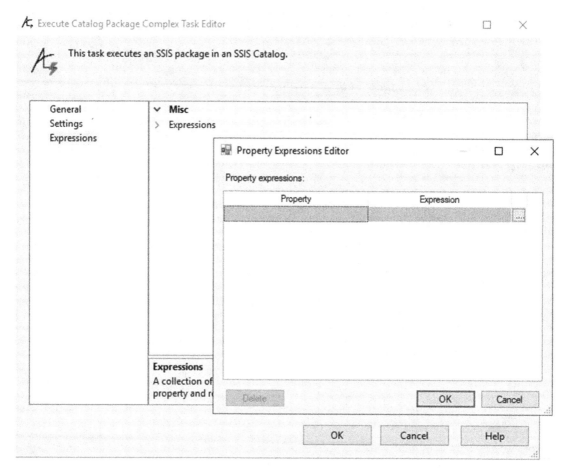

Figure 12-18. *Expressions*

Recall the goals of this section of the book, which are

- Surface a more "SSIS-y" experience for users of the task including a "pretty" editor with General and Settings pages "views"

- Enable the use of SSIS Expressions

- Add design-time validation of task settings

- Surface more SSIS Catalog execution properties in the editor

In this section, we begin to see the second bullet realized – enabling the use is SSIS expressions – as Figure 12-18 shows.

We added no code to create an "ExpressionsView," so where did this editor page come from? The ExpressionsView is inherited from the `Microsoft.DataTransformationServices.Controls` assembly. You may not believe it at this time, but the ability to manipulate SSIS custom task properties using SSIS expressions is worth all the work required to add an "SSIS-y" editor.

Conclusion

In this chapter, we focused on operations required to couple the new complex editor (ExecuteCatalogPackageTaskComplexUI) with the ExecuteCatalogPackageTask. Once coupled, we were able to test the minimally coded ExecuteCatalogPackageTask in a test SSIS package.

Now would be an excellent time to check in your code.

In the next chapter, we add properties.

CHAPTER 13

Implement Views and Properties

In Chapter 12, we built and tested a minimally coded ExecuteCatalogPackageTask sporting a new "SSIS-y" editor named ExecuteCatalogPackageTaskComplexUI. In this chapter, we will implement the IDTSTaskUIView editor interfaces for GeneralView and SettingsView, add editor properties, and conduct even more tests.

Implementing the GeneralView IDTSTaskUIView Interface

In Chapter 11, we used some nifty functionality built into Visual Studio 2019 to implement the required IDTSTaskUIView interface methods for the GeneralView with a single click, as shown in Figure 13-1:

© Andy Leonard 2021
A. Leonard, *Building Custom Tasks for SQL Server Integration Services*,
https://doi.org/10.1007/978-1-4842-6482-9_13

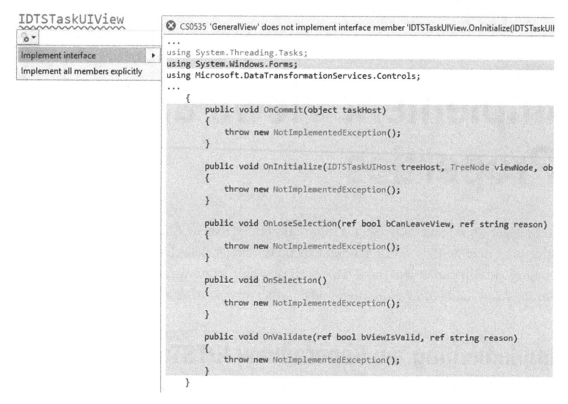

Figure 13-1. *Implementing required IDTSTaskUIView interface methods for GeneralView*

Near the end of the chapter, we commented out the throw statements so the ExecuteCatalogPackageTaskComplexUI project would build and pass some basic tests. The code now appears as shown in Listing 13-1:

Listing 13-1. IDTSTaskUIView interface methods for GeneralView, commented out

```
public void OnInitialize(IDTSTaskUIHost treeHost, TreeNode viewNode,
object taskHost, object connections)
  {
    // throw new NotImplementedException();
  }
```

```
public void OnValidate(ref bool bViewIsValid, ref string reason)
  {
    // throw new NotImplementedException();
  }
public void OnCommit(object taskHost)
  {
    // throw new NotImplementedException();
  }
public void OnSelection()
  {
    // throw new NotImplementedException();
  }
public void OnLoseSelection(ref bool bCanLeaveView, ref string reason)
  {
    // throw new NotImplementedException();
  }
```

The code above has also been rearranged to more closely resemble an order I prefer (see the earlier note on "CDO").

The next step is to implement the GeneralView OnInitialize method.

Implementing GeneralView OnInitialize

Implement the GeneralView OnInitialize method by replacing the current OnInitialize method code with the code in Listing 13-2:

Listing 13-2. Implementing OnInitialize for GeneralView

```
public virtual void OnInitialize(IDTSTaskUIHost treeHost
                                , System.Windows.Forms.TreeNode viewNode
                                , object taskHost
                                , object connections)
{
  if (taskHost == null)
```

```
{
throw new ArgumentNullException("Attempting to initialize the
ExecuteCatalogPackageTask UI with a null TaskHost");
  }

  if (!(((TaskHost)taskHost).InnerObject is ExecuteCatalogPackageTask.
  ExecuteCatalogPackageTask))
  {
throw new ArgumentException("Attempting to initialize the
ExecuteCatalogPackageTask UI with a task that is not an
ExecuteCatalogPackageTask.");
  }

  theTask = ((TaskHost)taskHost).InnerObject as ExecuteCatalogPackageTask.
  ExecuteCatalogPackageTask;

  this.generalNode = new GeneralNode(taskHost as TaskHost);

  generalPropertyGrid.SelectedObject = this.generalNode;

  generalNode.Name = ((TaskHost)taskHost).Name;
}
```

The GeneralView OnInitialize method appears as shown in Figure 13-2:

```
public virtual void OnInitialize(IDTSTaskUIHost treeHost
                       , System.Windows.Forms.TreeNode viewNode
                       , object taskHost
                       , object connections)
{
    if (taskHost == null)
    {
        throw new ArgumentNullException("Attempting to initialize the ExecuteCatalogPackageTask UI with a null TaskHost.");
    }

    if (!(((TaskHost)taskHost).InnerObject is ExecuteCatalogPackageTask.ExecuteCatalogPackageTask))
    {
        throw new ArgumentException("Attempting to initialize the ExecuteCatalogPackageTask UI with a task that is not an ExecuteCatalogPackageTask.");
    }

    theTask = ((TaskHost)taskHost).InnerObject as ExecuteCatalogPackageTask.ExecuteCatalogPackageTask;

    this.generalNode = new GeneralNode(taskHost as TaskHost);

    generalPropertyGrid.SelectedObject = this.generalNode;

    generalNode.Name = ((TaskHost)taskHost).Name;
}
```

Figure 13-2. *The GeneralView OnInitialize method*

Note TaskHost and GeneralNode are marked with red squiggly lines to indicate an issue with each. Hover over TaskHost, click the dropdown, and then click "using Microsoft.SqlServer.Dts.Runtime;" as shown in Figure 13-3:

```
if (!(((TaskHost)taskHost).InnerObject is ExecuteCatalogPackageTask.ExecuteCatalogPackageTask))
{
    th  using Microsoft.SqlServer.Dts.Runtime;  ▶   ⊗ CS0246 The type or namespace name 'TaskHost' could not be found    atalogPackageTask UI with a t
}       Microsoft.SqlServer.Dts.Runtime.TaskHost       (are you missing a using directive or an assembly reference?)
        Generate type 'TaskHost'  ▶                    ...
    theTas  Change 'TaskHost' to 'taskHost'.           using Microsoft.DataTransformationServices.Controls;    k.ExecuteCatalogPackageTask;
                                                        using Microsoft.SqlServer.Dts.Runtime;
    this.generalNode = new General                     ...
                                            Preview changes
    generalPropertyGrid.SelectedObject = this.generalNode;
```

Figure 13-3. *Adding "using Microsoft.SqlServer.Dts.Runtime;"*

This Visual Studio automation adds a using directive for the Microsoft.SqlServer.Dts.Runtime assembly reference, clearing a number of red squiggly lines in the GeneralView OnInitialize method, as shown in Figure 13-4:

```
59   public virtual void OnInitialize(IDTSTaskUIHost treeHost
60                                    , System.Windows.Forms.TreeNode viewNode
61                                    , object taskHost
62                                    , object connections)
63   {
64       if (taskHost == null)
65       {
66           throw new ArgumentNullException("Attempting to initialize the ExecuteCatalogPackageTask UI with a null TaskHost");
67       }
68
69       if (!(((TaskHost)taskHost).InnerObject is ExecuteCatalogPackageTask.ExecuteCatalogPackageTask))
70       {
71           throw new ArgumentException("Attempting to initialize the ExecuteCatalogPackageTask UI with a task that is not an ExecuteCatalogPackageTask.");
72       }
73
74       theTask = ((TaskHost)taskHost).InnerObject as ExecuteCatalogPackageTask.ExecuteCatalogPackageTask;
75
76       this.generalNode = new GeneralNode(taskHost as TaskHost);
77
78       generalPropertyGrid.SelectedObject = this.generalNode;
79
80       generalNode.Name = ((TaskHost)taskHost).Name;
81   }
```

Figure 13-4. *The using directive clears most design-time issues*

Visual Studio line numbers are included in Figure 13-4 to aid in code functionality discussion. Lines 59–63 are the GeneralView OnInitialize method's declaration and arguments.

Lines 64–67 check to see if the taskHost member is null and, if taskHost is null, throw an ArgumentNullException that includes the message: "Attempting to initialize the ExecuteCatalogPackageTask UI with a null TaskHost."

Lines 69–72 test whether the `GeneralView` `taskHost` member's `InnerObject` may *not* be cast to an instance of the `ExecuteCatalogPackageTask` type. If the `GeneralView` `taskHost` member's `InnerObject` cannot be cast to an `ExecuteCatalogPackageTask`, the code throws an `ArgumentException` that includes the message: "Attempting to initialize the ExecuteCatalogPackageTask UI with a task that is not an ExecuteCatalogPackageTask."

If the previous "type test" succeeds, the `GeneralView` `theTask` member's `InnerObject` is assigned to the `ExecuteCatalogPackageTask` object on line 74.

On line 76, the `GeneralView` `generalNode` member is initialized (the code here is currently broken, but we will fix it soon).

On line 78, the `GeneralView` `generalPropertyGrid` member is initialized as the `generalNode`.

Finally, the `generalNode.Name` is initialized as the value of the `taskHost.Name` property value on line 80. The taskHost may be thought of as the "task on the SSIS package Control Flow." This line of code helps keep the name of the ExecuteCatalogPackageTask in sync with the `taskHost.Name` property value displayed one the SSIS package Control Flow when the Execute Catalog Package Task editor is closed.

There are a lot of moving parts in the `GeneralView` `OnInitialize` method. A lot of what is occurring in the `OnInitialize` method is a *knitting together* of the SSIS task editor View ➤ Node ➤ Property Category ➤ Property hierarchy we originally discussed in Chapter 10.

An SSIS task editor surfaces properties in a hierarchy: View ➤ Node ➤ Property Category ➤ Property. *Views* are "pages" on an SSIS task editor. The following section appeared in Chapter 10. We present it here as a review.

Figure 13-5 visualizes the hierarchy for the Execute SQL Task Editor. As mentioned earlier, the General view (in the green box on the left) displays the General node – represented by the propertygrid control (in the blue box on the right). The property category named "General" is shown in the red box. The Name property is shown enclosed in the yellow box, as shown in Figure 13-5:

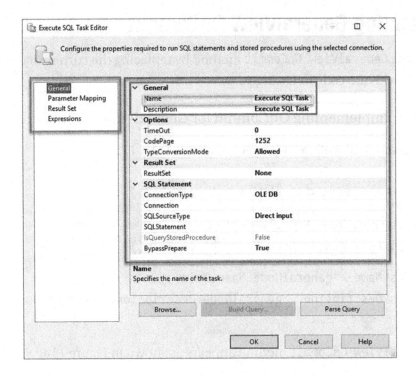

Figure 13-5. *Visualizing View ➤ Node ➤ Property Category ➤ Property*

Applied to the View ➤ Node ➤ Property Category ➤ Property hierarchy, the names of the entities for the Execute SQL Task Editor – shown in Figure 13-5 – are the following: General (View) ➤ General (Node) ➤ General (Property Category) ➤ Name (Property). That's a lot of General's, and one – the General node – is hiding beneath the propertygrid control.

The new `GeneralView OnInitialize` method is coupling the `ExecuteCatalogPackageTaskComplexUI` to the `ExecuteCatalogPackageTask` using the `GeneralView taskHost` member. Once that succeeds – and the code will throw an exception if the coupling is not possible – the `GeneralView`'s `generalNode` member is initialized (to a new `GeneralNode` object) and the `GeneralView`'s `generalPropertyGrid` is, in turn, initialized to the (new) `generalNode`.

Again, there are a *lot* of moving parts in the `GeneralView OnInitialize` method.

Implementing GeneralView OnCommit

Implement the GeneralView OnCommit method by replacing the current OnCommit method code with the code in Listing 13-3:

Listing 13-3. Implementing OnCommit for GeneralView

```
public virtual void OnCommit(object taskHost)
{
  TaskHost th = (TaskHost)taskHost;

  th.Name = generalNode.Name.Trim();
  th.Description = generalNode.Description.Trim();

  theTask.TaskName = generalNode.Name.Trim();
  theTask.TaskDescription = generalNode.Description.Trim();
}
```

The GeneralView OnCommit method appears as shown in Figure 13-6:

```
public virtual void OnCommit(object taskHost)
{
    TaskHost th = (TaskHost)taskHost;

    th.Name = generalNode.Name.Trim();
    th.Description = generalNode.Description.Trim();

    theTask.TaskName = generalNode.Name.Trim();
    theTask.TaskDescription = generalNode.Description.Trim();
}
```

Figure 13-6. *The GeneralView OnCommit method*

When the Name and Description members are added to the GeneralNode class, the red squiggly lines in Figure 13-6 – along with the errors the indicate – will resolve. Add the TaskName and TaskDescription properties to the ExecuteCatalogPackageTask using the code in Listing 13-4 to resolve the red squiggly lines beneath the TaskName and TaskDescription properties to the ExecuteCatalogPackageTask:

Listing 13-4. Adding the TaskName and TaskDescription properties to the ExecuteCatalogPackageTask

```
public string TaskName { get; set; } = "Execute Catalog Package Task";
public string TaskDescription { get; set; } = "Execute Catalog Package
Task";
```

Once added, the code appears as shown in Figure 13-7:

```
public string TaskName { get; set; } = "Execute Catalog Package Task";
1 reference
public string TaskDescription { get; set; } = "Execute Catalog Package Task";
```

Figure 13-7. Adding the TaskName and TaskDescription properties

Coding the GeneralNode

GeneralNode contains the ExecuteCatalogPackageTask properties surfaced on the General page of the Execute Catalog Package Task (complex) editor. Begin by adding members using the code in Listing 13-5:

Listing 13-5. Add taskHost and task members to GeneralNode

```
internal TaskHost taskHost = null;
private ExecuteCatalogPackageTask.ExecuteCatalogPackageTask task = null;
```

The GeneralNode class appears as shown in Figure 13-8:

```
internal class GeneralNode
{
    internal TaskHost taskHost = null;
    private ExecuteCatalogPackageTask.ExecuteCatalogPackageTask task = null;
}
```

Figure 13-8. The GeneralNode class members

Add a constructor to the GeneralNode class by adding the code in Listing 13-6:

Listing 13-6. Adding a GeneralNode class constructor

```
public GeneralNode(TaskHost taskHost)
{
  this.taskHost = taskHost;
  this.task = taskHost.InnerObject as ExecuteCatalogPackageTask.
ExecuteCatalogPackageTask;
}
```

Once the constructor is added, the GeneralNode class appears as shown in Figure 13-9:

```
internal class GeneralNode
{
    internal TaskHost taskHost = null;
    private ExecuteCatalogPackageTask.ExecuteCatalogPackageTask task = null;

    1 reference
    public GeneralNode(TaskHost taskHost)
    {
        this.taskHost = taskHost;
        this.task = taskHost.InnerObject as ExecuteCatalogPackageTask.ExecuteCatalogPackageTask;
    }
}
```

Figure 13-9. *GeneralNode class constructor*

After the GeneralNode constructor is implemented, the design-time error on line 76 clears, as shown in Figure 13-10:

```
76    this.generalNode = new GeneralNode(taskHost as TaskHost);
```

Figure 13-10. *No more error*

The next step is to code the GeneralNode properties.

Coding the GeneralNode Properties

In this section, we reach the Property Category ➤ Property portion of the View ➤ Node ➤ Property Category ➤ Property hierarchy. Properties of nodes are decorated to indicate property category and description. In the editor, the value of the property is paired with the property name, and this value is passed to the instantiation of the task. The pairing may be thought of as similar to a key-value mapping where the key is composed of the View ➤ Node ➤ Property Category ➤ Property hierarchy and the value is the value supplied by the SSIS developer during task (instance) edit. An example of a value is circled in Figure 13-11:

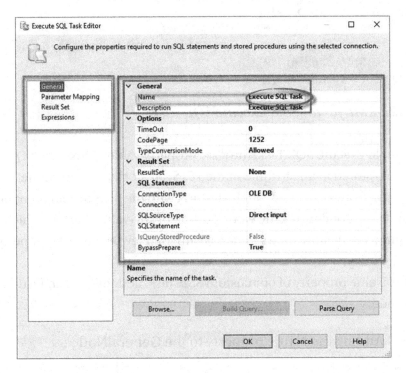

Figure 13-11. *The value of the key-value pair*

In the SSIS package, the value is configured during editing by an SSIS developer. When the SSIS developer clicks the OK button on the editor, the OnCommit method fires and stores the key-value property configurations in the SSIS package's XML, as shown in Figure 13-12:

```xml
<DTS:Executables>
  <DTS:Executable
    DTS:refId="Package\Execute SQL Task"
    DTS:CreationName="Microsoft.ExecuteSQLTask"
    DTS:Description="Execute SQL Task"
    DTS:DTSID="{B12AF18C-77FD-4164-9BA4-681FBA10D49D}"
    DTS:ExecutableType="Microsoft.ExecuteSQLTask"
    DTS:LocaleID="-1"
    DTS:ObjectName="Execute SQL Task"
    DTS:TaskContact="Execute SQL Task; Microsoft Corporation;
    DTS:ThreadHint="0">
    <DTS:Variables />
```

Figure 13-12. *XML for an SSIS Execute SQL Task*

In our sample Execute SQL Task, the Name property value is "Execute SQL Task." The property value is stored in an attribute named DTS:ObjectName. At runtime, SSIS XML is loaded, interpreted, and executed, but it all starts with the SSIS developer opening the task editor and then configuring the value portion of key-value pairs, in which the keys are visually surfaced in editor views that make up the View ➤ Node ➤ Property Category ➤ Property hierarchy.

To add the Name property of our custom SSIS task, add the code in Listing 13-7 to the GeneralNode:

Listing 13-7. Adding the Name property to the GeneralNode

```csharp
[
  Category("General"),
  Description("Specifies the name of the task.")
]
public string Name {
  get { return taskHost.Name; }
  set {
    if ((value == null) || (value.Trim().Length == 0))
    {
      throw new ApplicationException("Task name cannot be empty");
    }
    taskHost.Name = value;
  }
}
```

When added, the code appears as shown in Figure 13-13:

```
[
Category("General"),
Description("Specifies the name of the task.")
]
1 reference
public string Name {
    get { return taskHost.Name; }
    set {
        if ((value == null) || (value.Trim().Length == 0))
        {
            throw new ApplicationException("Task name cannot be empty");
        }

        taskHost.Name = value;
    }
}
```

Figure 13-13. *Adding the Name property*

The red squiggly lines under the decorations indicate an issue. Hovering over the code presents options to address the issue, as shown in Figure 13-14:

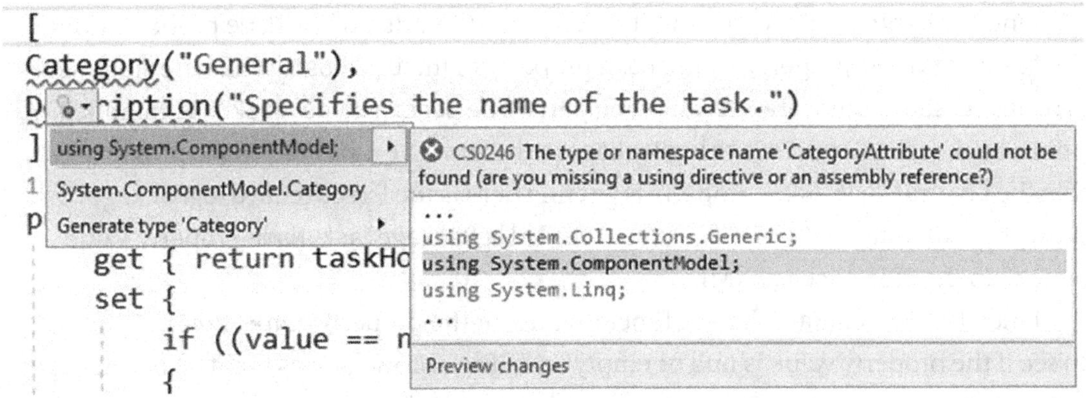

Figure 13-14. *Addressing the decoration issue*

Adding the using directive resolves the issue (you have to love Visual Studio 2019!), as shown in Figure 13-15:

```
117    [
118    Category("General"),
119    Description("Specifies the name of the task.")
120    ]
       1 reference
121    public string Name {
122        get { return taskHost.Name; }
123        set {
124            if ((value == null) || (value.Trim().Length == 0))
125            {
126                throw new ApplicationException("Task name cannot be empty");
127            }
128
129            taskHost.Name = value;
130        }
131    }
```

Figure 13-15. *The Name property with issues resolved*

The Category and Description decorations shown on lines 117-120 are used by the propertygrid control for Property Category – which may hold one or more properties – and the Property Description displayed at the bottom of the editor when the property is selected during edit. The Property Category is set to General in this case; the Property Description is set to Specifies the name of the task. The Property Name is derived from the name of the view member – Name in this case.

Line 122 contains a get statement that returns the value of the Name property from the taskHost.Name property, or the Name property of the taskHost. While the statement is relatively short, there are a few moving parts. The GeneralNode taskHost member points back to the ExecuteCatalogPackageTask class. The taskHost.Name property value that the GeneralNode Name property is getting here is the ExecuteCatalogPackageTask.Name property value. Where is the ExecuteCatalogPackageTask.Name property value stored? In the SSIS package XML.

Lines 123–130 contain the set functionality for the property. Lines 124–127 check to see if the property value is null or empty and, if so, throws an ApplicationException that returns the message "Task name cannot be empty".

If there is no exception, the value of the taskHost.Name is set on Line 129.

Add the Description property to the GeneralNode using the code in Listing 13-8:

Listing 13-8. Adding the GeneralNode Description property

```
[
  Category("General"),
  Description("Specifies the description for this task.")
]
public string Description {
  get { return taskHost.Description; }
  set { taskHost.Description = value; }
}
```

When added, the code appears as shown in Figure 13-16:

```
[
Category("General"),
Description("Specifies the description for this task.")
]
1 reference
public string Description {
    get { return taskHost.Description; }
    set { taskHost.Description = value; }
}
```

Figure 13-16. *The Description property*

When the Name and Description properties are added, errors in the OnCommit method clear (compare to Figure 13-6), as shown in Figure 13-17:

```
public virtual void OnCommit(object taskHost)
{
    TaskHost th = (TaskHost)taskHost;

    th.Name = generalNode.Name.Trim();
    th.Description = generalNode.Description.Trim();

    theTask.TaskName = generalNode.Name.Trim();
    theTask.TaskDescription = generalNode.Description.Trim();
}
```

Figure 13-17. OnCommit errors cleared

Testing GeneralView

Build the solution and then open a test SSIS project. Add an Execute Catalog Package Task to the control flow and open the editor. Observe the General page, as shown in Figure 13-18:

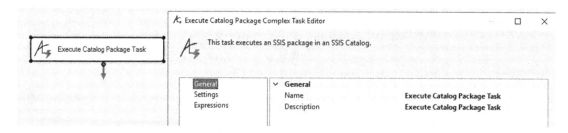

Figure 13-18. The GeneralView in action

The next step is to code the SettingsView.

Implementing the SettingsView IDTSTaskUIView Interface

In Chapter 11, we used the same nifty functionality built into Visual Studio 2019 to implement the required IDTSTaskUIView interface methods for the SettingsView as we used to implement the GeneralView interface, as shown in Figure 13-19:

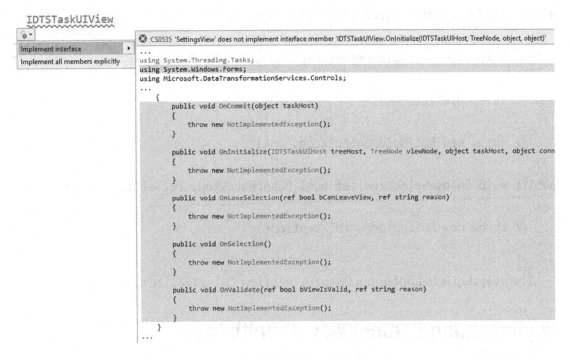

Figure 13-19. *Implementing required IDTSTaskUIView interface methods for SettingsView*

Near the end of the chapter, we commented out the throw statements so the ExecuteCatalogPackageTaskComplexUI project would build and pass some basic tests. The code – rearranged to suit my CDO – now appears as shown in Listing 13-9:

Listing 13-9. IDTSTaskUIView interface methods for SettingsView, commented out

```
public void OnInitialize(IDTSTaskUIHost treeHost, TreeNode viewNode,
object taskHost, object connections)
  {
    // throw new NotImplementedException();
  }
public void OnValidate(ref bool bViewIsValid, ref string reason)
  {
    // throw new NotImplementedException();
  }
```

```
public void OnCommit(object taskHost)
  {
    // throw new NotImplementedException();
  }
public void OnSelection()
  {
    // throw new NotImplementedException();
  }
public void OnLoseSelection(ref bool bCanLeaveView, ref string reason)
  {
    // throw new NotImplementedException();
  }
```

The next step is to implement the SettingsView OnInitialize method.

Implementing SettingsView OnInitialize

Implement the SettingsView OnInitialize method by replacing the current OnInitialize method code with the code in Listing 13-10:

Listing 13-10. Implementing OnInitialize for SettingsView

```
public virtual void OnInitialize(IDTSTaskUIHost treeHost
                          , System.Windows.Forms.TreeNode viewNode
                          , object taskHost
                          , object connections)
  {
    if (taskHost == null)
      {
        throw new ArgumentNullException("Attempting to initialize the
        ExecuteCatalogPackageTask UI with a null TaskHost");
      }
```

```
if (!(((TaskHost)taskHost).InnerObject is ExecuteCatalogPackageTask.
ExecuteCatalogPackageTask))
{
    throw new ArgumentException("Attempting to initialize the
    ExecuteCatalogPackageTask UI with a task that is not a
    ExecuteCatalogPackageTask.");
}

theTask = ((TaskHost)taskHost).InnerObject as ExecuteCatalogPackage
Task.ExecuteCatalogPackageTask;

this.settingsNode = new SettingsNode(taskHost as TaskHost,
connections);

settingsPropertyGrid.SelectedObject = this.settingsNode;
}
```

As when coding the GeneralView, repair the missing using directive to clear the TaskHost design-time warning (see Figure 13-3). We will clear the SettingsNode design-time warning – the red squiggly line – later.

The SettingsView OnInitialize method should now appear as shown in Figure 13-20:

```
59  public virtual void OnInitialize(IDTSTaskUIHost treeHost
60                          , System.Windows.Forms.TreeNode viewNode
61                          , object taskHost
62                          , object connections)
63  {
64      if (taskHost == null)
65      {
66          throw new ArgumentNullException("Attempting to initialize the ExecuteCatalogPackageTask UI with a null TaskHost");
67      }
68
69      if (!(((TaskHost)taskHost).InnerObject is ExecuteCatalogPackageTask.ExecuteCatalogPackageTask))
70      {
71          throw new ArgumentException("Attempting to initialize the ExecuteCatalogPackageTask UI with a task that is not a ExecuteCatalogPackageTask.");
72      }
73
74      theTask = ((TaskHost)taskHost).InnerObject as ExecuteCatalogPackageTask.ExecuteCatalogPackageTask;
75
76      this.settingsNode = new SettingsNode(taskHost as TaskHost, connections);
77
78      settingsPropertyGrid.SelectedObject = this.settingsNode;
79  }
```

Figure 13-20. *The SettingsView OnInitialize method*

Visual Studio line numbers are included in Figure 13-20 to aid in code functionality discussion. Lines 59–63 are the SettingsView OnInitialize method's declaration and arguments.

Lines 64–67 check to see if the `taskHost` member is null and, if `taskHost` is null, throw an `ArgumentNullException` that includes the message: "Attempting to initialize the ExecuteCatalogPackageTask UI with a null TaskHost."

Lines 69–72 test whether the `SettingsView` `taskHost` member's `InnerObject` may *not* be cast to an instance of the `ExecuteCatalogPackageTask` type. If the `SettingsView` `taskHost` member's `InnerObject` cannot be cast to an `ExecuteCatalogPackageTask`, the code throws an `ArgumentException` that includes the message: "Attempting to initialize the ExecuteCatalogPackageTask UI with a task that is not an ExecuteCatalogPackageTask."

If the previous "type test" succeeds, the `SettingsView` `theTask` member's `InnerObject` is assigned to the `ExecuteCatalogPackageTask` object on line 74.

On line 76, the `SettingsView` `generalNode` member is initialized (the code here is currently broken, but we will fix it soon).

Finally, the `SettingsView` `settingsPropertyGrid` member is initialized as the `settingsNode`.

As with the `GeneralView`, there are a lot of moving parts in the `SettingsView` `OnInitialize` method. The new `SettingsView` `OnInitialize` method is coupling the `ExecuteCatalogPackageTaskComplexUI` to the `ExecuteCatalogPackageTask` using the `SettingsView` `taskHost` member. Once that succeeds – and the code will throw an exception if the coupling is not possible – the `SettingsView`'s `settingsNode` member is initialized (to a new `SettingsNode` object), and the `SettingsView`'s `settingsPropertyGrid` is, in turn, initialized to the (new) `settingsNode`.

Adding ExecuteCatalogPackageTask Properties

Before implementing `SettingsView` `OnCommit`, we need to add a few properties to the `ExecuteCatalogPackageTask` class. Open the ExecuteCatalogPackageTask.cs file in the ExecuteCatalogPackageTask project, and then add the member declarations in Listing 13-11:

Listing 13-11. Adding ExecuteCatalogPackageTask members

```
public string ConnectionManagerName { get; set; } = String.Empty;
public bool Synchronized { get; set; } = false;
public bool Use32bit { get; set; } = false;
public string LoggingLevel { get; set; } = "Basic";
```

When added, the new `ExecuteCatalogPackageTask` members appear as shown in Figure 13-21:

```
public class ExecuteCatalogPackageTask : Microsoft.SqlServer.Dts.Runtime.Task
{
    // Public key: e86e33313a45419e
    //             e4f20b7aa35f375d -- key for simple UI
    //             a68173515d1ee3e3 -- key for complex UI

    18 references
    public string TaskName { get; set; } = "Execute Catalog Package Task";
    3 references
    public string TaskDescription { get; set; } = "Execute Catalog Package Task";
    5 references
    public string ConnectionManagerName { get; set; } = String.Empty;
    6 references
    public bool Synchronized { get; set; } = false;
    3 references
    public bool Use32bit { get; set; } = false;
    3 references
    public string LoggingLevel { get; set; } = "Basic";
    2 references
    public string ReferenceName { get; set; } = "NULL (-1)";
    4 references
    public long ReferenceID { get; set; } = -1;
    22 references
    public string ServerName { get; set; } = String.Empty;
    12 references
    private Server catalogServer { get; set; } = null;
```

Figure 13-21. *New ExecuteCatalogPackageTask members*

`SettingsView` surfaces the `ExecuteCatalogPackageTask` properties configured on the Settings page of the Execute Catalog Package Task (complex) editor. In this section, we introduce complexity into the complex editor, so we will take an incremental approach to coding, building, and testing. We begin by adding the FolderName, ProjectName, and PackageName properties.

Implementing SettingsView OnCommit for FolderName, ProjectName, and PackageName Properties

Return to the ExecuteCatalogPackageTaskComplexUI project and implement the `SettingsView OnCommit` method by replacing the current `OnCommit` method code with the code in Listing 13-12:

Listing 13-12. Implementing OnCommit for SettingsView

```
public virtual void OnCommit(object taskHost)
  {
    theTask.PackageFolder = settingsNode.FolderName;
    theTask.PackageProject = settingsNode.ProjectName;
    theTask.PackageName = settingsNode.PackageName;
  }
```

The SettingsView OnCommit method appears as shown in Figure 13-22:

```
public virtual void OnCommit(object taskHost)
{
    theTask.PackageFolder = settingsNode.FolderName;
    theTask.PackageProject = settingsNode.ProjectName;
    theTask.PackageName = settingsNode.PackageName;
}
```

Figure 13-22. *The SettingsView OnCommit method for FolderName, ProjectName, and PackageName Properties*

The next step is to code SettingsNode for the FolderName, ProjectName, and PackageName properties.

Coding SettingsNode for FolderName, ProjectName, and PackageName Properties

Begin by adding FolderName, ProjectName, and PackageName members to SettingsNode using the code in Listing 13-13:

Listing 13-13. Add members to SettingsNode

```
internal ExecuteCatalogPackageTask.ExecuteCatalogPackageTask _task = null;
private TaskHost _taskHost = null;
```

The SettingsNode class appears as shown in Figure 13-23:

```
internal class SettingsNode
{
    internal ExecuteCatalogPackageTask.ExecuteCatalogPackageTask _task = null;
    private TaskHost _taskHost = null;
}
```

Figure 13-23. *The SettingsNode class members*

Add a constructor to the SettingsNode class by adding the code in Listing 13-14:

Listing 13-14. Adding a SettingsNode class constructor

```
public SettingsNode(TaskHost taskHost
                    , object connections)
  {
    _taskHost = taskHost;
    _task = taskHost.InnerObject as ExecuteCatalogPackageTask.
    ExecuteCatalogPackageTask;
  }
```

Once the constructor is added, the SettingsNode class appears as shown in Figure 13-24:

```
public SettingsNode(TaskHost taskHost
                    , object connections)
{
    _taskHost = taskHost;
    _task = taskHost.InnerObject as ExecuteCatalogPackageTask.ExecuteCatalogPackageTask;
}
```

Figure 13-24. *SettingsNode class constructor*

After the SettingsNode constructor implementation, the design-time warning on line 78 clears, as shown in Figure 13-25:

```
78   this.settingsNode = new SettingsNode(taskHost as TaskHost, connections);
```

Figure 13-25. *No more error*

The next step is to code the SettingsNode FolderName, ProjectName, and PackageName properties.

Coding the SettingsNode FolderName, ProjectName, and PackageName Properties

Let's begin with SettingsNode members (properties) that identify the package in the SSIS Catalog we wish to execute:

- Folder name

- Project name

- Package name

To add the FolderName, ProjectName, and PackageName properties of our custom SSIS task, add the code in Listing 13-15 to the SettingsNode:

Listing 13-15. Adding FolderName, ProjectName, and PackageName properties to the SettingsNode

```
[
  Category("SSIS Catalog Package Properties"),
  Description("Enter SSIS Catalog Package folder name.")
]
public string FolderName {
  get { return _task.PackageFolder; }
  set {
      if (value == null)
      {
        throw new ApplicationException("Folder name cannot be empty");
      }

      _task.PackageFolder = value;
    }
}
```

```
[
  Category("SSIS Catalog Package Properties"),
  Description("Enter SSIS Catalog Package project name.")
]
public string ProjectName {
  get { return _task.PackageProject; }
  set {
      if (value == null)
      {
        throw new ApplicationException("Project name cannot be empty");
      }

      _task. PackageProject = value;
    }
}
[
  Category("SSIS Catalog Package Properties"),
  Description("Enter SSIS Catalog Package name.")
]
public string PackageName {
  get { return _task.PackageName; }
  set {
      if (value == null)
      {
        throw new ApplicationException("Package name cannot be empty");
      }

      _task. PackageName = value;
    }
}
```

When added, the code appears as shown in Figure 13-26:

```
public string FolderName {
    get { return _task.PackageFolder; }
    set {
        if (value == null)
        {
            throw new ApplicationException("Folder name cannot be empty");
        }

        _task.PackageFolder = value;
    }
}
[
    Category("SSIS Catalog Package Properties"),
    Description("Enter SSIS Catalog Package project name.")
]
2 references
public string ProjectName {
    get { return _task.PackageProject; }
    set {
        if (value == null)
        {
            throw new ApplicationException("Project name cannot be empty");
        }

        _task.PackageProject = value;
    }
}
[
    Category("SSIS Catalog Package Properties"),
    Description("Enter SSIS Catalog Package name.")
]
1 reference
public string PackageName {
    get { return _task.PackageName; }
    set {
        if (value == null)
        {
            throw new ApplicationException("Package name cannot be empty");
        }

        _task.PackageName = value;
    }
}
```

Figure 13-26. *Adding FolderName, ProjectName, and PackageName properties*

Note the value is checked for null, but not checked for 0 length. The reason for the omission of a 0-length string check is the code will eventually set the value of the FolderName, ProjectName, and PackageName properties to an empty string when "parent" properties are updated in the editor. For example, if the SSIS developer selects a *new* ProjectName property value, the code needs to set the current PackageName property value to an empty string. This functionality will be coded a few chapters hence.

As with adding initial properties to the GeneralNode, adding decorations requires adding the using System.ComponentModel; directive to the SettingsView.cs file.

FolderName, ProjectName, and PackageName SettingsNode members are validated by design time much the same way GeneralNode members were validated.

Testing SettingsView FolderName, ProjectName, and PackageName Properties

Build the solution and then open a test SSIS project. Add an Execute Catalog Package Task to the control flow and open the editor. Observe the Settings page, as shown in Figure 13-27:

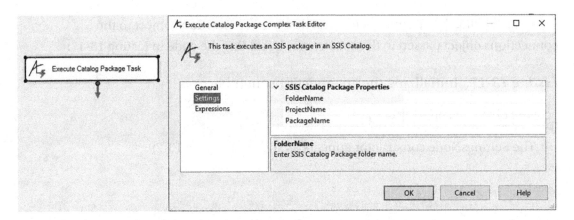

Figure 13-27. *The SettingsView FolderName, ProjectName, and PackageName properties in action*

The next step is to add connection-related properties to SettingsNode.

Coding SettingsNode for Connection-Related Members

To begin adding connection-related members to the SettingsNode, add a private member named _connections (of the object type) to the SettingsNode class using the code in Listing 13-16:

Listing 13-16. Adding the _connections object to SettingsNode

```
private object _connections = null;
```

Once added, SettingsNode members should appear as shown in Figure 13-28:

```
internal class SettingsNode
{
    internal ExecuteCatalogPackageTask.ExecuteCatalogPackageTask _task = null;
    private TaskHost _taskHost = null;
    private object _connections = null;
```

Figure 13-28. Adding _connections

In the SettingsNode constructor, initialize the _connections object to the connections object passed to the constructor by adding the code in Listing 13-17:

Listing 13-17. Initializing the _connections member

```
_connections = connections;
```

The SettingsNode constructor appears as shown in Figure 13-29:

```
public SettingsNode(TaskHost taskHost
                    , object connections)
{
    _taskHost = taskHost;
    _task = taskHost.InnerObject as ExecuteCatalogPackageTask.ExecuteCatalogPackageTask;
    _connections = connections;
}
```

Figure 13-29. Connections, initialized

The next step is isolating ADO.Net connections contained within the SSIS package.

Regarding SSIS Package Connections

The next few paragraphs are not intended to confuse you, but they *may confuse you* if you are reading about how SSIS packages surface collections to SSIS tasks for the very first time. The following statements are true about SSIS:

- SSIS packages and containers are *containers.*

- SSIS packages, containers, and tasks are *executables.*

- An SSIS package will always contain a collection of containers – and the containers collection will always have at least one member because the package itself is a container.

- An SSIS package will always contain a collection of executables – and the executables collection will always have at least one member because the package itself is an executable.

- An SSIS package will always contain a collection of connection managers – and the connections collection may contain 0, 1, or several connection managers.

The SSIS package connections collection is available to executables in case any given executable needs to consume an SSIS package connection manager. SSIS project connection managers are also members of SSIS package connections collections.

When the ExecuteCatalogPackageTaskComplexUIForm is instantiated, the ExecuteCatalogPackageTaskComplexUI's GetView method is called, and a member named connectionService (of the IDtsConnectionService type) is passed to the SettingsView OnInitialize method. The connections collection is passed to the SettingsNode constructor, where it may be used to populate lists of certain connection types.

Isolating SSIS Package ADO.Net Connections

To begin, add a Connections member to the SettingsNode using the code in Listing 13-18:

Listing 13-18. Adding a Connections object to SettingsNode

```
[
  Browsable(false)
]
internal object Connections {
  get { return _connections; }
  set { _connections = value; }
}
```

The SettingsNode Connections property is different from previous properties in two ways:

- Connections is an object type.

- The member decoration is Browsable(false), which means the Connections member is a property, but the Connections property is *not* surfaced in the SettingsNode propertygrid.

When added to the SettingsNode, the Connections property appears as shown in Figure 13-30:

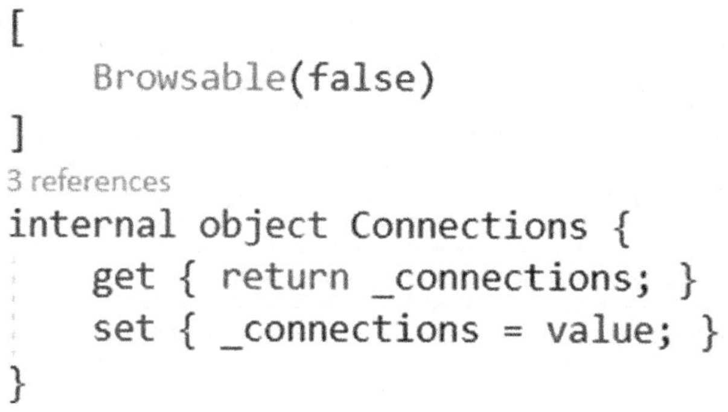

```
[
    Browsable(false)
]
3 references
internal object Connections {
    get { return _connections; }
    set { _connections = value; }
}
```

Figure 13-30. *The Connections property*

We want to only connect to the SSIS Catalog using an ADO.Net connection. To acquire a list of ADO.Net connection managers included in the SSIS package, add the code in Listing 13-19 to the `SettingsNode` constructor:

Listing 13-19. Acquiring a list of ADO.Net connection managers

```
_connections = ((IDtsConnectionService)connections).
GetConnectionsOfType("ADO.Net");
```

When added to the project, the code appears as shown in Figure 13-31:

```
public SettingsNode(TaskHost taskHost
                  , object connections)
{
    _taskHost = taskHost;
    _task = taskHost.InnerObject as ExecuteCatalogPackageTask.ExecuteCatalogPackageTask;
    _connections = ((IDtsConnectionService)connections).GetConnectionsOfType("ADO.Net");
```

Figure 13-31. *Adding the list of ADO.Net connection managers to _connections*

We now have a list of ADO.Net connection managers stored in the `_connections` object, which are hidden (not Browsable), internal `SettingsNode` property (member) named `Connections`.

The next step is to build a `TypeConverter` that builds a list of ADO.Net connection manager names.

Building the ADONetConnections TypeConverter

A `TypeConverter` "provides a unified way of converting types of values to other types, as well as for accessing standard values and subproperties," according to Microsoft's TypeConverter Class documentation (docs.microsoft.com/en-us/dotnet/api/system. componentmodel.typeconverter?view=netframework-4.7.2). A TypeConverter is used to create an *enumeration*, or list, of objects from a collection. Applied to the list of ADO. Net connection managers in the ExecuteCatalogPackageTaskComplexUI, we will build an `ArrayList` of string values containing the names of ADO.Net connection managers stored in the collection of `Connections` (of the `object` type).

To begin, add a new class named ADONetConnections to the SettingsView.cs file using the code in Listing 13-20:

Listing 13-20. Adding the ADONetConnections class

```
internal class ADONetConnections : StringConverter { }
```

When added, the code will appear as shown in Figure 13-32:

```
internal class ADONetConnections : StringConverter { }
```

Figure 13-32. *The new ADONetConnections StringConverter class*

StringConverter is one interface for TypeConverter.

Declare and initialize a `constant string` member named NEW_CONNECTION to the ADONetConnections class using the code in Listing 13-21:

Listing 13-21. Adding NEW_CONNECTION to ADONetConnections

```
private const string NEW_CONNECTION = "<New Connection...>";
```

ADONetConnections should appear as shown in Figure 13-33 after declaring the new member:

```
internal class ADONetConnections : StringConverter
{
    private const string NEW_CONNECTION = "<New Connection...>";
}
```

Figure 13-33. *Declaring ADONetConnections.NEW_CONNECTION*

A TypeConverter follows a general pattern, surfacing one object and three overridable methods:

- GetSpecializedObject (object)

- GetStandardValues (StandardValuesCollection)

- GetStandardValuesExclusive (bool)

- GetStandardValuesSupported (bool)

Implement these methods by adding the code in Listing 13-22 to the ADONetConnections class:

Listing 13-22. Adding TypeConverter methods to ADONetConnections

```
private object GetSpecializedObject(object contextInstance)
  {
    DTSLocalizableTypeDescriptor typeDescr = contextInstance as
    DTSLocalizableTypeDescriptor;

    if (typeDescr == null)
    {
      return contextInstance;
    }

    return typeDescr.SelectedObject;
  }
public override StandardValuesCollection GetStandardValues(ITypeDescriptor
Context context)
  {
    object retrievalObject = GetSpecializedObject(context.Instance) as
    object;

   return new StandardValuesCollection(getADONetConnections(retrieval
   Object));
  }
public override bool GetStandardValuesExclusive(ITypeDescriptorContext
context)
  {
    return true;
  }

public override bool GetStandardValuesSupported(ITypeDescriptorContext
context)
  {
    return true;
  }
```

When added, the code appears as shown in Figure 13-34:

```
1 reference
private object GetSpecializedObject(object contextInstance)
{
    DTSLocalizableTypeDescriptor typeDescr = contextInstance as DTSLocalizableTypeDescriptor;

    if (typeDescr == null)
    {
        return contextInstance;
    }

    return typeDescr.SelectedObject;
}

0 references
public override StandardValuesCollection GetStandardValues(ITypeDescriptorContext context)
{
    object retrievalObject = GetSpecializedObject(context.Instance) as object;

    return new StandardValuesCollection(getADONetConnections(retrievalObject));
}

0 references
public override bool GetStandardValuesExclusive(ITypeDescriptorContext context)
{
    return true;
}

0 references
public override bool GetStandardValuesSupported(ITypeDescriptorContext context)
{
    return true;
}
```

Figure 13-34. *Adding ADONetConnections methods*

A discussion of TypeConverter methods is an in-depth topic that the author chooses not to include in this example. The outcome of the TypeConverter implemented in the ADONetConnections StringConverter will be an ArrayList containing the names of ADO.Net connection managers configured in the SSIS package, plus the option to create a new ADO.Net connection manager.

The ADONetConnections StringConverter's GetStandardValues method calls getADONetConnections, which builds and returns the ArrayList, using the code in Listing 13-23:

Listing 13-23. getADONetConnections

```
private ArrayList getADONetConnections(object retrievalObject)
  {
    SettingsNode node = (SettingsNode)retrievalObject;
    ArrayList list = new ArrayList();
    ArrayList listConnections = new ArrayList();
    listConnections = (ArrayList)node.Connections;

    // adds the new connection item
    list.Add(NEW_CONNECTION);

    // adds each ADO.Net connection manager
    foreach (ConnectionManager cm in listConnections)
    {
      list.Add(cm.Name);
    }

    // sorts the connection manager list
    if ((list != null) && (list.Count > 0))
    {
      list.Sort();
    }

    return list;
  }
```

Clear the ArrayList type errors by adding the directive using System.Collections; to the SettingsView.cs file.

Once added, the code will appear as shown in Figure 13-35:

```
242    private ArrayList getADONetConnections(object retrievalObject)
243    {
244        SettingsNode node = (SettingsNode)retrievalObject;
245        ArrayList list = new ArrayList();
246        ArrayList listConnections = new ArrayList();
247
248        listConnections = (ArrayList)node.Connections;
249
250        // adds the new connection item
251        list.Add(NEW_CONNECTION);
252
253        // adds each ADO.Net connection manager
254        foreach (ConnectionManager cm in listConnections)
255        {
256            list.Add(cm.Name);
257        }
258
259        // sorts the connection manager list
260        if ((list != null) && (list.Count > 0))
261        {
262            list.Sort();
263        }
264
265        return list;
266    }
```

Figure 13-35. *getADONetConnections added*

A brief description of the code in getADONetConnections follows. An instance of
settingsNode is passed to the getADONetConnections method in the retrievalObject
(object) argument. A new internal SettingsNode variable named node and two ArrayList
variables – list and listConnections – are declared and initialized on lines 244–246.
listConnections is assigned the Connections object of the SettingsNode variable (node)
on line 248. NEW_CONNECTION is added to the list (ArrayList) on line 251.

On lines 254–257, a foreach loop enumerates each connection in listConnections
and adds the name of each connection manager to the list ArrayList. Remember,
per the SettingsNode constructor, Connections contains only ADO.Net connection
managers.

If the `list` `ArrayList` contains values, the code on lines 260–263 sorts the values contained in the `list` `ArrayList`.

On line 265, the `list` `ArrayList` is returned to the caller.

Surface the SourceConnection Property

The work in this section titled "Coding SettingsNode for Connection-Related Members" has all led to this point where we are (finally) able to add the SourceConnection property to `SettingsView`.

To surface the SourceConnection property, add the code in Listing 13-24 to the `SettingsNode` class:

Listing 13-24. Adding the SourceConnection property

```
[
  Category("Connections"),
  Description("The SSIS Catalog connection"),
  TypeConverter(typeof(ADONetConnections))
]
public string SourceConnection {
  get { return _task.ConnectionManagerName; }
  set { _task.ConnectionManagerName = value; }
  }
```

When added the code appears as shown in Figure 13-36:

```
[
    Category("Connections"),
    Description("The SSIS Catalog connection"),
    TypeConverter(typeof(ADONetConnections))
]
0 references
public string SourceConnection {
    get { return _task.ConnectionManagerName; }
    set {
        if ((value == null) || (value.Trim().Length == 0))
        {
            throw new ApplicationException("Connection Manager name cannot be empty");
        }

        _task.ConnectionManagerName = value;
    }
}
```

Figure 13-36. *SourceConnection member added to SettingsNode*

Testing the SourceConnection Property

Build the solution. If all goes well, the solution should build successfully. Open a test SSIS project and add the Execute Catalog Package Task to the control flow of a test SSIS package. Open the editor and click on the Settings page. The SourceConnection property appears in the Connections category and contains a list of the names of ADO.Net connection managers in the SSIS packages – plus the option to create a new connection – as shown in Figure 13-37:

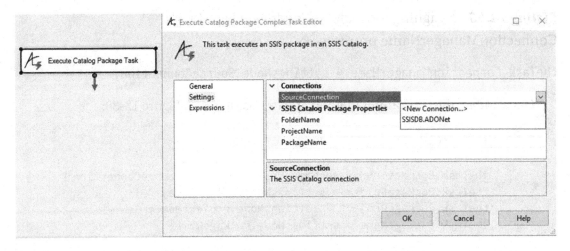

Figure 13-37. *The SourceConnection property is visible and populated*

SourceConnection surfaces a dropdown list because the SettingsNode
SourceConnection property decoration includes the TypeConverter attribute, informing
the SettingsView PropertyGrid that the values in the SourceConnection property are of
the ADONetConnections type. The ADONetConnections type is a StringConverter that
contains an ArrayList of strings, and the list of strings the ArrayList contains is the
names of all ADO.Net connection managers in the connections collection of the SSIS
package.

Reaching this point in development is *awesome*: We've surfaced the
SourceConnection property! That's the good news. The bad news is the
SourceConnection property doesn't do anything – yet. We are *almost* there, though.

The next step is to add code so the Execute Catalog Package Task uses the
SourceConnection property.

Now would be an excellent time to check in your code.

Using the SourceConnection Property

Update the SettingsView OnCommit method to send the SettingsNode
SourceConnection member value to the ExecuteCatalogPackageTask's
ConnectionManagerName property by adding the code in Listing 13-25 to the
SettingsView OnCommit method:

Listing 13-25. Assigning the ExecuteCatalogPackageTask's
ConnectionManagerName property

```
theTask.ConnectionManagerName = settingsNode.SourceConnection;
```

Once added, the OnCommit method appears as shown in Figure 13-38:

```
public virtual void OnCommit(object taskHost)
{
    theTask.ConnectionManagerName = settingsNode.SourceConnection;
    theTask.PackageFolder = settingsNode.FolderName;
    theTask.PackageProject = settingsNode.ProjectName;
    theTask.PackageName = settingsNode.PackageName;
}
```

Figure 13-38. *ConnectionManagerName property, assigned*

The OnCommit method fires when the view commits. In the case of the
SettingsView – at this point during development – the SourceConnection, FolderName,
ProjectName, and PackageName properties managed by the settingsNode will set the
values of the ExecuteCatalogPackageTask's ConnectionManagerName, PackageFolder,
PackageProject, and PackageName properties, respectively.

Extracting the ServerName from the SourceConnection

SourceConnection contains the name of an SSIS package connection manager
(an ADO.Net connection manager). We may extract the name of the SQL Server
instance contained in the connection manager's connection string using the
returnSelectedConnectionManagerDataSourceValue function code in Listing 13-26:

Listing 13-26. The returnSelectedConnectionManagerDataSourceValue function

```
private string returnSelectedConnectionManagerDataSourceValue(string
connectionManagerName, string connectionString = "")
  {
    string ret = String.Empty;

    ArrayList listConnections = (ArrayList)settingsNode.Connections;
    string connString = String.Empty;
```

```csharp
// match the selected ADO.Net connection manager
if (listConnections.Count > 0)
{
  foreach (ConnectionManager cm in listConnections)
  {
    if (cm.Name == connectionManagerName)
    {
      connString = cm.ConnectionString;
    }
  }
}
else
{
  connString = connectionString;
}

// parse if a match is found
if (connString!= String.Empty)
  {
    string dataSourceStartText = "Data Source=";
    string dataSourceEndText = ";";
    int dataSourceTagStart = connString.IndexOf(dataSourceStartText) +
    dataSourceStartText.Length;
    int dataSourceTagEnd = 0;
    int dataSourceTagLength = 0;
    if (dataSourceTagStart > 0)
    {
      dataSourceTagEnd = connString.IndexOf(dataSourceEndText,
      dataSourceTagStart);
```

```
            if (dataSourceTagEnd > dataSourceTagStart)
            {
                dataSourceTagLength = dataSourceTagEnd - dataSourceTagStart;
                ret = connString.Substring(dataSourceTagStart,
                dataSourceTagLength);
            }
        }
    }

    return ret;
}
```

When added to the SettingsView.cs file, the code appears as shown in Figure 13-39:

```
private string returnSelectedConnectionManagerDataSourceValue(string connectionManagerName)
{
    string ret = String.Empty;

    ArrayList listConnections = (ArrayList)settingsNode.Connections;
    string connectionString = String.Empty;

    // match the selected ADO.Net connection manager
    foreach (ConnectionManager cm in listConnections)
    {
        if (cm.Name == connectionManagerName)
        {
            connectionString = cm.ConnectionString;
        }
    }

    // parse if a match is found
    if (connectionString != String.Empty)
    {
        string dataSourceStartText = "Data Source=";
        string dataSourceEndText = ";";
        int dataSourceTagStart = connectionString.IndexOf(dataSourceStartText) + dataSourceStartText.Length;
        int dataSourceTagEnd = 0;
        int dataSourceTagLength = 0;
        if (dataSourceTagStart > 0)
        {
            dataSourceTagEnd = connectionString.IndexOf(dataSourceEndText, dataSourceTagStart);
            if (dataSourceTagEnd > dataSourceTagStart)
            {
                dataSourceTagLength = dataSourceTagEnd - dataSourceTagStart;
                ret = connectionString.Substring(dataSourceTagStart, dataSourceTagLength);
            }
        }
    }

    return ret;
}
```

Figure 13-39. *The returnSelectedConnectionManagerDataSourceValue function*

There are other ways to extract the Data Source attribute value from a connection string. Feel free to implement a better way in your code.

Update the `SettingsView OnCommit` method to send the value of the server name contained in the `SettingsNode SourceConnection ConnectionString`'s Data Source attribute value to the `ExecuteCatalogPackageTask`'s `ServerName` property by adding the code in Listing 13-27 to the `SettingsView OnCommit` method:

Listing 13-27. Assigning the ExecuteCatalogPackageTask's ServerName property

```
theTask.ServerName = returnSelectedConnectionManagerDataSourceValue(setting
sNode.SourceConnection);
```

Once added, the OnCommit method appears as shown in Figure 13-40:

```
public virtual void OnCommit(object taskHost)
{
    theTask.ConnectionManagerName = settingsNode.SourceConnection;
    theTask.ServerName = returnSelectedConnectionManagerDataSourceValue(settingsNode.SourceConnection);
    theTask.PackageFolder = settingsNode.FolderName;
    theTask.PackageProject = settingsNode.ProjectName;
    theTask.PackageName = settingsNode.PackageName;
}
```

Figure 13-40. *ServerName property, assigned*

Finally, edit the `SettingsView.propertyGridSettings_PropertyValueChanged` method so that changes to the `SourceConnection` property *also* trigger a call to the `returnSelectedConnectionManagerDataSourceValue` function – in two places (first, inside the New Connection functionality after assigning the SettingsNode. SourceConnection; second, add an `else` to the `if (e.ChangedItem.Value.Equals (NEW_CONNECTION))` and place a call there) – using the code in Listing 13-28:

Listing 13-28. Edit the response to SourceConnection property value changes

```
if (e.ChangedItem.PropertyDescriptor.Name.CompareTo("SourceConnection") == 0)
{
  if (e.ChangedItem.Value.Equals(NEW_CONNECTION))
  {
    ArrayList newConnection = new ArrayList();
    if (!((settingsNode.SourceConnection == null)
      || (settingsNode.SourceConnection == "")))
```

```
    {
      settingsNode.SourceConnection = null;
    }
    newConnection = connectionService.CreateConnection("ADO.Net");
    if ((newConnection != null) && (newConnection.Count > 0))
    {
      ConnectionManager cMgr = (ConnectionManager)newConnection[0];
      settingsNode.SourceConnection = cMgr.Name;
      theTask.ServerName = returnSelectedConnectionManagerDataSourceValue
      (settingsNode.SourceConnection , cMgr.ConnectionString);
      settingsNode.Connections = connectionService.
      GetConnectionsOfType("ADO.Net");
    }
    else
    {
      if (e.OldValue == null)
      {
        settingsNode.SourceConnection = null;
      }
      else
      {
        settingsNode.SourceConnection = (string)e.OldValue;
      }
    }
  }
  else
  {
    theTask.ServerName = returnSelectedConnectionManagerDataSourceValue
    (settingsNode.SourceConnection);
  }
}
```

Once added, the code appears as shown in Figure 13-41:

```
private void propertyGridSettings_PropertyValueChanged(object s
                                , System.Windows.Forms.PropertyValueChangedEventArgs e)
{
    if (e.ChangedItem.PropertyDescriptor.Name.CompareTo("SourceConnection") == 0)
    {
        if (e.ChangedItem.Value.Equals(NEW_CONNECTION))
        {
            ArrayList newConnection = new ArrayList();

            if (!((settingsNode.SourceConnection == null) || (settingsNode.SourceConnection == "")))
            {
                settingsNode.SourceConnection = null;
            }

            newConnection = connectionService.CreateConnection("ADO.Net");

            if ((newConnection != null) && (newConnection.Count > 0))
            {
                ConnectionManager cMgr = (ConnectionManager)newConnection[0];
                settingsNode.SourceConnection = cMgr.Name;
                theTask.ServerName = returnSelectedConnectionManagerDataSourceValue(settingsNode.SourceConnection, cMgr.ConnectionString);
                settingsNode.Connections = ConnectionService.GetConnectionsOfType("ADO.Net");
            }
            else
            {
                if (e.OldValue == null)
                {
                    settingsNode.SourceConnection = null;
                }
                else
                {
                    settingsNode.SourceConnection = (string)e.OldValue;
                }
            }
        }
        else
        {
            theTask.ServerName = returnSelectedConnectionManagerDataSourceValue(settingsNode.SourceConnection);
        }
    }
}
```

Figure 13-41. *Updated response to SourceConnection property value changes*

Let's Test It!

Build the solution. If all goes well, the solution should build successfully. Open a test SSIS project and add an ADO.Net connection manager aimed at an SSIS Catalog. Add the Execute Catalog Package Task to the control flow of a test SSIS package. Open the editor and click on the Settings page. Select the SSIS Catalog Ado.Net connection manager from the SourceConnection property dropdown.

Configure the SSIS Catalog FolderName, ProjectName, and PackageName properties – setting them to match a folder, project, and package in your SSIS Catalog, as shown in Figure 13-42:

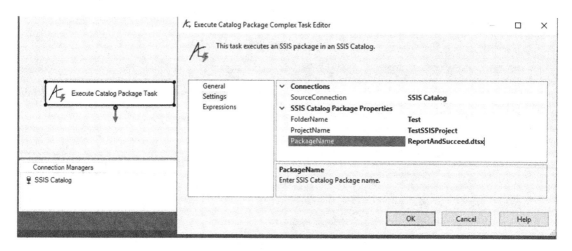

Figure 13-42. *Configuring the Execute Catalog Package Task*

Click the OK button to close the editor and then execute the SSIS package. If all goes as planned, the SSIS package execution succeeds. Open SQL Server Management Studio (SSMS) and connect to the SSIS Catalog's All Executions report. Verify the SSIS package executed, as shown in Figure 13-43:

Figure 13-43. *Successful execution*

We're not done coding SourceConnection functionality, but we have reached parity with the previous editor's functionality.

Conclusion

In this chapter, we implemented the IDTSTaskUIView editor interfaces for GeneralView and SettingsView, added properties (members) to each view, and conducted tests – where possible – each step along the way.

The next steps are completing the SourceConnection property functionality and adding more SettingsView members.

Now would be an excellent time to check in your code.

CHAPTER 14

Implement New Connection

In Chapter 13, we implemented GeneralView and made a good start of implementing SettingsView. This chapter is all about completing the SettingsView SourceConnection property implementation, which is the most complex part of building the Execute Catalog Package Task Complex editor (thus far, at least).

Implementing New Connection Functionality

To implement "<New Connection...>" functionality in the SourceConnection dropdown, we first need to add an event handler for changes to manage and respond changes in PropertyGrid values.

Begin by adding the code in Listing 14-1 to the SettingsView class:

Listing 14-1. Adding the propertyGridSettings_PropertyValueChanged event handler method

```
private void propertyGridSettings_PropertyValueChanged(object s, System.
Windows.Forms.PropertyValueChangedEventArgs e) { }
```

Once added, the code appears as shown in Figure 14-1:

```
private void propertyGridSettings_PropertyValueChanged(object s, System.Windows.Forms.PropertyValueChangedEventArgs e) { }
```

Figure 14-1. *The propertyGridSettings_PropertyValueChanged event handler method added*

© Andy Leonard 2021
A. Leonard, *Building Custom Tasks for SQL Server Integration Services*,
https://doi.org/10.1007/978-1-4842-6482-9_14

After adding the method to handle propertyGridSettings_PropertyValueChanged events, the next step is to update the SettingsView InitializeComponent method to assign the event handler to respond to the propertyGridSettings' PropertyValueChanged event, adding the code in Listing 14-2:

Listing 14-2. Assigning propertyGridSettings_PropertyValueChanged to propertyGridSettings.PropertyValueChanged

```
this.settingsPropertyGrid.PropertyValueChanged += new System.Windows.
Forms.PropertyValueChangedEventHandler(this.propertyGridSettings_
PropertyValueChanged);
```

Once added, the code appears as shown in Figure 14-2:

```
private void InitializeComponent()
{
    this.settingsPropertyGrid = new System.Windows.Forms.PropertyGrid();
    this.SuspendLayout();
    // settingsPropertyGrid
    this.settingsPropertyGrid.Anchor = ((System.Windows.Forms.AnchorStyles)((((System.Windows.Forms.AnchorStyles.Top
            | System.Windows.Forms.AnchorStyles.Bottom)
            | System.Windows.Forms.AnchorStyles.Left)
            | System.Windows.Forms.AnchorStyles.Right)));
    this.settingsPropertyGrid.Location = new System.Drawing.Point(3, 0);
    this.settingsPropertyGrid.Name = "settingsPropertyGrid";
    this.settingsPropertyGrid.PropertySort = System.Windows.Forms.PropertySort.Categorized;
    this.settingsPropertyGrid.Size = new System.Drawing.Size(387, 400);
    this.settingsPropertyGrid.TabIndex = 0;
    this.settingsPropertyGrid.ToolbarVisible = false;
    // SettingsView
    this.Controls.Add(this.settingsPropertyGrid);
    this.Name = "SettingsView";
    this.Size = new System.Drawing.Size(390, 400);
    this.ResumeLayout(false);
    this.settingsPropertyGrid.PropertyValueChanged += new System.Windows.Forms.PropertyValueChangedEventHandler(this.propertyGridSettings_PropertyValueChanged);
}
```

Figure 14-2. *The propertyGridSettings_PropertyValueChanged event handler method assigned to the propertyGridSettings.PropertyValueChanged event*

The propertyGridSettings_PropertyValueChanged event handler method is now called whenever *any* property value changes in the propertyGridSettings PropertyGrid.

The next step is tuning the logic of the propertyGridSettings_PropertyValueChanged event handler method so it responds as we desire to the value changing in *each* propertyGridSettings property. We begin with detecting – and responding to – changes in the SourceConnection property.

SourceConnection Property Value Changes

The first step in detecting and responding to changes in the SourceConnection property is detecting changes to the SourceConnection property. Add the code in Listing 14-3 to the propertyGridSettings_PropertyValueChanged event handler method:

Listing 14-3. Respond to SourceConnection property changes

```
if (e.ChangedItem.PropertyDescriptor.Name.CompareTo
("SourceConnection") == 0) { }
```

Once added, the propertyGridSettings_PropertyValueChanged event handler method appears as shown in Figure 14-3:

```
private void propertyGridSettings_PropertyValueChanged(object s
                            , System.Windows.Forms.PropertyValueChangedEventArgs e)
{
    if (e.ChangedItem.PropertyDescriptor.Name.CompareTo("SourceConnection") == 0) { }
}
```

Figure 14-3. *SourceConnection property changes only, please*

The next step is to check if "New Connection" was selected. Before proceeding, however, add the code in Listing 14-4 to define the NEW_CONNECTION string constant in SettingsView:

Listing 14-4. Add the NEW_CONNECTION string constant to SettingsView

```
private const string NEW_CONNECTION = "<New Connection...>";
```

Once added, the declarations in SettingsView appears as shown in Figure 14-4:

```
public partial class SettingsView : System.Windows.Forms.UserControl, IDTSTaskUIView
{
    private SettingsNode settingsNode = null;
    private System.Windows.Forms.PropertyGrid settingsPropertyGrid;
    private ExecuteCatalogPackageTask.ExecuteCatalogPackageTask theTask = null;
    private System.ComponentModel.Container components = null;

    private const string NEW_CONNECTION = "<New Connection...>";
```

Figure 14-4. *Declaring NEW_CONNECTION constant in SettingsView*

Add the code in Listing 14-5 inside the previous if conditional statement in the propertyGridSettings_PropertyValueChanged method to determine if "New Connection" was clicked:

Listing 14-5. Checking for "New Connection" click

```
if (e.ChangedItem.Value.Equals(NEW_CONNECTION)) { }
```

Once the check for a "New Connection" click is added, the propertyGridSettings_ PropertyValueChanged method appears as shown in Figure 14-5:

```
private void propertyGridSettings_PropertyValueChanged(object s
                                    , System.Windows.Forms.PropertyValueChangedEventArgs e)
{
    if (e.ChangedItem.PropertyDescriptor.Name.CompareTo("SourceConnection") == 0)
    {
        if (e.ChangedItem.Value.Equals(NEW_CONNECTION)) { }
    }
}
```

Figure 14-5. *Checking for New Connection clicks*

Before we add the code to create a new ADO.Net connection manager, we must first add and initialize (a little later) an IDtsConnectionService member named connectionService to the SettingsView class by adding the code in Listing 14-6 to declare the connectionService member:

Listing 14-6. Adding connectionService to SettingsView

```
private IDtsConnectionService connectionService;
```

When the code in Listing 14-6 is added, the SettingsView declarations appear as shown in Figure 14-6:

```
public partial class SettingsView : System.Windows.Forms.UserControl, IDTSTaskUIView
{
    private SettingsNode settingsNode = null;
    private System.Windows.Forms.PropertyGrid settingsPropertyGrid;
    private ExecuteCatalogPackageTask.ExecuteCatalogPackageTask theTask = null;
    private System.ComponentModel.Container components = null;

    private const string NEW_CONNECTION = "<New Connection...>";
    private IDtsConnectionService connectionService;
```

Figure 14-6. *connectionService added to SettingsView*

The next step is to initialize the `connectionService` `IDtsConnectionService` member by adding the code in Listing 14-7 to the `SettingsView` `OnInitialize` method:

Listing 14-7. Initializing connectionService in OnInitialize

```
connectionService = (IDtsConnectionService)connections;
```

When the code in Listing 14-7 is added, the `SettingsView` `OnInitialize` method appears as shown in Figure 14-7:

```
public virtual void OnInitialize(IDTSTaskUIHost treeHost
                              , System.Windows.Forms.TreeNode viewNode
                              , object taskHost
                              , object connections)
{
    if (taskHost == null)
    {
        throw new ArgumentNullException("Attempting to initialize the ExecuteCatalogPackageTask UI with a null TaskHost");
    }

    if (!(((TaskHost)taskHost).InnerObject is ExecuteCatalogPackageTask.ExecuteCatalogPackageTask))
    {
        throw new ArgumentException("Attempting to initialize the ExecuteCatalogPackageTask UI with a task that is not a ExecuteCatalogPackageTask.");
    }

    theTask = ((TaskHost)taskHost).InnerObject as ExecuteCatalogPackageTask.ExecuteCatalogPackageTask;

    this.settingsNode = new SettingsNode(taskHost as TaskHost, connections);

    settingsPropertyGrid.SelectedObject = this.settingsNode;

    connectionService = (IDtsConnectionService)connections;
}
```

Figure 14-7. *connectionService initialized in SettingsView OnInitialize*

Add the code in Listing 14-8 inside the previous `if` conditional statement – `if (e.ChangedItem.Value.Equals(NEW_CONNECTION))` – in the `propertyGridSettings_PropertyValueChanged` method to respond to "New Connection" clicks:

Listing 14-8. Respond to "New Connection" clicks

```
ArrayList newConnection = new ArrayList();

if (!((settingsNode.SourceConnection == null) || (settingsNode.SourceConnection == "")))
  {
    settingsNode.SourceConnection = null;
  }

newConnection = connectionService.CreateConnection("ADO.Net");
```

```
if ((newConnection != null) && (newConnection.Count > 0))
{
  ConnectionManager cMgr = (ConnectionManager)newConnection[0];
  settingsNode.SourceConnection = cMgr.Name;
  settingsNode.Connections = connectionService.GetConnectionsOfType
  ("ADO.Net");
}
else
{
  if (e.OldValue == null)
  {
    settingsNode.SourceConnection = null;
  }
  else
  {
    settingsNode.SourceConnection = (string)e.OldValue;
  }
}
```

When the code in Listing 14-8 is added, the propertyGridSettings_
PropertyValueChanged method appears as shown in Figure 14-8:

```
115   private void propertyGridSettings_PropertyValueChanged(object s
116                                                      , System.Windows.Forms.PropertyValueChangedEventArgs e)
117   {
118       if (e.ChangedItem.PropertyDescriptor.Name.CompareTo("SourceConnection") == 0)
119       {
120           if (e.ChangedItem.Value.Equals(NEW_CONNECTION))
121           {
122               ArrayList newConnection = new ArrayList();
123
124               if (!((settingsNode.SourceConnection == null) || (settingsNode.SourceConnection == "")))
125               {
126                   settingsNode.SourceConnection = null;
127               }
128
129               newConnection = connectionService.CreateConnection("ADO.Net");
130
131               if ((newConnection != null) && (newConnection.Count > 0))
132               {
133                   ConnectionManager cMgr = (ConnectionManager)newConnection[0];
134                   settingsNode.SourceConnection = cMgr.Name;
135                   settingsNode.Connections = connectionService.GetConnectionsOfType("ADO.Net");
136               }
137               else
138               {
139                   if (e.OldValue == null)
140                   {
141                       settingsNode.SourceConnection = null;
142                   }
143                   else
144                   {
145                       settingsNode.SourceConnection = (string)e.OldValue;
146                   }
147               }
148           }
149       }
150   }
```

Figure 14-8. *Responding to New Connection clicks*

On line 118, the code checks to see if the change that triggered the call to the propertyGridSettings_PropertyValueChanged method was a change to the SourceConnection property. Line 120 checks to see if the developer clicked the "<New Connection...>" item in the SourceConnection property dropdown. If the developer clicked the "<New Connection...>" item in the SourceConnection property dropdown, a new ArrayList variable named newConnection is declared on line 122.

On lines 124–127, the settingsNode SourceConnection value is set to null if and only if the current settingsNode SourceConnection value is *not* null or empty.

On line 129, a new ADO.Net connection manager is created. Creating a new ADO. Net connection manager involves

- Creating a new generic ADO.Net connection manager

- Adding the new generic ADO.Net connection manager to the SSIS package's connection collection

- Opening the editor for the new ADO.Net connection manager so the SSIS developer can configure the connection manager

On lines 131–136, the `settingsNode SourceConnection` value is assigned to the new connection if the `newConnection ArrayList` is not null and contains at least one value. The `settingsView.Connections` property is reloaded to add the new connection manager. If the `newConnection ArrayList` is null or contains no values, the code on lines 139–146 restores the previous value to the `settingsNode SourceConnection` value.

The next step is to test the code.

Let's Test It!

Before testing, let's define a couple use cases:

- Use case 1: As before, we may configure the Execute Catalog Package Task to use an ADO.Net connection manager that was previously configured in the test SSIS package. We may configure the FolderName, ProjectName, and PackageName properties on the Settings page to an SSIS package deployed to the SSIS Catalog.

  Assert: Test SSIS package debug execution succeeds and SSIS package deployed to the SSIS Catalog executes.

- Use case 2: We may configure the Execute Catalog Package Task to use a *new* ADO.Net connection manager by clicking "<New Connection…>" in the Settings page SourceConnection property dropdown. The "Configure New ADO.Net Connection" dialog will display and allow the developer to configure a new ADO.Net connection manager. As in use case 1, we configure the FolderName, ProjectName, and PackageName properties on the Settings page to an SSIS package deployed to the SSIS Catalog.

Assert: A new ADO.Net connection manager is added to the Test
SSIS package. Test SSIS package debug execution succeeds and
SSIS package deployed to the SSIS Catalog executes.

Use Case 1

Build the solution and then open the test SSIS project. To test use case 1, add an Execute
Catalog Package Task to the control, open the editor, and then configure the task to
execute an SSIS package in the SSIS Catalog, as shown in Figure 14-9:

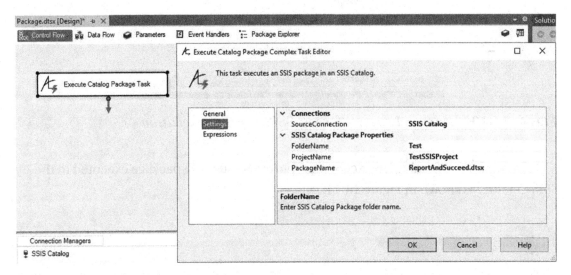

Figure 14-9. *The Execute Catalog Package Task configured for use case 1*

Execute the test SSIS package in the debugger. If all goes as planned, the test SSIS
package should succeed, as shown in Figure 14-10:

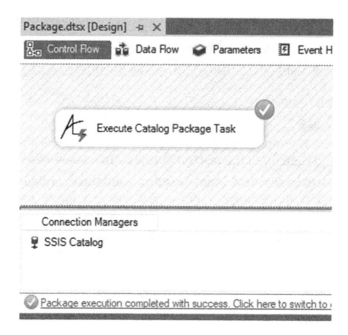

Figure 14-10. *Use case 1 success for test SSIS package execution*

Check the SSIS Catalog All Execution report to be sure the package executed in the SSIS Catalog, as shown in Figure 14-11:

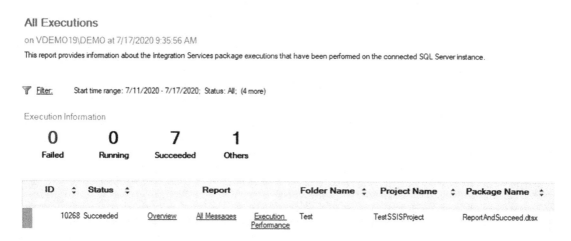

Figure 14-11. *Use case 1 success for configured package execution*

Success. It's not just for breakfast anymore.

Use Case 2

To test use case 2, add an Execute Catalog Package Task to the control, open the editor, and then select "<new Connection...>" from the SourceConnection property dropdown, as shown in Figure 14-12:

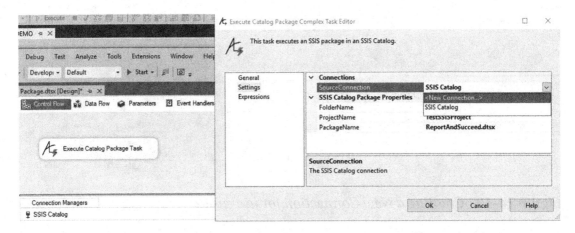

Figure 14-12. *The Execute Catalog Package Task configured for use case 2*

A new ASO.Net connection manager is created and displays in the Connection Managers pane of the SSIS package, and the "Configure ADO.NET Connection Manager" displays, as shown in Figure 14-13:

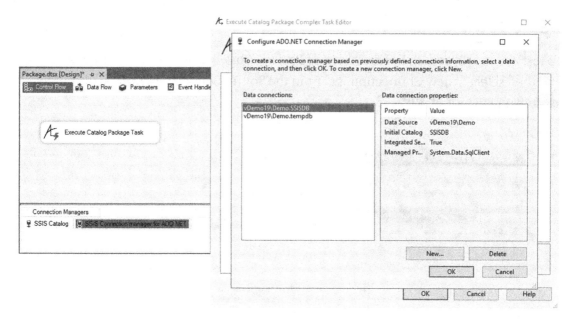

Figure 14-13. *Creating a New Connection for use case 2*

Configure an ADO.Net connection to the SSISDB database and then click the OK button. When the new connection is selected in the SourceConnection property, the Editor appears as shown in Figure 14-14:

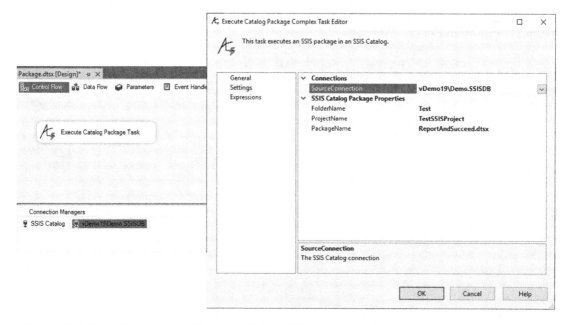

Figure 14-14. *New connection configured for use case 2*

Click the OK button to close the editor.

Execute the test SSIS package in the debugger. If all goes as planned, the test SSIS package should succeed, as shown in Figure 14-15:

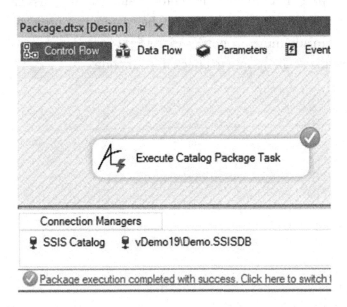

Figure 14-15. *Use case 2 success for test SSIS package execution*

Check the SSIS Catalog All Execution report to be sure the package executed in the SSIS Catalog, as shown in Figure 14-16:

Figure 14-16. *Use case 2 success for configured package execution*

Conclusion

The New Connection option makes building the `SettingsView SourceConnection` property a complex part of building the Execute Catalog Package Task Complex editor, which is why the author isolated this portion of the custom task project in its own chapter.

The next step is to add more properties to the `SettingsView`.

Now would be an excellent time to check in your code.

CHAPTER 15

Implement Use32bit, Synchronized, and LoggingLevel SettingsView Properties

In Chapters 13 and 14, we implemented GeneralView and SettingsView. In this chapter, we implement additional SettingsNode properties – Use32bit, Synchronized, and LoggingLevel. Adding the SourceConnection property was intense, so we begin this chapter by adding one straightforward and simple property implementation: User32bit. Be forewarned, the intensity increases.

Specifying a 32-Bit Interface

SSIS is provider-agnostic, which means SSIS can connect with just about any data provider installed on a server. If SSIS can connect to the provider, SSIS can read and write data through the said provider to resources for which the provider provides an interface.

Adding the Use32bit Property

Some providers surface 32-bit interfaces. A handful of providers surface *only* 32-bit interfaces. For this reason, the SSIS Catalog allows developers and operators to execute SSIS packages in 32-bit mode by setting a "use 32-bit" Boolean value to true at execution time.

253

© Andy Leonard 2021
A. Leonard, *Building Custom Tasks for SQL Server Integration Services*,
https://doi.org/10.1007/978-1-4842-6482-9_15

To add the Use32bit property to SettingsNode, we begin by adding the code in Listing 15-1 to the SettingsNode class:

Listing 15-1. Adding the Use32bit property to SettingsNode

```
[
 Category("SSIS Package Execution Properties"),
 Description("Enter SSIS Catalog Package Use32bit execution property
 value.")
]
public bool Use32bit {
  get { return _task.Use32bit; }
  set { _task.Use32bit = value; }
}
```

Once added, the SettingsNode Use32bit property code appears as shown in Figure 15-1:

```
[
    Category("SSIS Package Execution Properties"),
    Description("Enter SSIS Catalog Package Use32bit execution property value.")
]
0 references
public bool Use32bit {
    get { return _task.Use32bit; }
    set { _task.Use32bit = value; }
}
```

Figure 15-1. *The SettingsNode Use32bit property, implemented*

The next step is to update the ExecuteCatalogPackageTask Execute method to use the value set in the Use32bit property. Edit the catalogPackage.Execute(false, null); statement to match the code in Listing 15-2:

Listing 15-2. Configure the ExecuteCatalogPackageTask Execute method to use the Use32bit property

```
catalogPackage.Execute(Use32bit, null);
```

Once edited, the ExecuteCatalogPackageTask Execute method appears as shown in Figure 15-2:

```
public override DTSExecResult Execute(
    Connections connections,
    VariableDispenser variableDispenser,
    IDTSComponentEvents componentEvents,
    IDTSLogging log,
    object transaction)
{
    catalogServer = new Server(ServerName);
    integrationServices = new IntegrationServices(catalogServer);
    catalog = integrationServices.Catalogs[PackageCatalogName];
    catalogFolder = catalog.Folders[PackageFolder];
    catalogProject = catalogFolder.Projects[PackageProject];
    catalogPackage = catalogProject.Packages[PackageName];

    catalogPackage.Execute(Use32bit, null);

    return DTSExecResult.Success;
}
```

Figure 15-2. *The ExecuteCatalogPackageTask Execute method now uses the Use32bit property*

That's it. The Use32bit property is implemented. That wasn't so difficult, was it?

Test Use32bit

To test the Use32bit property, build the ExecuteCatalogPackageTask solution, open a test SSIS package, and configure the Execute Catalog Package Task to execute an SSIS package deployed to an SSIS Catalog. Set the Use32bit property to True, as shown in Figure 15-3:

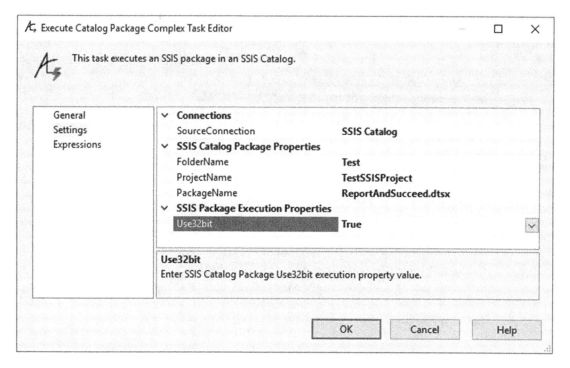

Figure 15-3. *Setting the Use32bit property to True*

Click the OK button and then execute the test SSIS package. If all goes as planned, the package execution will succeed in the SSIS Catalog. One way to check if the Use32bit property was set is to execute the T-SQL query in Listing 15-3:

Listing 15-3. Checking to see if Use32bit was set

```
Select folder_name
     , project_name
     , package_name
     , use32bitruntime
From SSISDB.catalog.executions
Order by execution_id DESC
```

Executing the T-SQL in Listing 15-3 returns results that confirm the Use32bit property works, as shown in Figure 15-4:

SQLQuery1.sql - vDe.... Ray Leonard (57))* ⇸ ✕

```
   1  ⊟Select folder_name
   2        , project_name
   3        , package_name
   4        , use32bitruntime
   5    From SSISDB.catalog.executions
   6    Order by execution_id desc
```

146 % ▾

⊞ Results Messages

	folder_name	project_name	package_name	use32bitruntime
1	Test	TestSSISProject	ReportAndSucceed.dtsx	1

Figure 15-4. *The Use32bit property in action*

The next property is Synchronized, and the implementation is as easy as the implementation of the Use32bit property.

Adding the Synchronized Property

By default, SSIS packages executed in the SSIS Catalog execute with the Synchronized execution parameter set to *false*. A false Synchronized execution parameter means the SSIS Catalog execution engine finds and starts the SSIS package and then returns. It's possible for the SSIS package to continue executing – for hours or days – and then fail. People who monitor SSIS executions must check the status of the SSIS package execution to determine the state of the instance of execution. One good way to monitor the state of an instance of execution for an SSIS package is to view the SSIS Catalog All Executions and Overview reports built into SQL Server Management Studio (SSMS).

If one desires an SSIS package execution process to remain "in process," or to continue to show the process as running until the instance of execution *completes*, one may set the Synchronized execution parameter to true. To add the Synchronized property to SettingsNode, we begin by adding the code in Listing 15-4 to the SettingsNode class:

Listing 15-4. Adding the Synchronized property to SettingsNode

```
[

  Category("SSIS Package Execution Properties"),
  Description("Enter SSIS Catalog Package SYNCHRONIZED execution parameter
  value.")
]
```

257

```
public bool Synchronized {
  get { return _task.Synchronized; }
  set { _task.Synchronized = value; }
}
```

Once added, the SettingsNode Synchronized property code appears as shown in Figure 15-5:

```
[
    Category("SSIS Package Execution Properties"),
    Description("Enter SSIS Catalog Package SYNCHRONIZED execution parameter value.")
]
0 references
public bool Synchronized {
    get { return _task.Synchronized; }
    set { _task.Synchronized = value; }
}
```

Figure 15-5. *The SettingsNode Synchronized property, implemented*

The next step is to update the ExecuteCatalogPackageTask Execute method to use the value set in the Synchronized property. Editing the Execute method is not as simple and straightforward as the edits to implement the Use32bit property; it's a little more involved. It all starts with a look at the Execute *statement* overloads in the ExecuteCatalogPackageTask Execute *method.*

Examining Execute() Overloads

To take a look at the available overloads for the SSIS package Execute method, find the Execute method in the ExecuteCatalogPackageTask code. Locate the line of code that calls the execution of the SSIS package – the line that we just updated when adding the Use32bit property. At this time, the line reads catalogPackage.Execute(Use32bit, null);. Select the opening parenthesis and type *another* opening parenthesis over it to open the overload options, as shown in Figure 15-6:

```
catalogPackage.Execute(Use32bit, null);
  ▲ 1 of 3 ▼  long Microsoft.SqlServer.Management.IntegrationServices.PackageInfo.Execute(bool use32RuntimeOn64, EnvironmentReference reference)
```

Figure 15-6. *Viewing Execute overload 1 of 3*

By viewing the overloads list, we know the `Execute` function has three overloads because the overloads tooltip tells us, "1 of 3." We also know overload 1 of 3 takes two arguments:

- A `Boolean` value named `use32RuntimeOn64` – for which we supplied our `Boolean` property named `Use32bit`

- An `EnvironmentReference` value named `reference`

If we click the "down arrow" to the right of the 1 of 3, we can view overload 2 of 3, as shown in Figure 15-7:

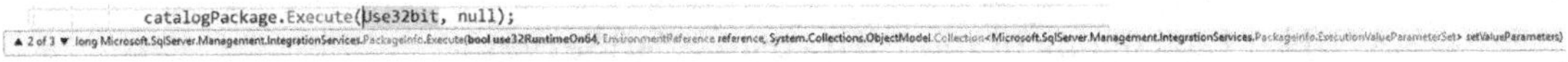

Figure 15-7. *Viewing Execute overload 2 of 3*

Viewing the overloads argument list for overload 2 of 3, we know this overload for the `Execute` takes three arguments, and the first two arguments are the same as overload 1 of 3:

- A `Boolean` value named `use32RuntimeOn64` – for which we supplied our `Boolean` property named `Use32bit`

- An `EnvironmentReference` value named `reference`

- A `Collection` of one or more `Microsoft.SqlServer.Management.IntegrationServices.PackageInfo.ExecutionValueParameterSet` value(s) named `setValueParameters`

This third argument – the `collection` of `ExecutionValueParameterSet` parameters named `setValueParameters` – is the argument that will hold the `Synchronized` property value we are now coding. But first, let's look at the Execute 3 of overload.

If we click the "down arrow" to the right of the 2 of 3, we can view Execute overload 3 of 3, as shown in Figure 15-8:

Figure 15-8. *Viewing Execute overload 3 of 3*

Viewing the overloads argument list for overload 3 of 3, we know this overload for the Execute takes four arguments, and the first three arguments are the same as overload 2 of 3:

- A Boolean value named use32RuntimeOn64 – for which we supplied our Boolean property named Use32bit

- An EnvironmentReference value named reference

- A Collection of one or more Microsoft.SqlServer.Management. IntegrationServices.PackageInfo.ExecutionValueParameterSet value(s) named setValueParameters

- A Collection of one or more Microsoft.SqlServer. Management.IntegrationServices.PackageInfo. PropertyOverrideParameterSet value(s) named propertyOverrideParameters

We will use the second overload – 2 of 3 – in this version of the ExecuteCatalogPackageTask.

There are two steps to adding the ExecutionValueParameterSet:

1. Build the ExecutionValueParameterSet.

2. Add the ExecutionValueParameterSet to the call to package. Execute().

Building the ExecutionValueParameterSet

The ExecutionValueParameterSet is a collection of the Microsoft.SqlServer. Management.IntegrationServices.PackageInfo.ExecutionValuearameterSet type. The first step is to create a function that builds and returns the ExecutionValueParameterSet, using the code in Listing 15-5:

Listing 15-5. Building the returnExecutionValueParameterSet function

```
using System.Collections.ObjectModel;
```
.
.
.

```
private Collection<Microsoft.SqlServer.Management.IntegrationServices.
PackageInfo.ExecutionValueParameterSet> returnExecutionValueParameterSet
(Microsoft.SqlServer.Management.IntegrationServices.PackageInfo
catalogPackage)
{

    // initialize the parameters collection
    Collection<Microsoft.SqlServer.Management.IntegrationServices.
    PackageInfo.ExecutionValueParameterSet> executionValueParameterSet =
    new Collection<Microsoft.SqlServer.Management.IntegrationServices.
    PackageInfo.ExecutionValueParameterSet>();

    // set SYNCHRONIZED execution parameter
    executionValueParameterSet.Add(new Microsoft.SqlServer.Management.
    IntegrationServices.PackageInfo.ExecutionValueParameterSet { ObjectType =
    50, ParameterName = "SYNCHRONIZED", ParameterValue = Synchronized });

    return executionValueParameterSet;
}
```

Add the using `System.Collections.ObjectModel;` directive to the ExecuteCatalogPackageTask.cs file header, along with other using directives.

Once added, the `returnExecutionValueParameterSet` function appears as shown in Figure 15-9:

```
82   private Collection<Microsoft.SqlServer.Management.IntegrationServices.PackageInfo.ExecutionValueParameterSet> returnExecutionValueParameterSet()
83   {
84
85       // initialize the parameters collection
86       Collection<Microsoft.SqlServer.Management.IntegrationServices.PackageInfo.ExecutionValueParameterSet> executionValueParameterSet =
87           new Collection<Microsoft.SqlServer.Management.IntegrationServices.PackageInfo.ExecutionValueParameterSet>();
88
89       // set SYNCHRONIZED execution parameter
90       executionValueParameterSet.Add(
91           new Microsoft.SqlServer.Management.IntegrationServices.PackageInfo.ExecutionValueParameterSet {
92               ObjectType = 50, ParameterName = "SYNCHRONIZED", ParameterValue = Synchronized });
93
94       return executionValueParameterSet;
95   }
```

Figure 15-9. *The returnExecutionValueParameterSet function*

The returnExecutionValueParameterSet function is declared to return a value of type Collection<Microsoft.SqlServer.Management.IntegrationServices.PackageInfo. ExecutionValueParameterSet> on line 82.

A new variable named executionValueParameterSet of Collection<Microsoft. SqlServer.Management.IntegrationServices.PackageInfo. ExecutionValueParameterSet> type is created on lines 86–87.

On lines 90–92, a new Collection<Microsoft.SqlServer.Management. IntegrationServices.PackageInfo.ExecutionValueParameterSet> object is initialized and added to the executionValueParameterSet collection.

On line 94, the executionValueParameterSet collection is returned to the caller, to which we now turn our attention.

Calling the returnExecutionValueParameterSet Function

Return to the ExecuteCatalogPackageTask Execute method, and overwrite the catalogPackage.Execute(Use32bit, null); statement with the code in Listing 15-6:

Listing 15-6. Updating package.Execute()

```
Collection<Microsoft.SqlServer.Management.IntegrationServices.
PackageInfo.ExecutionValueParameterSet> executionValueParameterSet =
returnExecutionValueParameterSet();

catalogPackage.Execute(Use32bit, null, executionValueParameterSet);
```

Once edited, the code near the end of the ExecuteCatalogPackageTask Execute method appears as shown in Figure 15-10:

```
Collection<Microsoft.SqlServer.Management.IntegrationServices.PackageInfo.ExecutionValueParameterSet> executionValueParameterSet =
    returnExecutionValueParameterSet();

catalogPackage.Execute(Use32bit, null, executionValueParameterSet);

return DTSExecResult.Success;
}
```

Figure 15-10. *Package.Execute(), updated to configure and use execution parameters*

The next step is to add the Synchronized Property to SettingsNode.

Adding the Synchronized Property to SettingsView

To add the Synchronized property to SettingsNode, begin by adding the code in
Listing 15-7 to the SettingsNode class:

Listing 15-7. Adding the Synchronized property to SettingsNode

```
[
  Category("SSIS Package Execution Properties"),
  Description("Enter SSIS Catalog Package SYNCHRONIZED execution parameter
  value.")
]
public bool Synchronized {
  get { return _task.Synchronized; }
  set { _task.Synchronized = value; }
}
```

Once added, the SettingsNode Synchronized property code appears as shown in
Figure 15-11:

```
[
    Category("SSIS Package Execution Properties"),
    Description("Enter SSIS Catalog Package SYNCHRONIZED execution parameter value.")
]
0 references
public bool Synchronized {
    get { return _task.Synchronized; }
    set { _task.Synchronized = value; }
}
```

Figure 15-11. *The SettingsNode Synchronized property, implemented*

The next step is to test the SettingsNode Synchronized property.

Test Synchronized

To test the Synchronized property, build the ExecuteCatalogPackageTask solution, open
a test SSIS package, and configure the Execute Catalog Package Task to execute an SSIS
package deployed to an SSIS Catalog. Set the Synchronized property to True, as shown in
Figure 15-12:

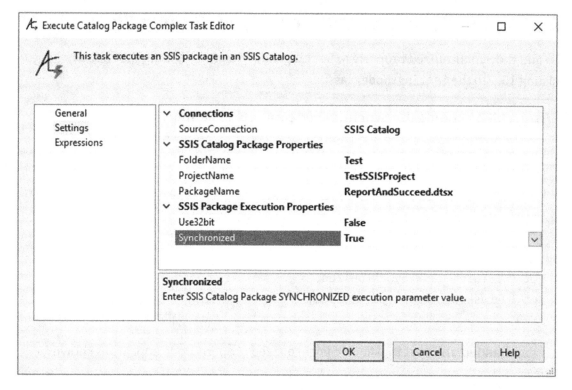

Figure 15-12. *Setting the Synchronized property to True*

Click the OK button and execute the test SSIS package in debug. If all goes as planned, the test SSIS package debug execution succeeds as shown in Figure 15-13:

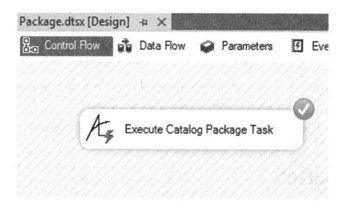

Figure 15-13. *Successful test execution*

Browse to the Overview report for this test execution in SSMS's Catalog Reports. The SYNCHRONIZED execution parameter – in the Parameters Used sub-report – should indicate the Synchronized execution parameter set to True, as shown in Figure 15-14:

Figure 15-14. *Synchronized execution parameter True*

Did you notice each implementation grow in complexity? The next property we will implement is Logging Level.

Adding the LoggingLevel Property

By default, SSIS packages executed in the SSIS Catalog execute with the Logging Level execution parameter set to *1* (Basic). Logging level is an enumeration of logging level name values that map to a list of integers. Do you smell something? I do. I smell another TypeConverter cooking...

Depending on the version of the SSIS Catalog in use, an SSIS developer may encounter four to five built-in logging level settings, and – perhaps – many more custom-defined logging levels. And logging level may be configured as the SSIS Catalog default logging level, but nearly all SSIS developers agree setting the default Catalog logging level to Basic is a best practice. Logging level may be altered for any SSIS package execution.

Building the LoggingLevel TypeConverter

Before adding the LoggingLevel property to SettingsNode, we need to add another TypeConverter class. TypeConverters follow a pattern that includes one type-specific function named GetSpecializedObject and three overridden functions: GetStandardValues, GetStandardValuesExclusive, and GetStandardValuesSupported. Begin by adding the code in Listing 15-8 to the SettingsNode class:

Listing 15-8. Adding the LoggingLevel TypeConverter (StringConverter)

```
internal class LoggingLevels : StringConverter
{
  private object GetSpecializedObject(object contextInstance)
  {
    DTSLocalizableTypeDescriptor typeDescr = contextInstance as
    DTSLocalizableTypeDescriptor;

    if (typeDescr == null)
    {
      return contextInstance;
    }

    return typeDescr.SelectedObject;
  }

  public override StandardValuesCollection GetStandardValues(
  ITypeDescriptorContext context)
  {
    object retrievalObject = GetSpecializedObject(context.Instance) as
    object;

    return new StandardValuesCollection(getLoggingLevels(retrievalObject));
  }

  public override bool GetStandardValuesExclusive(ITypeDescriptorContext
  context)
  {
    return true;
  }
```

```
public override bool GetStandardValuesSupported(ITypeDescriptorContext
context)
{
  return true;
}
}
```

Once added, the SettingsNode LoggingLevel StringConverter code appears as shown in Figure 15-15:

```
internal class LoggingLevels : StringConverter
{
    1 reference
    private object GetSpecializedObject(object contextInstance)
    {
        DTSLocalizableTypeDescriptor typeDescr = contextInstance as DTSLocalizableTypeDescriptor;

        if (typeDescr == null)
        {
            return contextInstance;
        }

        return typeDescr.SelectedObject;
    }

    1 reference
    public override StandardValuesCollection GetStandardValues(ITypeDescriptorContext context)
    {
        object retrievalObject = GetSpecializedObject(context.Instance) as object;

        return new StandardValuesCollection(getLoggingLevels(retrievalObject));
    }

    1 reference
    public override bool GetStandardValuesExclusive(ITypeDescriptorContext context)
    {
        return true;
    }

    1 reference
    public override bool GetStandardValuesSupported(ITypeDescriptorContext context)
    {
        return true;
    }
}
```

Figure 15-15. *The LoggingLevels StringConverter class*

All SSIS Catalog editions surface four logging levels:

- None (0)

- Basic (1)

- Performance (2)

- Verbose (3)

In all versions of the SSIS Catalog, Basic (1) is the default logging level. Complete the `LoggingLevels StringConverter` class by adding the `getLoggingLevels` function code in Listing 15-9:

Listing 15-9. Adding the getLoggingLevels function

```
private ArrayList getLoggingLevels(object retrievalObject)
{
  ArrayList logLevelsArray = new ArrayList();

  logLevelsArray.Add("None");
  logLevelsArray.Add("Basic");
  logLevelsArray.Add("Performance");
  logLevelsArray.Add("Verbose");

  return logLevelsArray;
}
```

Extending the ExecutionValueParameterSet with LoggingLevel

As we mentioned when adding the Synchronized execution parameter, the `ExecutionValueParameterSet` is a collection of the `Microsoft.SqlServer.Management.IntegrationServices.PackageInfo.ExecutionValuearameterSet` type. Like the Synchronized execution parameter, `LoggingLevel` is also an execution parameter.

Before adding the LoggingLevel integer value to the execution parameters collection, the value must be decoded using the code in Listing 15-10:

Listing 15-10. Adding the DecodeLoggingLevel function

```
private int decodeLoggingLevel(string loggingLevel)
{
  int ret = 1;

  switch (loggingLevel)
  {
    default:
      break;
    case "None":
      ret = 0;
      break;
    case "Performance":
      ret = 2;
      break;
    case "Verbose":
      ret = 3;
      break;
  }

  return ret;
}
```

When the decodeLoggingLevel function is added to the
ExecuteCatalogPackageTask class, the code appears as shown in Figure 15-16:

```
private int decodeLoggingLevel(string loggingLevel)
{
    int ret = 1;

    switch (loggingLevel)
    {
        default:
            break;
        case "None":
            ret = 0;
            break;
        case "Performance":
            ret = 2;
            break;
        case "Verbose":
            ret = 3;
            break;
    }

    return ret;
}
```

Figure 15-16. *The decodeLoggingLevel function*

To add the LoggingLevel value to the returnExecutionValueParameterSet function, edit the returnExecutionValueParameterSet function to match the code in Listing 15-11:

Listing 15-11. Editing the returnExecutionValueParameterSet function

```
private Collection<Microsoft.SqlServer.Management.
IntegrationServices.PackageInfo.ExecutionValueParameterSet>
returnExecutionValueParameterSet(          Microsoft.SqlServer.
Management.IntegrationServices.PackageInfo catalogPackage)
{

  // initialize the parameters collection
  Collection<Microsoft.SqlServer.Management.IntegrationServices.
  PackageInfo.ExecutionValueParameterSet> executionValueParameterSet =
  new Collection<Microsoft.SqlServer.Management.IntegrationServices.
  PackageInfo.ExecutionValueParameterSet>();
```

```
// set SYNCHRONIZED execution parameter
executionValueParameterSet.Add(new Microsoft.SqlServer.Management.
IntegrationServices.PackageInfo.ExecutionValueParameterSet { ObjectType =
50, ParameterName = "SYNCHRONIZED", ParameterValue = Synchronized });

// set LOGGING_LEVEL execution parameter
int LoggingLevelValue = decodeLoggingLevel(LoggingLevel);
executionValueParameterSet.Add(new Microsoft.SqlServer.Management.
IntegrationServices.PackageInfo.ExecutionValueParameterSet { ObjectType =
50, ParameterName = "LOGGING_LEVEL", ParameterValue = LoggingLevelValue
});

    return executionValueParameterSet;
}
```

Once added, the returnExecutionValueParameterSet function appears as shown in Figure 15-17:

```
private Collection<Microsoft.SqlServer.Management.IntegrationServices.PackageInfo.ExecutionValueParameterSet> returnExecutionValueParameterSet()
{

    // initialize the parameters collection
    Collection<Microsoft.SqlServer.Management.IntegrationServices.PackageInfo.ExecutionValueParameterSet> executionValueParameterSet =
        new Collection<Microsoft.SqlServer.Management.IntegrationServices.PackageInfo.ExecutionValueParameterSet>();

    // set SYNCHRONIZED execution parameter
    executionValueParameterSet.Add(
        new Microsoft.SqlServer.Management.IntegrationServices.PackageInfo.ExecutionValueParameterSet {
            ObjectType = 50, ParameterName = "SYNCHRONIZED", ParameterValue = Synchronized });

    // set LOGGING_LEVEL execution parameter
    int LoggingLevelValue = decodeLoggingLevel(LoggingLevel);
    executionValueParameterSet.Add(
        new Microsoft.SqlServer.Management.IntegrationServices.PackageInfo.ExecutionValueParameterSet {
            ObjectType = 50, ParameterName = "LOGGING_LEVEL", ParameterValue = LoggingLevelValue });

    return executionValueParameterSet;
}
```

Figure 15-17. *The returnExecutionValueParameterSet function, edited*

The next step is to add the SettingsView LoggingLevel property.

Adding the LoggingLevel Property to SettingsView

To add the LoggingLevel property to SettingsNode, begin by adding the code in Listing 15-12 to the SettingsNode class:

Listing 15-12. Adding the LoggingLevel property to SettingsNode

```
[
  Category("SSIS Package Execution Properties"),
  Description("Enter SSIS Catalog Package LOGGING_LEVEL execution parameter
  value."),
  TypeConverter(typeof(LoggingLevels))
]
public string LoggingLevel {
  get { return _task.LoggingLevel; }
  set { _task.LoggingLevel = value; }
}
```

Once added, the SettingsNode LoggingLevel property code appears as shown in Figure 15-18:

```
[
    Category("SSIS Package Execution Properties"),
    Description("Enter SSIS Catalog Package LOGGING_LEVEL execution parameter value."),
    TypeConverter(typeof(LoggingLevels))
]
0 references
public string LoggingLevel {
    get { return _task.LoggingLevel; }
    set { _task.LoggingLevel = value; }
}
```

Figure 15-18. *The SettingsNode LoggingLevel property, implemented*

The next step is to test the SettingsNode LoggingLevel property.

Test LoggingLevel

To test the LoggingLevel property, build the ExecuteCatalogPackageTask solution, open a test SSIS package, and configure the Execute Catalog Package Task to execute an SSIS package deployed to an SSIS Catalog. Set the LoggingLevel property to Verbose, as shown in Figure 15-19:

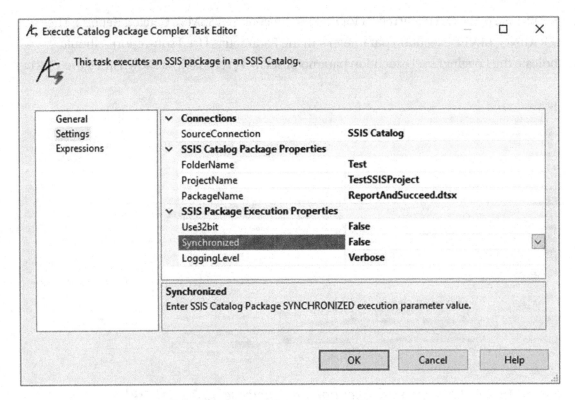

Figure 15-19. *Setting the LoggingLevel property to Verbose*

Click the OK button and execute the test SSIS package in debug. If all goes as planned, the test SSIS package debug execution succeeds as shown in Figure 15-20:

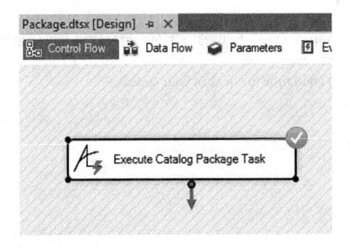

Figure 15-20. *Successful test execution*

Browse to the Overview report for this test execution in SSMS's Catalog Reports. The LOGGING_LEVEL execution parameter – in the Parameters Used sub-report – should indicate the LoggingLevel execution parameter set to 3 (Verbose), as shown in Figure 15-21:

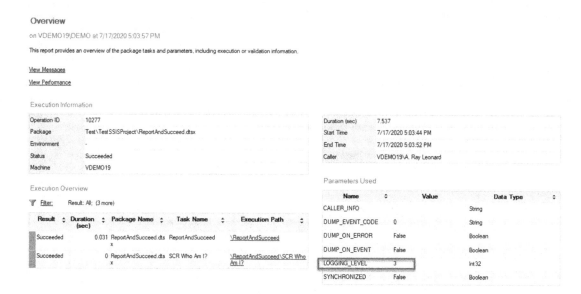

Figure 15-21. *LoggingLevel execution parameter set to 3 (Verbose)*

The next property to implement is Reference, which is the subject of the next chapter.

Conclusion

In this chapter, we implemented the Use32bit, Synchronized, and LoggingLevel SettingsView properties.

Now would be a good time to check in your code.

CHAPTER 16

Refactoring SourceConnection

The goal of this chapter is to refactor ExecuteCatalogPackageTask methods related to the SourceConnection property. The goals are

- Downgrade from SSIS 2019 to SSIS 2017 so as to run on the Azure platform.

- Refactor connection identification to support the Server ➤ Integration Services ➤ SSIS Catalog ➤ Folder ➤ Project ➤ Package hierarchy.

- Refactor the SettingsView.SourceConnection property.

- Identify catalog, folder, project, and package objects in the Server ➤ Integration Services ➤ SSIS Catalog ➤ Folder ➤ Project ➤ Package hierarchy.

We also refactor the Execute Catalog Package Task for two additional goals:

1. Using Expressions – which is one of the main goals for this edition of the book.

2. Executing the Execute Catalog Package Task in Azure-SSIS integration runtimes.

© Andy Leonard 2021
A. Leonard, *Building Custom Tasks for SQL Server Integration Services*,
https://doi.org/10.1007/978-1-4842-6482-9_16

Thinking Azure-SSIS

At the time of this writing (October 2020), Azure-SSIS does not support SSIS 2019. SSIS 2017 is supported, so we must downgrade the task and Visual Studio solution to run as an SSIS 2017 custom task. Azure-SSIS will likely support SSIS 2019 in the future (I don't know and I have no control over internal Microsoft decisions and priorities).

I advise you move your development effort to a machine configured with Microsoft SQL Server 2017 and not configured with Microsoft SQL Server 2019 to avoid collisions with assemblies in the Microsoft .Net Framework.

Begin by updating the ExecuteCatalogPackageTask project References by expanding the References virtual folder in Solution Explorer, as shown in Figure 16-1:

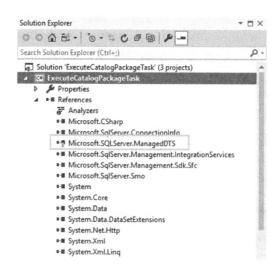

Figure 16-1. *ExecuteCatalogPackageTask References*

References to certain assemblies – such as the `Micrsoft.SQLServer.ManagedDTS` assembly outlined in Figure 16-1 – may display warning icons. The warning icon indicates an issue with the assembly. In this case, the issue is the SSIS 2019 of the `Micrsoft.SQLServer.ManagedDTS` assembly is not registered on the development server that has SQL Server 2017 (only) installed.

It is very important to note that your development server may be configured differently than the development server I am using. Your mileage may vary.

Click the reference to the `Micrsoft.SQLServer.ManagedDTS` assembly, and then press the F4 key to display its properties, as shown in Figure 16-2:

Figure 16-2. *Micrsoft.SQLServer.ManagedDTS assembly properties*

Note the Version property of the `Micrsoft.SQLServer.ManagedDTS` assembly displays the value "`0.0.0.0`" because the later version of the `Micrsoft.SQLServer.ManagedDTS` assembly cannot be located on this development server.

Delete the `Micrsoft.SQLServer.ManagedDTS` assembly from the ExecuteCatalogPackageTask References collection by right-clicking the assembly and then clicking Remove, as shown in Figure 16-3:

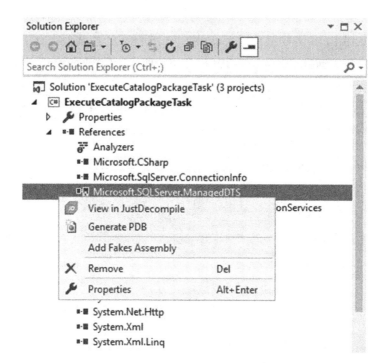

Figure 16-3. *Deleting the current version of the Micrsoft.SQLServer.ManagedDTS assembly*

As before, right-click the References virtual folder and click Add Reference to add a new reference (or, in this case, a new version of a reference), as shown in Figure 16-4:

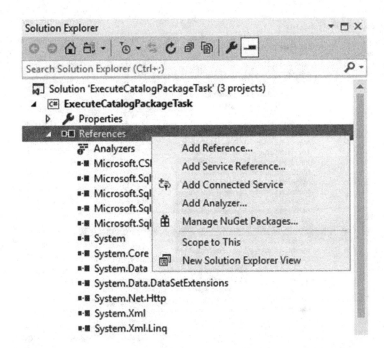

Figure 16-4. *Adding – replacing, really – a new reference*

Expand Assemblies and select Extensions. Navigate to the `Micrsoft.SQLServer.`
`ManagedDTS` assembly in the assemblies list, and select the `Micrsoft.SQLServer.`
`ManagedDTS` assembly, as shown in Figure 16-5:

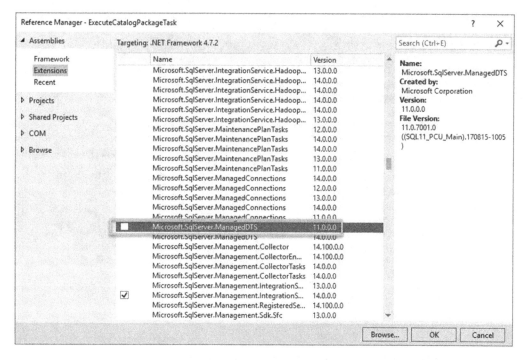

Figure 16-5. *Selecting Micrsoft.SQLServer.ManagedDTS*

Pay very close attention to the Version column and details in the Reference Manager's right pane. SSIS 2017 is version 14. The selected version of `Micrsoft.SQLServer.ManagedDTS` is version 11.0.0.0 – or version 11. Version 11 is SSIS 2012.

Click the Browse button and navigate to the location of the assembly file. On my server, the location is `C:\Windows\Microsoft.NET\assembly\GAC_MSIL\Microsoft.SqlServer.ManagedDTS\v4.0_14.0.0.0__89845dcd8080cc91`. Note the version of the `Micrsoft.SQLServer.ManagedDTS` assembly is `v4.0_14.0.0.0__89845dcd8080cc91`. We know the version because the folder which contains the `Micrsoft.SQLServer.ManagedDTS` assembly is named `v4.0_14.0.0.0__89845dcd8080cc91`, as shown in Figure 16-6:

Figure 16-6. *Selecting the SSIS 2017 version of the Micrsoft.SQLServer.*
ManagedDTS assembly

Add the reference to the `Micrsoft.SQLServer.ManagedDTS` assembly, and view the
properties to verify SSIS 2017 (version 14), as shown in Figure 16-7:

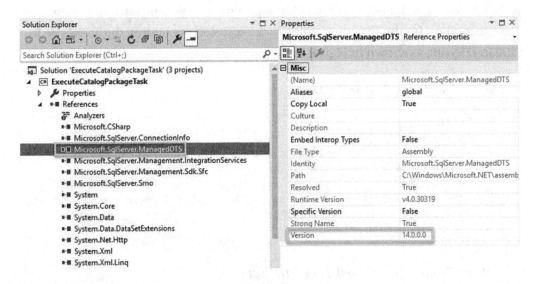

Figure 16-7. *The SSIS 2017 version of the Micrsoft.SQLServer.ManagedDTS*
assembly

Repeat this process, verifying each version of each referenced assembly in *both* the ExecuteCatalogPackageTask and the ExecuteCatalogPackageTaskComplexUI projects, as shown in Figure 16-8:

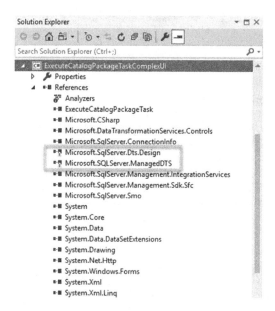

Figure 16-8. *Rinse and repeat*

Once the References are downgraded, open the ExecuteCatalogPackageTask project's ExecuteCatalogPackageTask.cs file. Update the TaskType attribute in the DtsTask decoration for the ExecuteCatalogPackageTask class, setting the TaskType from DTS150 to DTS140, as shown in Figure 16-9:

```
namespace ExecuteCatalogPackageTask
{
    [DtsTask(
        TaskType = "DTS140"
        , DisplayName = "Execute Catalog Package Task"
        , IconResource = "ExecuteCatalogPackageTask.ALCStrike.ico"
        , Description = "A task to execute packages stored in the SSIS Catalog."
        , UITypeName = "ExecuteCatalogPackageTaskComplexUI.ExecuteCatalogPackage
        , TaskContact = "ExecuteCatalogPackageTask; Building Custom Tasks for SQ
    13 references
    public class ExecuteCatalogPackageTask : Microsoft.SqlServer.Dts.Runtime.T
```

Figure 16-9. *Updating the TaskType attribute*

The ExecuteCatalogPackageTask solution has been downgraded, and the ExecuteCatalogPackageTask is now ready for Azure-SSIS.

Refactor Connection Identification

Connection manager identification is vital – especially when the connection string property is managed dynamically or overridden at execution time. The first step in refactoring connection identification is to add connection-related properties to the ExecuteCatalogPackageTask code using the code in Listing 16-1:

Listing 16-1. Adding Connections, ConnectionManagerIndex, and ConnectionManagerId to the ExecuteCatalogPackageTask class

```
public Connections Connections;
public string ConnectionManagerId { get; set; } = String.Empty;
public int ConnectionManagerIndex { get; set; } = -1;
```

Once added, the code appears as shown in Figure 16-10:

```
30 references | Andy Leonard, 39 days ago | 1 author, 1 change
public string TaskName { get; set; } = "Execute Catalog Package Task";
3 references | Andy Leonard, 39 days ago | 1 author, 1 change
public string TaskDescription { get; set; } = "Execute Catalog Package Task";
public Connections Connections;
18 references | Andy Leonard, 39 days ago | 1 author, 2 changes
public string ConnectionManagerName { get; set; } = String.Empty;
17 references | Andy Leonard, 6 days ago | 1 author, 1 change
public string ConnectionManagerId { get; set; } = String.Empty;
2 references | Andy Leonard, 3 days ago | 1 author, 6 changes
public int ConnectionManagerIndex { get; set; } = -1;
19 references | Andy Leonard, 62 days ago | 1 author, 1 change
public bool Synchronized { get; set; } = false;
```

Figure 16-10. *Connections, ConnectionManagerId, and ConnectionManagerIndex added to the ExecuteCatalogPackageTask class*

Initialize the Connections variable by adding the code in Listing 16-2 to the ExecuteCatalogPackageTask.InitializeTask method:

Listing 16-2. Initializing Connections

```
// init Connections
Connections = connections;
```

Once added, the `ExecuteCatalogPackageTask.InitializeTask` method appears as shown in Figure 16-11:

```
public override void InitializeTask(
    Connections connections,
    VariableDispenser variableDispenser,
    IDTSInfoEvents events,
    IDTSLogging log,
    EventInfos eventInfos,
    LogEntryInfos logEntryInfos,
    ObjectReferenceTracker refTracker)
{
    // init Connections
    Connections = connections;
}
```

Figure 16-11. *The ExecuteCatalogPackageTask.InitializeTask method, updated*

Initialize the `ConnectionManagerIndex` property value by creating the `returnConnectionManagerIndex` method using the code in Listing 16-3:

Listing 16-3. The returnConnectionManagerIndex method

```
private int returnConnectionManagerIndex(Connections connections
                                , string connectionManagerName)
{
  int ret = -1;

  try
  {
    ConnectionManagerId = GetConnectionID(connections,
    ConnectionManagerName);
    Microsoft.SqlServer.Dts.Runtime.ConnectionManager connectionManager =
    connections[ConnectionManagerId];
    ConnectionManagerName = connectionManager.Name;
```

```
  if (connectionManager != null)
  {
    for (int i = 0; i <= connections.Count; i++)
    {
      if (connections[i].Name == connectionManager.Name)
      {
        ret = i;
        break;
      }
    }
  }
}
catch (Exception ex)
{
  string message = "Unable to locate connection manager: " +
  ConnectionManagerName;
  throw new Exception(message, ex.InnerException);
}

return ret;
}
```

Once added, the returnConnectionManagerIndex method appears as shown in Figure 16-12:

```
94   private int returnConnectionManagerIndex(Connections connections
95                                        , string connectionManagerName)
96   {
97       int ret = -1;
98
99       try
100      {
101          ConnectionManagerId = GetConnectionID(connections, ConnectionManagerName);
102          Microsoft.SqlServer.Dts.Runtime.ConnectionManager connectionManager = connections[ConnectionManagerId];
103          ConnectionManagerName = connectionManager.Name;
104
105          if (connectionManager != null)
106          {
107              for (int i = 0; i <= connections.Count; i++)
108              {
109                  if (connections[i].Name == connectionManager.Name)
110                  {
111                      ret = i;
112                      break;
113                  }
114              }
115          }
116      }
117      catch (Exception ex)
118      {
119          string message = "Unable to locate connection manager: " + ConnectionManagerName;
120          throw new Exception(message, ex.InnerException);
121      }
122
123      return ret;
124  }
```

***Figure 16-12.** The returnConnectionManagerIndex method*

Examining the code shown in Figure 16-12, a return variable named ret of the
int type is declared and initialized to -1 on line 97. A try-catch block spans lines
99–121, after which – on line 123 – the value of the ret variable is returned from the
returnConnectionManagerIndex method. On line 101, the code attempts to set the
value of the ExecuteCatalogPackageTask.ConnectionManagerId string type property
by calling the GetConnectionID method included in the Microsoft.SqlServer.Dts.
Runtime.Task object methods. On line 102, a variable named connectionManager, of
the Microsoft.SqlServer.Dts.Runtime.ConnectionManager type, is declared and
initialized using the value of the ConnectionManagerId property to identify a member
of the connections collection. On line 103, the value of the ConnectionManagerName
property is set (or reset) to the name of the connectionManager object using
connectionManager.Name. An if condition starts on line 105 and verifies the
connectionManager object is not null. If the connectionManager object is not null,
a for loop starts on line 107. The for loop iterates the number of connections. On
line 109, an if condition uses the iterator i to compare the value of the Name property
of the currently iterating connection – connection(i).Name – to the value of the
connectionManager.Name property. If the value of the connection(i).Name equals the

value of the `connectionManager.Name` property, the value of the `ret` variable is set to the current value of the iterator, `i`.

To set the value of the ConnectionManagerIndex property, add a call to the `returnConnectionManagerIndex` method in the ExecuteCatalogPackageTask.Execute method using the code in Listing 16-4:

Listing 16-4. Calling the returnConnectionManagerIndex method

```
ConnectionManagerIndex = returnConnectionManagerIndex(connections,
ConnectionManagerName);
```

Once added, the code appears as shown in Figure 16-13:

```
public override DTSExecResult Execute(
    Connections connections,
    VariableDispenser variableDispenser,
    IDTSComponentEvents componentEvents,
    IDTSLogging log,
    object transaction)
{
    ConnectionManagerIndex = returnConnectionManagerIndex(connections, ConnectionManagerName);

    catalogServer = new Server(ServerName);
    integrationServices = new IntegrationServices(catalogServer);
    catalog = integrationServices.Catalogs[PackageCatalogName];
    catalogFolder = catalog.Folders[PackageFolder];
    catalogProject = catalogFolder.Projects[PackageProject];
    catalogPackage = catalogProject.Packages[PackageName];

    Collection<Microsoft.SqlServer.Management.IntegrationServices.PackageInfo.ExecutionValueParameterSet>
        executionValueParameterSet = returnExecutionValueParameterSet();

    catalogPackage.Execute(Use32bit, null, executionValueParameterSet);

    return DTSExecResult.Success;
}
```

Figure 16-13. *Calling returnConnectionManagerIndex in the ExecuteCatalogPackageTask.Execute method*

Setting the `ConnectionManagerIndex` property value in this manner supports property management by expressions, which we will cover later.

Refactor the SettingsView.SourceConnection Property

Since connection manager properties may be overridden at execution time, connection manager identification is crucial. Begin refactoring the SettingsView. SourceConnection property by replacing the declaration of the IDtsConnectionService type SettingsView variable named connectionService with the code in Listing 16-5:

Listing 16-5. Replacing the connectionService variable with the ConnectionService property

```
protected IDtsConnectionService ConnectionService { get; set; }
```

Once the connectionService variable is replaced, the code appears as shown in Figure 16-14:

```
public partial class SettingsView : System.Windows.Forms.UserControl, IDTSTaskUIView
{
    private SettingsNode settingsNode = null;
    private System.Windows.Forms.PropertyGrid settingsPropertyGrid;
    private ExecuteCatalogPackageTask.ExecuteCatalogPackageTask theTask = null;
    private System.ComponentModel.Container components = null;

    private const string NEW_CONNECTION = "<New Connection...>";
    0 references | Andy Leonard, 1 day ago | 1 author, 4 changes
    protected IDtsConnectionService ConnectionService { get; set; }
```

Figure 16-14. *Updating to the ConnectionService property*

Changing the connectionService variable to the ConnectionService property causes errors in the SettingsView class. Fix the first error in the SettingsView.OnInitialize method by updating the line connectionService = (IDtsConnectionService)connections; with the code in Listing 16-6:

Listing 16-6. Updating SettingsView.OnInitialize

```
ConnectionService = (IDtsConnectionService)connections;
```

Once updated, the code appears as shown in Figure 16-15:

```
this.settingsNode = new SettingsNode(taskHost as TaskHost, connections);

settingsPropertyGrid.SelectedObject = this.settingsNode;

ConnectionService = (IDtsConnectionService)connections;
}
```

Figure 16-15. *ConnectionService updated*

Two locations in the SettingsView.propertyGridSettings_PropertyValueChanged method require an update, using the code shown in Listing 16-7:

Listing 16-7. Updating SettingsView.propertyGridSettings_PropertyValueChanged

```
newConnection = ConnectionService.CreateConnection("ADO.Net");

.

.

.

settingsNode.Connections = ConnectionService.GetConnectionsOfType("ADO.Net");
```

Once updated, the code appears as shown in Figure 16-16:

```
private void propertyGridSettings_PropertyValueChanged(object s
                                        , System.Windows.Forms.PropertyValueChangedEventArgs e)
{
    if (e.ChangedItem.PropertyDescriptor.Name.CompareTo("SourceConnection") == 0)
    {
        if (e.ChangedItem.Value.Equals(NEW_CONNECTION))
        {
            ArrayList newConnection = new ArrayList();

            if (!((settingsNode.SourceConnection == null) || (settingsNode.SourceConnection == "")))
            {
                settingsNode.SourceConnection = null;
            }

            newConnection = ConnectionService.CreateConnection("ADO.Net");

            if ((newConnection != null) && (newConnection.Count > 0))
            {
                ConnectionManager cMgr = (ConnectionManager)newConnection[0];
                settingsNode.SourceConnection = cMgr.Name;
                settingsNode.Connections = ConnectionService.GetConnectionsOfType("ADO.Net");
            }
        }
```

Figure 16-16. *SettingsView.propertyGridSettings_PropertyValueChanged updated*

Continue updating the SettingsView.propertyGridSettings_
PropertyValueChanged method by adding the code in Listing 16-8 to the if conditional
if ((newConnection != null) && (newConnection.Count > 0)):

Listing 16-8. Updating the SettingsView.propertyGridSettings_
PropertyValueChanged method's new connection code

```
theTask.ServerName = returnSelectedConnectionManagerDataSourceValue(setting
sNode.SourceConnection);
theTask.ConnectionManagerName = settingsNode.SourceConnection;
theTask.ConnectionManagerId = theTask.GetConnectionID(theTask.Connections,
theTask.ConnectionManagerName);
```

Once added, the code appears as shown in Figure 16-17:

```
if ((newConnection != null) && (newConnection.Count > 0))
{
    ConnectionManager cMgr = (ConnectionManager)newConnection[0];
    settingsNode.SourceConnection = cMgr.Name;
    theTask.ServerName = returnSelectedConnectionManagerDataSourceValue(settingsNode.SourceConnection);
    theTask.ConnectionManagerName = settingsNode.SourceConnection;
    theTask.ConnectionManagerId = theTask.GetConnectionID(theTask.Connections, theTask.ConnectionManagerName);
    settingsNode.Connections = ConnectionService.GetConnectionsOfType("ADO.Net");
}
```

Figure 16-17. *SettingsView.propertyGridSettings_PropertyValueChanged
method's new connection code, updated*

Refactor the SettingsView.propertyGridSettings_PropertyValueChanged method
by adding the code in Listing 16-9 by adding an else statement to the if conditional if
(e.ChangedItem.Value.Equals(NEW_CONNECTION)):

Listing 16-9. Adding the SettingsView.propertyGridSettings_
PropertyValueChanged method's not-new connection code

```
else
{
  theTask.ServerName = returnSelectedConnectionManagerDataSourceValue(
  settingsNode.SourceConnection);
  theTask.ConnectionManagerName = settingsNode.SourceConnection;
```

```
theTask.ConnectionManagerId = theTask.GetConnectionID(theTask.
Connections, theTask.ConnectionManagerName);
settingsNode.Connections = ConnectionService.GetConnectionsOfType("ADO.
Net");
}
```

Once added, the code appears as shown in Figure 16-18:

```
else // if not a new connection
{
    theTask.ServerName = returnSelectedConnectionManagerDataSourceValue(settingsNode.SourceConnection);
    theTask.ConnectionManagerName = settingsNode.SourceConnection;
    theTask.ConnectionManagerId = theTask.GetConnectionID(theTask.Connections, theTask.ConnectionManagerName);
    settingsNode.Connections = ConnectionService.GetConnectionsOfType("ADO.Net");
}
```

Figure 16-18. *SettingsView.propertyGridSettings_PropertyValueChanged method's not-new connection code, added*

The next step is to refactor the way we identify the catalog, folder, project, and package in the ExecuteCatalogPackageTask.

Identifying Catalog, Folder, Project, and Package

"What is the problem we are trying to solve?" This is a question I learned from a mentor. It is a good question. The problem we are trying to solve is *better* connection management. Until now, connection management has been...*adequate*. Connection management in the current design ignores two valid use cases (at least):

1. Connecting to an Azure-SSIS Catalog hosted by an Azure SQL DB that requires a SQL login (username and password) for authentication

2. Using property expressions to override the ConnectionManagerName property value

We begin with a second look at how the task code assigns the catalogProject property value, found in the ExecuteCatalogPackageTask's Execute() method. In the ExecuteCatalogPackageTask's Execute() method, the task currently populates the Server ➤ Integration Services ➤ SSIS Catalog ➤ Folder ➤ Project ➤ Package hierarchy using the code shown in Listing 16-10 and shown in Figure 16-19:

```
public override DTSExecResult Execute(
    Connections connections,
    VariableDispenser variableDispenser,
    IDTSComponentEvents componentEvents,
    IDTSLogging log,
    object transaction)
{
    catalogServer = new Server(ServerName);
    integrationServices = new IntegrationServices(catalogServer);
    catalog = integrationServices.Catalogs[PackageCatalogName];
    catalogFolder = catalog.Folders[PackageFolder];
    catalogProject = catalogFolder.Projects[PackageProject];
    catalogPackage = catalogProject.Packages[PackageName];

    Collection<Microsoft.SqlServer.Management.IntegrationServices.PackageInfo.ExecutionValueParameterSet>
        executionValueParameterSet = returnExecutionValueParameterSet();

    EnvironmentReference environmentReference = returnEnvironmentReference(catalogProject);

    catalogPackage.Execute(Use32bit, null, executionValueParameterSet);

    return DTSExecResult.Success;
}
```

Figure 16-19. *The Execute() method*

Listing 16-10. Populating the Server ➤ Integration Services ➤ SSIS Catalog ➤ Folder ➤ Project ➤ Package hierarchy, currently

```
catalogServer = new Server(ServerName);
integrationServices = new IntegrationServices(catalogServer);
catalog = integrationServices.Catalogs[PackageCatalogName];
catalogFolder = catalog.Folders[PackageFolder];
catalogProject = catalogFolder.Projects[PackageProject];
```

The code in Listing 16-10 – shown in Figure 16-19 – identifies one SSIS project based on property values configured from the SettingsNode in SettingsView. At execution time, this code is prone to errors if one or more of the SettingsNode properties are improperly configured. Identifying key artifacts – such as catalog, folder, project, and package objects – is important in the Server ➤ Integration Services ➤ SSIS Catalog ➤ Folder ➤ Project ➤ Package hierarchy. In this section, the code to identify catalog, folder, project, and package is collected and refactored into more robust and independent methods.

Let's refactor this code by moving it to a new function named returnCatalogProject in the ExecuteCatalogPackageTask class.

Adding the returnCatalogProject Method

Continue refactoring the Execute() method by adding the returnCatalogProject method to the ExecuteCatalogPackageTask using the code in Listing 16-11:

Listing 16-11. Adding ExecuteCatalogPackageTask.returnCatalogProject

```
public ProjectInfo returnCatalogProject(string ServerName
                                      , string FolderName
                                      , string ProjectName)
{

  ProjectInfo catalogProject = null;

  SqlConnection cn = (SqlConnection)Connections[ConnectionManagerId].
  AcquireConnection(null);
  integrationServices = new IntegrationServices(cn);
  if (integrationServices != null)
  {
    catalog = integrationServices.Catalogs[PackageCatalogName];
    if (catalog != null)
    {
      catalogFolder = catalog.Folders[FolderName];
      if (catalogFolder != null)
      {
        catalogProject = catalogFolder.Projects[ProjectName];
      }
    }
  }
  return catalogProject;
}
```

Once added, the new function appears as shown in Figure 16-20:

```
public ProjectInfo returnCatalogProject(string ServerName
                            , string FolderName
                            , string ProjectName)
{
    ProjectInfo catalogProject = null;

    SqlConnection cn = (SqlConnection)Connections[ConnectionManagerId].AcquireConnection(null);
    integr o- onServices = new IntegrationServices(cn);
    if (in
    {
        ca
        if
        {
```

using System.Data.SqlClient;
System.Data.SqlClient.SqlConnection
Generate class 'SqlConnection' in new file
Generate class 'SqlConnection'
Generate nested class 'SqlConnection'
Generate new type...

CS0246 The type or namespace name 'SqlConnection' could not be found (are you missing a using directive or an assembly reference?)

...
using System.Collections.ObjectModel;
using System.Data.SqlClient;
using System.Linq;
...

Preview changes

```
            if (catalogFolder != null)
            {
                catalogProject = catalogFolder.Projects[ProjectName];
            }
        }
    }
    return catalogProject;
}
```

Figure 16-20. *The returnCatalogProject function*

If "SqlConnection" has a red squiggly line beneath it, right-click SqlConnection, expand Quick Actions, and then click using System.Data.SqlClient; to add the using System.Data.SqlClient; directive near the top of the ExecuteCatalogPackageTask.cs file.

Once the using System.Data.SqlClient; directive is added, the code appears as shown in Figure 16-21:

```
public ProjectInfo returnCatalogProject(string ServerName
                                      , string FolderName
                                      , string ProjectName)
{
    ProjectInfo catalogProject = null;

    SqlConnection cn = (SqlConnection)Connections[ConnectionManagerId].AcquireConnection(null);
    integrationServices = new IntegrationServices(cn);
    if (integrationServices != null)
    {
        catalog = integrationServices.Catalogs[PackageCatalogName];
        if (catalog != null)
        {
            catalogFolder = catalog.Folders[FolderName];
            if (catalogFolder != null)
            {
                catalogProject = catalogFolder.Projects[ProjectName];
            }
        }
    }

    return catalogProject;
}
```

Figure 16-21. *The returnCatalogProject function*

Declaring the returnCatalogProject function as public allows access to the ExecuteCatalogPackageTask.returnCatalogProject function from the ExecuteCatalogPackageTaskComplexUI project.

Additional "returnCatalog*" methods are similar and demonstrate a very helpful pattern for interacting with SSIS connection managers: The Connections. AcquireConnection method returns a SqlConnection type object. Acquiring a SqlConnection by calling the Connections.AcquireConnection method is one way – perhaps the only way – to obtain a connection that requires a username and password from a connection manager.

Later in this book, we demonstrate connecting an ExecuteCatalogPackageTask to an Azure-SSIS Catalog deployed on an Azure SQL DB instance. One way to connect to Azure SQL DB instances uses a SQL Login with username and password.

Edit the code in the Execute() method, replacing the code that populates the Server ➤ Integration Services ➤ SSIS Catalog ➤ Folder ➤ Project hierarchy using the code shown in Listing 16-12:

Listing 16-12. Updating the Execute() method

```
catalogProject = returnCatalogProject(ServerName, PackageFolder,
PackageProject);
```

Once updated, the new Execute() method appears as shown in Figure 16-22:

```
public override DTSExecResult Execute(
    Connections connections,
    VariableDispenser variableDispenser,
    IDTSComponentEvents componentEvents,
    IDTSLogging log,
    object transaction)
{
    ConnectionManagerIndex = returnConnectionManagerIndex(connections, ConnectionManagerName);

    catalogProject = returnCatalogProject(ServerName, PackageFolder, PackageProject);
    catalogPackage = catalogProject.Packages[PackageName];
```

Figure 16-22. *A portion of the updated Execute() method*

The next step is to add a method to return the catalog package in a similar fashion.

Adding the returnCatalogPackage Method

Next, add the returnCatalogPackage function using the code in Listing 16-13:

Listing 16-13. Adding the returnCatalogPackage function

```
public Microsoft.SqlServer.Management.IntegrationServices.PackageInfo
returnCatalogPackage(
    string ServerName
  , string FolderName
  , string ProjectName
  , string PackageName)
{
  Microsoft.SqlServer.Management.IntegrationServices.PackageInfo
  catalogPackage = null;

  SqlConnection cn = (SqlConnection)Connections[ConnectionManagerId].
  AcquireConnection(null);
  integrationServices = new IntegrationServices(cn);
```

```
if (integrationServices != null)
{
  catalog = integrationServices.Catalogs[PackageCatalogName];
  if (catalog != null)
  {
    catalogFolder = catalog.Folders[FolderName];
    if (catalogFolder != null)
    {
      catalogProject = catalogFolder.Projects[ProjectName];
      if (catalogProject != null)
      {
        catalogPackage = catalogProject.Packages[PackageName];
      }
    }
  }
}

return catalogPackage;
}
```

Once added, the code appears as shown in Figure 16-23:

```
public Microsoft.SqlServer.Management.IntegrationServices.PackageInfo returnCatalogPackage(
                                  string ServerName
                                , string FolderName
                                , string ProjectName
                                , string PackageName)
{
    Microsoft.SqlServer.Management.IntegrationServices.PackageInfo catalogPackage = null;

    SqlConnection cn = (SqlConnection)Connections[ConnectionManagerId].AcquireConnection(null);
    integrationServices = new IntegrationServices(cn);
    if (integrationServices != null)
    {
        catalog = integrationServices.Catalogs[PackageCatalogName];
        if (catalog != null)
        {
            catalogFolder = catalog.Folders[FolderName];
            if (catalogFolder != null)
            {
                catalogProject = catalogFolder.Projects[ProjectName];
                if (catalogProject != null)
                {
                    catalogPackage = catalogProject.Packages[PackageName];
                }
            }
        }
    }

    return catalogPackage;
}
```

Figure 16-23. *The returnCatalogPackage function*

Edit the code in the Execute() method, replacing the code that populates the Server ➤ Integration Services ➤ SSIS Catalog ➤ Folder ➤ Project ➤ Package hierarchy using the code shown in Listing 16-14:

Listing 16-14. Updating the Execute() method

```
catalogPackage = returnCatalogPackage(ServerName, PackageFolder,
PackageProject, PackageName);
```

Once updated, the new Execute() method appears as shown in Figure 16-24:

```
public override DTSExecResult Execute(
    Connections connections,
    VariableDispenser variableDispenser,
    IDTSComponentEvents componentEvents,
    IDTSLogging log,
    object transaction)
{
    ConnectionManagerIndex = returnConnectionManagerIndex(connections, ConnectionManagerName);

    catalogProject = returnCatalogProject(ServerName, PackageFolder, PackageProject);
    catalogPackage = returnCatalogPackage(ServerName, PackageFolder, PackageProject, PackageName);
```

Figure 16-24. *A portion of the updated Execute() method*

The returnCatalogProject and returnCatalogPackage methods are all we need at this point in the development of the ExecuteCatalogPackageTask. While we are here, though, we might as well build the additional methods we will require in the future: returnCatalog and returnCatalogFolder.

Adding the returnCatalog Method

Continue by adding the returnCatalog function to the ExecuteCatalogPackageTask code using the code in Listing 16-15:

Listing 16-15. Adding the returnCatalog function to ExecuteCatalogPackageTask

```
public Catalog returnCatalog(string ServerName)
{
  Catalog catalog = null;

  SqlConnection cn = (SqlConnection)Connections[ConnectionManagerId].
  AcquireConnection(null);
  integrationServices = new IntegrationServices(cn);
  if (integrationServices != null)
  {
    catalog = integrationServices.Catalogs[PackageCatalogName];
  }

  return catalog;
}
```

The returnCatalog function is modeled from the returnCatalogProject function. The difference is a Catalog type object is returned instead of a ProjectInfo type object. Once added, the code appears as shown in Figure 16-25:

```
public Catalog returnCatalog(string ServerName)
{
    Catalog catalog = null;

    SqlConnection cn = (SqlConnection)Connections[ConnectionManagerId].AcquireConnection(null);
    integrationServices = new IntegrationServices(cn);
    if (integrationServices != null)
    {
        catalog = integrationServices.Catalogs[PackageCatalogName];
    }

    return catalog;
}
```

Figure 16-25. *The returnCatalog function added to ExecuteCatalogPackageTask*

Adding the returnCatalogFolder Method

The next step is adding the returnCatalogFolder function to the ExecuteCatalogPackageTask code using the code in Listing 16-16:

Listing 16-16. Adding the returnCatalogFolder function to ExecuteCatalogPackageTask

```
public CatalogFolder returnCatalogFolder(string ServerName
                                , string FolderName)
{
  CatalogFolder catalogFolder = null;

  SqlConnection cn = (SqlConnection)Connections[ConnectionManagerId].
  AcquireConnection(null);
  integrationServices = new IntegrationServices(cn);
  if (integrationServices != null)
  {
    catalog = integrationServices.Catalogs[PackageCatalogName];
```

```
  if (catalog != null)
  {
    catalogFolder = catalog.Folders[FolderName];
  }
}

return catalogFolder;
}
```

The returnCatalog function is utterly and completely modeled from the
returnCatalogProject function. The difference is the Catalog is returned instead of a
ProjectInfo object. Once added, the code appears as shown in Figure 16-26:

```
public CatalogFolder returnCatalogFolder(string ServerName
                                       , string FolderName)
{
    CatalogFolder catalogFolder = null;

    catalogServer = new Server(ServerName);
    if (catalogServer != null)
    {
        integrationServices = new IntegrationServices(catalogServer);
        if (integrationServices != null)
        {
            catalog = integrationServices.Catalogs[PackageCatalogName];
            if (catalog != null)
            {
                catalogFolder = catalog.Folders[FolderName];
            }
        }
    }
    return catalogFolder;
}
```

Figure 16-26. *The returnCatalogFolder function added to
ExecuteCatalogPackageTask*

The "returnCatalog*" methods are helpful for the next step in our design, which is
initializing the SettingsNode References collection.

Let's Test It!

Build the ExecuteCatalogPackageTask solution, and then open a test SSIS project. Add an Execute Catalog Package Task to the control flow, open the editor, and configure the task to execute an SSIS package stored in an SSIS Catalog, as shown in Figure 16-27:

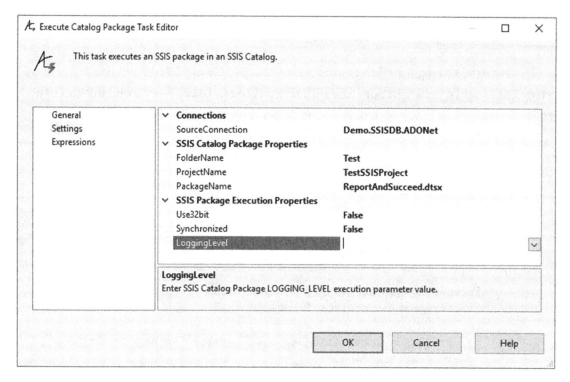

Figure 16-27. *Configuring the Execute Catalog Package Task for a test execution*

Click the OK button to close the editor and then execute the package in the SSIS debugger. If all goes as planned, the test debug execution succeeds, as shown in Figure 16-28:

Figure 16-28. *Success!*

Open SQL Server Management Studio's Object Explorer. Navigate to the Integration Services Catalogs node and expand to the SSISDB node. Right-click the SSISDB node, hover over Reports, and click All Executions to view the results of the test SSIS package execution, as shown in Figure 16-29:

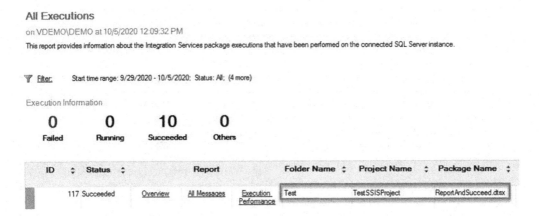

Figure 16-29. *Successful test execution, verified*

The new SSIS Catalog identification methods are cleaner and more robust. The code is in much better shape for additional functionality.

Conclusion

In this chapter, we made connection management more robust and refactored ExecuteCatalogPackageTask methods that assist with identifying object in the Server ➤ Integration Services ➤ SSIS Catalog ➤ Folder ➤ Project ➤ Package hierarchy. Two of these methods – returnCatalogProject and returnCatalogPackage – are used in the ExecuteCatalogPackageTask's Execute method.

Now would be an excellent time to check in your code.

CHAPTER 17

Refactoring the SSIS Package Hierarchy

The goal of this chapter is to refactor ExecuteCatalogPackageTask methods to prepare for adding and testing the Reference property. The goals are

- Refactor the SettingsView catalog, folder, project, and package properties.

- Test folder, project, and package property expressions.

Refactor the SettingsView Catalog, Folder, Project, and Package Properties

Are you tired of typing the folder name, project name, and package name each time we configure an instance of the Execute Catalog Package Task? I am. Let's add properties and functionality to allow us to *select* folders, projects, and packages.

In this section, we add object type members to manage three collections – folders, projects, and packages – to the SettingsNode class. To do so, we will follow this pattern for each collection:

- Declare SettingsNode object type members (properties) to contain the collection.

- Add a new property for each level in the Folder ➤ Project ➤ Package hierarchy.

- Add a hidden (non-browsable) property for each collection.

- Add a method to populate a list for each object collection.

305

© Andy Leonard 2021
A. Leonard, *Building Custom Tasks for SQL Server Integration Services,*
https://doi.org/10.1007/978-1-4842-6482-9_17

- Add a method to update each object collection.

- Centralize the call to update all related collections.

- Add calls to the propertyGridSettings_PropertyValueChanged to populate the *next* property collections in the hierarchy when certain property hierarchy values change.

- Add calls to the propertyGridSettings_PropertyValueChanged to clear properties *lower* in the hierarchy when certain property hierarchy values change.

- Hide the original property.

We begin by declaring the three objects for _folders, _projects, and _packages in the SettingsNode class using the code in Listing 17-1:

Listing 17-1. Adding _folders, _projects, and _packages collection objects to SettingsNode

```
private object _folders = null;
private object _projects = null;
private object _packages = null;
```

Once added, the new objects appear as shown in Figure 17-1:

```
internal class SettingsNode
{
    internal ExecuteCatalogPackageTask.ExecuteCatalogPackageTask _task = null;
    private TaskHost _taskHost = null;
    private object _connections = null;

    private object _folders = null;
    private object _projects = null;
    private object _packages = null;

    private const string NEW_CONNECTION = "<New Connection...>";
```

Figure 17-1. *Adding _folders, _projects, and _packages collection objects*

The next step is to add hidden (non-browsable) properties for each collection.

The Folder Property and Folders Collection

The relationship between the Folder property and the Folders collection is similar to the relationship between the SourceConnection property and the connections collection. One difference is the connections collection is passed to the task from the SSIS package hosting the Execute Catalog Package Task. Our code sets the value of a Connections property in the ExecuteCatalogPackageTask.InitializeTask method (see Figures 16-10 and 16-11 in Chapter 16). The SSIS package is unaware of a collection of SSIS Catalog Folders. We must, therefore, manage the collection of SSIS Catalog Folders in our code.

Add a new Folder property to the SettingsNode class using the code in Listing 17-2:

Listing 17-2. Add the SettingsNode.Folder property

```
[
  Category("SSIS Catalog Package Properties"),
  Description("Select SSIS Catalog Package folder name."),
  TypeConverter(typeof(Folders))
]
public string Folder {
  get { return _task.PackageFolder; }
  set {
    if (value == null)
    {
      throw new ApplicationException("Folder name cannot be empty");
    }

    _task.PackageFolder = value;
  }
}
```

Once added, the code appears as shown in Figure 17-2:

```
[
    Category("SSIS Catalog Package Properties"),
    Description("Select SSIS Catalog Package folder name."),
    TypeConverter(typeof(Folders))
]
0 references | Andy Leonard, 4 days ago | 1 author, 3 changes
public string Folder {
    get { return _task.PackageFolder; }
    set {
        if (value == null)
        {
            throw new ApplicationException("Folder name cannot be empty");
        }

        _task.PackageFolder = value;
    }
}
```

Figure 17-2. *Adding the SettingsNode.Folder property*

Note the Folders TypeConverter has a red squiggly line beneath it, indicating an error condition. In this case, the Folders TypeConverter does not yet exist. Add the Folders TypeConverter – modeled after the LoggingLevels TypeConverter – using the code in Listing 17-3:

Listing 17-3. The Folders TypeConverter

```
internal class Folders : StringConverter
{
  private object GetSpecializedObject(object contextInstance)
  {
    DTSLocalizableTypeDescriptor typeDescr = contextInstance as
    DTSLocalizableTypeDescriptor;

    if (typeDescr == null)
    {
      return contextInstance;
    }
```

```csharp
    return typeDescr.SelectedObject;
}
public override StandardValuesCollection GetStandardValues(
ITypeDescriptorContext context)
{
  object retrievalObject = GetSpecializedObject(context.Instance) as
  object;

  return new StandardValuesCollection(getFolders(retrievalObject));
}

public override bool GetStandardValuesExclusive(ITypeDescriptorContext
context)
{
  return true;
}

public override bool GetStandardValuesSupported(ITypeDescriptorContext
context)
{
  return true;
}

private ArrayList getFolders(object retrievalObject)
{
  SettingsNode node = (SettingsNode)retrievalObject;
  ArrayList list = new ArrayList();
  ArrayList listFolders;

  listFolders = (ArrayList)node.Folders;
  if (listFolders == null)
  {
    listFolders = new ArrayList();
  }
```

```
    if (listFolders != null)
    {
      // adds each folder
      foreach (string fld in listFolders)
      {
        list.Add(fld); // Folder name
      }

      // sorts the folder list
      if ((list != null) && (list.Count > 0))
      {
        list.Sort();
      }
    }

    return list;
  }
}
```

Once added, the Folders TypeConverter code appears as shown in Figure 17-3:

```csharp
internal class Folders : StringConverter
{
    1 reference | Andy Leonard, 20 hours ago | 1 author, 3 changes
    private object GetSpecializedObject(object contextInstance)
    {
        DTSLocalizableTypeDescriptor typeDescr = contextInstance as DTSLocalizableTypeDescriptor;

        if (typeDescr == null)
        {
            return contextInstance;
        }

        return typeDescr.SelectedObject;
    }

    3 references | Andy Leonard, 20 hours ago | 1 author, 3 changes
    public override StandardValuesCollection GetStandardValues(ITypeDescriptorContext context)
    {
        object retrievalObject = GetSpecializedObject(context.Instance) as object;

        return new StandardValuesCollection(getFolders(retrievalObject));
    }

    3 references | Andy Leonard, 20 hours ago | 1 author, 3 changes
    public override bool GetStandardValuesExclusive(ITypeDescriptorContext context)
    {
        return true;
    }

    3 references | Andy Leonard, 20 hours ago | 1 author, 3 changes
    public override bool GetStandardValuesSupported(ITypeDescriptorContext context)
    {
        return true;
    }

    1 reference | Andy Leonard, 20 hours ago | 1 author, 3 changes
    private ArrayList getFolders(object retrievalObject)
    {
        SettingsNode node = (SettingsNode)retrievalObject;
        ArrayList list = new ArrayList();
        ArrayList listFolders;

        listFolders = (ArrayList)node.Folders;
        if (listFolders == null)
        {
            listFolders = new ArrayList();
        }

        if (listFolders != null)
        {
            // adds each folder
            foreach (string fld in listFolders)
            {
                list.Add(fld); // Folder name
            }

            // sorts the folder list
            if ((list != null) && (list.Count > 0))
            {
                list.Sort();
            }
        }

        return list;
    }
}
```

Figure 17-3. *The Folders TypeConverter*

Note the getFolders method displays an error – a red squiggly line under node.
Folders. We correct that error in the coming pages by adding the Folders property to the
SettingsNode class.

When the Folders TypeConverter is added, the error in the Folder property
declaration is resolved, as shown in Figure 17-4 (compare to Figure 17-2):

```
[
    Category("SSIS Catalog Package Properties"),
    Description("Select SSIS Catalog Package folder name."),
    TypeConverter(typeof(Folders))
]
0 references | Andy Leonard, 4 days ago | 1 author, 3 changes
public string Folder {
    get { return _task.PackageFolder; }
    set {
        if (value == null)
        {
            throw new ApplicationException("Folder name cannot be empty");
        }

        _task.PackageFolder = value;
    }
}
```

Figure 17-4. *Folders TypeConverter error cleared*

Add the Folders property using the code in Listing 17-4:

Listing 17-4. Adding the Folders property

```
[
  Category("SSIS Catalog Package Path Collections"),
  Description("Enter SSIS Catalog Package folders collection."),
  Browsable(false)
]
public object Folders {
  get { return _folders; }
  set { _folders = value; }
}
```

Once added, the Folders property appears as shown in Figure 17-5:

```
public string FolderName {
    get { return _task.PackageFolder; }
    set {
        if ((value == null) || (value.Trim().Length == 0))
        {
            throw new ApplicationException("Folder name cannot be empty");
        }

        _task.PackageFolder = value;
    }
}
```

```
[
    Category("SSIS Catalog Package Path Collections"),
    Description("Enter SSIS Catalog Package folders collection."),
    Browsable(false)
]
1 reference
internal object Folders {
    get { return _folders; }
    set { _folders = value; }
}
```

Figure 17-5. *Folders property added*

The next step is to add a method to populate a list of folders using the code in Listing 17-5:

Listing 17-5. Populate the Folders collection

```
internal ArrayList GetFoldersFromCatalog()
{
  ArrayList foldersList = new ArrayList();

  if ((_task.ServerName != null) && (_task.ServerName != ""))
  {
    Catalog catalog = _task.returnCatalog(_task.ServerName);

    if (catalog != null)
    {
      foreach (CatalogFolder cf in catalog.Folders)
```

```
      {
         foldersList.Add(cf.Name);
      }
    }
  }
  return foldersList;
}
```

Once added, the code appears as shown in Figure 17-6:

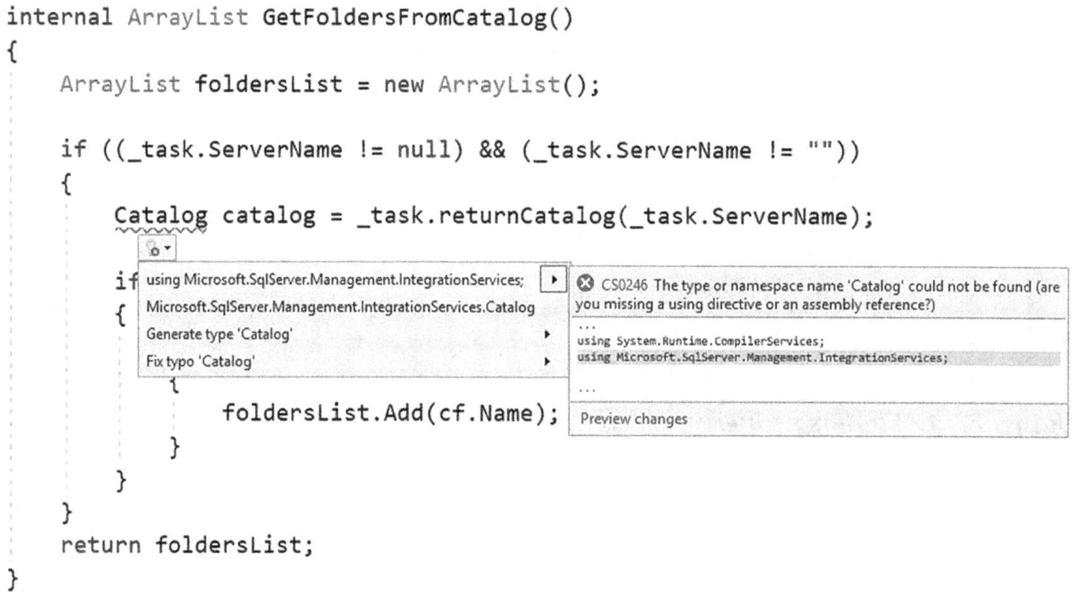

```
internal ArrayList GetFoldersFromCatalog()
{
    ArrayList foldersList = new ArrayList();

    if ((_task.ServerName != null) && (_task.ServerName != ""))
    {
        Catalog catalog = _task.returnCatalog(_task.ServerName);
```

```
        if                                                                foldersList.Add(cf.Name);
        {
        }
      }
    }
    return foldersList;
}
```

Figure 17-6. *Adding the GetFoldersFromCatalog method*

The Catalog (and hidden CatalogFolder) objects are underlined with red squiggly lines. Click the Quick Actions dropdown and then click using Microsoft.SqlServer. Management.IntegrationServices; to add the directive. Once the directive is added, the code appears as shown in Figure 17-7:

```
internal ArrayList GetFoldersFromCatalog()
{
    ArrayList foldersList = new ArrayList();

    if ((_task.ServerName != null) && (_task.ServerName != ""))
    {
        Catalog catalog = _task.returnCatalog(_task.ServerName);

        if (catalog != null)
        {
            foreach (CatalogFolder cf in catalog.Folders)
            {
                foldersList.Add(cf.Name);
            }
        }
    }
    return foldersList;
}
```

Figure 17-7. *The GetFoldersFromCatalog method after adding the using directive*

The GetFoldersFromCatalog method constructs and populates an ArrayList type variable that contains a list of SSIS Catalog Folders hosted in the SSIS Catalog surfaced by the SourceConnection property.

The next step is to add a method to populate the Folders collection property with the contents returned from the GetFoldersFromCatalog method, and then refresh the SettingsView propertygrid. The code for the new method named updateFolders is in Listing 17-6:

Listing 17-6. Adding the updateFolders method

```
private void updateFolders()
{
  if (settingsNode.SourceConnection != "")
  {
    settingsNode.Folders = settingsNode.GetFoldersFromCatalog();
    this.settingsPropertyGrid.Refresh();
  }
}
```

Once added, the code appears as shown in Figure 17-8:

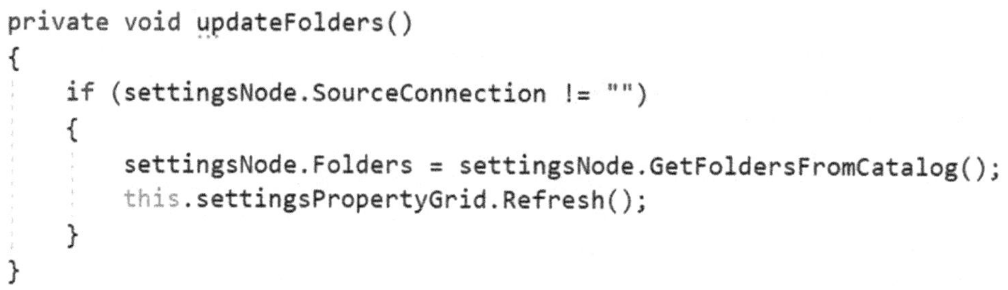

```
private void updateFolders()
{
    if (settingsNode.SourceConnection != "")
    {
        settingsNode.Folders = settingsNode.GetFoldersFromCatalog();
        this.settingsPropertyGrid.Refresh();
    }
}
```

Figure 17-8. *The updateFolders method, added*

The next step is to begin centralizing the call to update all related collections using the code in Listing 17-7:

Listing 17-7. Centralize the call to update the folders collection

```
private void updateCollections()
{
  Cursor = Cursors.WaitCursor;

  updateFolders();
  Cursor = Cursors.Default;
}
```

Once added, the code appears as shown in Figure 17-9:

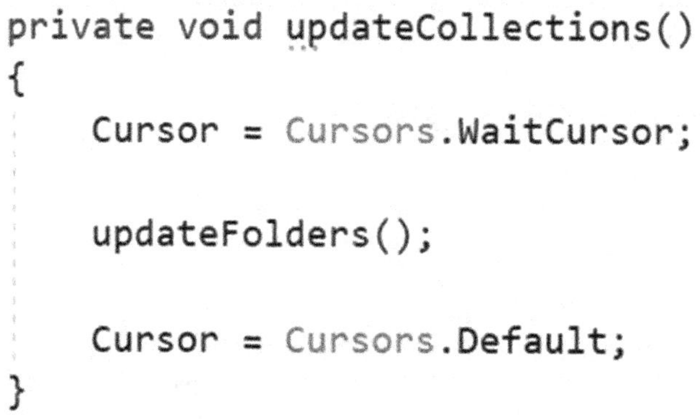

```
private void updateCollections()
{
    Cursor = Cursors.WaitCursor;

    updateFolders();

    Cursor = Cursors.Default;
}
```

Figure 17-9. *Centralizing the call to update the folders collection*

We start the updateCollections method by setting the cursor to a wait cursor because later, when we connect to Azure-SSIS catalogs, populating the folders collection will take a few seconds. After calling the updateFolders method, the cursor is reset to the default cursor.

Updates to the Folders collection make sense when the SourceConnection property is initially selected or updated. Add a call to the updateCollections method at the bottom of the SourceConnection property section of the SettingsView. propertyGridSettings_PropertyValueChanged method, as shown in Figure 17-10:

```
        if (e.ChangedItem.PropertyDescriptor.Name.CompareTo("Folder") == 0)
        {
            updateCollections();
        }
    }


  else // if not a new connection
  {
      theTask.ServerName = returnSelectedConnectionManagerDataSourceValue(settingsNode.SourceConnection);
      theTask.ConnectionManagerName = settingsNode.SourceConnection;
      theTask.ConnectionManagerId = theTask.GetConnectionID(theTask.Connections, theTask.ConnectionManagerName);
      settingsNode.Connections = ConnectionService.GetConnectionsOfType("ADO.Net");
  }
  updateCollections();
  }
}
```

Figure 17-10. *Adding a call to updateCollections to SourceConnection section of the SettingsView.propertyGridSettings_PropertyValueChanged*

The next step is to add a call to the updateCollections method in the propertyGridSettings_PropertyValueChanged method, a call that populates the folders property collection when the Folder property value changes, by adding the code in Listing 17-8 to the SettingsView.propertyGridSettings_PropertyValueChanged method:

Listing 17-8. Add code to respond to changes in the Folder property

```
if (e.ChangedItem.PropertyDescriptor.Name.CompareTo("Folder") == 0)
{
  updateCollections();
}
```

Once added, the code appears as shown in Figure 17-11:

```
if (e.ChangedItem.PropertyDescriptor.Name.CompareTo("Folder") == 0)
{
    updateCollections();
}
}
```

Figure 17-11. *Adding code to respond to changes in the Folder property*

Add a call to the updateCollections method at the bottom of the SettingsView. OnInitialize method, as shown in Figure 17-12:

```
settingsPropertyGrid.SelectedObject = this.settingsNode;

ConnectionService = (IDtsConnectionService)connections;

updateCollections();
}
```

Figure 17-12. *Adding a call to updateCollections to SettingsView.OnInitialize*

To test the functionality, build the ExecuteCatalogPackageTask solution, open a test SSIS package in a test SSIS project, add an Execute Catalog Package Task to the control flow canvas, open the editor, and configure a SourceConnection. After configuring a SourceConnection, the Folder property should be populated with the names of SSIS Catalog Folders, as shown in Figure 17-13:

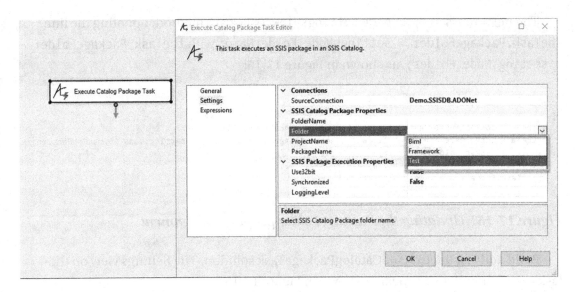

Figure 17-13. *Folders*

The next step is to hide the FolderName property. To hide the FolderName property, simply comment out the FolderName property declaration by selecting the code, holding the Ctrl key, and pressing the K key, followed by the C key. The selected code is commented out as shown in Figure 17-14:

```
//[
//    Category("SSIS Catalog Package Properties"),
//    Description("Enter SSIS Catalog Package folder name.")
//]
//public string FolderName {
//    get { return _task.PackageFolder; }
//    set {
//        if ((value == null) || (value.Trim().Length == 0))
//        {
//            throw new ApplicationException("Folder name cannot be empty");
//        }

//        _task.PackageFolder = value;
//    }
//}
```

Figure 17-14. *The FolderName property, commented out*

The next step is to update the SettingsView.OnCommit method, updating the line theTask.PackageFolder = settingsNode.FolderName; with theTask.PackageFolder = settingsNode.Folder;, as shown in Figure 17-15:

```
public virtual void OnCommit(object taskHost)
{
    theTask.ConnectionManagerName = settingsNode.SourceConnection;
    theTask.ServerName = returnSelectedConnectionManagerDataSourceValue(settingsNode.SourceConnection);
    theTask.PackageFolder = settingsNode.Folder;
    theTask.PackageProject = settingsNode.ProjectName;
    theTask.PackageName = settingsNode.PackageName;
}
```

Figure 17-15. *Updating the PackageFolder property assignment*

Build and test the ExecuteCatalogPackageTask solution. The Settings view on the task editor should now appear as shown in Figure 17-16:

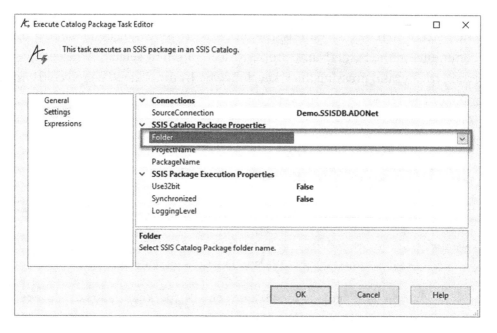

Figure 17-16. *The Folder property*

The Folder and Folders collection properties are now configured. The next steps are to configure the Project and Projects collection properties and the Package and Packages collection properties.

Now would be an excellent time to check in your code.

The Project Property and Projects Collection

The relationship between the Project property and the Projects collection is identical to the relationship between the Folder property and the Folders collection. The only difference is the objects themselves. As with the Folders collection, we must manage the collection of SSIS Catalog Projects in our code.

Add a new Project property to the SettingsNode class using the code in Listing 17-9:

Listing 17-9. Add the SettingsNode.Project property

```
[
  Category("SSIS Catalog Package Properties"),
  Description("Select SSIS Catalog Package project name."),
  TypeConverter(typeof(Projects))
]
public string Project {
  get { return _task.PackageProject; }
  set {
    if (value == null)
    {
      throw new ApplicationException("Project name cannot be empty");
    }
    _task. PackageProject = value;
  }
}
```

Once added, the code appears as shown in Figure 17-17:

```
[
    Category("SSIS Catalog Package Properties"),
    Description("Select SSIS Catalog Package project name."),
    TypeConverter(typeof(Projects))
]
0 references | Andy Leonard, 5 days ago | 1 author, 3 changes
public string Project {
    get { return _task.PackageProject; }
    set {
        if (value == null)
        {
            throw new ApplicationException("Project name cannot be empty");
        }

        _task.PackageProject = value;
    }
}
```

Figure 17-17. *Adding the SettingsNode.Project property*

As before with the Folder TypeConverter, please note the Projects TypeConverter has a red squiggly line beneath it, indicating the same error condition as before: The Projects TypeConverter does not yet exist. Add the Projects TypeConverter using the code in Listing 17-10:

Listing 17-10. The Projects TypeConverter

```
internal class Projects : StringConverter
{
  private object GetSpecializedObject(object contextInstance)
  {
    DTSLocalizableTypeDescriptor typeDescr = contextInstance as
    DTSLocalizableTypeDescriptor;

    if (typeDescr == null)
    {
      return contextInstance;
    }

    return typeDescr.SelectedObject;
  }
```

```csharp
public override StandardValuesCollection GetStandardValues(
ITypeDescriptorContext context)
{
  object retrievalObject = GetSpecializedObject(context.Instance) as
  object;

  return new StandardValuesCollection(getProjects(retrievalObject));
}

public override bool GetStandardValuesExclusive(ITypeDescriptorContext
context)
{
  return true;
}

public override bool GetStandardValuesSupported(ITypeDescriptorContext
context)
{
  return true;
}

private ArrayList getProjects(object retrievalObject)
{
  SettingsNode node = (SettingsNode)retrievalObject;
  ArrayList list = new ArrayList();
  ArrayList listProjects;

  listProjects = (ArrayList)node.Projects;
  if (listProjects == null)
  {
    listProjects = new ArrayList();
  }

  if (listProjects!= null)
  {
    // adds each project
    foreach (string fld in listProjects)
    {
```

```
      list.Add(fld); // Project name
    }

    // sorts the project list
    if ((list != null) && (list.Count > 0))
    {
      list.Sort();
    }
  }

  return list;
  }
}
```

Once added, the Projects TypeConverter code appears as shown in Figure 17-18:

```
internal class Projects : StringConverter
{
    1 reference | Andy Leonard, 5 days ago | 1 author, 2 changes
    private object GetSpecializedObject(object contextInstance)
    {
        DTSLocalizableTypeDescriptor typeDescr = contextInstance as DTSLocalizableTypeDescriptor;

        if (typeDescr == null)
        {
            return contextInstance;
        }

        return typeDescr.SelectedObject;
    }

    3 references | Andy Leonard, 5 days ago | 1 author, 2 changes
    public override StandardValuesCollection GetStandardValues(ITypeDescriptorContext context)
    {
        object retrievalObject = GetSpecializedObject(context.Instance) as object;

        return new StandardValuesCollection(getProjects(retrievalObject));
    }

    3 references | Andy Leonard, 5 days ago | 1 author, 2 changes
    public override bool GetStandardValuesExclusive(ITypeDescriptorContext context)
    {
        return true;
    }

    3 references | Andy Leonard, 5 days ago | 1 author, 2 changes
    public override bool GetStandardValuesSupported(ITypeDescriptorContext context)
    {
        return true;
    }

    1 reference | Andy Leonard, 5 days ago | 1 author, 2 changes
    private ArrayList getProjects(object retrievalObject)
    {
        SettingsNode node = (SettingsNode)retrievalObject;
        ArrayList list = new ArrayList();
        ArrayList listProjects;

        listProjects = (ArrayList)node.Projects;
        if (listProjects == null)
        {
            listProjects = new ArrayList();
        }

        if (listProjects != null)
        {
            // adds each project
            foreach (string fld in listProjects)
            {
                list.Add(fld); // Project name
            }

            // sorts the project list
            if ((list != null) && (list.Count > 0))
            {
                list.Sort();
            }
        }

        return list;
    }
}
```

Figure 17-18. *The Projects TypeConverter*

Note the getProjects method displays an error – a red squiggly line under node. Projects. We correct that error in the coming pages by adding the Projects property to the SettingsNode class.

When the Projects TypeConverter is added, the error in the Project property declaration is resolved, as shown in Figure 17-19 (compare to Figure 17-17):

```
[
    Category("SSIS Catalog Package Properties"),
    Description("Select SSIS Catalog Package project name."),
    TypeConverter(typeof(Projects))
]
O references | Andy Leonard, 5 days ago | 1 author, 3 changes
public string Project {
    get { return _task.PackageProject; }
    set {
        if (value == null)
        {
            throw new ApplicationException("Project name cannot be empty");
        }

        _task.PackageProject = value;
    }
}
```

Figure 17-19. *Projects TypeConverter error cleared*

Add the Projects property using the code in Listing 17-11:

Listing 17-11. Adding the Projects property

```
[
  Category("SSIS Catalog Package Path Collections"),
  Description("Enter SSIS Catalog Package projects collection."),
  Browsable(false)
]
public object Projects {
  get { return _projects; }
  set { _projects = value; }
}
```

Once added, the Projects property appears as shown in Figure 17-20:

```
[
    Category("SSIS Catalog Package Properties"),
    Description("Enter SSIS Catalog Package project name.")
]
1 reference | Andy Leonard, 5 days ago | 1 author, 4 changes
public string ProjectName {
    get { return _task.PackageProject; }
    set {
        if ((value == null) || (value.Trim().Length == 0))
        {
            throw new ApplicationException("Project name cannot be empty");
        }

        _task.PackageProject = value;
    }
}


[
    Category("SSIS Catalog Package Path Collections"),
    Description("Enter SSIS Catalog Package projects collection."),
    Browsable(false)
]
1 reference | Andy Leonard, 5 days ago | 1 author, 2 changes
public object Projects {
    get { return _projects; }
    set { _projects = value; }
}
```

Figure 17-20. *Projects property added*

The next step is to add a method to populate a list of projects using the code in Listing 17-12:

Listing 17-12. Populate the Projects collection

```
internal ArrayList GetProjectsFromCatalog()
{
  ArrayList projectsList = new ArrayList();

  if (((_task.ServerName != null) && (_task.ServerName != ""))
   && ((_task.PackageFolder != null) && (_task.PackageFolder != "")))
```

```
    {
      CatalogFolder catalogFolder = _task.returnCatalogFolder(_task.
      ServerName, _task.PackageFolder);
      if (catalogFolder != null)
      {
        foreach (ProjectInfo pr in catalogFolder.Projects)
        {
          projectsList.Add(pr.Name);
        }
      }
    }
  return projectsList;
}
```

Once added, the code appears as shown in Figure 17-21:

```
internal ArrayList GetProjectsFromCatalog()
{
    ArrayList projectsList = new ArrayList();

    if (((_task.ServerName != null) && (_task.ServerName != ""))
     && ((_task.PackageFolder != null) && (_task.PackageFolder != "")))
    {
        CatalogFolder catalogFolder = _task.returnCatalogFolder(_task.ServerName
                                                    , _task.PackageFolder);

        if (catalogFolder != null)
        {
            foreach (ProjectInfo pr in catalogFolder.Projects)
            {
                projectsList.Add(pr.Name);
            }
        }
    }
    return projectsList;
}
```

Figure 17-21. *Adding the GetProjectsFromCatalog method*

The GetProjectsFromCatalog method constructs and populates an ArrayList type variable that contains a list of SSIS Catalog Projects hosted in the SSIS Catalog folder configured previously.

The next step is to add a method to populate the Projects collection property with the contents returned from the GetProjectsFromCatalog method, and then refresh the SettingsView propertygrid. The code for the new method named updateProjects is in Listing 17-13:

Listing 17-13. Adding the updateProjects method

```
private void updateProjects()
{
  if ((settingsNode.SourceConnection != "")
   && (settingsNode.Folder != ""))

  {
    settingsNode.Projects = settingsNode.GetProjectsFromCatalog();
    this.settingsPropertyGrid.Refresh();
  }
}
```

Once added, the code appears as shown in Figure 17-22:

```
private void updateProjects()
{
    if ((settingsNode.SourceConnection != "")
     && (settingsNode.Folder != ""))

    {
        settingsNode.Projects = settingsNode.GetProjectsFromCatalog();
        this.settingsPropertyGrid.Refresh();
    }
}
```

Figure 17-22. *The updateProjects method, added*

The next step is to add a call to the updateProjects method in the updateCollections method using the code in Listing 17-14:

Listing 17-14. Update the updateCollections method

```
private void updateCollections()
{
  Cursor = Cursors.WaitCursor;

  updateFolders();
  updateProjects();

  Cursor = Cursors.Default;
}
```

Once added, the code appears as shown in Figure 17-23:

```
private void updateCollections()
{
    Cursor = Cursors.WaitCursor;

    updateFolders();
    updateProjects();

    Cursor = Cursors.Default;
}
```

Figure 17-23. *Centralizing the call to update the folders and projects collections*

Updates to the Projects collection make sense when the Folder property is initially selected or updated. In the previous section, we added code in the propertyGridSettings_PropertyValueChanged method to call the updateCollections method when the Folder property value changes. The next step is to add a call to the updateCollections method in the propertyGridSettings_PropertyValueChanged method when the Project property value changes by adding the code in Listing 17-15 to the SettingsView.propertyGridSettings_PropertyValueChanged method:

Listing 17-15. Add code to respond to changes in the Project property

```
if (e.ChangedItem.PropertyDescriptor.Name.CompareTo("Project") == 0)
{
  updateCollections();
}
```

Once added, the code appears as shown in Figure 17-24:

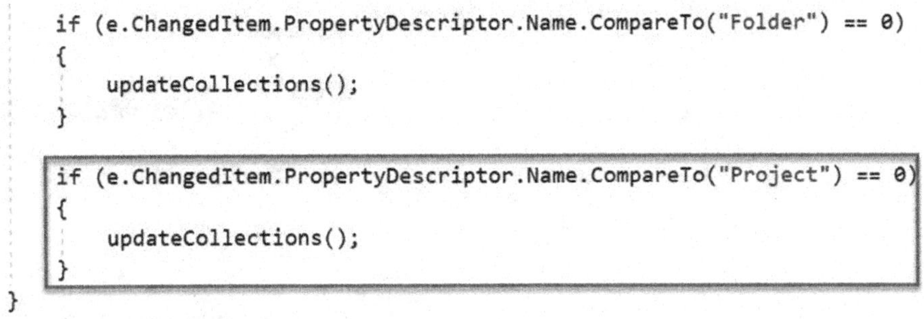

```
if (e.ChangedItem.PropertyDescriptor.Name.CompareTo("Folder") == 0)
{
    updateCollections();
}

if (e.ChangedItem.PropertyDescriptor.Name.CompareTo("Project") == 0)
{
    updateCollections();
}
}
```

Figure 17-24. Adding code to respond to changes in the Project property

To test the functionality, build the ExecuteCatalogPackageTask solution, open a test SSIS package in a test SSIS project, add an Execute Catalog Package Task to the control flow canvas, open the task editor, and configure a SourceConnection and SSIS Catalog Folder. After configuring a SourceConnection and SSIS Catalog Folder, the Project property should be populated with the names of SSIS Catalog Projects, as shown in Figure 17-25:

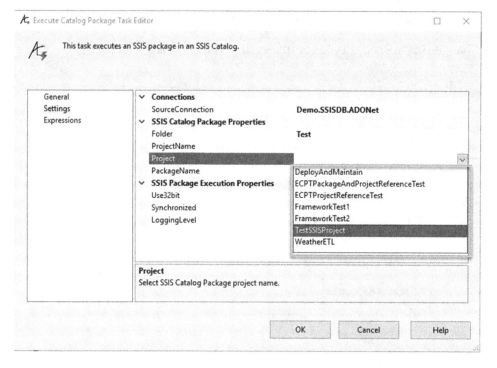

Figure 17-25. *Projects*

The next step is to hide the ProjectName property. To hide the ProjectName property, simply comment out the ProjectName property declaration by selecting the code, holding the Ctrl key, and pressing the K key, followed by the C key. The selected code is commented out as shown in Figure 17-26:

```
//[
//  Category("SSIS Catalog Package Properties"),
//  Description("Enter SSIS Catalog Package project name.")
//]
//public string ProjectName {
//     get { return _task.PackageProject; }
//     set {
//          if ((value == null) || (value.Trim().Length == 0))
//          {
//               throw new ApplicationException("Project name cannot be empty");
//          }

//          _task.PackageProject = value;
//     }
//}
```

Figure 17-26. *The ProjectName property, commented out*

The next step is to update the SettingsView.OnCommit method, updating the line theTask.PackageProject = settingsNode.ProjectName; with theTask. PackageProject = settingsNode.Project;, as shown in Figure 17-27:

```
public virtual void OnCommit(object taskHost)
{
    theTask.ConnectionManagerName = settingsNode.SourceConnection;
    theTask.ServerName = returnSelectedConnectionManagerDataSourceValue(settingsNode.SourceConnection);
    theTask.PackageFolder = settingsNode.Folder;
    theTask.PackageProject = settingsNode.Project;
    theTask.PackageName = settingsNode.PackageName;
}
```

Figure 17-27. *Updating the PackageProject property assignment*

Build and test the ExecuteCatalogPackageTask solution. The Settings view on the task editor should now appear as shown in Figure 17-28:

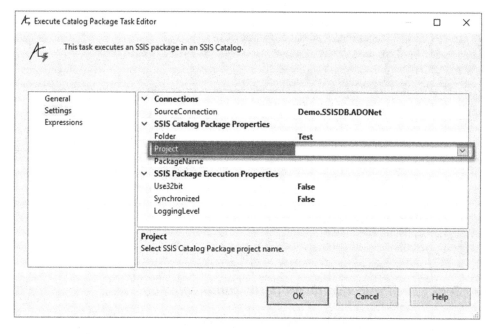

Figure 17-28. *The Project property*

The Project and Projects collection properties are now configured. The next steps are to configure the Package and Packages collection properties.

Now would be an excellent time to check in your code.

The Package Property and Packages Collection

The relationship between the Package property and the Packages collection is identical to the relationship between the Project property and the Projects collection. The only difference is the objects themselves. As with the Projects collection, we must manage the collection of SSIS Catalog Packages in our code.

Add a new Package property to the SettingsNode class using the code in Listing 17-16:

Listing 17-16. Add the SettingsNode.Package property

```
[
  Category("SSIS Catalog Package Properties"),
  Description("Select SSIS Catalog Package name."),
  TypeConverter(typeof(Packages))
]
```

```
public string Package {
  get { return _task.PackageName; }
  set {
    if (value == null)
    {
      throw new ApplicationException("Package name cannot be empty");
    }

    _task. PackageName = value;
  }
}
```

Once added, the code appears as shown in Figure 17-29:

```
[
    Category("SSIS Catalog Package Properties"),
    Description("Select SSIS Catalog Package name."),
    TypeConverter(typeof(Packages))
]
0 references | Andy Leonard, 6 days ago | 1 author, 3 changes
public string Package {
    get { return _task.PackageName; }
    set {
        if (value == null)
        {
            throw new ApplicationException("Package name cannot be empty");
        }

        _task.PackageName = value;
    }
}
```

Figure 17-29. *Adding the SettingsNode.Package property*

As before with the Folder and Project TypeConverters, please note the Packages
TypeConverter has a red squiggly line beneath it, indicating the same error condition as
before: The Packages TypeConverter does not yet exist. Add the Packages TypeConverter
using the code in Listing 17-17:

Listing 17-17. The Packages TypeConverter

```csharp
internal class Packages : StringConverter
{
  private object GetSpecializedObject(object contextInstance)
  {
    DTSLocalizableTypeDescriptor typeDescr = contextInstance as
    DTSLocalizableTypeDescriptor;

    if (typeDescr == null)
    {
      return contextInstance;
    }

    return typeDescr.SelectedObject;
  }

  public override StandardValuesCollection GetStandardValues(
  ITypeDescriptorContext context)
  {
    object retrievalObject = GetSpecializedObject(context.Instance) as
    object;

    return new StandardValuesCollection(getPackages(retrievalObject));
  }

  public override bool GetStandardValuesExclusive(ITypeDescriptorContext
  context)
  {
    return true;
  }

  public override bool GetStandardValuesSupported(ITypeDescriptorContext
  context)
  {
    return true;
  }
```

```csharp
private ArrayList getPackages(object retrievalObject)
{
  SettingsNode node = (SettingsNode)retrievalObject;
  ArrayList list = new ArrayList();
  ArrayList listPackages;

  listPackages = (ArrayList)node.Packages;
  if (listPackages == null)
  {
    listPackages = new ArrayList();
  }

  if (listPackages != null)
  {
    // adds each package
    foreach (string pkg in listPackages)
    {
      list.Add(pkg); // Package name
    }

    // sorts the package list
    if ((list != null) && (list.Count > 0))
    {
      list.Sort();
    }
  }

  return list;
  }
}
```

Once added, the Projects TypeConverter code appears as shown in Figure 17-30:

```
internal class Packages : StringConverter
{
    1 reference | Andy Leonard, 6 days ago | 1 author, 2 changes
    private object GetSpecializedObject(object contextInstance)
    {
        DTSLocalizableTypeDescriptor typeDescr = contextInstance as DTSLocalizableTypeDescriptor;

        if (typeDescr == null)
        {
            return contextInstance;
        }

        return typeDescr.SelectedObject;
    }

    4 references | Andy Leonard, 6 days ago | 1 author, 2 changes
    public override StandardValuesCollection GetStandardValues(ITypeDescriptorContext context)
    {
        object retrievalObject = GetSpecializedObject(context.Instance) as object;

        return new StandardValuesCollection(getPackages(retrievalObject));
    }

    4 references | Andy Leonard, 6 days ago | 1 author, 2 changes
    public override bool GetStandardValuesSupported(ITypeDescriptorContext context)
    {
        return true;
    }

    1 reference | Andy Leonard, 6 days ago | 1 author, 2 changes
    private ArrayList getPackages(object retrievalObject)
    {
        SettingsNode node = (SettingsNode)retrievalObject;
        ArrayList list = new ArrayList();
        ArrayList listPackages;

        listPackages = (ArrayList)node.Packages;
        if (listPackages == null)
        {
            listPackages = new ArrayList();
        }

        if (listPackages != null)
        {
            // adds each package
            foreach (string pkg in listPackages)
            {
                list.Add(pkg); // Package name
            }

            // sorts the package list
            if ((list != null) && (list.Count > 0))
            {
                list.Sort();
            }
        }

        return list;
    }
}
```

Figure 17-30.   *The Packages TypeConverter*

Note the getPackages method displays an error – a red squiggly line under node.
Packages. We correct that error in the coming pages by adding the Packages property to
the SettingsNode class.

When the Packages TypeConverter is added, the error in the Package property
declaration is resolved, as shown in Figure 17-31 (compare to Figure 17-29):

```
[
    Category("SSIS Catalog Package Properties"),
    Description("Select SSIS Catalog Package name."),
    TypeConverter(typeof(Packages))
]
0 references | Andy Leonard, 6 days ago | 1 author, 3 changes
public string Package {
    get { return _task.PackageName; }
    set {
        if (value == null)
        {
            throw new ApplicationException("Package name cannot be empty");
        }

        _task.PackageName = value;
    }
}
```

Figure 17-31. *Packages TypeConverter error cleared*

Add the Packages property using the code in Listing 17-18:

Listing 17-18. Adding the Packages property

```
[
  Category("SSIS Catalog Package Path Collections"),
  Description("Enter SSIS Catalog Packages collection."),
  Browsable(false)
]
public object Packages {
  get { return _packages; }
  set { _packages = value; }
}
```

Once added, the Packages property appears as shown in Figure 17-32:

```
[
    Category("SSIS Catalog Package Path Collections"),
    Description("Enter SSIS Catalog Packages collection."),
    Browsable(false)
]
```
1 reference | Andy Leonard, 6 days ago | 1 author, 2 changes
```
public object Packages {
    get { return _packages; }
    set { _packages = value; }
}
```

Figure 17-32. *Packages property added*

The next step is to add a method to populate a list of packages using the code in Listing 17-19:

Listing 17-19. Populate the Packages collection

```
internal ArrayList GetPackagesFromCatalog()
{
  ArrayList packagesList = new ArrayList();

  if ((( _task.ServerName != null) && (_task.ServerName != ""))
   && ((_task.PackageFolder != null) && (_task.PackageFolder != ""))
   && ((_task.PackageProject != null) && (_task.PackageProject != "")))
  {
    ProjectInfo catalogProject = _task.returnCatalogProject(_task.ServerName
                                    , _task.PackageFolder
                                    , _task.PackageProject);

    if (catalogProject != null)
    {
      foreach (Microsoft.SqlServer.Management.IntegrationServices.
      PackageInfo
                pkg in catalogProject.Packages)
      {
        packagesList.Add(pkg.Name);
      }
```

```
        }
    }
    return packagesList;
}
```

Once added, the code appears as shown in Figure 17-33:

```
internal ArrayList GetPackagesFromCatalog()
{
    ArrayList packagesList = new ArrayList();

    if (((_task.ServerName != null) && (_task.ServerName != ""))
     && ((_task.PackageFolder != null) && (_task.PackageFolder != ""))
     && ((_task.PackageProject != null) && (_task.PackageProject != "")))
    {
        ProjectInfo catalogProject = _task.returnCatalogProject(_task.ServerName
                                            , _task.PackageFolder
                                            , _task.PackageProject);

        if (catalogProject != null)
        {
            foreach (Microsoft.SqlServer.Management.IntegrationServices.PackageInfo
                        pkg in catalogProject.Packages)
            {
                packagesList.Add(pkg.Name);
            }
        }
    }
    return packagesList;
}
```

Figure 17-33. *Adding the GetPackagesFromCatalog method*

The GetPackagesFromCatalog method constructs and populates an ArrayList type variable that contains a list of SSIS Catalog Packages hosted in the SSIS Catalog project previously configured.

The next step is to add a method to populate the Packages collection property with the contents returned from the GetPackagesFromCatalog method, and then refresh the SettingsView propertygrid. The code for the new method named updatePackages is in Listing 17-20:

Listing 17-20. Adding the updatePackages method

```
private void updatePackages()
{
  if ((settingsNode.SourceConnection != "")
   && (settingsNode.Folder != "")
   && (settingsNode.Project != ""))
  {
    settingsNode.Packages = settingsNode.GetPackagesFromCatalog();
    this.settingsPropertyGrid.Refresh();
  }
}
```

Once added, the code appears as shown in Figure 17-34:

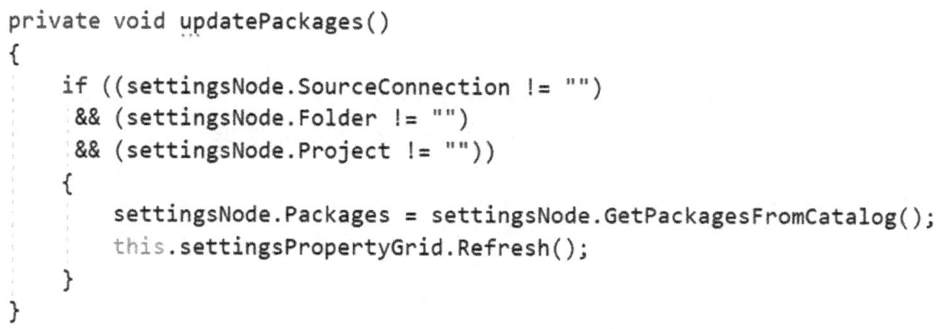

```
private void updatePackages()
{
    if ((settingsNode.SourceConnection != "")
     && (settingsNode.Folder != "")
     && (settingsNode.Project != ""))
    {
        settingsNode.Packages = settingsNode.GetPackagesFromCatalog();
        this.settingsPropertyGrid.Refresh();
    }
}
```

Figure 17-34. *The updatePackages method, added*

The next step is to add a call to the updatePackages method in the updateCollections method using the code in Listing 17-21:

Listing 17-21. Update the updateCollections method

```
private void updateCollections()
{
  Cursor = Cursors.WaitCursor;

  updateFolders();
  updateProjects();
```

```
    updatePackages();

    Cursor = Cursors.Default;
}
```

Once added, the code appears as shown in Figure 17-35:

```
private void updateCollections()
{
    Cursor = Cursors.WaitCursor;

    updateFolders();
    updateProjects();
    updatePackages();

    Cursor = Cursors.Default;
}
```

Figure 17-35. *Centralizing the call to update the folders, projects, and packages collections*

Updates to the Packages collection make sense when the Project property is initially selected or updated. In previous sections, we added code in the propertyGridSettings_ PropertyValueChanged method to call the updateCollections method when the Folder or Project property values change. The next step is to add a call to the updateCollections method in the propertyGridSettings_PropertyValueChanged method when the Package property value changes by adding the code in Listing 17-22 to the SettingsView.propertyGridSettings_PropertyValueChanged method:

Listing 17-22. Add code to respond to changes in the Package property

```
if (e.ChangedItem.PropertyDescriptor.Name.CompareTo("Package") == 0)
{
    updateCollections();
}
```

Once added, the code appears as shown in Figure 17-36:

```
if (e.ChangedItem.PropertyDescriptor.Name.CompareTo("Package") == 0)
{
    updateCollections();
}
```

Figure 17-36. *Adding code to respond to changes in the Package property*

To test the functionality, build the ExecuteCatalogPackageTask solution, open a test SSIS package in a test SSIS project, add an Execute Catalog Package Task to the control flow canvas, open the task editor, and configure a SourceConnection, folder, and project. After configuring a SourceConnection, folder, and project, the Package property should be populated with the names of SSIS Catalog Packages, as shown in Figure 17-37:

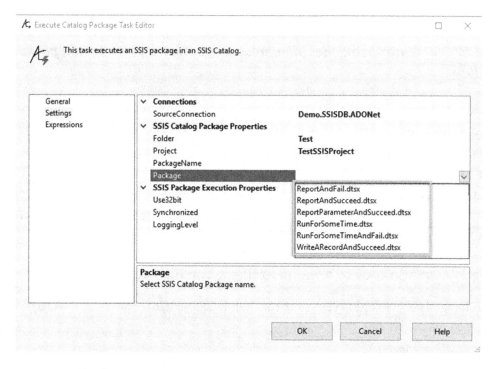

Figure 17-37. *Packages*

The next step is to hide the PackageName property. To hide the PackageName property, simply comment out the PackageName property declaration by selecting the code, holding the Ctrl key, and pressing the K key, followed by the C key. The selected code is commented out as shown in Figure 17-38:

```
//[
//  Category("SSIS Catalog Package Properties"),
//  Description("Enter SSIS Catalog Package name.")
//]
//public string PackageName {
//    get { return _task.PackageName; }
//    set {
//        if ((value == null) || (value.Trim().Length == 0))
//        {
//            throw new ApplicationException("Package name cannot be empty");
//        }

//        _task.PackageName = value;
//    }
//}
```

Figure 17-38. *The PackageName property, commented out*

The next step is to update the `SettingsView.OnCommit` method, updating the line `theTask.PackageName = settingsNode.PackageName;` with `theTask.PackageName = settingsNode.Package;`, as shown in Figure 17-39:

```
public virtual void OnCommit(object taskHost)
{
    theTask.ConnectionManagerName = settingsNode.SourceConnection;
    theTask.ServerName = returnSelectedConnectionManagerDataSourceValue(settingsNode.SourceConnection);
    theTask.PackageFolder = settingsNode.Folder;
    theTask.PackageProject = settingsNode.Project;
    theTask.PackageName = settingsNode.Package;
}
```

Figure 17-39. *Updating the PackageName property assignment*

Build and test the ExecuteCatalogPackageTask solution. The Settings view on the task editor should now appear as shown in Figure 17-40:

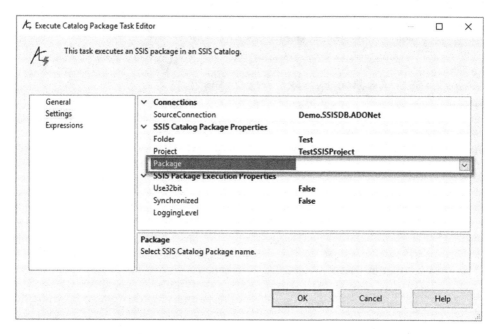

Figure 17-40. *The Package property*

The Package and Packages collection properties are now configured.
Now would be an excellent time to check in your code.

Resetting Collections

Resetting collections is important because it makes the SourceConnection ➤ Folder ➤ Project ➤ Package hierarchy more manageable while editing. Implement the resetCollections method in SettingsView class using the code in Listing 17-23:

Listing 17-23. Add the SettingsView.resetCollections method

```
private void resetCollections(string collectionName)
{
  Cursor = Cursors.WaitCursor;

  switch (collectionName)
```

```
{
  default:
    break;
  case "Connections":
    settingsNode.Folder = "";
    settingsNode.Project = "";
    settingsNode.Package = "";
    break;
  case "Folders":
    settingsNode.Project = "";
    settingsNode.Package = "";
    break;
   case "Projects":
    settingsNode.Package = "";
    break;
  }

  Cursor = Cursors.Default;
}
```

Once added, the code appears as shown in Figure 17-41:

```
private void resetCollections(string collectionName)
{
    Cursor = Cursors.WaitCursor;

    switch (collectionName)
    {
        default:
            break;
        case "Connections":
            settingsNode.Folder = "";
            settingsNode.Project = "";
            settingsNode.Package = "";
            break;
        case "Folders":
            settingsNode.Project = "";
            settingsNode.Package = "";
            break;
        case "Projects":
            settingsNode.Package = "";
            break;
    }

    Cursor = Cursors.Default;
}
```

Figure 17-41. *Adding the SettingsView.resetCollections method*

How does the resetCollections method work? A string type argument
named collectionName is passed to the resetCollections method. Just inside the
resetCollections method, the cursor is set to a WaitCursor, and just before the
resetCollections method exits, the cursor is reset to the Default cursor.

A switch statement, driven by the collectionName argument value, is sandwiched in
between these cursor "sets." The hierarchy is SourceConnection ➤ Folder ➤ Project ➤
Package. switch statement cases exist for "Connections," "Folders," and "Projects."

The "Connections" case resets the settingsNode.Folder, settingsNode.Project,
and settingsNode.Package property values to an empty string. The "Folders" case resets
the settingsNode.Project and settingsNode.Package property values to an empty
string. The "Projects" case resets the settingsNode.Package property value to an empty
string.

The next step is to add calls to the resetCollections method to the SettingsView.
propertyGridSettings_PropertyValueChanged method's response code for the
SourceConnection, Folder, and Project properties, as shown in Figure 17-42:

```
    else // if not a new connection
    {
        theTask.ServerName = returnSelectedConnectionManagerDataSourc
        theTask.ConnectionManagerName = settingsNode.SourceConnection
        theTask.ConnectionManagerId = theTask.GetConnectionID(theTask
        settingsNode.Connections = ConnectionService.GetConnectionsOf
    }
    updateCollections();
    resetCollections("Connections");
}

if (e.ChangedItem.PropertyDescriptor.Name.CompareTo("Folder") == 0)
{
    updateCollections();
    resetCollections("Folders");
}

if (e.ChangedItem.PropertyDescriptor.Name.CompareTo("Project") == 0)
{
    updateCollections();
    resetCollections("Projects");
}

if (e.ChangedItem.PropertyDescriptor.Name.CompareTo("Package") == 0)
{
    updateCollections();
}
```

Figure 17-42. *Adding calls to the resetCollections method*

Test the resetCollections method by building the ExecuteCatalogPackageTask,
opening a test SSIS package, and then adding an Execute Catalog Package Task to the
Control Flow surface. Open the Execute Catalog Package Task Editor and configure an
SSIS package execution, as shown in Figure 17-43:

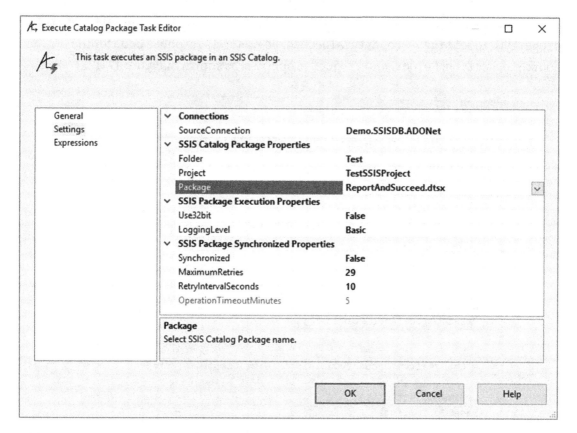

Figure 17-43. *An SSIS package execution, configured*

Test the resetCollections method's Project response by selecting a different Project from the dropdown, as shown in Figure 17-44:

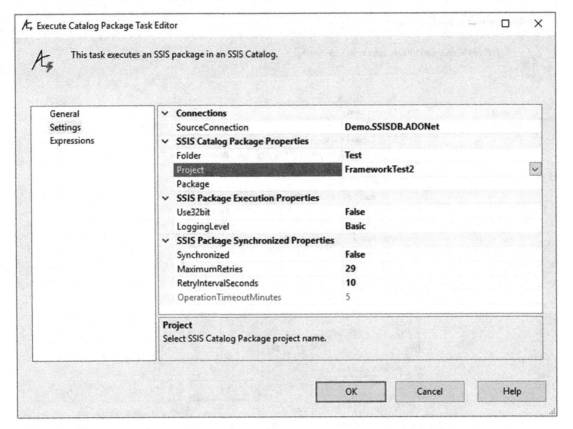

Figure 17-44. *The Package property reset on Project property value change*

Test the resetCollections method's Folder response by selecting a different Folder from the dropdown, as shown in Figure 17-45:

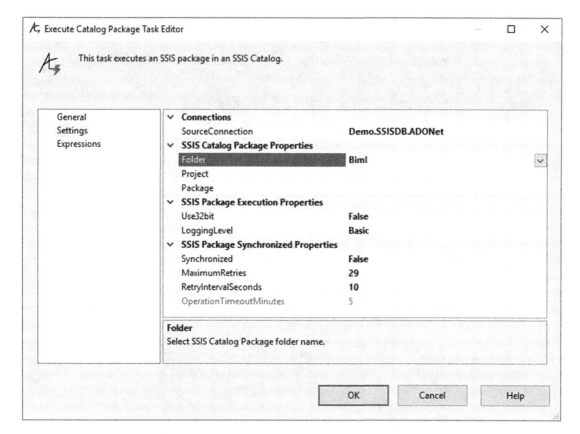

Figure 17-45. *The Project property reset on Folder property value change*

Test the resetCollections method's SourceConnection response by selecting a different SourceConnection from the dropdown, as shown in Figure 17-46:

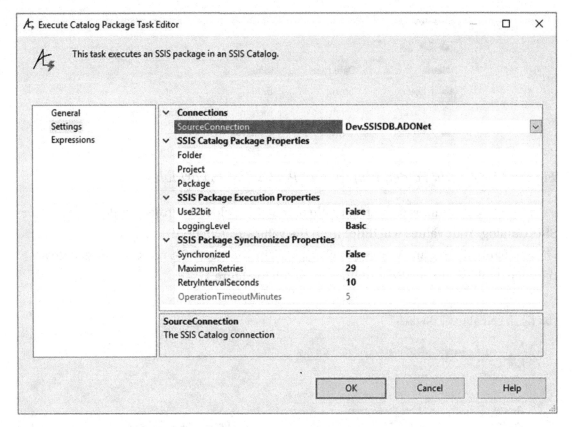

Figure 17-46. *The Folder property reset on SourceConnection property value change*

The resetCollections method works as designed.

Let's Test Expressions!

The code is in no shape, at present, to execute the Execute Catalog Package Task in an Azure-SSIS integration runtime. We may, however, use Expressions.

To test expressions, add three String data type variables to your test SSIS package named Folder, Project, and Package, as shown in Figure 17-47:

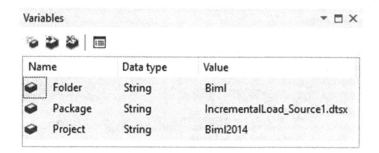

Figure 17-47. *Add Folder, Project, and Package SSIS variables*

Configure the values of each variable to match a Folder ➤ Project ➤ Package in your SSIS Catalog. Your values will differ from the values shown here.

Configure an Execute Catalog Package Task in your test SSIS package to execute a package deployed to an SSIS Catalog, as shown in Figure 17-48:

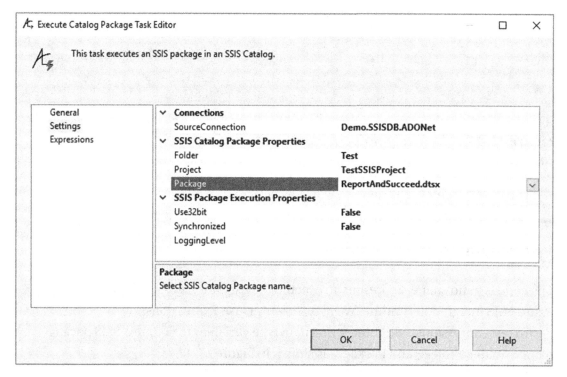

Figure 17-48. *A configured Execute Catalog Package Task*

The next step is to click Expressions in the left list to open the Expression view, as shown in Figure 17-49:

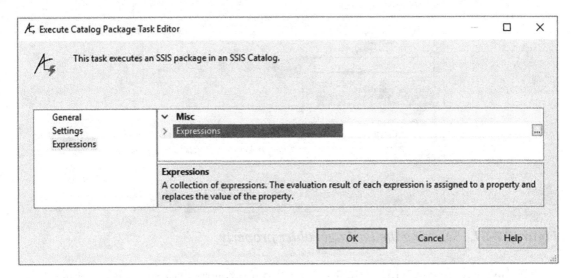

Figure 17-49. *The Expressions view*

Click the ellipsis to the right of the Expressions property (collection) value to open the Property Expressions Editor dialog, as shown in Figure 17-50:

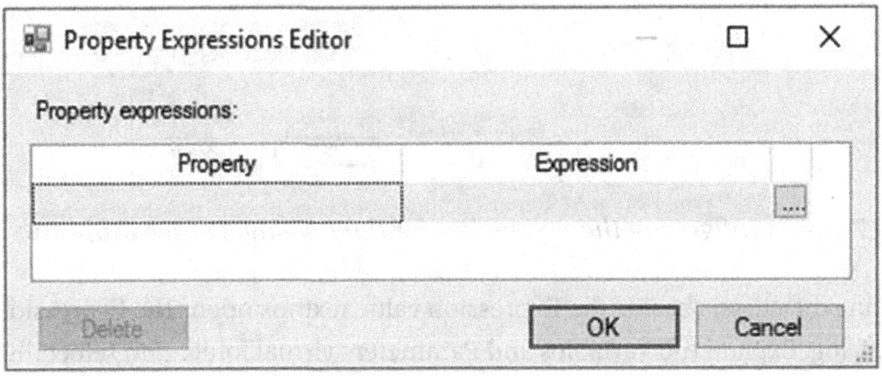

Figure 17-50. *The Property Expressions Editor*

Click the Property dropdown and select PackageFolder, as shown in Figure 17-51:

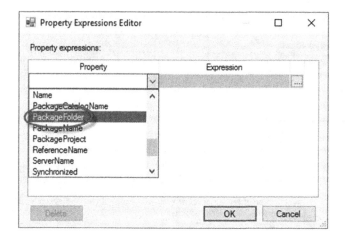

Figure 17-51. *Selecting the PackageFolder property*

The next step in configuring the PackageFolder property expression is clicking the ellipsis beside the Expression value textbox, as shown in Figure 17-52:

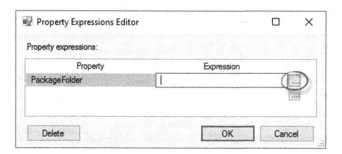

Figure 17-52. *Configuring the expression for the PackageFolder property*

Clicking the ellipsis beside the Expression value textbox opens the Expression Builder dialog. Expand the Variables and Parameters virtual folder and select the User::Folder SSIS variable, as shown in Figure 17-53:

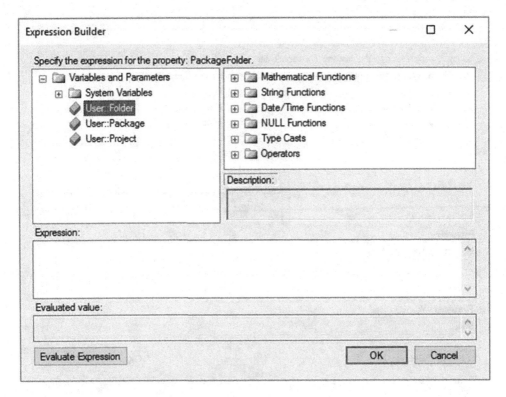

Figure 17-53. *Selecting the User::Folder SSIS variable*

Drag the User::Folder SSIS variable into the Expression textbox. Click the Evaluate Expression button and observe the default value of the User::Folder SSIS variable in the Evaluated Value textbox, as shown in Figure 17-54:

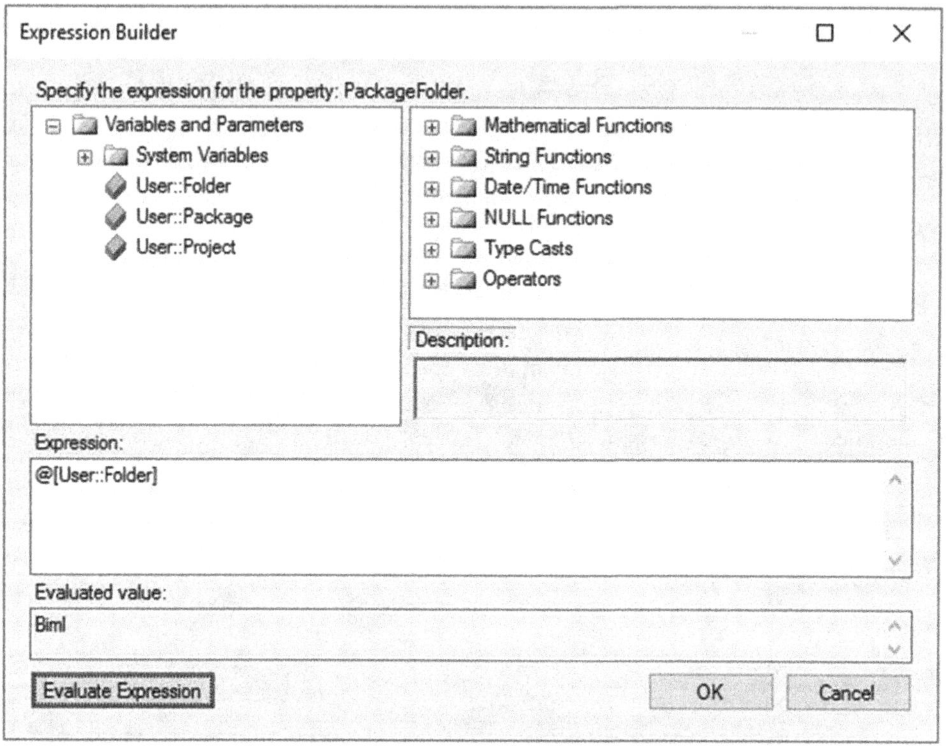

Figure 17-54. *User::Folder SSIS variable selected and evaluated*

Click the OK button to close the Expression Builder dialog. Note the property expression value for PackageFolder property is now configured to the User::Folder SSIS variable, as shown in Figure 17-55:

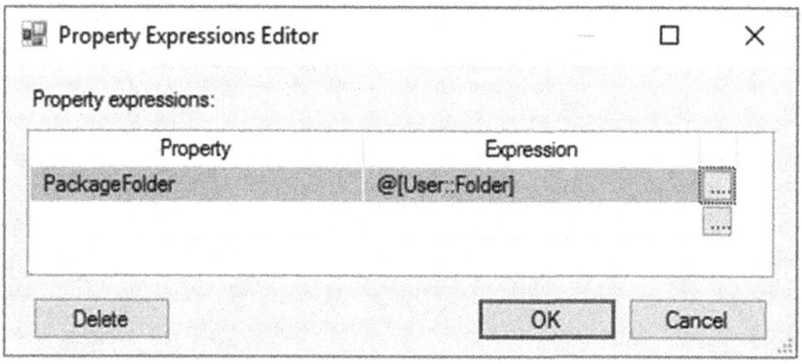

Figure 17-55. *The User::Folder SSIS variable assigned to the PackageFolder property*

At execution time, the value in the User::Folder SSIS variable will override the PackageFolder property.

Repeat the procedure to assign the PackageProject property to the User::Project SSIS variable value, and the PackageName property to the User::Package SSIS variable value, as shown in Figure 17-56:

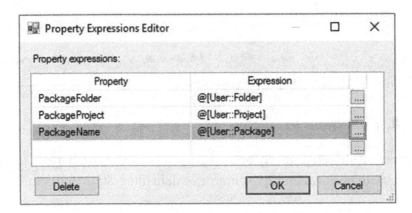

Figure 17-56. *PackageProject and PackageName properties assigned to User::Project and User::Package SSIS variables, respectively*

Execute the test SSIS package. If all goes as planned, the test execution succeeds, as shown in Figure 17-57:

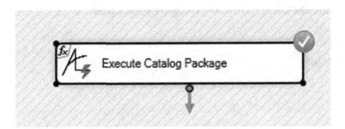

Figure 17-57. *A successful test execution*

Check the All Executions report to verify the Folder ➤ Project ➤ Package path matches the values configure in your test SSIS package's variables, as shown in Figure 17-58:

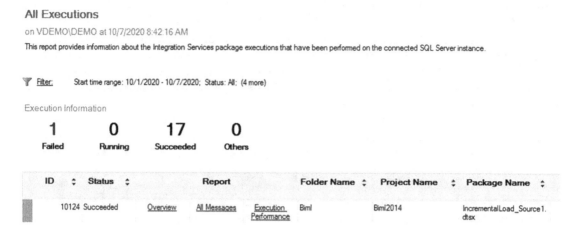

Figure 17-58. *Expressions test success*

SSIS Expression-driven property overrides are a powerful mechanism for reusing one SSIS package to perform multiple enterprise data integration operations.

Conclusion

In this chapter, we made package path management more robust by surfacing pre-populated lists of folders, projects, and packages. We tested the refactored properties with Expressions, and they work!

Now would be an excellent time to check in your code.

CHAPTER 18

Instrumentation and Validation

Instrumentation is a sub-science of engineering which originally meant collecting physical data from industrial processes. In software engineering, instrumentation refers to the art and science of surfacing key indicators of the settings, state, and performance of software.

Validation is checking values to make certain the values are in a usable state. In the context of the Execute Catalog Package Task, certain properties *must* be configured using non-empty and non-default values.

In this chapter, we will add instrumentation and validation to the Execute Catalog Package Task.

Instrumentation

In its most basic form, instrumentation is how code "talks" to developers and operators – it informs developers and operators of the status of an operation. In the case of the ExecuteCatalogPackageTask, it is expected that the task inform developers and operators if the SSIS Catalog package executed successfully or not.

Adding Instrumentation

Open the ExecuteCatalogPackageTask.cs file in the ExecuteCatalogPackageTask project in the ExecuteCatalogPackageTask solution, and create a new function named `logMessage` in the `ExecuteCatalogPackageTask` class using the code in Listing 18-1:

361

© Andy Leonard 2021
A. Leonard, *Building Custom Tasks for SQL Server Integration Services*,
https://doi.org/10.1007/978-1-4842-6482-9_18

Listing 18-1. Adding logMessage

```
private void logMessage(
  IDTSComponentEvents componentEvents
, string messageType
, int messageCode
, string subComponent
, string message)
{
  bool fireAgain = true;
  switch(messageType)
  {
    default:
      break;
    case "Information":
      componentEvents.FireInformation(messageCode, subComponent, message,
      "", 0, ref fireAgain);
      break;
    case "Warning":
      componentEvents.FireWarning(messageCode, subComponent, message, "", 0);
      break;
    case "Error":
      componentEvents.FireError(messageCode, subComponent, message, "", 0);
      break;
  }
}
```

Once added, the code appears as shown in Figure 18-1:

```
private void logMessage(IDTSComponentEvents componentEvents
    , string messageType
    , int messageCode
    , string subComponent
    , string message)
{
    bool fireAgain = true;
    switch(messageType)
    {
        default:
            break;
        case "Information":
            componentEvents.FireInformation(messageCode, subComponent, message, "", 0, ref fireAgain);
            break;
        case "Warning":
            componentEvents.FireWarning(messageCode, subComponent, message, "", 0);
            break;
        case "Error":
            componentEvents.FireError(messageCode, subComponent, message, "", 0);
            break;
    }
}
```

Figure 18-1. *The logMessage function*

Add a process "starting" information message to the Execute method using the code in Listing 18-2:

Listing 18-2. Adding a process "starting" message

```
string packagePath = "\\SSISDB\\" + PackageFolder + "\\"
                    + PackageProject + "\\"
                    + PackageName;
string msg = "Starting " + packagePath + " on " + ServerName;
logMessage(componentEvents, "Information", 1001, TaskName, msg);
```

Once added, the code appears as shown in Figure 18-2:

```
public override DTSExecResult Execute(
    Connections connections,
    VariableDispenser variableDispenser,
    IDTSComponentEvents componentEvents,
    IDTSLogging log,
    object transaction)
{
    ConnectionManagerIndex = returnConnectionManagerIndex(connections, ConnectionManagerName);

    catalogProject = returnCatalogProject(ServerName, PackageFolder, PackageProject);
    catalogPackage = returnCatalogPackage(ServerName, PackageFolder, PackageProject, PackageName);

    Collection<Microsoft.SqlServer.Management.IntegrationServices.PackageInfo.ExecutionValueParameterSet>
        executionValueParameterSet = returnExecutionValueParameterSet();

    string packagePath = "\\SSISDB\\" + PackageFolder + "\\"
            + PackageProject + "\\"
            + PackageName;
    string msg = "Starting " + packagePath + " on " + ServerName;
    logMessage(componentEvents, "Information", 1001, TaskName, msg);

    catalogPackage.Execute(Use32bit, null, executionValueParameterSet);

    return DTSExecResult.Success;
}
```

Figure 18-2. *Adding a "starting" message*

Add an "ended" message using the code in Listing 18-3:

Listing 18-3. Adding an "ended" message

```
msg = packagePath + " on " + ServerName + " completed";
logMessage(componentEvents, "Information", 1002, TaskName, msg);
```

Once added, the code appears as shown in Figure 18-3:

```
public override DTSExecResult Execute(
    Connections connections,
    VariableDispenser variableDispenser,
    IDTSComponentEvents componentEvents,
    IDTSLogging log,
    object transaction)
{
    ConnectionManagerIndex = returnConnectionManagerIndex(connections, ConnectionManagerName);

    catalogProject = returnCatalogProject(ServerName, PackageFolder, PackageProject);
    catalogPackage = returnCatalogPackage(ServerName, PackageFolder, PackageProject, PackageName);

    Collection<Microsoft.SqlServer.Management.IntegrationServices.PackageInfo.ExecutionValueParameterSet>
        executionValueParameterSet = returnExecutionValueParameterSet();

    string packagePath = "\\SSISDB\\" + PackageFolder + "\\"
            + PackageProject + "\\"
            + PackageName;
    string msg = "Starting " + packagePath + " on " + ServerName;
    logMessage(componentEvents, "Information", 1001, TaskName, msg);

    catalogPackage.Execute(Use32bit, null, executionValueParameterSet);

    msg = packagePath + " on " + ServerName + " completed";
    logMessage(componentEvents, "Information", 1002, TaskName, msg);

    return DTSExecResult.Success;
}
```

Figure 18-3. *Adding an "ended" message*

Build and test the Execute Catalog Package Task, observing the Execution Results tab as shown in Figure 18-4:

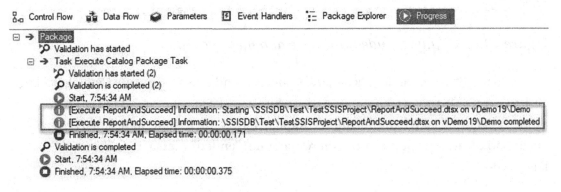

Figure 18-4. *Observing the messages*

The code executes and reports as designed, but the report code is designed inaccurately. When the Execute Catalog Package Task executes an SSIS package in the SSIS Catalog, the Synchronized execution parameter governs the behavior of the package.Execute() method. If Synchronized is false (which is the default), the SSIS Catalog finds the package and then returns from execution. If Synchronized is true, the SSIS Catalog executes the package *in-process*, returning from execution only *after* the SSIS package execution completes in the SSIS Catalog. The message should stand out, so change the messageType argument in the logMessage method from "Information" to "Warning."

The "ended" message is currently inaccurate. Update the "ended" message logic using the code in Listing 18-4:

Listing 18-4. Updating the "ended" message

```
msg = packagePath + " on " + ServerName
 + (Synchronized ? " completed." : " started. Check SSIS Catalog Reports
for package execution results.");
logMessage(componentEvents, "Warning", 1002, TaskName, msg);
```

Once added, the code appears as shown in Figure 18-5:

```
msg = packagePath + " on " + ServerName + (Synchronized ? " completed."
    : " started. Check SSIS Catalog Reports for package execution results.");
logMessage(componentEvents, "Warning", 1002, TaskName, msg);
```

Figure 18-5. *Updated "ended" message and message type*

Build the ExecuteCatalogPackageTask solution and add the Execute Catalog Package Task to a test SSIS project, configured to execute a package with the Synchronized property set to False. When execution completes, view the Execution Results/Progress tab to find the newly updated (and more accurate) "ended" message, as shown in Figure 18-6:

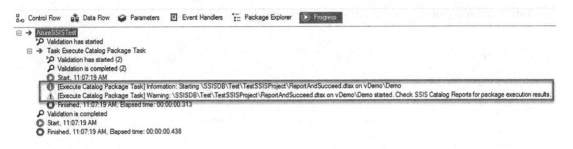

Figure 18-6. *The new "ended" message*

The "ended" message should also include execution time instrumentation, and the message could be flagged as a warning instead of information by implementing the code in Listing 18-5:

Listing 18-5. Adding execution time and warning

```
Stopwatch sw = new Stopwatch();
sw.Start();
.

.

.

sw.Stop();
string swMsg = String.Empty;
if(Synchronized)
{
  swMsg = " Package Execution Time: " + sw.Elapsed.ToString();
}

msg = packagePath + " on " + ServerName + (Synchronized ?
    (" completed." + swMsg.Substring(0, (swMsg.Length - 4))) :
    (" started. Check SSIS Catalog Reports for package execution
    results."));
logMessage(componentEvents, (Synchronized ? "Information" : "Warning"),
1002, TaskName, msg);
```

When added, the code appears as shown in Figure 18-7:

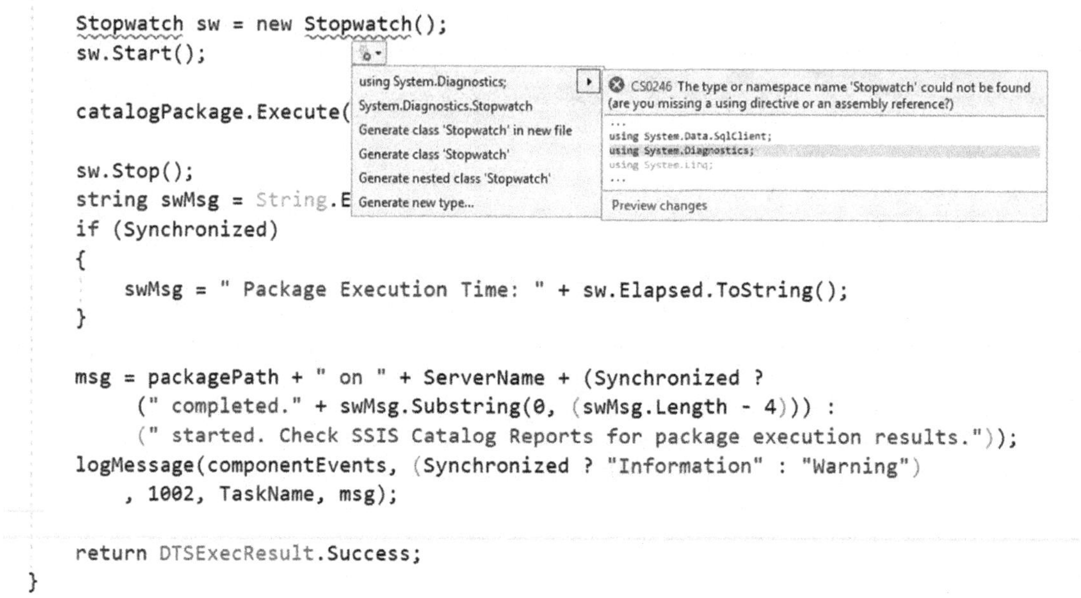
Stopwatch sw = new Stopwatch();
sw.Start();
using System.Diagnostics;
System.Diagnostics.Stopwatch
Generate class 'Stopwatch' in new file
Generate class 'Stopwatch'
Generate nested class 'Stopwatch'
Generate new type...
CS0246 The type or namespace name 'Stopwatch' could not be found (are you missing a using directive or an assembly reference?)
...
using System.Data.SqlClient;
using System.Diagnostics;
using System.Linq;
...
Preview changes
catalogPackage.Execute(
sw.Stop();
string swMsg = String.E
if (Synchronized)
{
swMsg = " Package Execution Time: " + sw.Elapsed.ToString();
}
msg = packagePath + " on " + ServerName + (Synchronized ?
(" completed." + swMsg.Substring(0, (swMsg.Length - 4))) :
(" started. Check SSIS Catalog Reports for package execution results."));
logMessage(componentEvents, (Synchronized ? "Information" : "Warning")
, 1002, TaskName, msg);
return DTSExecResult.Success;
}

Figure 18-7. *Updating the "ended" message, again*

As before, a directive is missing but Visual Studio knows what we need, the `using System.Diagnostics;` directive. Use Quick Actions to add the `using System.Diagnostics;` directive. Once added, the code appears as shown in Figure 18-8:

```
92    Stopwatch sw = new Stopwatch();
93    sw.Start();
94
95    catalogPackage.Execute(Use32bit, null, executionValueParameterSet);
96
97    sw.Stop();
98    string swMsg = String.Empty;
99    if (Synchronized)
100   {
101       swMsg = " Package Execution Time: " + sw.Elapsed.ToString();
102   }
103
104   msg = packagePath + " on " + ServerName + (Synchronized ?
105       (" completed." + swMsg.Substring(0, (swMsg.Length - 4))) :
106       (" started. Check SSIS Catalog Reports for package execution results."));
107   logMessage(componentEvents, (Synchronized ? "Information" : "Warning")
108       , 1002, TaskName, msg);
109
110
111   return DTSExecResult.Success;
112 }
```

Figure 18-8. *The updated message code, after adding the using System.*
Diagnostics; directive

Stopwatch is a member of the System.Diagnostics .Net Framework assembly that
allows developers to measure the elapsed time between two events. The Stopwatch type
variable named sw is declared and initialized on line 92. The sw Stopwatch variable is
started on line 93, just before the Execute method for the PackageInfo variable named
catalogPackage is called on line 95.

Immediately after the Execute method returns, the Stopwatch is stopped on line 97.
A string variable named swMsg is declared and initialized to an empty string on line 98.
If the package was executed with the Synchronized property set to true (line 99), the
swMsg string variable is populated with a message to inform developers and operators
of the package execution elapsed time captured by the Stopwatch variable named sw.

The string variable named msg is populated on lines 104–106 and begins with the
value of the packagePath string variable concatenated with the literal string value " on ",
followed by the value of the ServerName property.

If the `Synchronized` property set to true – meaning the code *waited* until the SSIS package execution was completed before reaching this line of code – `" completed."` and the value of the `swMsg string` variable are concatenated to the value of the `msg` variable. If the `Synchronized` property set to false – meaning the code found the SSIS package and continued (also known as "fire and forget") – `" started. Check SSIS Catalog Reports for package execution results."` is concatenated to the value of the `msg` variable.

The if-then-else functionality is controlled using the ternary conditional operator: `<expression> ? <if true> : <if false>`. The expression must evaluate to either true or false. The expression portion is simply the `Synchronized` property, which is a Boolean value. The "if true" operation of the ternary operation is (`" completed."` `+ swMsg.Substring(0, (swMsg.Length - 4)))`, which builds a message informing developers and operators of the package execution elapsed time. The `swMsg.Length - 4` code truncates the elapsed time at milliseconds. The "if false" operation of the ternary operation is (`" started. Check SSIS Catalog Reports for package execution results."))`, which builds a message informing developers and operators that the package has started executing asynchronously and that they should look elsewhere for package execution results.

A different ternary conditional operation, found on line 107, checks the value of the `Synchronized` property to determine whether to return an Information or Warning messageType.

Let's Test It!

To test, build the task solution and configure an Execute Catalog package Task with the `Synchronized` property set to False. When execution completes, view the Execution Results/Progress tab to find the newly-updated-again "ended" message, as shown in Figure 18-9:

Figure 18-9. *The new, new "ended" message*

Execute Catalog Package Task instrumentation now surfaces "start" and "ended" messages.

Set the Execute Catalog Package Task Synchronized property to true, as shown in Figure 18-10:

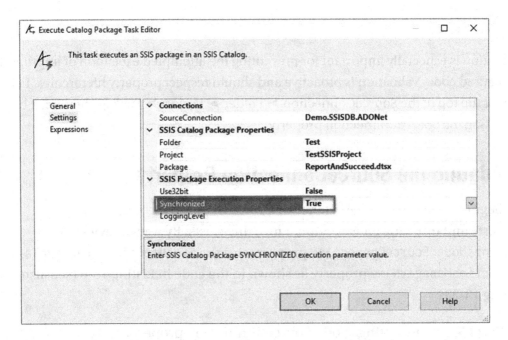

Figure 18-10. *Setting the Execute Catalog Package Task Synchronized property to true*

Execute the test SSIS package and view the Progress/Execution Results tab, shown in Figure 18-11:

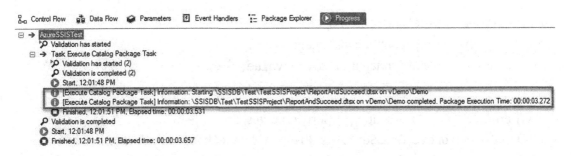

Figure 18-11. *Synchronized execution instrumentation*

Instrumentation is a great way to mitigate the total cost of ownership. Providing accurate and timely feedback to developers and operators reduces the time required to identify the root cause of a fault or failure.

Validation

Validation is especially important for preventing the attempted execution of improperly configured code. Validation is proactive and should respect property hierarchies. Let's start at the top of the SourceConnection ➤ Folder ➤ Project ➤ Package hierarchy by validating the SourceConnection property.

Validating the SourceConnection Property

We begin by testing for the existence of a value in the SourceConnection property and throwing an exception if no value exists. By way of review, the SettingsNode.SourceConnection property sets the ExecuteCatalogPackageTask. ConnectionManagerName property as shown in the code in Listing 18-6 (see also Listing 13-23):

Listing 18-6. The SettingsNode SourceConnection property

```
[
  Category("Connections"),
  Description("The SSIS Catalog connection"),
  TypeConverter(typeof(ADONetConnections))
]
public string SourceConnection {
  get { return _task.ConnectionManagerName; }
  set { _task.ConnectionManagerName = value; }
}
```

When the SourceConnection property changes, the code in SettingsView.propertyGridSettings_PropertyValueChanged updates the ExecuteCatalogPackageTask.ConnectionManagerName property using the code in Listing 18-7 (see also Listing 13-27):

Listing 18-7. Updating the ExecuteCatalogPackageTask's ServerName property

```
theTask.ServerName = returnSelectedConnectionManagerDataSourceValue(setting
sNode.SourceConnection);
```

The ExecuteCatalogPackageTask's `ConnectionManagerName` and `ServerName` properties are initialized as String.Empty as shown in Listing 18-8:

Listing 18-8. SourceConnection-related properties initialized as String.Empty

```
public string ConnectionManagerName { get; set; } = String.Empty;
.
.
.
public string ServerName { get; set; } = String.Empty;
```

The ExecuteCatalogPackageTask `Validate` method is called by the SSIS execution engine. Our validation code, therefore, belongs in the ExecuteCatalogPackageTask `Validate` method.

Begin validating the SourceConnection property by testing the `ConnectionManagerName` and `ServerName` property values for non-empty string values using the code in Listing 18-9:

Listing 18-9. Begin validating SourceConnection

```
// test for SourceConnection (ConnectionManagerName and ServerName)
existence
if((ConnectionManagerName == "") || (ServerName == ""))
{
  throw new Exception("Source Connection property is not configured.");
}
```

Once added, the `Validate()` appears as shown in Figure 18-12:

```
public override DTSExecResult Validate(
    Connections connections,
    VariableDispenser variableDispenser,
    IDTSComponentEvents componentEvents,
    IDTSLogging log)
{

    // test for SourceConnection (ConnectionManagerName and ServerName) existence
    if((ConnectionManagerName == "") || (ServerName == ""))
    {

        throw new Exception("Source Connection property is not configured.");
    }

    return DTSExecResult.Success;
}
```

Figure 18-12. *The Validate method, updated*

Build the Execute Catalog Package Task solution and test the updated version of the task by adding the Execute Catalog Package Task to a test SSIS package, as shown in Figure 18-13:

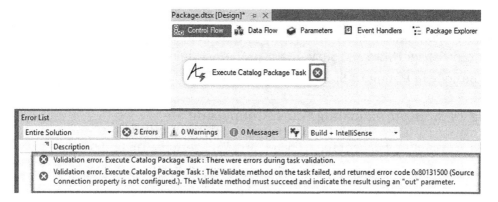

Figure 18-13. *Testing the latest version of the Execute Catalog Package Task*

Two changes are noteworthy:

1. The Execute Catalog Package Task now indicates an error state.

2. The Error List indicates two errors. The "root" error is listed second in the Error List window and reads: Validation error. Execute Catalog Package Task: The Validate method on the task failed, and returned error code 0x80131500 (Source Connection property is not configured.). The Validate method must succeed and indicate the result using an "out" parameter.

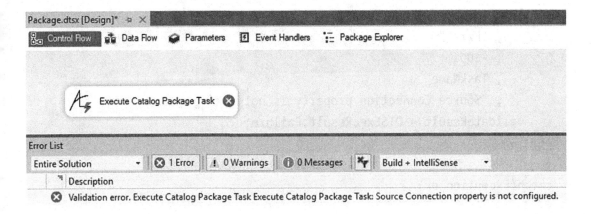

Figure 18-14. *Cleaning up validation errors*

Error-checking – and validation – code should *never* fail. Try-catch functionality elegantly manages failures in code execution. Rather than throwing exceptions in logic, we should leverage our recently added instrumentation functionality to inform developers of validation issues.

Refactor the Validate method using the code in Listing 18-10:

Listing 18-10. Refactoring Validate

```
public override DTSExecResult Validate(
          Connections connections,
          VariableDispenser variableDispenser,
          IDTSComponentEvents componentEvents,
          IDTSLogging log)
{

  // init validateResult
  DTSExecResult validateResult = DTSExecResult.Success;

  // test for SourceConnection (ConnectionManagerName and ServerName)
  existence
  try
  {
    if ((ConnectionManagerName == "") || (ServerName == ""))
    {
```

```
      logMessage(componentEvents
          , "Error"
          , -1001
          , TaskName
          , "Source Connection property is not configured.");
      validateResult = DTSExecResult.Failure;
    }
  }
  catch(Exception ex)
  {
    if(componentEvents != null)
    {
      // fire a generic error containing exception details
      logMessage(componentEvents
          , "Error"
          , -1001
          , TaskName
          , ex.Message);
    }

    // manage validateResult state
    validateResult = DTSExecResult.Failure;
  }

  return validateResult;
}
```

Once refactored, the Validate() method appears as shown in Figure 18-15:

```
59    public override DTSExecResult Validate(
60        Connections connections,
61        VariableDispenser variableDispenser,
62        IDTSComponentEvents componentEvents,
63        IDTSLogging log)
64    {
65        // init validateResult
66        DTSExecResult validateResult = DTSExecResult.Success;
67
68        // test for SourceConnection (ConnectionManagerName and ServerName) existence
69        try
70        {
71            if ((ConnectionManagerName == "") || (ServerName == ""))
72            {
73                logMessage(componentEvents
74                    , "Error"
75                    , -1001
76                    , TaskName
77                    , "Source Connection property is not configured.");
78
79                validateResult = DTSExecResult.Failure;
80            }
81        }
82        catch (Exception ex)
83        {
84            if (componentEvents != null)
85            {
86                // fire a generic error containing exception details
87                logMessage(componentEvents
88                    , "Error"
89                    , -1001
90                    , TaskName
91                    , ex.Message);
92            }
93
94            // manage validation state
95            validateResult = DTSExecResult.Failure;
96        }
97
98        return validateResult;
99    }
```

Figure 18-15. *Validate, refactored*

The refactored Validate() method declares and initializes a DTSExecResult type variable named validateResult on line 66. The validateResult variable manages validation state throughout the Validate() method – see lines 79 and 95 – and is returned from the Validate() method on line 98.

A `try` block is initiated on line 69 and covers the code on lines 71–81.

The code on line 71 tests the `ConnectionManagerName` and `ServerName` properties for non-empty string values. If non-empty string values are detected in the `ConnectionManagerName` and `ServerName` properties, the code calls the `logMessage` function which fires an error event in the SSIS package.

The `catch` block starts on line 82 and covers the code on lines 83–96.

The code on line 84 checks to make sure the `componentEvents` argument (passed to the `Validate()` method) is not null. If not null, the `logMessage` function is called to raise an error event that contains details of any *other* error raised by the code in the `try` block in the SSIS package.

Taken together, this validation design pattern checks for a specific condition, answering the question, "Is the SourceConnection property configured with values?" If the SourceConnection property is *not* configured with values, an error is raised in the SSIS package. If any other error occurs when checking to see if the SourceConnection property is configured with values, the `catch` block raises an error event configured to report the error message. If the SourceConnection property *is* configured with values and no additional error occurs when checking to see if the SourceConnection property is configured with values, the `Validate()` method returns a `Success DTSExecResult` value.

As before, build the solution and test the updated ExecuteCatalogPackageTask functionality using a test SSIS package.

Once the SourceConnection property is configured, the `Validate()` method indicates no error, as shown in Figure 18-16:

Figure 18-16. *A validated SourceConnection property*

The validation logic for the `ConnectionManagerName` and `ServerName` property values work as designed.

Building the Connection Validation Helper Function

The next step is to make sure the Execute Catalog Package Task can connect to the SSIS Catalog configured by the ConnectionManagerName and ServerName property values. Validating the connection will require several *helper* functions. Add the returnConnection and attemptConnection helper functions in Listing 18-11:

Listing 18-11. Connection validation helper functions: returnConnection and attemptConnection

```
private SqlConnection returnConnection()
{
  return (SqlConnection)Connections[ConnectionManagerId].
  AcquireConnection(null);
}
private bool attemptConnection(Connections connections
                              , int connectionManagerIndex)
{
  bool ret = false;

  try
  {
    using (System.Data.SqlClient.SqlConnection con = returnConnection())
    {
      if (con.State != System.Data.ConnectionState.Open)
      {
        con.Open();
      }
      ret = true;
    }
  }
  catch (Exception ex)
  {
    ret = false;
  }

  return ret;
}
```

To support connection manager connection string overrides, returnConnection returns a SqlConnection obtained by calling the AcquireConnection method for the Connections collection object defined using the ConnectionManagerId value. If the Connection Manager connects to an instance Azure SQL Database – which can require a username and password (SQL Login) – converting the AcquireConnection method return value to a SqlConnection may be the only way to acquire this connection.

The returnConnection method is used to set the connection used by the Execute Catalog Package Task when the attemptConnection method is called. The attemptConnection is called early in the task properties Validate process.

Once added, the `returnConnection` and `attemptConnection` helper functions appear as shown in Figure 18-17:

```
149    private SqlConnection returnConnection()
150    {
151        return (SqlConnection)Connections[ConnectionManagerId].AcquireConnection(null);
152    }
153

       0 references | Andy Leonard, 7 days ago | 1 author, 8 changes
154    private bool attemptConnection(Connections connections
155                                 , int connectionManagerIndex)
156    {
157        bool ret = false;
158
159        try
160        {
161            using (System.Data.SqlClient.SqlConnection con = returnConnection())
162            {
163                if (con.State != System.Data.ConnectionState.Open)
164                {
165                    con.Open();
166                }
167                ret = true;
168            }
169        }
170        catch (Exception ex)
171        {
172            ret = false;
173        }
174
175        return ret;
176    }
```

Figure 18-17. *The attemptConnection helper function*

The return value for the `returnConnection` method is a `SqlConnection`. The code in the `returnConnection` method is a single line, but that line of code is *busy*. Let's unpack that line of code.

An SSIS Connection Manager's `AcquireConnection` method returns a `SqlConnection` type value. It is possible to connect to an SSIS Catalog hosted in Azure SQL DB. Later in the book, we will cover more about using the Execute Catalog Package Task to execute an SSIS package deployed to an Azure Data Factory (ADF) SSIS Integration Runtime (IR), often referred to as "Azure-SSIS." Although SSIS Catalogs hosted on on-premises require Windows Authentication for interaction (deployment, execution), it's possible to interact with an SSIS Catalog hosted on Azure SQL DB using a SQL Login. Connection managers *never* surface passwords. One way – perhaps the only way – to establish a connection to Azure SQL DB using a login is to call the Connection Manager's `AcquireConnection` method.

The code on line 151 returns the connection manager's `AcquireConnection` method, to which it passes a `null` value for the `txn` (transaction) `object` argument. The connection manager is identified by the ConnectionManagerId – a unique identifier populated earlier in the response to changes in the `SourceConnection` property value detected in the `SettingsView propertyGridSettings_PropertyValueChanged` method. There are two calls to set the `ExecuteCatalogPackageTask ConnectionManagerId` property – one for when a new connection is created and one for when an existing connection manager is selected. The line of code that sets the `ConnectionManagerId` is the same for both use cases: `theTask.ConnectionManagerId = theTask.GetConnectionID(theTask.Connections, theTask.ConnectionManagerName);`. The `GetConnectionID` method is built into the `Microsoft.SqlServer.Dts.Runtime.Task` .Net Framework assembly.

The `returnConnection` method returns a `SqlConnection` type value, regardless of authentication method.

The return value for the `attemptConnection` method is a Boolean (`bool`) type variable named `ret`. The `ret` variable is declared and initialized to `false` on line 157. `ret` is set to `true` on line 167 if the code is able to open the connection on line 165 – or finds the connection already open on line 163. A try-catch block catches exceptions and sets `ret` to `false` on line 172 if an error occurs. `ret` is returned from the function on line 175.

Calling attemptConnection in the Validate Method

The next step is to add logic to the Validate method to test SourceConnection property connectivity to the SSIS Catalog by calling the attemptConnection helper function using the code in Listing 18-12:

Listing 18-12. Calling attemptConnection

```
// attempt to connect
bool connectionAttempt = attemptConnection(connections
        , ConnectionManagerIndex);
if (!connectionAttempt)
{
  logMessage(componentEvents
          , "Error"
          , -1002
          , TaskName
          , "SQL Server Instance Connection attempt failed.");
  validateResult = DTSExecResult.Failure;
}
```

Once added, the code appears as shown in Figure 18-18:

```
public override DTSExecResult Validate(
    Connections connections,
    VariableDispenser variableDispenser,
    IDTSComponentEvents componentEvents,
    IDTSLogging log)
{
    // init validateResult
    DTSExecResult validateResult = DTSExecResult.Success;

    // test for SourceConnection (ConnectionManagerName and ServerName) existence
    try
    {
        if ((ConnectionManagerName == "") || (ServerName == ""))
        {
            logMessage(componentEvents
                , "Error"
                , -1001
                , TaskName
                , "Source Connection property is not configured.");
            validateResult = DTSExecResult.Failure;

            // attempt to connect
            bool connectionAttempt = attemptConnection(connections
                , ConnectionManagerIndex);
            if (!connectionAttempt)
            {
                logMessage(componentEvents
                    , "Error"
                    , -1002
                    , TaskName
                    , "SQL Server Instance Connection attempt failed.");

                validateResult = DTSExecResult.Failure;
            }
        }
    }
    catch (Exception ex)
    {
        if (componentEvents != null)
        {
            // fire a generic error containing exception details
            logMessage(componentEvents
                , "Error"
                , -1001
                , TaskName
                , ex.Message);
        }

        // manage validateResult state
        validateResult = DTSExecResult.Failure;
    }

    return validateResult;
}
```

Figure 18-18. *Calling the attemptConnection helper function*

How I Tested the attemptConnection Validation

To test the attemptConnection helper function, build the ExecuteCatalogPackageTask solution. I provisioned a new SQL Server instance named "HadACatalog" on a virtual machine named vDemo19. I created an SSIS Catalog on the HadACatalog instance, as shown in Figure 18-19:

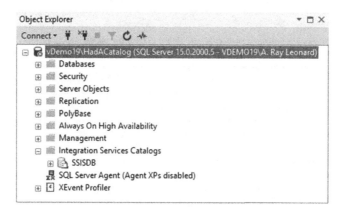

Figure 18-19. *An SSIS Catalog on vDemo19\HadACatalog*

I next configured an instance of the Execute Catalog Package Task in a test SSIS package to connect to the SSIS Catalog on the HadACatalog SQL Server instance, saved the test SSIS package, and then closed the solution, as shown in Figure 18-20:

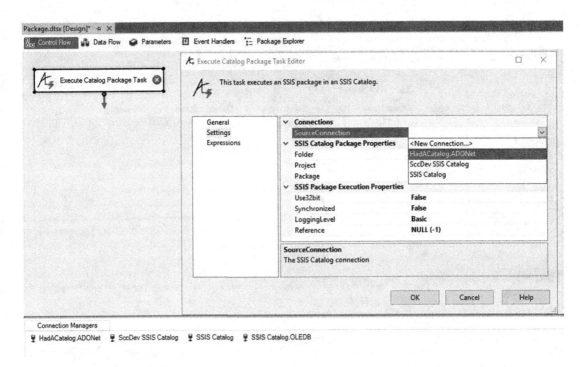

Figure 18-20. *Execute Catalog Package Task configured to use the HadACatalog instance*

I next deleted the SSIS Catalog on the HadACatalog SQL Server instance, as shown in Figure 18-21:

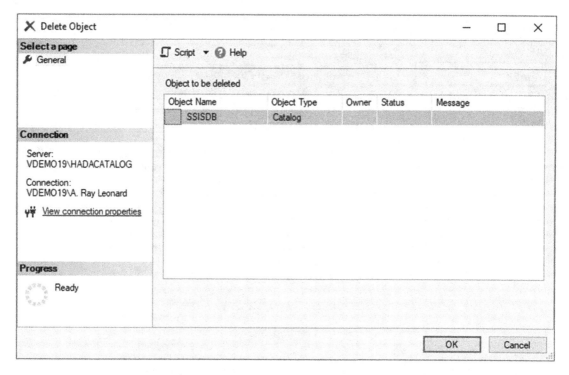

Figure 18-21. *Deleting the SSIS Catalog on the HadACatalog SQL Server instance*

When I reopened the test SSIS package (and waited for the connectivity to complete testing), the Validation error message displayed "SQL Server Instance Connection attempt failed," as shown in Figure 18-22:

Figure 18-22. *The attemptConnection validation error*

The SourceConnection property validation using the attemptConnection method is code complete.

The next step is to validate the required Folder, Project, and Package properties.

Validating Folder, Project, and Package Properties

The validation for SourceConnection represents a good design pattern for implementing validation for the Execute Catalog Package Task properties: Folder, Project, and Package.

Begin Folder property validation by adding the code in Listing 18-13:

Listing 18-13. Add Folder validation

```
// test for Folder property existence
try
{
  if (PackageFolder == "")
  {
    logMessage(componentEvents
      , "Error"
      , -1003
      , TaskName
      , "Folder property is not configured.");
    validateResult = DTSExecResult.Failure;
  }

  // attempt to retrieve folder
  CatalogFolder validateFolder = returnCatalogFolder(
      ServerName
    , PackageFolder);

  if (validateFolder == null)
  {
    logMessage(componentEvents
      , "Error"
      , -1003
      , TaskName
```

```
      , "Failed to retrieve Catalog Folder.");
    validateResult = DTSExecResult.Failure;
  }

}
catch (Exception exf)
{
  if (componentEvents != null)
  {
    // fire a generic error containing exception details
    logMessage(componentEvents
        , "Error"
        , -1003
        , TaskName
        , exf.Message);
  }

  // manage validateResult state
  validateResult = DTSExecResult.Failure;
}
```

Once added, the folder validation code appears as shown in Figure 18-23:

```
105    // test for Folder property existence
106    try
107    {
108        if (PackageFolder == "")
109        {
110            logMessage(componentEvents
111                , "Error"
112                , -1003
113                , TaskName
114                , "Folder property is not configured.");
115            validateResult = DTSExecResult.Failure;
116        }
117
118        // attempt to retrieve folder
119        CatalogFolder validateFolder = returnCatalogFolder(
120                                        ServerName
121                                        , PackageFolder);
122
123        if (validateFolder == null)
124        {
125            logMessage(componentEvents
126                , "Error"
127                , -1003
128                , TaskName
129                , "Failed to retrieve Catalog Folder.");
130            validateResult = DTSExecResult.Failure;
131        }
132    }
133    catch (Exception exf)
134    {
135        if (componentEvents != null)
136        {
137            // fire a generic error containing exception details
138            logMessage(componentEvents
139                , "Error"
140                , -1003
141                , TaskName
142                , exf.Message);
143        }
144
145        // manage validateResult state
146        validateResult = DTSExecResult.Failure;
    }
```

Figure 18-23. *Folder validation code*

The code checks for the existence of a value in the PackageFolder property on line 108. If the PackageFolder value is an empty string, the code raises an error event. On lines 119–121, the code attempts to configure a CatalogFolder object variable named validateFolder using the configured values for ServerName and PackageFolder. If the validateFolder variable cannot be configured, the validateFolder variable value will be null. The code on line 123 tests the validateFolder variable value for a null value, and if the validateFolder variable value is null, an error event is raised. Lines 133–147 catch other error conditions and raise an error event if other errors occur.

Validation for Project and Package properties follows this same pattern.

Implement Project validation using the code in Listing 18-14:

Listing 18-14. Project property validation

```
// test for Project property existence
try
{
  if (PackageProject == "")
  {
    logMessage(componentEvents
      , "Error"
      , -1004
      , TaskName
      , "Project property is not configured.");
    validateResult = DTSExecResult.Failure;
  }

  // attempt to retrieve project
  ProjectInfo validateProject = returnCatalogProject(
    ServerName
    , PackageFolder
    , PackageProject);
```

```
  if (validateProject == null)
  {
    logMessage(componentEvents
        , "Error"
        , -1004
        , TaskName
        , "Failed to retrieve Catalog Project.");
    validateResult = DTSExecResult.Failure;
  }
}
catch (Exception expr)
{
  if (componentEvents != null)
  {
    // fire a generic error containing exception details
    logMessage(componentEvents
        , "Error"
        , -1004
        , TaskName
        , expr.Message);
  }

  // manage validateResult state
  validateResult = DTSExecResult.Failure;
}
```

Once added, the project validation code appears as shown in Figure 18-24:

```
// test for Project property existence
try
{
    if (PackageProject == "")
    {
        logMessage(componentEvents
            , "Error"
            , -1004
            , TaskName
            , "Project property is not configured.");
        validateResult = DTSExecResult.Failure;
    }

    // attempt to retrieve project
    ProjectInfo validateProject = returnCatalogProject(
                                    ServerName
                                  , PackageFolder
                                  , PackageProject);

    if (validateProject == null)
    {
        logMessage(componentEvents
            , "Error"
            , -1004
            , TaskName
            , "Failed to retrieve Catalog Project.");
        validateResult = DTSExecResult.Failure;
    }

}
catch (Exception expr)
{
    if (componentEvents != null)
    {
        // fire a generic error containing exception details
        logMessage(componentEvents
            , "Error"
            , -1004
            , TaskName
            , expr.Message);
    }

    // manage validateResult state
    validateResult = DTSExecResult.Failure;
}
```

Figure 18-24. *Project validation code*

Implement Project validation using the code in Listing 18-15:

Listing 18-15. Package property validation

```
// test for Package property existence
try
{
  if (PackageName == "")
  {
    logMessage(componentEvents
        , "Error"
        , -1005
        , TaskName
        , "Package property is not configured.");
    validateResult = DTSExecResult.Failure;
  }

  // attempt to retrieve package
  Microsoft.SqlServer.Management.IntegrationServices.PackageInfo
      validatePackage = returnCatalogPackage(
          ServerName
        , PackageFolder
        , PackageProject
        , PackageName);

  if (validatePackage == null)
  {
    logMessage(componentEvents
        , "Error"
        , -1005
        , TaskName
        , "Failed to retrieve Catalog Package.");
    validateResult = DTSExecResult.Failure;
  }
}
```

```
catch (Exception expkg)
{
  if (componentEvents != null)
  {
    // fire a generic error containing exception details
    logMessage(componentEvents
        , "Error"
        , -1005
        , TaskName
        , expkg.Message);
  }

  // manage validateResult state
  validateResult = DTSExecResult.Failure;
}
```

Once added, the package validation code appears as shown in Figure 18-25:

```csharp
// test for Package property existence
try
{
    if (PackageName == "")
    {
        logMessage(componentEvents
            , "Error"
            , -1005
            , TaskName
            , "Package property is not configured.");
        validateResult = DTSExecResult.Failure;
    }

    // attempt to retrieve package
    Microsoft.SqlServer.Management.IntegrationServices.PackageInfo
        validatePackage = returnCatalogPackage(
                                    ServerName
                                  , PackageFolder
                                  , PackageProject
                                  , PackageName);

    if (validatePackage == null)
    {
        logMessage(componentEvents
            , "Error"
            , -1005
            , TaskName
            , "Failed to retrieve Catalog Package.");
        validateResult = DTSExecResult.Failure;
    }

}
catch (Exception expkg)
{
    if (componentEvents != null)
    {
        // fire a generic error containing exception details
        logMessage(componentEvents
            , "Error"
            , -1005
            , TaskName
            , expkg.Message);
    }

    // manage validateResult state
    validateResult = DTSExecResult.Failure;
}
```

Figure 18-25. *Package validation code*

The Folder, Project, and Package property validations are code complete. Build the ExecuteCatalogPackageTask solution, and then add the Execute Catalog Package Task to a test SSIS package. As the validation is currently coded, adding an Execute Catalog Package Task to a test SSIS package takes more time than before. Once validated, the Execute Catalog Package Task raises several errors, as shown in Figure 18-26:

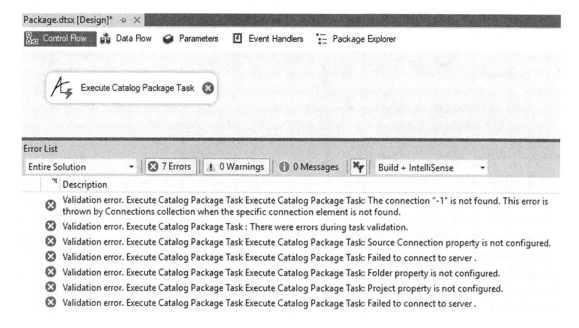

Figure 18-26. *Error raised when adding an Execute Catalog Package Task*

Because the properties being validated are hierarchical (SourceConnection ➤ Folder ➤ Project ➤ Package), it makes no sense to attempt validation of properties *lower* in the hierarchy if properties *higher* in the hierarchy are invalid. One way to correct validation behavior is to check the value of the validateResult DTSExecResult variable before validating subsequent properties by adding the conditional statement in Listing 18-16 prior to Folder, Project, and Package validation code:

Listing 18-16. Check the value of validateResult DTSExecResult variable

```
if (validateResult != DTSExecResult.Failure)
{
.
.
.
}
```

Applied to the Folder property validation, the code appears as shown in Figure 18-27:

```
if (validateResult != DTSExecResult.Failure)
{
    // test for Folder property existence
    try
    {
        if (PackageFolder == "")
        {
            logMessage(componentEvents
                , "Error"
                , -1003
                , TaskName
                , "Folder property is not configured.");
            validateResult = DTSExecResult.Failure;
        }

        // attempt to retrieve folder
        CatalogFolder validateFolder = returnCatalogFolder(
                                        ServerName
                                        , PackageFolder);

        if (validateFolder == null)
        {
            logMessage(componentEvents
                , "Error"
                , -1003
                , TaskName
                , "Failed to retrieve Catalog Folder.");
            validateResult = DTSExecResult.Failure;
        }
    }
    catch (Exception exf)
    {
        if (componentEvents != null)
        {
            // fire a generic error containing exception details
            logMessage(componentEvents
                , "Error"
                , -1003
                , TaskName
                , exf.Message);
        }

        // manage validateResult state
        validateResult = DTSExecResult.Failure;
    }
}
```

Figure 18-27. *Applying validateResult conditional to Folder property*

Checking the value of the `validateResult` variable works because each property validation sets `validateResult` to `DTSExecResult.Failure` if the property is invalid.

Build the ExecuteCatalogPackageTask solution and then add the Execute Catalog Package Task to a test SSIS package. Validation completes faster and tests only SourceConnection, as shown in Figure 18-28:

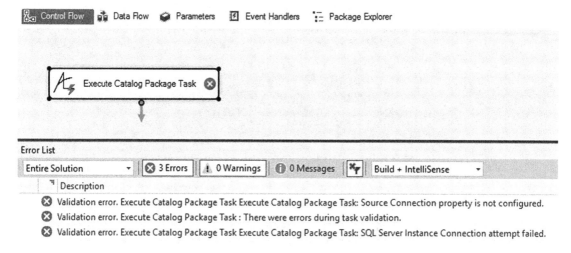

Figure 18-28. *Faster and better validation*

The validation code is complete.

Conclusion

In this chapter, we added instrumentation and validation to the ExecuteCatalogPackageTask solution.

In the next chapter, we identify and address two egregious bugs.

Now would be an excellent time to check in your code.

CHAPTER 19

Crushing Bugs

Two egregious bugs remain in the Execute Catalog Package Task code:

1. The Execute Catalog Package Task reports success, even when the SSIS package execution fails.

2. If the SSIS package executes for longer than 30 seconds, the ExecuteCatalogPackageTask.Execute returns an error message that reads "The Execute method on the task returned error code 0x80131904 (Execution Timeout Expired. The timeout period elapsed prior to completion of the operation or the server is not responding.). The Execute method must succeed, and indicate the result using an 'out' parameter."

The root cause of both bugs lies in the Execute method, so the solution is blended. Let's start with the second bug, Execution Timeout Expired.

Execution Timeout Expired

Why does the ExecuteCatalogPackageTask.Execute method time out at 30 seconds? I do not know. Just because I do not know or understand why some functionality is coded the way it is coded does *not* mean the functionality is coded incorrectly. I simply do not know why the ExecuteCatalogPackageTask.Execute method times out at 30 seconds. I *do*, however, need to work around this limitation.

The solution I found uses the WaitHandle.WaitAny method.

© Andy Leonard 2021
A. Leonard, *Building Custom Tasks for SQL Server Integration Services*,
https://doi.org/10.1007/978-1-4842-6482-9_19

Threading, Briefly

The `WaitHandle.WaitAny` method is a threading topic, which is part of the `System.Threading` .Net Framework namespace. You do not need to master threading to write most .Net applications, but the more you know, the better. Thread management is a topic to which data professionals can relate. Think database *transactions*.

A database transaction would not allow two account owners of a joint banking account to withdraw all funds from the bank account just because they execute a withdrawal request at precisely the same time. A database transaction *blocks* one withdrawal request until the other withdrawal request completes, making the second withdrawal request *wait* until the first withdrawal request completes. When the first withdrawal request completes its transaction, the database engine notifies – or *signals* – the second withdrawal request that the blocking process is complete. The second withdrawal request executes and fails because the account is empty – the first withdrawal request already removed the funds from the account while blocking the second withdrawal request.

The terms emphasized in the previous paragraph relate to both data transactions and thread safety.

An application is considered *threadsafe* if the application includes state management functionality similar database transactions. A threadsafe application manages thread safety like a database transaction maintains atomicity as a mechanism for protecting code execution and delivering accurate results.

A threadsafe application achieves atomicity by allowing some code to only execute serially while managing queues of waiting threads. Waiting threads receive signals when their turn to execute arrives. Threadsafe applications are the heart of multi-threaded functionality. Learn more at `docs.microsoft.com/en-us/dotnet/api/system.threading?view=netframework-4.7.2`.

Multi-threaded applications share *resources* – chunks of functionality which are coded for *exclusive* access, like a `WithdrawFunds()` method in a banking application. It is common for a multi-threaded application to manage more than one exclusive resource to complete execution. A `WaitHandle` manages a collection of resources executing in a related operation, and the `WaitAny` method waits for a signal to *any* member of the collection in the `WaitHandle`. Learn more about the `WaitHandle.WaitAny` method at `docs.microsoft.com/en-us/dotnet/api/system.threading.waithandle.waitany?view=netframework-4.7.2`.

A `ManualResetEvent` object is derived from the `WaitHandle` object. The state of a `ManualResetEvent` object is a Boolean value: false or true; and this state is managed by calling the `ManualResetEvent.Set()` and `ManualResetEvent.Reset()` methods. The `ManualResetEvent.Reset()` method *resets* (sets the Boolean state to *false*), *manually* blocking any additional threads that show up to use the shared resource, letting these threads know they have to wait for their turn to execute. The `ManualResetEvent.Set()` method *signals* (sets the Boolean state to *true*) waiting threads, *manually* letting waiting threads know they may now execute.

The previous two sentences are important. You may need to come back to this section as we work through the examples to come. Don't feel bad. Threading is hard. Thread safety is harder.

ExecuteCatalogPackageTask.Execute

The SSIS Catalog `Synchronized` execution parameter – A Boolean value – controls how the `ExecuteCatalogPackageTask.Execute` method returns from execution. The default `Synchronized` execution parameter value is false, which means the `ExecuteCatalogPackageTask.Execute` method functions as "fire and forget." If you start an SSIS package with the `Synchronized` execution parameter value set to false, the package starts executing, and the `ExecuteCatalogPackageTask.Execute` method returns "success" almost immediately. Because the `ExecuteCatalogPackageTask.Execute` method behaves as "fire and forget" and returns "success" almost immediately, the `ExecuteCatalogPackageTask.Execute` method's default 30-second timeout does not affect SSIS packages executed with the `Synchronized` execution parameter value set to false.

The 30-second timeout for the `ExecuteCatalogPackageTask.Execute` method is only an issue when an SSIS package is executed with the `Synchronized` execution parameter value set to true.

The implementation of the `WaitHandle.WaitAny`-based solution, then, applies only to SSIS package executions when the `Synchronized` execution parameter value set to true.

Designing a Test SSIS Package

To test 30-second timeout errors for the ExecuteCatalogPackageTask.Execute method, add a new test SSIS package named RunForSomeTime.dtsx to a test SSIS project, as shown in Figure 19-1:

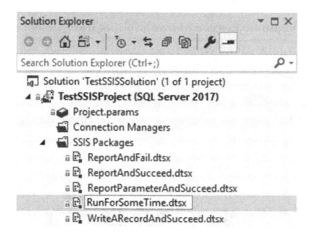

Figure 19-1. *Adding the RunForSomeTime.dtsx test SSIS package*

Add a package parameter named DelayString of the String data type as shown in Figure 19-2:

Figure 19-2. *Adding the DelayString package parameter*

Add an SSIS variable named WaitForQuery of the String data type. Set the value of the WaitForQuery using the T-SQL statement shown in Listing 19-1:

Listing 19-1. Adding the WaitForQuery SSIS variable value

```
WaitFor Delay '00:00:30'
```

Once the T-SQL statement is added to the variable value, the WaitForQuery variable appears as shown in Figure 19-3:

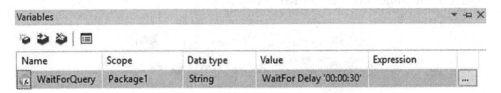

Figure 19-3. *Adding the WaitForQuery SSIS variable*

Click the ellipsis beside the Expression textbox to open the Expression Builder dialog, and then enter the SSIS Expression Language statement in Listing 19-2 in the Expression textbox:

Listing 19-2. the WaitForQuery SSIS variable expression

```
"WaitFor Delay '" + @[$Package::DelayString]  + "'"
```

When added, the WaitForQuery SSIS variable expression appears as shown in Figure 19-4:

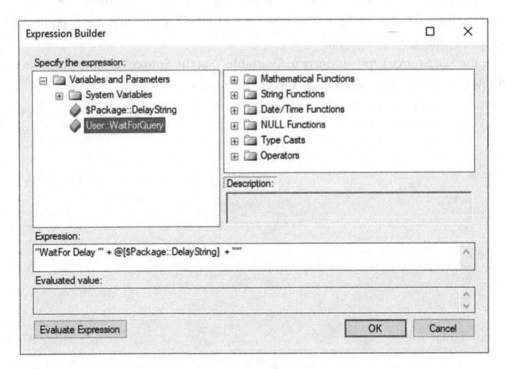

Figure 19-4. *The WaitForQuery SSIS variable expression*

Click the OK button to close the Expression Builder dialog.

Add an Execute SQL Task to RunForSomeTime.dtsx and rename the execute SQL task "SQL Run for some time," as shown in Figure 19-5:

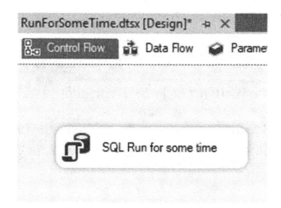

Figure 19-5. *Adding the SQL Run for some time Execute SQL Task*

Open the SQL Run for some time execute SQL task editor and set the ConnectionType to ADO.NET. Click the Connection dropdown and click "<New connection...>." Configure an ADO.Net connection manager to *any* database – this package will not use the configured connection, but the Execute SQL Task requires a connection manager configured.

Set the SQLSourceType property to "Variable." Set the SourceVariable property to the User::WaitForQery SSIS variable, as shown in Figure 19-6:

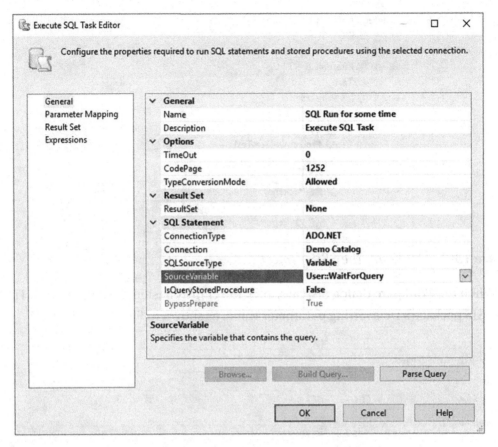

Figure 19-6. *Configuring SQL Run for some time execute SQL task*

Click the OK button to close the execute SQL task editor, and then deploy the SSIS project to an SSIS Catalog.

Next, open SSMS and connect to the SSIS Catalog to which you deployed the SSIS project. Navigate to the SSIS project in the SSMS Object Explorer Integration Services Catalogs node, right-click the project, and then click Configure, as shown in Figure 19-7:

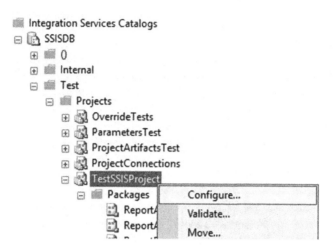

Figure 19-7. Configure the SSIS project

When the Configure dialog displays, click the ellipsis beside the RunForSomeTime.
dtsx SSIS package's DelayString parameter value, as shown in Figure 19-8:

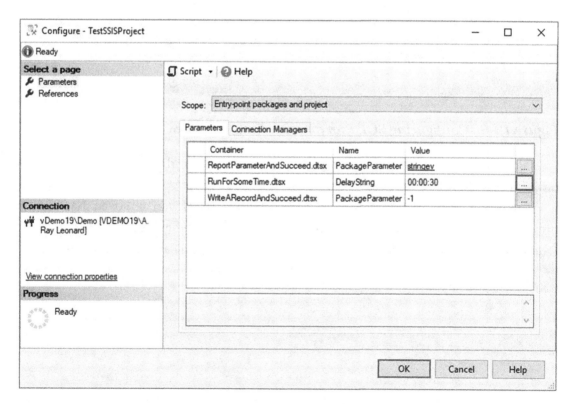

*Figure 19-8. Preparing to override the RunForSomeTime.dtsx SSIS package
DelayString parameter*

Configure a literal override of the RunForSomeTime.dtsx SSIS package DelayString parameter by clicking the "Edit value" option and entering "00:00:45" in the literal override textbox, as shown in Figure 19-9:

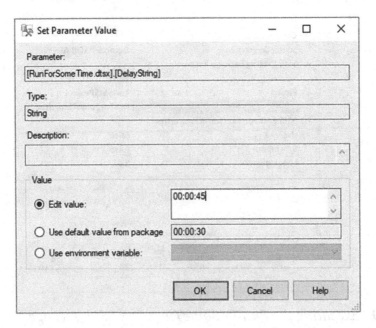

Figure 19-9. *Configure a literal override of the RunForSomeTime.dtsx SSIS package DelayString parameter*

Click the OK button to save the literal override.

Open a test SSIS package, add an Execute Catalog Package Task, and configure the Execute Catalog Package Task to execute the RunForSomeTime.dtsx SSIS package. Be sure to leave the Synchronized property set to false, as shown in Figure 19-10:

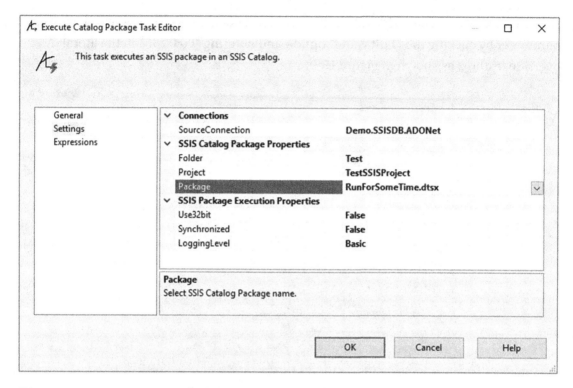

Figure 19-10. *Executing the RunForSomeTime.dtsx SSIS package*

Execute the test SSIS package and review the Progress tab when execution completes (and succeeds, if all goes as planned), as shown in Figure 19-11:

Figure 19-11. *Reviewing the Progress tab*

Note the Execute Catalog Package Task reports finished after less than one second.

Open the SSIS Catalog Reports All Executions report in SSMS, as shown in Figure 19-12:

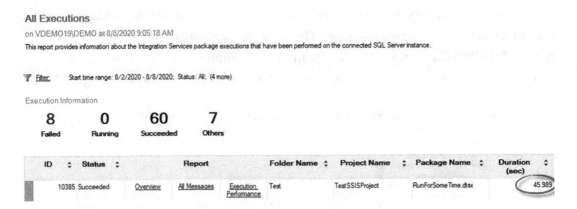

All Executions

on VDEMO19\DEMO at 8/8/2020 9:05:18 AM

This report provides information about the Integration Services package executions that have been performed on the connected SQL Server instance.

▼ Filter: Start time range: 8/2/2020 - 8/8/2020; Status: All; (4 more)

Execution Information

8	0	60	7
Failed	**Running**	**Succeeded**	**Others**

ID ⇕	Status ⇕	Report			Folder Name ⇕	Project Name ⇕	Package Name ⇕	Duration (sec) ⇕
10385	Succeeded	Overview	All Messages	Execution Performance	Test	TestSSISProject	RunForSomeTime.dtsx	45.989

Figure 19-12. *Viewing the All Executions SSIS Catalog report*

Note the RunForSomeTime.dtsx SSIS package executed for just over 45 seconds, which is how it was configured earlier.

Return to the test SSIS package's Execute Catalog Package Task editor, and set the Synchronized property to True, as shown in Figure 19-13:

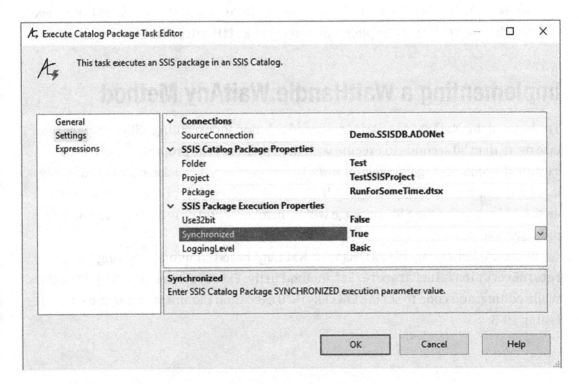

Figure 19-13. *Setting the Synchronized property to true*

Execute the test SSIS package. After 30 seconds, note the test SSIS package execution fails with the error message "The Execute method on the task returned error code 0x80131904 (Execution Timeout Expired. The timeout period elapsed prior to completion of the operation or the server is not responding.)," as shown in Figure 19-14:

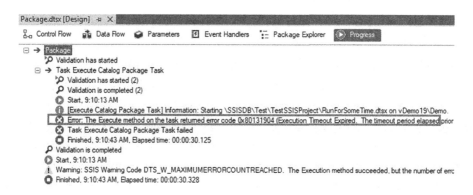

Figure 19-14. *Execution timeout at 30 seconds*

This is the behavior we wish to overcome. The RunForSomeTime.dtsx SSIS package may now be used to test the implementation of the WaitHandle.WaitAny-based solution.

Implementing a WaitHandle.WaitAny Method

The heart of this WaitHandle.WaitAny-based solution for executing SSIS packages that take more than 30 seconds to execute with the Synchronized property set to true is to execute the SSIS package *asynchronously*. Executing the SSIS package asynchronously is, well, executing the SSIS package as if the Synchronized property set to *false*, so this method of executing the SSIS package will be invoked if and only if the Synchronized property is set to *true*.

Begin implementing this WaitHandle.WaitAny-based solution by editing the returnExecutionValueParameterSet method in the ExecuteCatalogPackageTask class. While editing, add code to set the CALLER_INFO execution parameter using the code in Listing 19-3:

Listing 19-3. Editing the returnExecutionValueParameterSet method in ExecuteCatalogPackageTask

```
private Collection<Microsoft.SqlServer.Management.IntegrationServices.
PackageInfo.ExecutionValueParameterSet> returnExecutionValueParameterSet()
{

 // initialize the parameters collection
  Collection<Microsoft.SqlServer.Management.IntegrationServices.
  PackageInfo.ExecutionValueParameterSet> executionValueParameterSet =
  new Collection<Microsoft.SqlServer.Management.IntegrationServices.
  PackageInfo.ExecutionValueParameterSet>();

  // set SYNCHRONIZED execution parameter
  executionValueParameterSet.Add(new Microsoft.SqlServer.Management.
  IntegrationServices.PackageInfo.ExecutionValueParameterSet
  {
    ObjectType = 50,
    ParameterName = "SYNCHRONIZED",
    ParameterValue = false // always execute with the Synchronized
                                  property false
  });

  // set LOGGING_LEVEL execution parameter
  int LoggingLevelValue = decodeLoggingLevel(LoggingLevel);
  executionValueParameterSet.Add(new Microsoft.SqlServer.Management.
  IntegrationServices.PackageInfo.ExecutionValueParameterSet
  {
    ObjectType = 50,
    ParameterName = "LOGGING_LEVEL",
    ParameterValue = LoggingLevelValue
  });

  // set CALLER_INFO execution parameter
  string machineName = Environment.MachineName.Replace('"', '\'').
  Replace("\\", "//");
  string userName = Environment.UserName;
```

```
executionValueParameterSet.Add(new Microsoft.SqlServer.Management.
IntegrationServices.PackageInfo.ExecutionValueParameterSet
{
  ObjectType = 50,
  ParameterName = "CALLER_INFO",
  ParameterValue = machineName + "\\" + userName
});
return executionValueParameterSet;
}
```

Once edited, the returnExecutionValueParameterSet method appears as shown in Figure 19-15:

```
private Collection<Microsoft.SqlServer.Management.IntegrationServices.PackageInfo.ExecutionValueParameterSet> returnExecutionValueParameterSet()
{
    // initialize the parameters collection
    Collection<Microsoft.SqlServer.Management.IntegrationServices.PackageInfo.ExecutionValueParameterSet> executionValueParameterSet =
        new Collection<Microsoft.SqlServer.Management.IntegrationServices.PackageInfo.ExecutionValueParameterSet>();

    // set SYNCHRONIZED execution parameter
    executionValueParameterSet.Add(
        new Microsoft.SqlServer.Management.IntegrationServices.PackageInfo.ExecutionValueParameterSet
        {
            ObjectType = 50,
            ParameterName = "SYNCHRONIZED",
            ParameterValue = false // always execute with the Synchronized property false
        });

    // set LOGGING_LEVEL execution parameter
    int LoggingLevelValue = decodeLoggingLevel(LoggingLevel);
    executionValueParameterSet.Add(
        new Microsoft.SqlServer.Management.IntegrationServices.PackageInfo.ExecutionValueParameterSet
        {
            ObjectType = 50,
            ParameterName = "LOGGING_LEVEL",
            ParameterValue = LoggingLevelValue
        });

    // set CALLER_INFO execution parameter
    string machineName = Environment.MachineName.Replace('"', '\'').Replace("\\", "//");
    string userName = Environment.UserName;
    executionValueParameterSet.Add(
        new Microsoft.SqlServer.Management.IntegrationServices.PackageInfo.ExecutionValueParameterSet
        {
            ObjectType = 50,
            ParameterName = "CALLER_INFO",
            ParameterValue = machineName + "\\" + userName
        });
    return executionValueParameterSet;
}
```

Figure 19-15. *Editing the returnExecutionValueParameterSet method*

Continue implementing this WaitHandle.WaitAny-based solution by editing the ExecuteCatalogPackageTask.Execute method catalogPackage.Execute call by editing the call to catalogPackage.Execute, adding the code in Listing 19-4:

Listing 19-4. Checking for execution configured for Synchronized execution

```
long executionId = catalogPackage.Execute(Use32bit
                                  , null
                                  , executionValueParameterSet);
if (Synchronized)
{
  ManualResetEvent manualResetState = new ManualResetEvent(false);
}
```

When added, the code appears as shown in Figure 19-16:

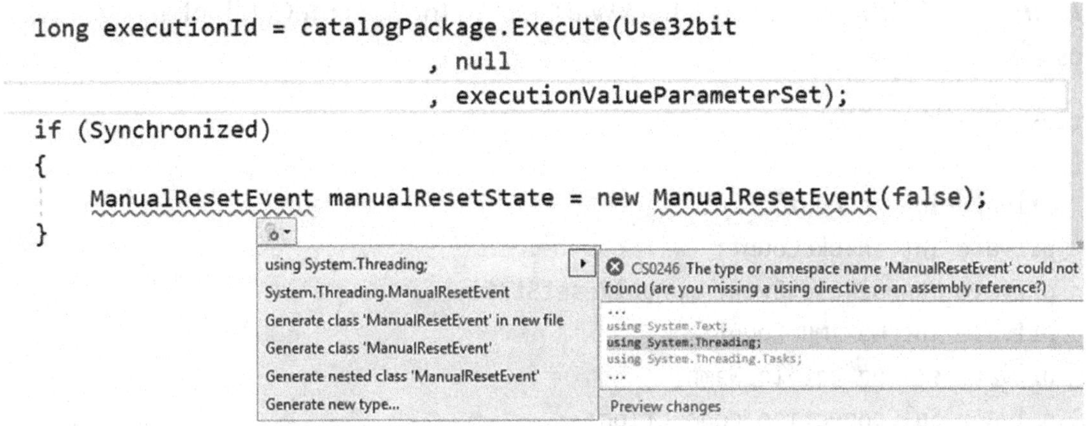

Figure 19-16. *Implementing the WaitHandle.WaitAny-based solution*

Use Visual Studio Quick Actions to add the using System.Threading; directive by hovering over the ManualResetEvent type declaration, clicking the Quick Actions dropdown, and then clicking the using System.Threading; directive. After the using System.Threading; directive is added, the code appears as shown in Figure 19-17:

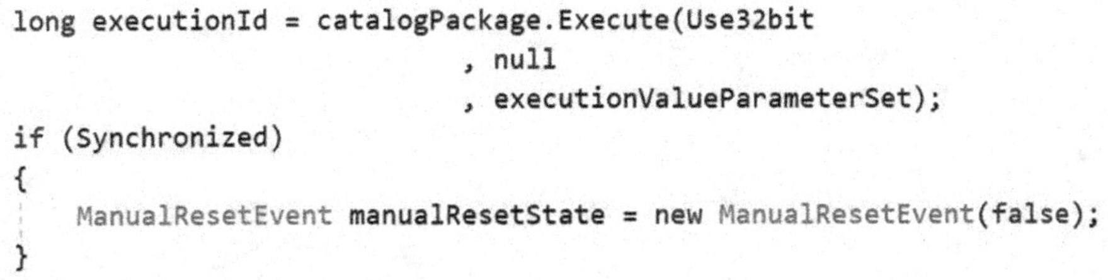

Figure 19-17. *Error cleared after adding the directive*

413

If the package execution is *not* configured for Synchronized execution, the code executes the package as before. If the package execution *is* configured for Synchronized execution, a ManualResetEvent named manualResetState is declared, and the state of manualResetState is initialized as false. Remember, a ManualResetEvent set to false begins *waiting* (blocking) any other threads that show up to use the shared resource assigned to the ManualResetEvent.

The next step is to configure the Timer, which *ticks* based on interval configuration. When the timer ticks, the timer will call a method named CheckStatus in a class named CheckWaitState. Add the CheckWaitState class to the ExecuteCatalogPackageTask.cs file and declare private members using the code in Listing 19-5:

Listing 19-5. Implementing CheckWaitState in the ExecuteCatalogPackageTask. cs file

```
class CheckWaitState
{
  private long executionId;
  private int invokeCount;
  private ManualResetEvent manualResetState;
  private int maximumCount;
  private string catalogName;
  private SqlConnection connection;
  private ExecuteCatalogPackageTask task;
  public Operation.ServerOperationStatus OperationStatus { get; set; }
}
```

Once the code is added, it appears as shown in Figure 19-18:

```
class CheckWaitState
{
    private long executionId;
    private int invokeCount;
    private ManualResetEvent manualResetState;
    private int maximumCount;
    private string catalogName;
    private SqlConnection connection;
    private ExecuteCatalogPackageTask task;
    0 references | Andy Leonard, 8 days ago | 1 author, 4 changes
    public Operation.ServerOperationStatus OperationStatus { get; set; }
}
```

Figure 19-18. *Implementing the CheckWaitState class*

Implement the CheckWaitState constructor using the code in Listing 19-6:

Listing 19-6. Implementing the CheckWaitState constructor

```
public CheckWaitState(long executionId
    , int maxCount
    , SqlConnection connection
    , string catalogName
    , ExecuteCatalogPackageTask task)
{
  this.executionId = executionId;
  this.invokeCount = 0;
  this.maximumCount = maxCount;
  this.connection = connection;
  this.catalogName = catalogName;
  this.task = task;
}
```

Once the constructor is implemented, the CheckWaitState class appears as shown in Figure 19-19:

```
class CheckWaitState
{
    private long executionId;
    private int invokeCount;
    private ManualResetEvent manualResetState;
    private int maximumCount;
    private string catalogName;
    private SqlConnection connection;
    private ExecuteCatalogPackageTask task;
    0 references | Andy Leonard, 8 days ago | 1 author, 4 changes
    public Operation.ServerOperationStatus OperationStatus { get; set; }


    0 references | Andy Leonard, 8 days ago | 1 author, 2 changes
    public CheckWaitState(long executionId
                        , int maxCount
                        , SqlConnection connection
                        , string catalogName
                        , ExecuteCatalogPackageTask task)
    {
        this.executionId = executionId;
        this.invokeCount = 0;
        this.maximumCount = maxCount;
        this.connection = connection;
        this.catalogName = catalogName;
        this.task = task;
    }
}
```

Figure 19-19. *The CheckWaitState class with the constructor implemented*

Implement the CheckTimerState class using the code in Listing 19-7:

Listing 19-7. Implementing the TimerCheckerState class

```
class TimerCheckerState
{
  public ManualResetEvent manualResetState { get; private set; }

  public TimerCheckerState(ManualResetEvent manualResetState)
  {
    this.manualResetState = manualResetState;
  }
}
```

Once added, the code appears as shown in Figure 19-20:

```
class TimerCheckerState
{
    2 references
    public ManualResetEvent manualResetState { get; private set; }

    1 reference
    public TimerCheckerState(ManualResetEvent manualResetState)
    {
        this.manualResetState = manualResetState;
    }
}
```

Figure 19-20. *The TimerCheckerState class*

The next step is to implement a helper function named returnOperationStatus in the CheckWaitState class using the code in Listing 19-8:

Listing 19-8. Coding the CheckWaitState.returnOperationStatus helper function

```
public Operation.ServerOperationStatus returnOperationStatus()
{
  CatalogCollection catalogCollection = new
  IntegrationServices(connection).Catalogs;
  Catalog catalog = catalogCollection[catalogName];
  OperationCollection operationCollection = catalog.Operations;
  Operation operation = operationCollection[executionId];
  Operation.ServerOperationStatus operationStatus = operation.Status;

  return operationStatus;
}
```

Once added to the CheckWaitState class, the returnOperationStatus helper function appears as shown in Figure 19-21:

```
public Operation.ServerOperationStatus returnOperationStatus()
{
    CatalogCollection catalogCollection = new IntegrationServices(connection).Catalogs;
    Catalog catalog = catalogCollection[catalogName];
    OperationCollection operationCollection = catalog.Operations;
    Operation operation = operationCollection[executionId];
    Operation.ServerOperationStatus operationStatus = operation.Status;

    return operationStatus;
}
```

Figure 19-21. *The CheckWaitState.returnOperationStatus helper function*

The returnOperationStatus method first connects to the CatalogCollection type named catalogCollection. A Catalog type named catalog is derived from the catalogCollection by the catalogName property (defaulted to "SSISDB").

An OperationCollection type named operationCollection is assigned from the catalog.Operations type collection. An Operation type named operation is read from the operationCollection[executionId]. The operationStatus variable, a variable of the Operation.ServerOperationStatus type, is read from the operation.Status property.

The next step is to code the checkOperationStatus method to the CheckWaitState class to respond to the ServerOperationStatus of the SSIS package execution using the code in Listing 19-9:

Listing 19-9. Add the CheckWaitState.CheckOperationStatus method

```
public void checkOperationStatus(Operation.ServerOperationStatus
operationStatus)
{
  // check for package execution "finished" states
  if (
      (operationStatus == Operation.ServerOperationStatus.Canceled)
   || (operationStatus == Operation.ServerOperationStatus.Completion)
   || (operationStatus == Operation.ServerOperationStatus.Failed)
   || (operationStatus == Operation.ServerOperationStatus.Stopping)
   || (operationStatus == Operation.ServerOperationStatus.Success)
   || (operationStatus == Operation.ServerOperationStatus.UnexpectTerminated)
      )
```

```
{
    // reset counter
    invokeCount = 0;
    // signal thread
    manualResetState.Set();
  }
}
```

Once added, the code appears as shown in Figure 19-22:

```
public void checkOperationStatus(Operation.ServerOperationStatus operationStatus)
{
    // check for package execution "finished" states
    if (
            (operationStatus == Operation.ServerOperationStatus.Canceled)
        || (operationStatus == Operation.ServerOperationStatus.Completion)
        || (operationStatus == Operation.ServerOperationStatus.Failed)
        || (operationStatus == Operation.ServerOperationStatus.Stopping)
        || (operationStatus == Operation.ServerOperationStatus.Success)
        || (operationStatus == Operation.ServerOperationStatus.UnexpectTerminated)
      )
    {
        // reset counter
        invokeCount = 0;
        // signal thread
        manualResetState.Set();
    }
}
```

Figure 19-22. *Adding the CheckWaitState.CheckOperationStatus method*

The checkOperationStatus method receives an Operation.ServerOperationStatus type argument named operationStatus. An if conditional checks to see if the operationStatus argument value is in a "finished" operational state. "Finished" operation states include

- Canceled

- Completion

- Failed

- Stopping

- Success

- UnexpectTerminated

If the operationStatus argument value is in a "finished" operational state, the timer tick counter named invokeCount is reset to 0, and the ManualResetEvent type property named manualResetState is Set. As stated earlier: The ManualResetEvent.Set() method *signals* (sets the Boolean state to *true*) waiting threads, *manually* letting waiting threads know they may now execute.

Refactoring logMessage to raiseEvent

Return to the ExecuteCatalogPackageTask class and refactor the logMessage method, starting with the name of the method. The logMessage method doesn't actually log a message. Instead, the logMessage method raises an event. Refactor the logMessage method by renaming it to raiseEvent and replacing it with the code in Listing 19-10:

Listing 19-10. Refactoring the logMessage method to the raiseEvent method

```
public void raiseEvent(string messageType
                     , int messageCode
                     , string subComponent
                     , string message)
{
  bool fireAgain = true;
  switch (messageType)
  {
    default:
      break;
    case "Information":
      componentEvents.FireInformation(messageCode, subComponent, message,
      "", 0, ref fireAgain);
      break;
    case "Warning":
      componentEvents.FireWarning(messageCode, subComponent, message, "", 0);
      break;
```

```
  case "Error":
    componentEvents.FireError(messageCode, subComponent, message, "", 0);
    break;
  }
}
```

Once replaced, the code appears as shown in Figure 19-23:

```
public void raiseEvent(
      string messageType
    , int messageCode
    , string subComponent
    , string message)
{
    bool fireAgain = true;
    switch (messageType)
    {
        default:
            break;
        case "Information":
            componentEvents.FireInformation(messageCode, subComponent, message, ""
                , 0, ref fireAgain);
            break;
        case "Warning":
            componentEvents.FireWarning(messageCode, subComponent, message, "", 0);
            break;
        case "Error":
            componentEvents.FireError(messageCode, subComponent, message, "", 0);
            break;
    }
}
```

Figure 19-23. *Replacing the logMessage method with the raiseEvent method*

The componentEvents property introduces an error, denoted by the red squiggly line beneath the property name. In the logMessage method, componentEvents was passed as an argument. The short version of a longer story is: Until now, every method from which we called the logMessage method had access to componentEvents, which was passed to those methods by the Task object.

In the next section, we want to raise event messages from methods *outside* the Task object, methods that are not part of the ExecuteCatalogPackageTask Task object class; we want to raise event messages from the CheckWaitState class.

The renaming of the `logMessage` method to `raiseEvent` triggers a refactoring effort, and the refactoring effort appears out of order. The reason the refactoring effort appears out of order is because it *is*, in fact, out of order. Refactoring isn't always orderly. Welcome to software development.

A major difference between the `logMessage` method and the `raiseEvent` method is the number of arguments. The `logMessage` method had five arguments: componentEvents, messageType, messageCode, subComponent, and message. The `raiseEvent` method has four arguments: messageType, messageCode, subComponent, and message. The four shared arguments have the same type in both methods. The componentEvents argument in the `logMessage` method is missing from the `raiseEvent` method.

Our first step in refactoring is addressing the componentEvents argument, and we do that by adding a `componentEvents` property to the `ExecuteCatalogPackageTask` class using the code in Listing 19-11:

Listing 19-11. Add the componentEvents property to the ExecuteCatalogPackageTask class

```
private IDTSComponentEvents componentEvents { get; set; } = null;
```

Once added, the new componentEvents property appears as shown in Figure 19-24:

```
    private IDTSComponentEvents componentEvents { get; set; } = null;
```

Figure 19-24. *Adding the ExecuteCatalogPackageTask.componentEvents property*

Once the componentEvents property is added to the `ExecuteCatalogPackageTask` class, earlier errors are cleared in the raiseEvent method, as shown in Figure 19-25 (compare to Figure 19-23):

```
public void raiseEvent(
      string messageType
    , int messageCode
    , string subComponent
    , string message)
{
    bool fireAgain = true;
    switch (messageType)
    {
        default:
            break;
        case "Information":
            componentEvents.FireInformation(messageCode, subComponent, message, ""
                , 0, ref fireAgain);
            break;
        case "Warning":
            componentEvents.FireWarning(messageCode, subComponent, message, "", 0);
            break;
        case "Error":
            componentEvents.FireError(messageCode, subComponent, message, "", 0);
            break;
    }
}
```

Figure 19-25. *Errors cleared*

Initialize the componentEvents property in the ExecuteCatalogPackageTask.
Validate method using the code in Listing 19-12:

Listing 19-12. Initialize the componentEvents property in the ExecuteCatalogPa
ckageTask.Validate method

```
// initialize componentEvents
this.componentEvents = componentEvents;
```

Once added, the code appears as shown in Figure 19-26:

423

```
public override DTSExecResult Validate(
    Connections connections,
    VariableDispenser variableDispenser,
    IDTSComponentEvents componentEvents,
    IDTSLogging log)
{
    // initialize componentEvents
    this.componentEvents = componentEvents;
```

Figure 19-26. *Initializing the componentEvents property value in the ExecuteCata logPackageTask.Validate method*

According to the Error List (in my project, at least), 19 errors remain. Most errors display the same message: "The name 'logMessage' does not exist in the current context," as shown in Figure 19-27:

Error List		
Entire Solution ▾	⊗ 19 Errors	⚠ 1 Warning	ⓘ 0 of 24 Messages

	Code	Description
⊗	CS0103	The name 'logMessage' does not exist in the current context
⊗	CS0103	The name 'logMessage' does not exist in the current context

Figure 19-27. *19 errors*

The next step is to update each call to the raiseEvent method, and there are several in the ExecuteCatalogPackageTask.Validate method. Edit the logMessage method call by replacing the name "logMessage" with "raiseEvent," as shown in Figure 19-28:

```
// test for SourceConnection (ConnectionManagerName and ServerName) existence
try
{
    if ((ConnectionManagerName == "") || (ServerName == ""))
    {
        raiseEvent(componentEvents
            , "Error"
            , -1001
            , TaskName
            , "Source Connection property is not configured.");
        validateResult = DTSExecResult.Failure;
```

Figure 19-28. *Replacing "logMessage" with "raiseEvent"*

Next, delete the first argument (componentEvents) and the first comma, as shown in Figure 19-29:

```
// test for SourceConnection (ConnectionManagerName and ServerName) existence
try
{
    if ((ConnectionManagerName == "") || (ServerName == ""))
    {
        raiseEvent("Error"
            , -1001
            , TaskName
            , "Source Connection property is not configured.");
        validateResult = DTSExecResult.Failure;
```

Figure 19-29. *Removing the first argument*

According to the Error List, only 18 more errors remain to resolve (your error count may vary) – shown in Figure 19-30:

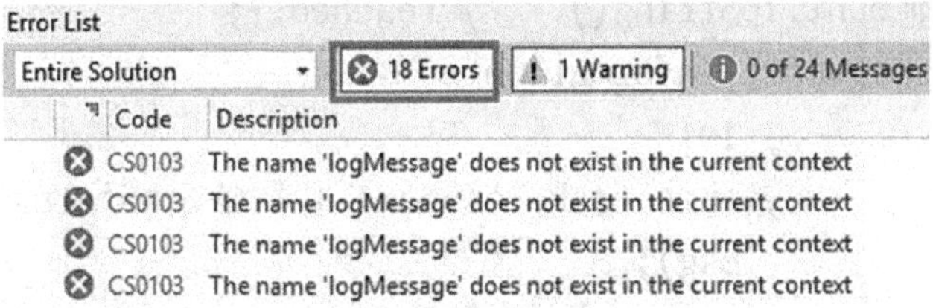

Figure 19-30. *18 errors remain*

Repeat the rename of "logMessage" to "raiseEvent," and the removal of the first argument, in each of the remaining 18 calls (your error count may vary) with the error message "The name 'logMessage' does not exist in the current context".

The next step is to implement the CheckWaitState.CheckStatus method, which is the method called when the timer ticks (which will be implemented soon) using the code in Listing 19-13:

Listing 19-13. Implementing the CheckWaitState.CheckStatus method

```
public void CheckStatus(object state)
{
  TimerCheckerState localState = ((TimerCheckerState)state);
  this.manualResetState = localState.manualResetState;
```

```
// increment the counter
invokeCount++;

// log this tick
string msg = "Asynchronous Execution Retry Count: " + invokeCount.
ToString() + " (Maximum Retry Count: " + maximumCount.ToString() + ")";

this.task.raiseEvent("Information"
                    , 101
                    , this.task.TaskName + ".CheckStatus"
                    , msg);

// check for package execution reached max count
if (invokeCount == maximumCount)
{
  // log maximumCount reached
  msg = "Asynchronous Execution Maximum Retry Count ("
      + maximumCount.ToString() + ") reached.";
  this.task.raiseEvent("Information"
                    , 101
                    , this.task.TaskName + ".CheckStatus"
                    , msg);

  // set OperationStatus
  OperationStatus = Operation.ServerOperationStatus.Canceled;

  // reset counter
  invokeCount = 0;

  // signal thread
  manualResetState.Set();
}
else
{
  OperationStatus = returnOperationStatus();

  checkOperationStatus(OperationStatus);
}
}
```

Once added, the code appears as shown in Figure 19-31:

```
576   public void CheckStatus(object state)
577   {
578       TimerCheckerState localState = ((TimerCheckerState)state);
579       this.manualResetState = localState.manualResetState;
580
581       // increment the counter
582       invokeCount++;
583
584       // log this tick
585       string msg = "Asynchronous Execution Retry Count: " + invokeCount.ToString()
586               + " (Maximum Retry Count: " + maximumCount.ToString() + ")";
587
588       this.task.raiseEvent("Information"
589                           , 101
590                           , this.task.TaskName + ".CheckStatus"
591                           , msg);
592
593       // check for package execution reached max count
594       if (invokeCount == maximumCount)
595       {
596           // log maximumCount reached
597           msg = "Asynchronous Execution Maximum Retry Count ("
598               + maximumCount.ToString() + ") reached.";
599           this.task.raiseEvent("Information"
600                           , 101
601                           , this.task.TaskName + ".CheckStatus"
602                           , msg);
603
604           // set OperationStatus
605           OperationStatus = Operation.ServerOperationStatus.Canceled;
606
607           // reset counter
608           invokeCount = 0;
609
610           // signal thread
611           manualResetState.Set();
612       }
613       else
614       {
615           OperationStatus = returnOperationStatus();
616
617           checkOperationStatus(OperationStatus);
618       }
619   }
```

Figure 19-31. *The CheckWaitState.CheckStatus method, implemented*

With each tick of the timer (the timer code will be implemented next), the CheckWaitState.CheckStatus method is called. Perhaps the most important part of this code is found on lines 578–579. On line 578, a variable of the TimerCheckerState class named localState is declared and initialized with the value of the state object argument, converted to a TimerCheckerState type. The value of the CheckWaitState.manualResetState variable of the ManualResetEvent type is next set to the localState.manualResetState on line 579. On line 582, a variable named invokeCount, which tracks the number of times the CheckWaitState.CheckStatus method has been called by the timer, is incremented.

On lines 584–591, a message is generated and an event raised. The message variable – named msg – includes the values of the invokeCount and maximumCount variables on lines 585–586. The ExecuteCatalogPackageTask.raiseEvent method is called, passing the msg variable, to raise an event message in the SSIS package.

On lines 594–618, the value of the invokeCount variable value is checked to see if invokeCount variable value has reached the value of the maximumCount variable. If the invokeCount has reached the value of the maximumCount variable, the msg variable value is configured to send a message indicating the maximumCount variable value has been reached on lines 597–598, an event is raised on lines 599–602, and the CheckWaitState.OperationStatus property value is set to Operation.ServerOperationStatus.Canceled on line 605. The invokeCount variable value is reset to 0 on line 608, and the manualResetState calls its Set() method on line 611. The manualResetState.Set() call on line 611 notifies waiting threads, informing them that the current thread has completed the current thread's exclusive operation, which lets the next waiting thread know it may now execute.

If the invokeCount has not reached the value of the maximumCount variable, the CheckWaitState.OperationStatus property value is set by calling the CheckWaitState.returnOperationStatus method (see Listing 19-8 and Figure 19-21). The CheckWaitState.checkOperationStatus method (see Listing 19-9 and Figure 19-22) is next called to determine if the current Operation Status has reached a "finished" state on line 617. As discussed earlier, if the CheckWaitState.checkOperationStatus method determines the SSIS package execution has reached a "finished" state, the execution is stopped.

Refactoring the Execute Method

Returning to the ExecuteCatalogPackageTask.Execute method, the code is getting...
busy. It's time for more refactoring. Begin by migrating the ManualResetEvent
declaration and initialization code in Listing 19-4 to a new helper function named
executeSynchronous using the code in Listing 19-14:

Listing 19-14. Coding the executeSynchronous helper function in the
ExecuteCatalogPackageTask

```
private Operation.ServerOperationStatus executeSynchronous(long executionId
                              , SqlConnection connection)
{
  Operation.ServerOperationStatus ret = Operation.ServerOperationStatus.
  UnexpectTerminated;
  ManualResetEvent manualResetState = new ManualResetEvent(false);
  return ret;
}
```

Once added, the ExecuteCatalogPackageTask.executeSynchronous helper function
appears as shown in Figure 19-32:

```
private Operation.ServerOperationStatus executeSynchronous(long executionId
                                        , SqlConnection connection)
{
    Operation.ServerOperationStatus ret = Operation.ServerOperationStatus.UnexpectTerminated;
    ManualResetEvent manualResetState = new ManualResetEvent(false);
    return ret;
}
```

Figure 19-32. *The ExecuteCatalogPackageTask.executeSynchronous helper
function*

The code in the ExecuteCatalogPackageTask.executeSynchronous
helper function begins with the declaration and initialization of an Operation.
ServerOperationStatus type variable named ret, which is initialized to the Operation.
ServerOperationStatus.UnexpectTerminated value. A ManualResetEvent type variable
named manualResetState is declared and initialized as a new ManualResetEvent set to
false.

The ExecuteCatalogPackageTask.executeSynchronous helper function is declared to return an Operation.ServerOperationStatus type value, and the ret variable is returned to satisfy the declaration.

Build out the ExecuteCatalogPackageTask.executeSynchronous helper function, adding the code in Listing 19-15 after the ManualResetEvent declaration and before the return ret; statement:

Listing 19-15. Completing ExecuteCatalogPackageTask.executeSynchronous

```
int maximumRetries = 20;
int retryIntervalSeconds = 10;
int operationTimeoutMinutes = 10;

CheckWaitState statusChecker = new CheckWaitState(executionId
                                          , maximumRetries
                                          , connection
                                          , PackageCatalogName
                                          , this);
TimeSpan dueTime = new TimeSpan(0, 0, 0);
TimeSpan period = new TimeSpan(0, 0, retryIntervalSeconds);

object timerState = new TimerCheckerState(manualResetState);
TimerCallback timerCallback = statusChecker.CheckStatus;
Timer timer = new Timer(timerCallback, timerState, dueTime, period);

WaitHandle[] manualResetStateWaitHandleCollection = new WaitHandle[]
            { manualResetState };
int timeoutMillseconds = (int)new TimeSpan(0, operationTimeoutMinutes
                                          , 0).TotalMilliseconds;
bool exitContext = false;

// wait here, please
WaitHandle.WaitAny(manualResetStateWaitHandleCollection
                , timeoutMillseconds
                , exitContext);

ret = statusChecker.OperationStatus;
manualResetState.Dispose();
timer.Dispose();
```

Once added, the ExecuteCatalogPackageTask.executeSynchronous helper function appears as shown in Figure 19-33:

```
449   private Operation.ServerOperationStatus executeSynchronous(long executionId
450                                             , SqlConnection connection)
451   {
452       Operation.ServerOperationStatus ret = Operation.ServerOperationStatus.UnexpectTerminated;
453       ManualResetEvent manualResetState = new ManualResetEvent(false);
454
455       int maximumRetries = 20;
456       int retryIntervalSeconds = 10;
457       int operationTimeoutMinutes = 10;
458
459       CheckWaitState statusChecker = new CheckWaitState(executionId
460                                             , maximumRetries
461                                             , connection
462                                             , PackageCatalogName
463                                             , this);
464       TimeSpan dueTime = new TimeSpan(0, 0, 0);
465       TimeSpan period = new TimeSpan(0, 0, retryIntervalSeconds);
466
467       object timerState = new TimerCheckerState(manualResetState);
468       TimerCallback timerCallback = statusChecker.CheckStatus;
469       Timer timer = new Timer(timerCallback, timerState, dueTime, period);
470
471       WaitHandle[] manualResetStateWaitHandleCollection = new WaitHandle[]
472        { manualResetState };
473       int timeoutMillseconds = (int)new TimeSpan(0, operationTimeoutMinutes, 0).TotalMilliseconds;
474       bool exitContext = false;
475
476       // wait here, please
477       WaitHandle.WaitAny(manualResetStateWaitHandleCollection
478                       , timeoutMillseconds
479                       , exitContext);
480
481       ret = statusChecker.OperationStatus;
482
483       manualResetState.Dispose();
484       timer.Dispose();
485
486       return ret;
487   }
```

Figure 19-33. *The ExecuteCatalogPackageTask.executeSynchronous helper function, code complete*

Implementing this WaitHandle.WaitAny-based solution requires a ManualResetEvent to check the status of the executing package. Each time the Timer *ticks* (configured on line 469), the Timer calls the method named CheckStatus in the CheckWaitState class (see Listing 19-13 and Figure 19-31) – configured as the

TimerCallback type variable named timerCallback on line 468 – that checks the status of the SSIS package execution. Timer ticks are configured to also pass three additional variables:

- timerState: A TimerCheckerState variable initialized with the manualResetState (ManualResetEvent type) variable on line 467

- dueTime: A TimeSpan variable initialized to "right now" (TimeSpan(0, 0, 0);) on line 464

- period: A TimeSpan variable initialized on line 465 to the number of seconds in the retryIntervalSeconds int variable (initialized as 10 seconds on line 456)

A WaitHandle collection named manualResetStateWaitHandleCollection is declared and initialized to the collection of WaitHandles in manualResetState variable on lines 471–472. An int type variable named timeoutMilliseconds is declared and initialized to the number of milliseconds in the operationTimeoutMinutes int type variable (declared and initialized on line 457) – on line 473. A bool type variable named exitContext is declared and initialized to false on line 474.

On lines 477–479, WaitHandle.WaitAny is called passing the value of the manualResetStateWaitHandleCollection, timeoutMilliseconds, and exitContext variables. It is here that the package execution thread starts *waiting* (blocking) any additional calls to the ExecuteCatalogPackageTask.executeSynchronous helper function.

In *synchronous* execution, the CheckWaitState.CheckStatus method is called with each timer tick until the ManualResetEvent variable named manualResetState is manually reset. The manual reset occurs when one of two conditions is met:

1. The operationStatus variable in the CheckWaitState.CheckStatus method indicates a "finished" state for the SSIS package execution.

2. The number of retries (captured by the invokeCount variable in the CheckWaitState.CheckStatus method) reaches the maximumRetries variable value.

The first case occurs when the CheckWaitState.CheckStatus method indicates the number of retries (invokeCount) has *not* reached the maximumRetries variable value, and a call to the CheckWaitState.returnOperationStatus method returns the SSIS package execution OperationStatus of a "finished" state. The SSIS package execution OperationStatus is evaluated by the CheckWaitState.checkOperationStatus method. If the SSIS package execution OperationStatus is found to be in a "finished" state, execution is halted by setting the CheckWaitState.manualResetState variable value to true.

The second case occurs when the CheckWaitState.CheckStatus method indicates the number of retries (invokeCount) *has* reached the maximumRetries variable value.

In *asynchronous* SSIS package execution, there is no call to the CheckWaitState. CheckStatus method. The ExecuteCatalogPackageTask.evaluateStatus method – which we build next – supports both synchronous and asynchronous SSIS package executions.

The next step is to check the operationStatus variable in the CheckWaitState. CheckStatus method for a "finished" state by refactoring SSIS package execution, using the code in Listing 19-16 to build the evaluateStatus helper method:

Listing 19-16. Adding the ExecuteCatalogPackageTask.evaluateStatus helper method

```
private DTSExecResult evaluateStatus(Operation.ServerOperationStatus os
                              , string packagePath
                              , string elapsed)
{
  DTSExecResult ret = DTSExecResult.Success;
  string msg = String.Empty;
  string swMsg = String.Empty;

  if (Synchronized)
  {
    swMsg = " Package Execution Time: " + elapsed;
  }

  switch (os)
  {
    default:
      break;
```

```
case Operation.ServerOperationStatus.Success:
  msg = packagePath + " on " + ServerName + (Synchronized ?
      (" succeeded." + swMsg.Substring(0, (swMsg.Length - 4))) :
      (" started. Check SSIS Catalog Reports for package execution
      results."));
  raiseEvent((Synchronized ? "Information" : "Warning")
    , 1099, TaskName, msg);
  ret = DTSExecResult.Success;
  break;
case Operation.ServerOperationStatus.Created:
case Operation.ServerOperationStatus.Pending:
case Operation.ServerOperationStatus.Running:
  msg = packagePath + " on " + ServerName + (Synchronized ?
      (" " + os.ToString().ToLower() + "." + swMsg.Substring(0,
      (swMsg.Length - 4))) :
      (" started. Check SSIS Catalog Reports for package execution
      results."));
  raiseEvent((Synchronized ? "Information" : "Warning")
    , 1099, TaskName, msg);
  ret = DTSExecResult.Success;
  break;
case Operation.ServerOperationStatus.Failed:
  msg = packagePath + " on " + ServerName + (Synchronized ?
      (" failed." + swMsg.Substring(0, (swMsg.Length - 4))) :
      (" started. Check SSIS Catalog Reports for package execution
      results."));
  raiseEvent("Error", -1099, TaskName, msg);
  ret = DTSExecResult.Failure;
  break;
case Operation.ServerOperationStatus.UnexpectTerminated:
  msg = packagePath + " on " + ServerName + (Synchronized ?
      (" terminated unexpectedly." + swMsg.Substring(0, (swMsg.
      Length - 4))) :
      (" started. Check SSIS Catalog Reports for package execution
      results."));
```

```
        raiseEvent("Error", -1099, TaskName, msg);
        ret = DTSExecResult.Failure;
        break;
    case Operation.ServerOperationStatus.Canceled:
        msg = packagePath + " on " + ServerName + (Synchronized ?
            (" was canceled." + swMsg.Substring(0, (swMsg.Length - 4))) :
            (" started. Check SSIS Catalog Reports for package execution
            results."));
        raiseEvent("Error", -1099, TaskName, msg);
        ret = DTSExecResult.Failure;
        break;
    }

    return ret;
}
```

Once added, the ExecuteCatalogPackageTask.evaluateStatus method appears as shown in Figure 19-34:

```
307    private DTSExecResult evaluateStatus(Operation.ServerOperationStatus os
308                             , string packagePath
309                             , string elapsed)
310    {
311        DTSExecResult ret = DTSExecResult.Success;
312        string msg = String.Empty;
313        string swMsg = String.Empty;
314
315        if (Synchronized)
316        {
317            swMsg = " Package Execution Time: " + elapsed;
318        }
319
320        switch (os)
321        {
322            default:
323                break;
324            case Operation.ServerOperationStatus.Success:
325                msg = packagePath + " on " + ServerName + (Synchronized ?
326                    (" succeeded." + swMsg.Substring(0, (swMsg.Length - 4))) :
327                    (" started. Check SSIS Catalog Reports for package execution results."));
328                raiseEvent((Synchronized ? "Information" : "Warning"), 1099, TaskName, msg);
329                ret = DTSExecResult.Success;
330                break;
331            case Operation.ServerOperationStatus.Created:
332            case Operation.ServerOperationStatus.Pending:
333            case Operation.ServerOperationStatus.Running:
334                msg = packagePath + " on " + ServerName + (Synchronized ?
335                    (" " + os.ToString().ToLower() + "." + swMsg.Substring(0, (swMsg.Length - 4)))
336                    (" started. Check SSIS Catalog Reports for package execution results."));
337                raiseEvent((Synchronized ? "Information" : "Warning"), 1099, TaskName, msg);
338                ret = DTSExecResult.Success;
339                break;
340            case Operation.ServerOperationStatus.Failed:
341                msg = packagePath + " on " + ServerName + (Synchronized ?
342                    (" failed." + swMsg.Substring(0, (swMsg.Length - 4))) :
343                    (" started. Check SSIS Catalog Reports for package execution results."));
344                raiseEvent("Error", -1099, TaskName, msg);
345                ret = DTSExecResult.Failure;
346                break;
347            case Operation.ServerOperationStatus.UnexpectTerminated:
348                msg = packagePath + " on " + ServerName + (Synchronized ?
349                    (" terminated unexpectedly." + swMsg.Substring(0, (swMsg.Length - 4))) :
350                    (" started. Check SSIS Catalog Reports for package execution results."));
351                raiseEvent("Error", -1099, TaskName, msg);
352                ret = DTSExecResult.Failure;
353                break;
354            case Operation.ServerOperationStatus.Canceled:
355                msg = packagePath + " on " + ServerName + (Synchronized ?
356                    (" was canceled." + swMsg.Substring(0, (swMsg.Length - 4))) :
357                    (" started. Check SSIS Catalog Reports for package execution results."));
358                raiseEvent("Error", -1099, TaskName, msg);
359                ret = DTSExecResult.Failure;
360                break;
361        }
362
363        return ret;
364    }
```

Figure 19-34. The ExecuteCatalogPackageTask.evaluateStatus method

The `ExecuteCatalogPackageTask.evaluateStatus` method receives three arguments:

- `Os`: An `Operation.ServerOperationStatus` type argument containing the current operation status of the executing package

- `packagePath`: A `string` type argument that contains the SSIS Catalog path to the executing package

- `elapsed`: A `string` type argument that represents the execution time of the SSIS package

The `evaluateStatus` method begins on line 311 with the declaration and initialization of the `DTSExecResult` variable named `ret`, which is initialized to `DTSExecResult.Success`. A `string` variable named `msg` is declared and initialized to `String.Empty` on line 312, and another `string` variable named `swMsg` is declared and initialized to `String.Empty` on line 313.

If the `ExecuteCatalogPackageTask.Synchronized` property is set to true (checked on 315), `swMsg` is set to `" Package Execution Time: " + elapsed;`.

A `switch` statement, based on the value of the `os` argument, spans lines 320–361. Cases for several `Operation.ServerOperationStatus` values are used to decide `msg` variable values, call the `raiseEvent` method, and set the `ret` variable value. The `ret` variable value is returned from the `evaluateStatus` method.

If the SSIS package is executing synchronously and the `CheckWaitState` retry count (`invokeCount`) reaches the `maximumCount` value, the `CheckWaitState.OperationStatus` property is set to `Operation.ServerOperationStatus.Canceled` (see Listing 19-13 and Figure 19-31). Setting the value of the `CheckWaitState.OperationStatus` property has no effect on the execution of the SSIS package. Our code must respond to the `CheckWaitState.OperationStatus` property value set to `Operation.ServerOperationStatus.Canceled`.

The next step is to implement a helper function to stop package execution using the code in Listing 19-17:

Listing 19-17. Add the ExecuteCatalogPackageTask.stopExecution helper function

```
private void stopExecution(long executionId
                      , SqlConnection connection)
{
  CatalogCollection catalogCollection = new
  IntegrationServices(connection).Catalogs;
  Catalog catalog = catalogCollection[PackageCatalogName];
  ExecutionOperationCollection executionCollection = catalog.Executions;
  ExecutionOperation executionOperation = executionCollection[executionId];
  executionOperation.Stop();
}
```

Once added, the code appears as shown in Figure 19-35:

```
private void stopExecution(long executionId
                      , SqlConnection connection)
{
    CatalogCollection catalogCollection = new IntegrationServices(connection).Catalogs;
    Catalog catalog = catalogCollection[PackageCatalogName];
    ExecutionOperationCollection executionCollection = catalog.Executions;
    ExecutionOperation executionOperation = executionCollection[executionId];
    executionOperation.Stop();
}
```

Figure 19-35. *Adding the ExecuteCatalogPackageTask.stopExecution helper function*

Once we refactor the ExecuteCatalogPackageTask.Execute method, we will need to ascertain the operation status of asynchronous SSIS package executions. To determine the operation status of asynchronous SSIS package execution, use the code in Listing 19-18 to build a slightly different version of the returnOperationStatus method for the ExecuteCatalogPackageTask class:

Listing 19-18. The ExecuteCatalogPackageTask.returnOperationStatus method

```
private Operation.ServerOperationStatus returnOperationStatus(
                                        SqlConnection connection
                                      , long executionId)
{
```

```
CatalogCollection catalogCollection = new
IntegrationServices(connection).Catalogs;
Catalog catalog = catalogCollection[PackageCatalogName];
OperationCollection operationCollection = catalog.Operations;
Operation operation = operationCollection[executionId];
Operation.ServerOperationStatus operationStatus = (Operation.
ServerOperationStatus)operation.Status;
return operationStatus;
}
```

Once added, the code appears as shown in Figure 19-36:

```
private Operation.ServerOperationStatus returnOperationStatus(SqlConnection connection
                                                     , long executionId)
{
    CatalogCollection catalogCollection = new IntegrationServices(connection).Catalogs;
    Catalog catalog = catalogCollection[PackageCatalogName];
    OperationCollection operationCollection = catalog.Operations;
    Operation operation = operationCollection[executionId];
    Operation.ServerOperationStatus operationStatus = (Operation.ServerOperationStatus)operation.Status;

    return operationStatus;
}
```

Figure 19-36. *A copy of the CheckWaitState.returnOperationStatus helper method implemented in the ExecuteCatalogPackageTask class*

The CheckWaitState.returnOperationStatus method is called only when the SSIS package is executing synchronously. The ExecuteCatalogPackageTask. returnOperationStatus method is needed to determine the operation status of the executing SSIS package when the package is executing asynchronously.

Continue refactoring the ExecuteCatalogPackageTask.Execute by building the ExecuteCatalogPackage helper function using the code in Listing 19-19:

Listing 19-19. Coding the ExecuteCatalogPackage helper function

```
private DTSExecResult ExecuteCatalogPackage()
{
  DTSExecResult executionResult;

  ConnectionManagerIndex = returnConnectionManagerIndex(Connections
                                        , ConnectionManagerName);
```

```
catalogProject = returnCatalogProject(ServerName
                                    , PackageFolder
                                    , PackageProject);
catalogPackage = returnCatalogPackage(ServerName
                                    , PackageFolder
                                    , PackageProject
                                    , PackageName);
Collection<Microsoft.SqlServer.Management.IntegrationServices.
PackageInfo.ExecutionValueParameterSet>
executionValueParameterSet = returnExecutionValueParameterSet();
string packagePath = "\\SSISDB\\" + PackageFolder + "\\"
                    + PackageProject + "\\"
                    + PackageName;
string msg = "Starting " + packagePath + " on " + ServerName + ".";
raiseEvent("Information", 1001, TaskName, msg);

Stopwatch sw = new Stopwatch();
sw.Start();

long executionId = catalogPackage.Execute(Use32bit
                                        , null
                                        , executionValueParameterSet);

SqlConnection connection = returnConnection();

Operation.ServerOperationStatus operationStatus;

if (Synchronized)
{
  operationStatus = executeSynchronous(executionId
                                    , connection);

  if (operationStatus == Operation.ServerOperationStatus.Canceled)
  {
    stopExecution(executionId
              , connection);
  }
  sw.Stop();
}
```

```
else
{
  sw.Stop();
  operationStatus = returnOperationStatus(connection
                                  , executionId);
}

executionResult = evaluateStatus(operationStatus
                          , packagePath
                          , sw.Elapsed.ToString());

return executionResult;
}
```

Once added, the ExecuteCatalogPackage helper function code appears as shown in Figure 19-37:

```
307    private DTSExecResult ExecuteCatalogPackage()
308    {
309        DTSExecResult executionResult;
310
311        ConnectionManagerIndex = returnConnectionManagerIndex(Connections, ConnectionManagerName);
312
313        catalogProject = returnCatalogProject(ServerName, PackageFolder, PackageProject);
314        catalogPackage = returnCatalogPackage(ServerName, PackageFolder, PackageProject, PackageName);
315
316        Collection<Microsoft.SqlServer.Management.IntegrationServices.PackageInfo.ExecutionValueParameterSet>
317            executionValueParameterSet = returnExecutionValueParameterSet();
318
319        string packagePath = "\\SSISDB\\" + PackageFolder + "\\"
320                           + PackageProject + "\\"
321                           + PackageName;
322        string msg = "Starting " + packagePath + " on " + ServerName + ".";
323        raiseEvent("Information", 1001, TaskName, msg);
324
325        Stopwatch sw = new Stopwatch();
326        sw.Start();
327
328        long executionId = catalogPackage.Execute(Use32bit
329                                            , null
330                                            , executionValueParameterSet);
331
332        SqlConnection connection = returnConnection();
333
334        Operation.ServerOperationStatus operationStatus;
335
336        if (Synchronized)
337        {
338            operationStatus = executeSynchronous(executionId
339                                            , connection);
340
341            if (operationStatus == Operation.ServerOperationStatus.Canceled)
342            {
343                stopExecution(executionId
344                            , connection);
345            }
346            sw.Stop();
347        }
348        else
349        {
350            sw.Stop();
351            operationStatus = returnOperationStatus(connection, executionId);
352        }
353
354        executionResult = evaluateStatus(operationStatus
355                                    , packagePath
356                                    , sw.Elapsed.ToString());
357
358        return executionResult;
359    }
```

Figure 19-37. *The ExecuteCatalogPackage helper function*

The ExecuteCatalogPackage helper function is essentially the code that was previously found in the ExecuteCatalogPackageTask.Execute method. The ExecuteCatalogPackage helper function returns a DTSExecResult type and begins by declaring the variable executionResult of the DTSExecResult type on line 309. The ExecuteCatalogPackageTask.ConnectionManagerIndex property value is set by a call to the returnConnectionManagerIndex function on line 311. The values of two ExecuteCatalogPackageTask internal properties – catalogProject and catalogPackage – are set on lines 313–314 by calling returnCatalogProject and returnCatalogPackage, respectively.

On lines 316–317, the executionValueParameterSet variable (of the Collection<Microsoft.SqlServer.Management.IntegrationServices.PackageInfo. ExecutionValueParameterSet> type) is populated by calling the helper function named returnExecutionValueParameterSet.

On lines 319–321, the packagePath (string) variable is declared and initialized to SSIS Catalog package path value in the format \SSISDB\<*Catalog Folder*>\<*SSIS Project*>\<*SSIS Package*>. The packagePath variable is then used in the msg (string) variable on line 322, and the msg variable is used to raise an SSIS package event in the call to the raiseEvent method on line 323.

A new Stopwatch type variable – named sw – is declared and initialized on line 325 and then started on line 326.

The SSIS package execution starts on lines 328–330. The result of the call to catalogPackage.Execute is captured by a long type variable named executionId.

On line 332, a SqlConnection variable named connection is declared and initialized by the returnConnection helper function. The operationStatus variable, of Operation. ServerOperationStatus type, is declared on line 334.

If the Synchronized property is set to true on line 336, the executeSynchronous helper function is called on lines 338–339, and the results are captured by the operationStatus variable. If the operationStatus variable value is Operation. ServerOperationStatus.Canceled on line 341, the stopExecution method is called and passed executionId and connection arguments on lines 343–344. The Stopwatch sw is stopped on line 346.

If the Synchronized property is set to false on line 336, the Stopwatch sw is stopped on line 350, and the operationStatus variable value is set by a call to the ExecuteCatalogPackageTask.returnOperationStatus method.

On lines 354–356, the executionResult variable value is set by calling the evaluateStatus method, and the ExecuteCatalogPackage helper function returns the value of the evaluateStatus helper function to the calling function on line 358.

Once coded, the ExecuteCatalogPackage helper function is called by the ExecuteCatalogPackageTask.Execute method using the code in Listing 19-20:

Listing 19-20. The ExecuteCatalogPackageTask.Execute method, refactored

```
public override DTSExecResult Execute(
          Connections connections,
          VariableDispenser variableDispenser,
          IDTSComponentEvents componentEvents,
          IDTSLogging log,
          object transaction)
{
  return ExecuteCatalogPackage();
}
```

Once edited, the ExecuteCatalogPackageTask.Execute method appears as shown in Figure 19-38:

```
public override DTSExecResult Execute(
    Connections connections,
    VariableDispenser variableDispenser,
    IDTSComponentEvents componentEvents,
    IDTSLogging log,
    object transaction)
{

    return ExecuteCatalogPackage();
}
```

Figure 19-38. The ExecuteCatalogPackageTask.Execute method, refactored

Build the ExecuteCatalogPackageTask solution. The next step is to test the code.

Let's Test It!

Open a test SSIS package and add an Execute Catalog Package Task to the Control
Flow. Open the Execute Catalog Package Task editor and configure the Execute Catalog
Package Task to execute the RunForSomeTime.dtsx SSIS package. Configure the
Synchronized property to True, as shown in Figure 19-39:

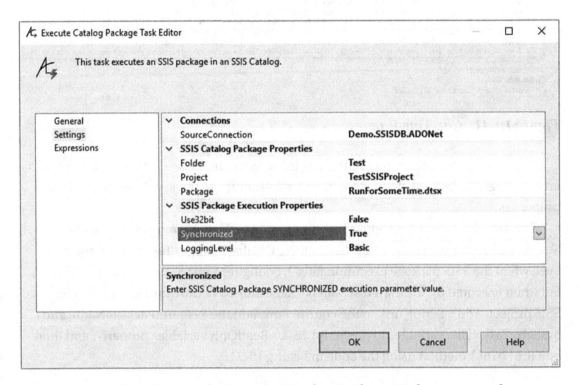

Figure 19-39. *Configuring the Execute Catalog Package Task to execute the*
RunForSomeTime.dtsx SSIS package

Execute the test SSIS package in the debugger. If all goes as planned, the test SSIS
package execution should succeed, as shown in Figure 19-40:

Figure 19-40. *Successful test*

Click the Progress tab to make sure the desired event messages were raised, as shown in Figure 19-41:

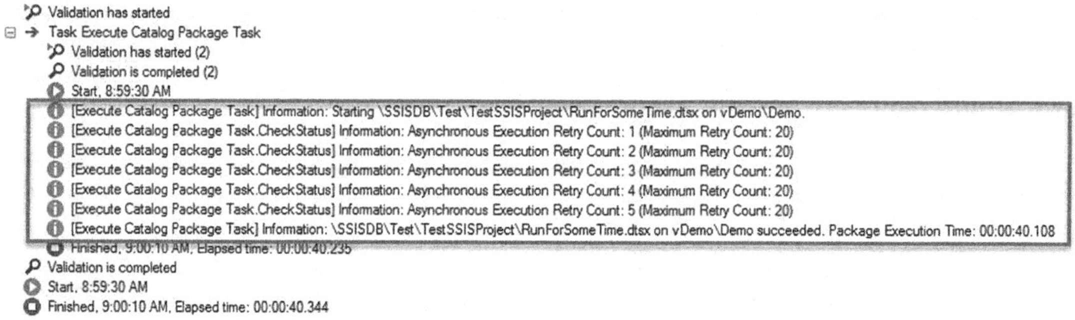

Figure 19-41. *Checking Progress*

The code is instrumented to return a start message, messages for each "tick," and an end message. In the next chapter, we add more flexibility to the synchronous execution properties.

This satisfies the first egregious bug mentioned at the beginning of this chapter. To test the second egregious bug ("the Execute Catalog Package Task reports success, even when the SSIS package execution fails"), configure a test SSIS package to always fail when executed by adding a test SSIS package named ReportAndFail.dtsx to a test SSIS project. Add a Script Task to the control flow, add the System::PackageName and System::TaskName variables to the Script Task's ReadOnlyVariables property, and then edit the Main() method using the code in Listing 19-21:

Listing 19-21. The ReportAndFail.dtsx Script Task Main() method code

```
public void Main()
{
  string packageName = Dts.Variables["System::PackageName"].Value.ToString();
  string taskName = Dts.Variables["System::TaskName"].Value.ToString();
  string subComponent = packageName + "." + taskName;
  int informationCode = 1001;
  bool fireAgain = true;
  string msg = "I am " + packageName;
```

```
Dts.Events.FireInformation(informationCode, subComponent, msg, "", 0,
ref fireAgain);
msg = "The package is intended to fail for test purposes.";
Dts.Events.FireError(informationCode, subComponent, msg, "", 0);

Dts.TaskResult = (int)ScriptResults.Success;
}
```

Once added, the Script Task's Main() method code appears as shown in Figure 19-42:

```
public void Main()
{
    string packageName = Dts.Variables["System::PackageName"].Value.ToString();
    string taskName = Dts.Variables["System::TaskName"].Value.ToString();
    string subComponent = packageName + "." + taskName;
    int informationCode = 1001;
    bool fireAgain = true;

    string msg = "I am " + packageName;

    Dts.Events.FireInformation(informationCode, subComponent, msg, "", 0, ref fireAgain);
    msg = "The package is intended to fail for test purposes.";
    Dts.Events.FireError(informationCode, subComponent, msg, "", 0);

    Dts.TaskResult = (int)ScriptResults.Success;
}
```

Figure 19-42. *The ReportAndFail.dtsx SSIS package Script Task Main() method code*

The Main() method in the Script Task raises two events: an Information event and an Error event. The Information event supplies the message "I am ReportAndFail". Raising the Error event fails the SSIS package execution and surfaces the message, "The package is intended to fail for test purposes."

Deploy the ReportAndFail.dtsx package to a test SSIS Catalog instance. Open a test SSIS package and add an Execute Catalog Package Task configured to execute the freshly deployed ReportAndFail.dtsx SSIS package, as shown in Figure 19-43:

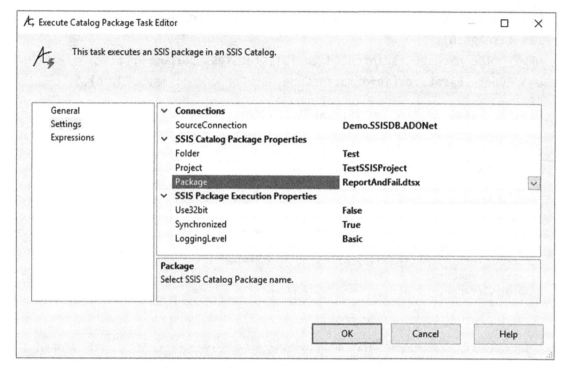

Figure 19-43. Configured to execute ReportAndFail.dtsx

Be sure to set the Synchronized property to True, or the ReportAndFail.dtsx SSIS package execution will start in the SSIS Catalog and then return "success" to the test SSIS package.

When the ReportAndFail.dtsx execution completes, the Execute Catalog Package Task should report failure on the Control Flow, as shown in Figure 19-44:

Figure 19-44. Failed execution, successful test

The Progress tab should indicate the ReportAndFail.dtsx SSIS package execution failed, as shown in Figure 19-45:

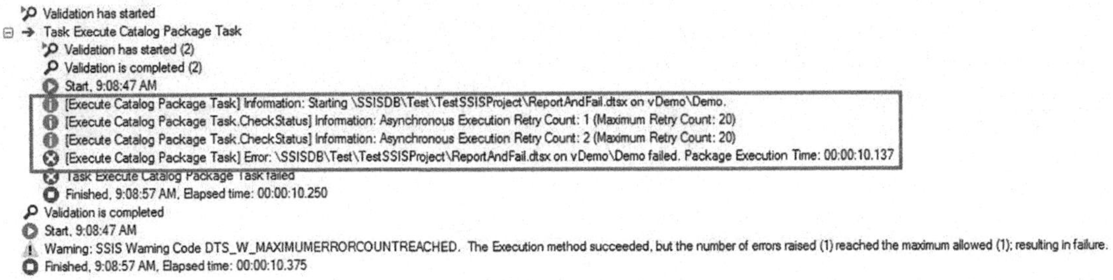

Figure 19-45. *Execute Catalog Package Task failure, logged*

Testing reveals the code no longer suffers from the two egregious errors mentioned at the start of this chapter.

Conclusion

In this chapter, we identified and corrected two errors in the Execute Catalog Package Task. The solutions were complex and involved adding a *lot* of code to the execute process. The solution, however, is not yet complete. We surface three properties that drive synchronous execution in the next chapter.

Now would be an excellent time to check in your code.

CHAPTER 20

Adding Synchronous Execution Properties

Chapter 19 included solutions for two egregious bugs:

1. If the SSIS package executes for longer than 30 seconds, the PackageInfo Execute() returns an error message that reads: "The Execute method on the task returned error code 0x80131904 (Execution Timeout Expired. The timeout period elapsed prior to completion of the operation or the server is not responding.). The Execute method must succeed, and indicate the result using an 'out' parameter."

2. The Execute Catalog Package Task reports success, even when the SSIS package execution fails.

The solution for the first bug involves asynchronous execution. Three settings required for the WaitHandle.WaitAny solution are

- maximumRetries: An int variable that sets the number of times the timer is allowed to "tick" before the SSIS Catalog Package execution operation is terminated.

- retryIntervalSeconds: An int variable that sets the number seconds between timer "ticks," or retries.

- operationTimeoutMinutes: An int variable that sets the number of minutes permitted before the SSIS Catalog Package execution operation is terminated.

At this point in development, the maximumRetries, retryIntervalSeconds, and operationTimeoutMinutes variables and their values are hard-coded into the

451

© Andy Leonard 2021
A. Leonard, *Building Custom Tasks for SQL Server Integration Services*,
https://doi.org/10.1007/978-1-4842-6482-9_20

executeSynchronous helper function in the ExecuteCatalogPackageTask class. The maximumRetries, retryIntervalSeconds, and operationTimeoutMinutes variables should really be ExecuteCatalogPackageTask class properties so SSIS developers may configure these values when Synchronous SSIS package execution exceeds 30 seconds.

In addition, the property values are related in that maximumRetries * retryIntervalSeconds should be less than the value operationTimeoutMinutes / 60 in order to avoid execution timeouts.

Surfacing the New Properties

The new properties should be visually linked to the Synchronized property setting in SettingsNode, and the Synchronized property should be separated from the "SSIS Package Execution Properties" category in SettingsNode. Begin by editing the Synchronized property in SettingsNode to appear in its own category named "SSIS Package Synchronized Properties" using the code in Listing 20-1:

Listing 20-1. Editing the Synchronized property category

```
[
  Category("SSIS Package Synchronized Properties"),
  Description("Enter SSIS Catalog Package SYNCHRONIZED execution parameter
  value.")
]
public bool Synchronized {
  get { return _task.Synchronized; }
  set { _task.Synchronized = value; }
}
```

Once edited, the code appears as shown in Figure 20-1:

```
[
    Category("SSIS Package Synchronized Properties"),
    Description("Enter SSIS Catalog Package SYNCHRONIZED execution parameter value.")
]
0 references
public bool Synchronized {
    get { return _task.Synchronized; }
    set { _task.Synchronized = value; }
}
```

Figure 20-1. *The Synchronized property is now in the SSIS Package Synchronized Properties category*

Build the ExecuteCatalogPackageTask solution and then add the Execute Catalog Package Task to a test SSIS package. Open the Execute Catalog Package Task editor, and note the new location of the Synchronized property, as shown in Figure 20-2:

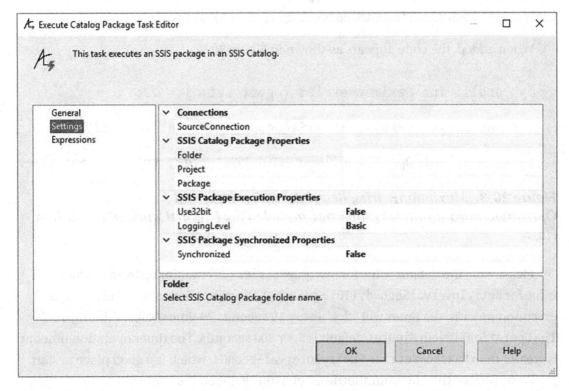

Figure 20-2. *The Synchronized property, edited*

The Synchronized property now has its own property category named "SSIS Package Synchronized Properties."

The next step is to add properties to manage the maximumRetries, retryIntervalSeconds, and operationTimeoutMinutes values.

Adding MaximumRetries, RetryIntervalSeconds, and OperationTimeoutMinutes

Add new properties to the ExecuteCatalogPackageTask object using the code in Listing 20-2:

Listing 20-2. Adding MaximumRetries, RetryIntervalSeconds, and OperationTimeoutMinutes properties to the ExecuteCatalogPackageTask class

```
public int MaximumRetries { get; set; } = 29;
public int RetryIntervalSeconds { get; set; } = 10;
public int OperationTimeoutMinutes { get; set; } = 5;
```

When added, the code appears as shown in Figure 20-3:

```
public int MaximumRetries { get; set; } = 29;

public int RetryIntervalSeconds { get; set; } = 10;

public int OperationTimeoutMinutes { get; set; } = 5;
```

Figure 20-3. *MaximumRetries, RetryIntervalSeconds, and OperationTimeoutMinutes properties, added to the ExecuteCatalogPackageTask class*

Please note the default value for MaximumRetries (29) multiplied by the default value for RetryIntervalSeconds (10) equals 290. When applied to the SSIS package execution process, the timer will "tick" every 10 seconds 29 times before "timing out." The OperationTimeoutMinutes default is 5, or 300 seconds. The timer operation timeout is greater than MaximumRetries * RetryIntervalSeconds, which is a good place to start.

Next, surface the MaximumRetries, RetryIntervalSeconds, and OperationTimeoutMinutes properties on SettingsNode by adding the code in Listing 20-3 to the SettingsView.cs file:

Listing 20-3. Surfacing the MaximumRetries, RetryIntervalSeconds, and OperationTimeoutMinutes properties

```
[
  Category("SSIS Package Synchronized Properties"),
  Description("Enter SSIS Catalog Package Maximum Retries " +
              "for the timer \"tick\" when SYNCHRONIZED is true.")
]
public int MaximumRetries {
  get { return _task.MaximumRetries; }
  set { _task.MaximumRetries = value; }
}

[
  Category("SSIS Package Synchronized Properties"),
  Description("Enter SSIS Catalog Package Retry Interval Seconds " +
          "to wait between timer \"tick\" retries when SYNCHRONIZED is true.")
]
public int RetryIntervalSeconds {
  get { return _task.RetryIntervalSeconds; }
  set { _task.RetryIntervalSeconds = value; }
}

[
  Category("SSIS Package Synchronized Properties"),
  Description("The SSIS Catalog Package Operation Timeout Minutes - " +
              "managed by RetryIntervalSeconds and MaximumRetires when
              SYNCHRONIZED is true."),
              ReadOnly(true)
]
public int OperationTimeoutMinutes {
  get { return _task.OperationTimeoutMinutes; }
  set { _task.OperationTimeoutMinutes = value; }
}
```

Once added, the code appears as shown in Figure 20-4:

```
[
    Category("SSIS Package Synchronized Properties"),
    Description("Enter SSIS Catalog Package Maximum Retries " +
    "for the timer \"tick\" when SYNCHRONIZED is true.")
]
0 references
public int MaximumRetries {
    get { return _task.MaximumRetries; }
    set { _task.MaximumRetries = value; }
}


[
    Category("SSIS Package Synchronized Properties"),
    Description("Enter SSIS Catalog Package Retry Interval Seconds " +
    "to wait between timer \"tick\" retries when SYNCHRONIZED is true.")
]
0 references
public int RetryIntervalSeconds {
    get { return _task.RetryIntervalSeconds; }
    set { _task.RetryIntervalSeconds = value; }
}


[
    Category("SSIS Package Synchronized Properties"),
    Description("The SSIS Catalog Package Operation Timeout Minutes - " +
    "managed by RetryIntervalSeconds and MaximumRetires when SYNCHRONIZED is true."),
    ReadOnly(true)
]
1 reference
public int OperationTimeoutMinutes {
    get { return _task.OperationTimeoutMinutes; }
    set { _task.OperationTimeoutMinutes = value; }
}
```

Figure 20-4. *Surfacing the MaximumRetries, RetryIntervalSeconds, and OperationTimeoutMinutes properties*

Note the OperationTimeoutMinutes property ReadOnly attribute is true, which means the value appears in the Execute Catalog Package Task editor, but is not editable. The OperationTimeoutMinutes property is managed mathematically and available for viewing only.

Test the new properties by building the ExecuteCatalogPackageTask solution, opening a test SSIS package, adding an Execute Catalog Package Task, and configuring the new MaximumRetries, RetryIntervalSeconds, and OperationTimeoutMinutes properties on the Settings page, as shown in Figure 20-5:

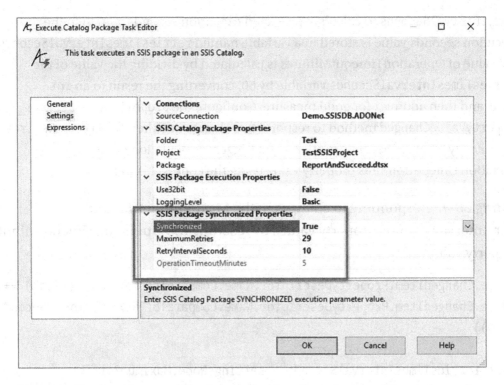

Figure 20-5. *Testing the new MaximumRetries, RetryIntervalSeconds, and OperationTimeoutMinutes properties*

Configure the Execute Catalog Package Task to execute a short-running (less than 5 minutes) SSIS package. Set the Synchronized property to True (because the new MaximumRetries, RetryIntervalSeconds, and OperationTimeoutMinutes properties are not used unless the Synchronized property is set to True), and then close the editor. Execute the test SSIS package. If all goes as planned, the test SSIS package should succeed when executed in the debugger, as shown in Figure 20-6:

Figure 20-6. *Successful execution*

The next step is to use the values of the MaximumRetries and RetryIntervalSeconds properties to manage the OperationTimeoutMinutes property. The OperationTimeoutMinutes property value is set by multiplying maximumRetries * retryIntervalSeconds to calculate projected execution seconds, and then the execution seconds value is stored in a variable named retriesTimesIntervalSeconds. The value of OperationTimeoutMinutes is calculated by dividing the value of the retriesTimesIntervalSeconds variable by 60, converting the result to an int value, and then adding 1 for good measure. Configure the propertyGridSettings_ PropertyValueChanged method to respond to a change in either the MaximumRetires or the RetryIntervalSeconds property and trigger recalculation of the OperationTimeoutMinutes property value using the code in Listing 20-4:

Listing 20-4. Responding to changes in the MaximumRetries and RetryIntervalSeconds property values by resetting the OperationTimeoutMinutes property value

```
if ((e.ChangedItem.PropertyDescriptor.Name.CompareTo("MaximumRetries") == 0)
 || (e.ChangedItem.PropertyDescriptor.Name.CompareTo("RetryIntervalSeconds")
 == 0))
{
  int retriesTimesIntervalSeconds = settingsNode.MaximumRetries
      * settingsNode.RetryIntervalSeconds;
  int operationTimeoutSeconds = settingsNode.OperationTimeoutMinutes * 60;
  settingsNode.OperationTimeoutMinutes = (int)((retriesTimesIntervalSeconds
  / 60) + 1);
  this.settingsPropertyGrid.Refresh();
}
```

When added to the propertyGridSettings_PropertyValueChanged method, the code appears as shown in Figure 20-7:

```
if ((e.ChangedItem.PropertyDescriptor.Name.CompareTo("MaximumRetries") == 0)
    || (e.ChangedItem.PropertyDescriptor.Name.CompareTo("RetryIntervalSeconds") == 0))
{
    int retriesTimesIntervalSeconds = settingsNode.MaximumRetries
        * settingsNode.RetryIntervalSeconds;
    int operationTimeoutSeconds = settingsNode.OperationTimeoutMinutes * 60;
    settingsNode.OperationTimeoutMinutes = (int)((retriesTimesIntervalSeconds / 60) + 1);
    this.settingsPropertyGrid.Refresh();
}
```

Figure 20-7. *Auto-reset the OperationTimeoutMinutes property value*

One could just as easily make the MaximumRetries property read-only and manage the MaximumRetries property value by calculating the MaximumRetries property value using the values of the RetryIntervalSeconds and the OperationTimeoutMinutes properties. The goal is the same: we want to surface wait-related properties in the Execute Catalog Package Task editor so SSIS developers who use the Execute Catalog Package Task can configure the wait-related properties to stop execution if the SSIS package has not completed execution in some amount of time.

Cleaning Up Outdated Asynchronous Execution

The next step is to clean up the (now) outdated local maximumRetries, retryIntervalSeconds, and operationTimeoutMinutes variables in the executeSynchronous method. Delete the code highlighted in Figure 20-8:

```
private Operation.ServerOperationStatus executeSynchronous(long executionId
                         , SqlConnection connection)
{
    Operation.ServerOperationStatus ret = Operation.ServerOperationStatus.UnexpectTerminated;
    ManualResetEvent manualResetState = new ManualResetEvent(false);

    int maximumRetries = 20;
    int retryIntervalSeconds = 10;
    int operationTimeoutMinutes = 10;
```

Figure 20-8. *Deleting local variables*

Once the local asynchronous-related variables are deleted, the executeSynchronous method appears as shown in Figure 20-9:

```
private Operation.ServerOperationStatus executeSynchronous(long executionId
                    , SqlConnection connection)
{
    Operation.ServerOperationStatus ret = Operation.ServerOperationStatus.UnexpectTerminated;
    ManualResetEvent manualResetState = new ManualResetEvent(false);

    CheckWaitState statusChecker = new CheckWaitState(executionId
                                        , maximumRetries
                                        , connection
                                        , PackageCatalogName
                                        , this);
    TimeSpan dueTime = new TimeSpan(0, 0, 0);
    TimeSpan period = new TimeSpan(0, 0, retryIntervalSeconds);

    object timerState = new TimerCheckerState(manualResetState);
    TimerCallback timerCallback = statusChecker.CheckStatus;
    Timer timer = new Timer(timerCallback, timerState, dueTime, period);

    WaitHandle[] manualResetStateWaitHandleCollection = new WaitHandle[]
                { manualResetState };
    int timeoutMillseconds = (int)new TimeSpan(0, operationTimeoutMinutes
                                    , 0).TotalMilliseconds;
    bool exitContext = false;

    // wait here, please
    WaitHandle.WaitAny(manualResetStateWaitHandleCollection
                    , timeoutMillseconds
                    , exitContext);

    ret = statusChecker.OperationStatus;

    manualResetState.Dispose();
    timer.Dispose();

    return ret;
}
```

Figure 20-9. *The executeSynchronous method after variables are deleted*

In the executeSynchronous method, replace maximumRetries with MaximumRetries, retryIntervalSeconds with RetryIntervalSeconds, and operationTimeoutMinutes with OperationTimeoutMinutes using the code in Listing 20-5:

Listing 20-5. Updating local variables with new properties

```
private Operation.ServerOperationStatus executeSynchronous(long executionId
                                    , SqlConnection connection)
{
```

```
Operation.ServerOperationStatus ret = Operation.ServerOperationStatus.
UnexpectTerminated;
ManualResetEvent manualResetState = new ManualResetEvent(false);

CheckWaitState statusChecker = new CheckWaitState(executionId
                                            , MaximumRetries
                                            , connection
                                            , PackageCatalogName
                                            , this);
TimeSpan dueTime = new TimeSpan(0, 0, 0);
TimeSpan period = new TimeSpan(0, 0, RetryIntervalSeconds);

object timerState = new TimerCheckerState(manualResetState);
TimerCallback timerCallback = statusChecker.CheckStatus;
Timer timer = new Timer(timerCallback, timerState, dueTime, period);

WaitHandle[] manualResetStateWaitHandleCollection = new WaitHandle[]
                        { manualResetState };
int timeoutMillseconds = (int)new TimeSpan(0, OperationTimeoutMinutes
                                        , 0).TotalMilliseconds;
bool exitContext = false;

// wait here, please
WaitHandle.WaitAny(manualResetStateWaitHandleCollection
                            , timeoutMillseconds
                            , exitContext);

ret = statusChecker.OperationStatus;

manualResetState.Dispose();
timer.Dispose();

return ret;
}
```

Once updated, the code appears as shown in Figure 20-10:

```
private Operation.ServerOperationStatus executeSynchronous(long executionId
                        , SqlConnection connection)
{
    Operation.ServerOperationStatus ret = Operation.ServerOperationStatus.UnexpectTerminated;
    ManualResetEvent manualResetState = new ManualResetEvent(false);

    CheckWaitState statusChecker = new CheckWaitState(executionId
                                                    , MaximumRetries
                                                    , connection
                                                    , PackageCatalogName
                                                    , this);
    TimeSpan dueTime = new TimeSpan(0, 0, 0);
    TimeSpan period = new TimeSpan(0, 0, RetryIntervalSeconds);

    object timerState = new TimerCheckerState(manualResetState);
    TimerCallback timerCallback = statusChecker.CheckStatus;
    Timer timer = new Timer(timerCallback, timerState, dueTime, period);

    WaitHandle[] manualResetStateWaitHandleCollection = new WaitHandle[]
                { manualResetState };
    int timeoutMillseconds = (int)new TimeSpan(0, OperationTimeoutMinutes
                                                , 0).TotalMilliseconds;
    bool exitContext = false;

    // wait here, please
    WaitHandle.WaitAny(manualResetStateWaitHandleCollection
                    , timeoutMillseconds
                    , exitContext);

    ret = statusChecker.OperationStatus;

    manualResetState.Dispose();
    timer.Dispose();

    return ret;
}
```

Figure 20-10.   *The updated executeSynchronous method*

Let's Test It!

Build the ExecuteCatalogPackageTask solution, open a test SSIS project and package, and then add a new Execute Catalog Package Task to the Control Flow. Configure the Execute Catalog Package Task to execute an SSIS package that takes some time to run, such as the RunForSomeTime.dtsx package, and set the Synchronized property to True, the MaximumRetries property to 50, and the RetryIntervalSeconds property to 2, as shown in Figure 20-11:

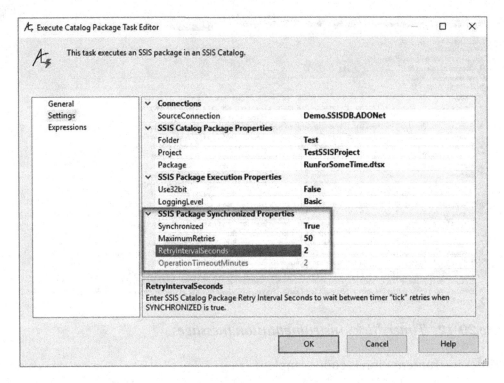

Figure 20-11. *Configuring the Execute Catalog Package Task for a timer instrumentation test*

Execute the test SSIS package and view the Progress tab. Timer "tick" instrumentation messages should appear similar to those shown in Figure 20-12:

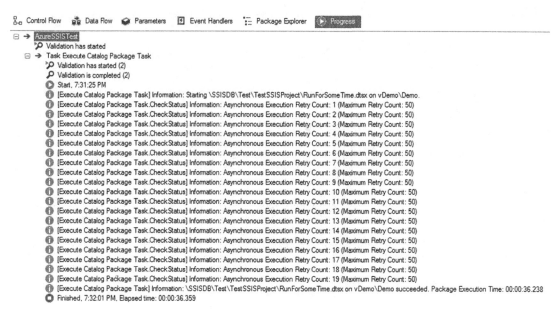

Figure 20-12. *Timer "tick" instrumentation messages*

Timer instrumentation is code complete.

Conclusion

In this chapter, we converted three hard-coded variables – maximumRetries, retryIntervalSeconds, and operationTimeoutMinutes – into ExecuteCatalogPackageTask class properties and then added code to the SettingsView and SettingsNode classes to surface the new properties to SSIS developers.

In the next chapter, we test the Execute Catalog Package Task functionality.

Now would be an excellent time to check in your code.

CHAPTER 21

Testing the Task

In previous chapters, we've coded features for the version of the Execute Catalog Package Task built in this second edition of the book. It's now time to test the Execute Catalog Package Task.

Manually Testing Use Cases

Test frameworks that automate redundancies in test generation, execution, and reporting exist. If your job is developing software all day every day, you either know about test frameworks or you will. You will occasionally encounter a testing requirement for which your chosen test framework is either incapable or "clunky." In that case, you will need to build a manual test.

All good testing is a series of scenarios, expected answers or results (assertions), and measurement of the actual results. The combination of a scenario and assertion is referred to as a *use case*. A single use case may contain several assertions. When we perform testing, we work through each use case, measure results, and record the measurements.

I have a maxim: "All software is tested. Some intentionally." I occasionally post this maxim in social media, as shown in Figure 21-1:

**"All software is tested.
Some intentionally."
- Andy Leonard**

***Figure 21-1.** Andy's software testing maxim*

A. Leonard, *Building Custom Tasks for SQL Server Integration Services*,
https://doi.org/10.1007/978-1-4842-6482-9_21

Software testing is meticulous and demanding work. We test some, not all, use cases in this chapter. If we tested all use cases, this chapter would be 150 pages, and my editor would (rightly) point out that this is a chapter, not a test plan.

Use Cases

In this section, we explore the following use cases for the Execute Catalog Package Task:

1. Task existence

2. Task validation

3. Task Editor – General

The first few use cases involve visual inspection – simply checking to see if the Execute Catalog Package Task appears in the SSIS Toolbox and, if so, selecting the Execute Catalog Package Task in the SSIS Toolbox and verifying the toolbox description.

The tests are documented using a manual testing documentation format. The author has seen similar manual testing documentation presented in an Excel spreadsheet and prefers Word documentation for manual test documentation.

Testing Task Existence

Scenario: Build the ExecuteCatalogPackageTask solution, open a test SSIS project, and then open a test SSIS package. The Execute Catalog Package Task should appear in the SSIS Toolbox, as shown in Figure 21-2:

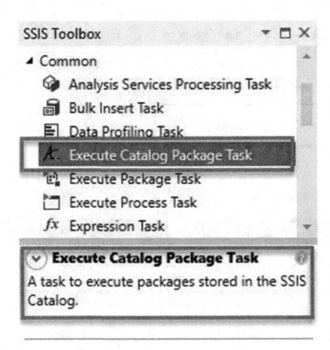

Figure 21-2. *Does the Execute Catalog Package Task appear in the SSIS Toolbox?*

Assertion: The Execute Catalog Package Task appears in the SSIS Toolbox.

Measurement: True.

Assertion: When the Execute Catalog Package Task is selected in the SSIS Toolbox, the Execute Catalog Package Task description appears in the Information portion of the SSIS Toolbox.

Measurement: True.

Testing Task Validation

Scenario: Drag an Execute Catalog Package Task to the Control Flow canvas of a test SSIS package. Examine the Error List dialog, as shown in Figure 21-3:

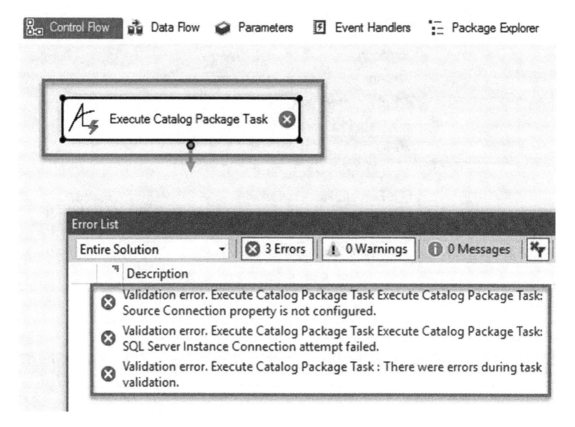

Figure 21-3. *Does the Execute Catalog Package Task appear – in error – on the Control Flow canvas?*

Assertion: An Execute Catalog Package Task may be added to the Control Flow canvas of a test SSIS package.

Measurement: True.

Assertion: A newly added Execute Catalog Package Task raises validation errors.

Measurement: True.

Assertion: The validation errors raised by a newly added Execute Catalog Package Task are

- Source Connection property is not properly configured.

- SQL Server Instance Connection attempt failed.

Measurement: True.

Assertion: The earlier validation errors raised by a newly added Execute Catalog Package Task trigger an SSIS validation error:

- There were errors during the task validation.

Measurement: True.

Testing the Task Editor

In the following test sections, we exercise the Execute Catalog Package Task Editor. Appearance and function are tested.

Scenario: Open the Execute Catalog Package Task Editor, as shown in Figure 21-4:

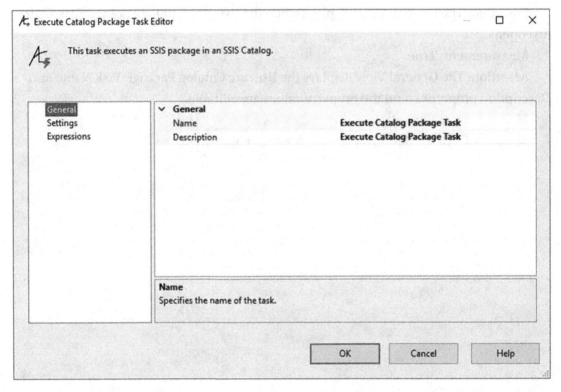

Figure 21-4. *Does the Execute Catalog Package Task Editor display without error?*

Sometimes the solution build succeeds, and one (or more than one) value is misaligned between the ExecuteCatalogPackageTask and ExecuteCatalogPackageTaskComplexUI classes. When such misalignment occurs, the editor will not display. Instead, an error will display.

Assertion: The Execute Catalog Package Task Editor opens without error.

Measurement: True, the Execute Catalog Package Task Editor opens without error.

Assertion: The Execute Catalog Package Task Editor surfaces three Views:

1. General

2. Settings

3. Expressions

Measurement: True.

Assertion: The General View displays when the Execute Catalog Package Task Editor first opens.

Measurement: True.

Assertion: The General View displays the Execute Catalog Package Task Name and Description properties, and the property values are editable.

Measurement: True.

Scenario: Click the Settings view, as shown in Figure 21-5:

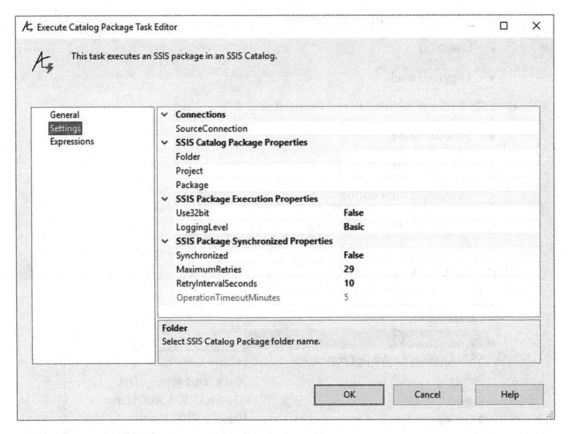

Figure 21-5. *Does the Execute Catalog Package Task Editor SettingsView display without error?*

Assertion: The Settings View displays without error when Settings is selected.

Measurement: True.

Assertion: When Settings is selected, the Settings View displays the following categories and properties:

- Connections

  - SourceConnection

- SSIS Catalog Package Properties

  - Folder

  - Project

  - Package

- SSIS Package Execution Properties

  - Use32bit

  - LoggingLevel

- SSIS Package Synchronized Properties

  - Synchronized

  - MaximumRetries

  - RetryIntervalSeconds

  - OperationTimeoutMinutes

Measurement: True

Scenario: Click the SourceConnection property dropdown, as shown in Figure 21-6:

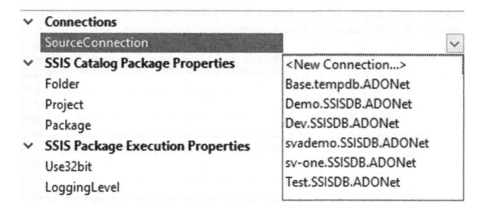

Figure 21-6. *Does the SourceConnection dropdown list display all available ADO. Net connection managers without error?*

Assertion: The SourceConnection dropdown list displays all available ADO.Net connection managers without error.

Measurement: True.

Scenario: Configure the SourceConnection property value from the SourceConnection property dropdown, as shown in Figure 21-7:

Figure 21-7. *Selecting a value for the SourceConnection property*

Scenario: Close the Execute Catalog Package Task Editor, as shown in Figure 21-8:

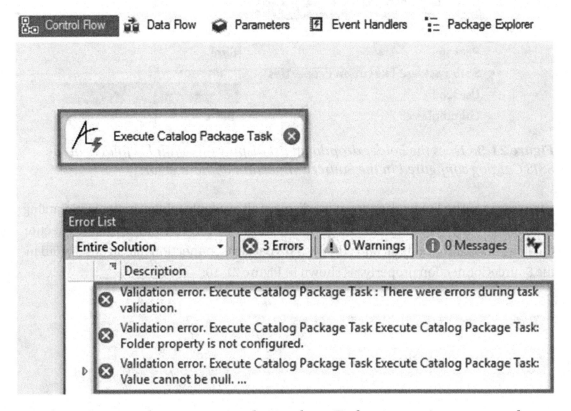

Figure 21-8. *Does the Execute Catalog Package Task appear – in error – on the Control Flow canvas?*

Assertion: The validation errors raised by the Execute Catalog Package Task as currently configured are

- There were errors during the task validation.

- Folder property is not properly configured.

- Value cannot be null.

Measurement: True.

Scenario: Open the Execute Catalog Package Task and navigate to the Settings view. Click the Folder property dropdown, as shown in Figure 21-9:

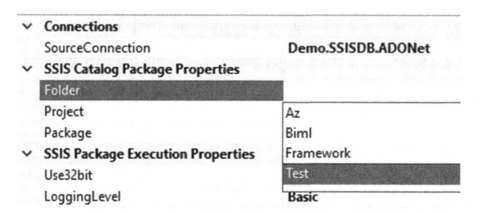

Figure 21-9. *Does the Folder dropdown list display all available folders in the SSIS Catalog configured in the SourceConnection without error?*

Assertion: The Folder dropdown list displays all available folders in the SSIS Catalog configured in the SourceConnection property without error. To verify, close the Execute Catalog Package Task Editor, and edit the SSIS package connection manager selected in the SourceConnection property, as shown in Figure 21-10:

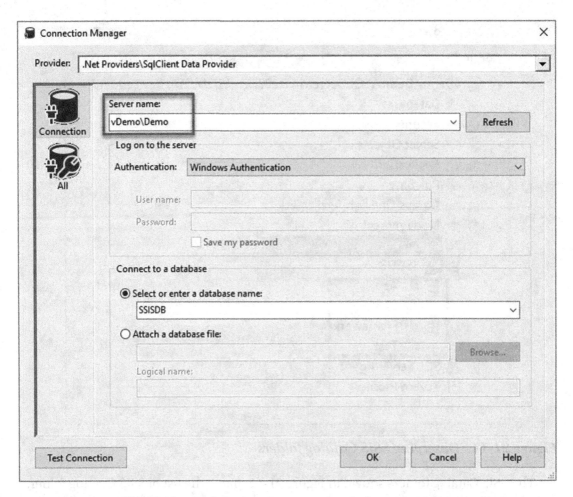

Figure 21-10. *Obtain the SQL Server instance from the SourceConnection connection manager*

Use SQL Server Management Studio (SSMS) to connect to the SourceConnection SQL Server instance. Open SSMS Object Explorer and expand Integration Services Catalogs. Expand the SSISDB node and observe SSIS Catalog folders, as shown in Figure 21-11:

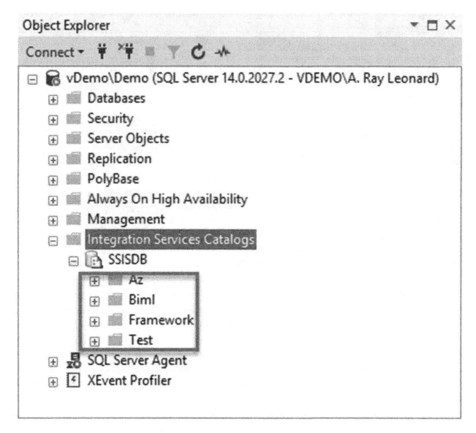

Figure 21-11. *Observing SSIS Catalog folders*

The SSIS Catalog folders shown in Figure 21-11 match the list of SSIS Catalog folders shown in Figure 21-9.

Measurement: True.

Scenario: Configure the Folder property value from the Folder property dropdown, as shown in Figure 21-12:

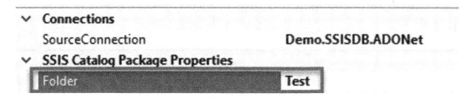

Figure 21-12. *Selecting a value for the Folder property*

Scenario: Close the Execute Catalog Package Task Editor, as shown in Figure 21-13:

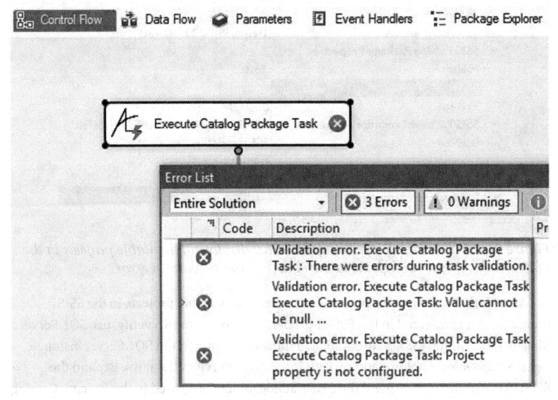

Figure 21-13. *Does the Execute Catalog Package Task appear – in error – on the Control Flow canvas?*

Assertion: The validation errors raised by the Execute Catalog Package Task as currently configured are

- There were errors during the task validation.

- Value cannot be null.

- Project property is not properly configured.

Measurement: True.

Scenario: Open the Execute Catalog Package Task and navigate to the Settings view. Click the Project property dropdown, as shown in Figure 21-14:

⌄ **Connections**	
SourceConnection	**Demo.SSISDB.ADONet**
⌄ **SSIS Catalog Package Properties**	
Folder	**Test**
Project	
Package	DeployAndMaintain
⌄ **SSIS Package Execution Properties**	ECPTPackageAndProjectReferenceTest
Use32bit	ECPTProjectReferenceTest
LoggingLevel	FrameworkTest1
⌄ **SSIS Package Synchronized Properties**	FrameworkTest2
Synchronized	TestSSISProject
MaximumRetries	WeatherETL

Figure 21-14. *Does the Project dropdown list display all available projects in the SSIS Catalog folder configured in the Folder property without error?*

Assertion: The Project dropdown list displays all available projects in the SSIS Catalog folder configured in the Folder property without error. To verify, use SQL Server Management Studio (SSMS) to connect to the SourceConnection SQL Server instance. Open SSMS Object Explorer and expand Integration Services Catalogs. Expand the SSISDB node, and then expand the SSIS Catalog folder configured in the Execute Catalog Package Task Folder property, as shown in Figure 21-15:

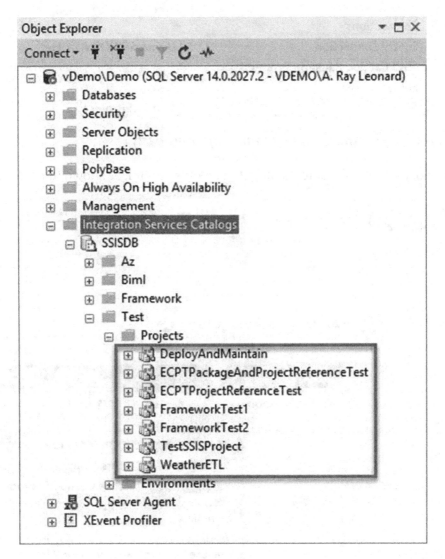

Figure 21-15. *Observing SSIS Catalog projects in the configured SSIS folder*

The SSIS Catalog projects shown in Figure 21-15 match the list of SSIS Catalog projects shown in Figure 21-14.

Measurement: True.

Scenario: Configure the Project property value from the Project property dropdown, as shown in Figure 21-16:

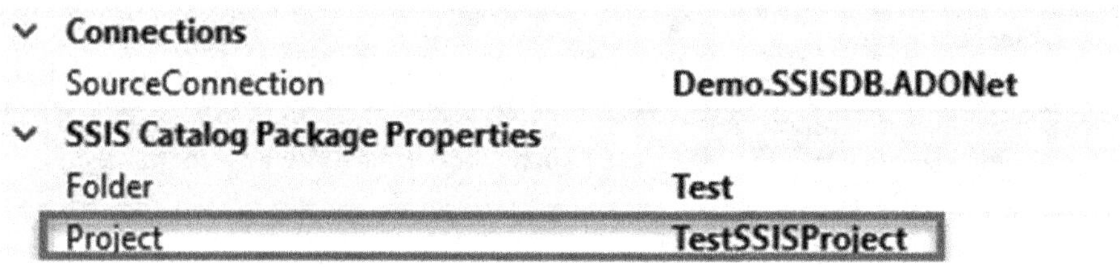

﹀ **Connections**
   SourceConnection   **Demo.SSISDB.ADONet**
﹀ **SSIS Catalog Package Properties**
   Folder   **Test**
   Project   **TestSSISProject**

Figure 21-16. *Selecting a value for the Project property*

Scenario: Close the Execute Catalog Package Task Editor, as shown in Figure 21-17:

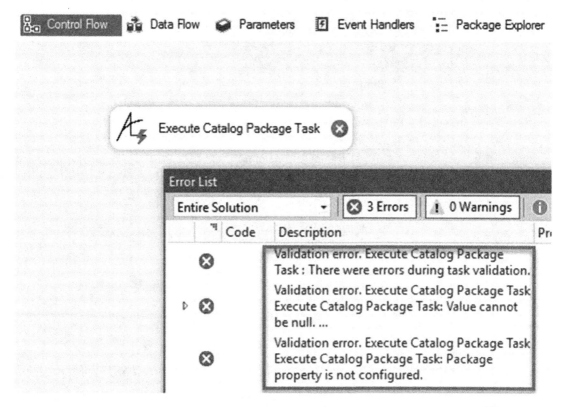

Figure 21-17. *Does the Execute Catalog Package Task appear – in error – on the Control Flow canvas?*

Assertion: The validation errors raised by the Execute Catalog Package Task as currently configured are

- There were errors during the task validation.

- Value cannot be null.

- Package property is not properly configured.

Measurement: True.

Scenario: Open the Execute Catalog Package Task and navigate to the Settings view. Click the Package property dropdown, as shown in Figure 21-18:

∨ **Connections**	
SourceConnection	**Demo.SSISDB.ADONet**
∨ **SSIS Catalog Package Properties**	
Folder	**Test**
Project	**TestSSISProject**
Package	
∨ **SSIS Package Execution Properties**	ReportAndFail.dtsx
Use32bit	ReportAndSucceed.dtsx
LoggingLevel	ReportParameterAndSucceed.dtsx
∨ **SSIS Package Synchronized Properties**	RunForSomeTime.dtsx
Synchronized	RunForSomeTimeAndFail.dtsx
MaximumRetries	WriteARecordAndSucceed.dtsx

Figure 21-18. *Does the Package dropdown list display all available packages in the SSIS Catalog project configured in the Project property without error?*

Assertion: The Package dropdown list displays all available packages in the SSIS Catalog project configured in the Project property without error. To verify, use SQL Server Management Studio (SSMS) to connect to the SourceConnection SQL Server instance. Open SSMS Object Explorer and expand Integration Services Catalogs. Expand the SSISDB node, expand the SSIS Catalog folder configured in the Execute Catalog Package Task Folder property, and then expand the SSIS Catalog project configured in the Execute Catalog Package Task Project property, as shown in Figure 21-19:

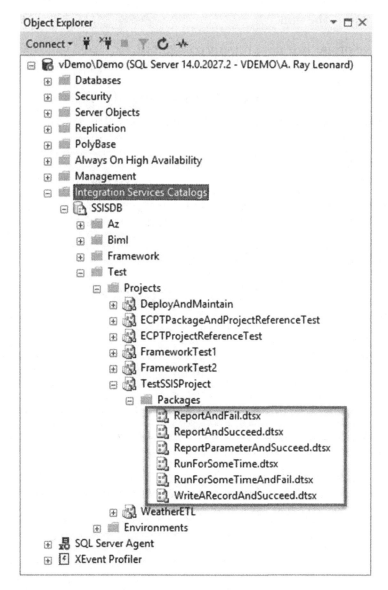

Figure 21-19. *Observing SSIS Catalog packages in the configured SSIS project*

The SSIS Catalog packages shown in Figure 21-19 match the list of SSIS Catalog projects shown in Figure 21-18.

Measurement: True.

Scenario: Close the Execute Catalog Package Task Editor and view the Execute Catalog Package Task on the SSIS test package Control Flow, as shown in Figure 21-20:

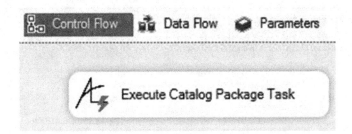

Figure 21-20. *The Execute Catalog Package Task, minimally configured to pass validation*

Assertion: No validation errors are raised by the Execute Catalog Package Task as currently configured.

Measurement: True.

Testing Execution

We shift gears at this point in the test process. While I dearly love manual software testing and documenting test results in "test-speak" for posterity, not everyone shares my passion. Starting here, we switch to prose.

Currently, the Execute Catalog Package Task is configured as shown in Figure 21-21:

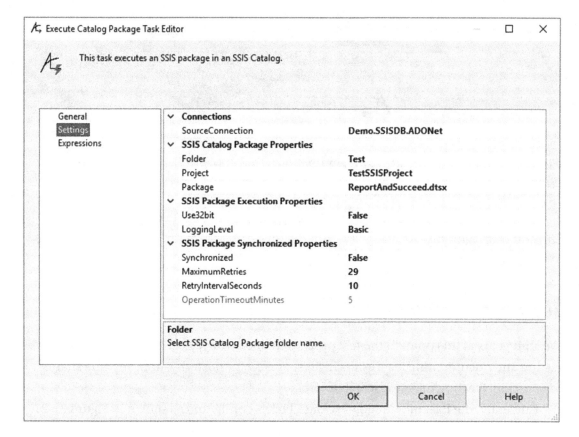

Figure 21-21. *The Execute Catalog Package Task, as configured*

The current configuration tests asynchronous SSIS package execution because the
Synchronized property – which maps to the SSIS Catalog execution parameter – is set to
false, which is the default.

Execute the test SSIS package. If all goes as planned, the test SSIS package with the
Execute Catalog Package Task will succeed, as shown in Figure 21-22:

Figure 21-22. *A successful test execution*

Observe the Progress/Execution Results tab to validate the instrumentation messages raised as events, as shown in Figure 21-23:

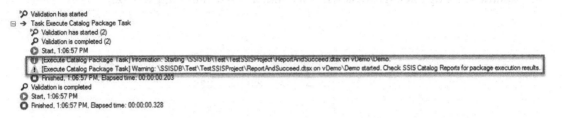

Figure 21-23. *Validating events*

Test synchronous SSIS package execution by opening the Execute Catalog Package Task editor and updating the Synchronized property to True, as shown in Figure 21-24:

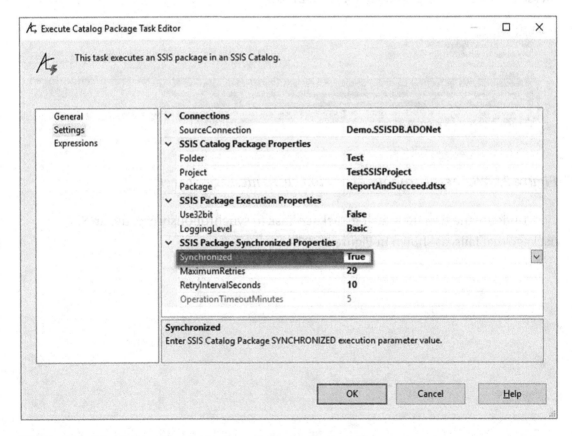

Figure 21-24. *Preparing to test synchronized execution*

Click the OK button to close the Execute Catalog Package Task Editor, and execute the test SSIS package in the debugger. If all goes as planned, the test SSIS package with the Execute Catalog Package Task will succeed, as shown in Figure 21-25:

Figure 21-25. *Another successful test execution*

View the Progress/Execution Results tab to validate asynchronous execution event messages are present, as shown in Figure 21-26:

Figure 21-26. *Asynchronous execution event messages: check*

Configure the Execute Catalog Package Task to synchronously execute an SSIS package that fails, as shown in Figure 21-27:

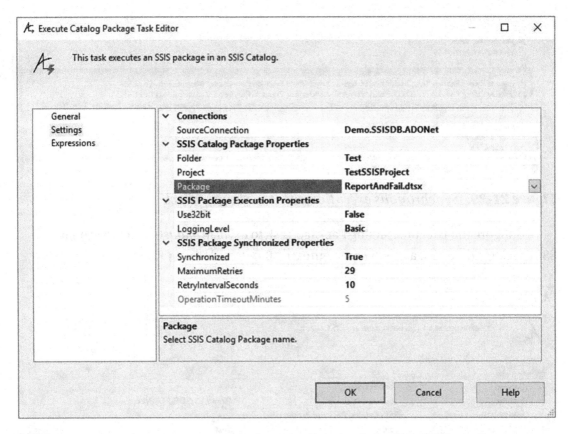

Figure 21-27. *Preparing to test synchronized execution of an SSIS package built to fail*

As expected, the SSIS package and Execute Catalog Package Task fail, as shown in Figure 21-28:

Figure 21-28. *A failed execution, as expected*

Observe the Progress/Execution Results tab as shown in in Figure 21-29:

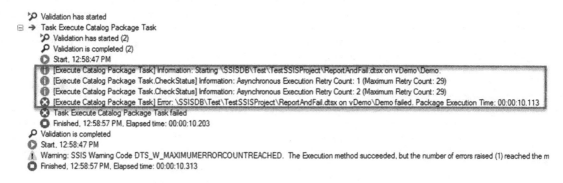

Figure 21-29. *Synchronous execution event messages, check*

Configure the Execute Catalog Package Task to *asynchronously* execute the same SSIS package that fails, as shown in Figure 21-30:

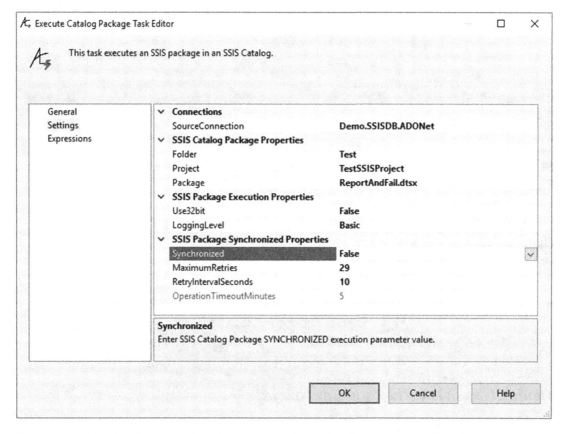

Figure 21-30. *Preparing to test a non-synchronized execution of an SSIS package built to fail*

As expected, the SSIS package and Execute Catalog Package Task *succeed*, as shown in Figure 21-31:

Figure 21-31. *A successful execution of a package, or is it?*

Verify the instrumentation messages found on the Progress/Execution Results tab are accurate for asynchronous execution, as shown in Figure 21-32:

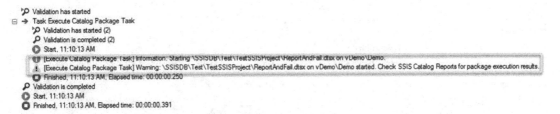

Figure 21-32. *Asynchronous execution instrumentation events*

Examine the SSIS Catalog All Executions Report.

Configure a longer-running (greater than 30 seconds) SSIS package built to succeed. Configure the SSIS package to execute synchronously, as shown in Figure 21-33:

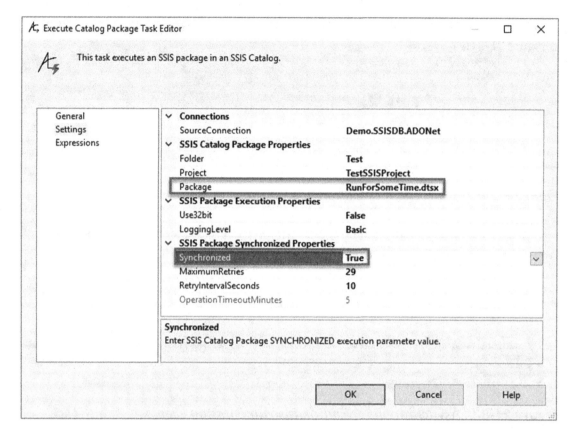

Figure 21-33. *Configuring a longer-running synchronous SSIS package execution*

If all goes according to plan, the SSIS package and Execute Catalog Package Task succeed, as shown in Figure 21-34:

Figure 21-34. *Yet another successful execution*

Observe the Progress/Execution Results to verify the instrumentation messages accurately reflect the progress of the execution, as shown in Figure 21-35:

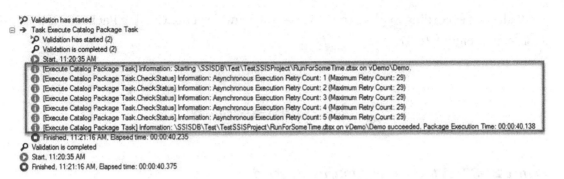

Figure 21-35. *Event messages for a synchronous execution of a longer-running execution*

Configure a longer-running (greater than 30 seconds) SSIS package built to fail. Configure the SSIS package to execute synchronously, as shown in Figure 21-36:

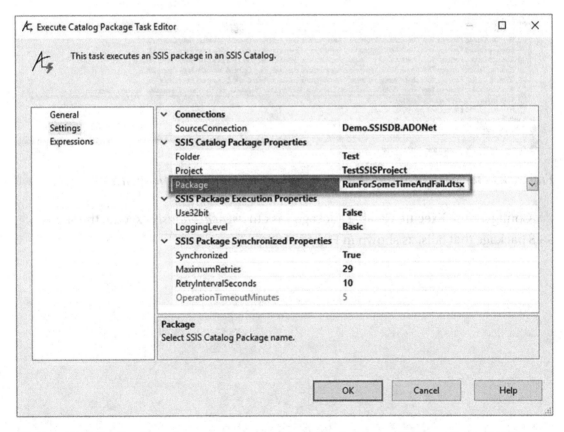

Figure 21-36. *Configuring a longer-running synchronous SSIS package built to fail*

If all goes according to plan, the SSIS package and Execute Catalog Package Task fail, as shown in Figure 21-37:

Figure 21-37. *A failed execution, as expected*

Verify the instrumentation messages found on the Progress/Execution Results tab are accurate for synchronous execution, as shown in Figure 21-38:

Figure 21-38. *Synchronous failed execution instrumentation events*

Configure the Execute Catalog Package Task to *asynchronously* execute the same SSIS package that fails, as shown in Figure 21-39:

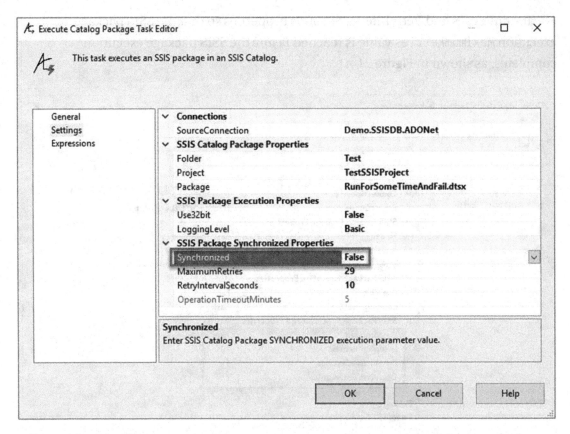

Figure 21-39. *Preparing to test a non-synchronized execution of the same SSIS package built to fail*

As expected, the SSIS package and Execute Catalog Package Task succeed, as shown in Figure 21-40:

Figure 21-40. *A successful execution*

Test timeout functionality by configuring a long-running SSIS package built to succeed. Set the Synchronized property to True, and then configure the

MaximumRetries and RetryIntervalSeconds properties so that the SSIS package execution `MaximumRetries` value is reached *before* the SSIS package execution completes, as shown in Figure 21-41:

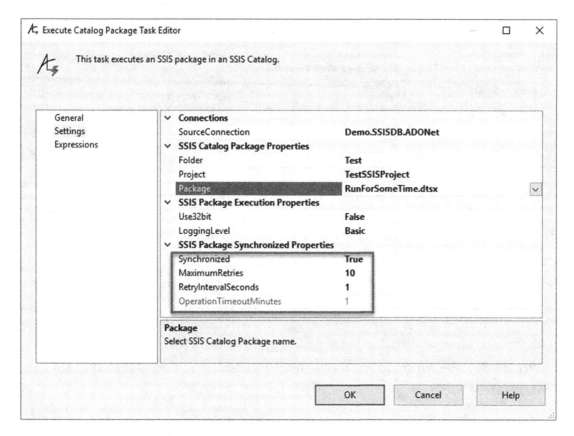

Figure 21-41. *Testing MaximumRetries*

If all goes according to plan, the SSIS package and Execute Catalog Package Task fail, as shown in Figure 21-42:

Figure 21-42. *A failed execution, as expected*

Examine the Progress/Execution Results tab to verify the correct event message – the event message indicating the SSIS package execution was canceled – displays, as shown in Figure 21-43:

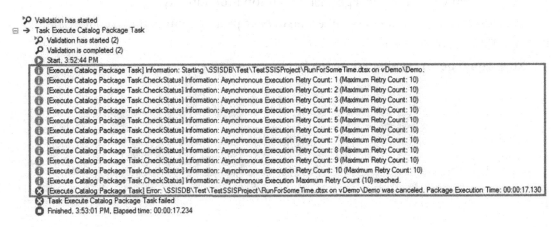

Figure 21-43. *The SSIS Package execution was canceled*

The next step is to verify that the SSIS package execution was canceled in the SSIS Catalog. Open SSMS and connect to the SQL Server instance that hosts the SSIS Catalog. Open the All Executions report to view the status of the SSIS package execution, as shown in Figure 21-44:

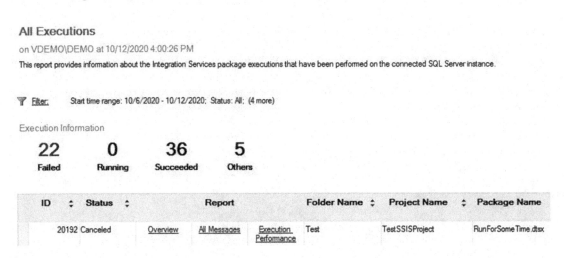

Figure 21-44. *The SSIS package execution status in the SSIS Catalog*

If all goes according to plan, the All Executions SSIS Catalog report in SSMS should indicate the SSIS package execution was canceled.

Conclusion

In this chapter, we applied one manual testing technique for testing validation and then tested the Execute Catalog Package Task execution functionality.

The next step is to build an installer file to ease propagation of the Execute Catalog Package Task in an enterprise.

Now would be an excellent time to check in your code.

CHAPTER 22

Building the Setup Project

Setup projects, or installer projects, allow developers to manage distribution of code in an enterprise and to share code with other enterprises. SSIS has long promoted a healthy community of third-party task and component developers. In this chapter, we add a setup project to the ExecuteCatalogPackageTask solution and configure the setup project to install the Execute Catalog Package Task on other servers using the following steps:

- Add the ExecuteCatalogPackageTaskSetup project.

- Add References.

- Configure the Product tag.

  - Configure the Package tag.

  - Configure the Installation Path Property tags.

  - Configure the MajorUpgrade and MediaTemplate tags.

  - Initialize the UIRef and License file tags.

  - Configure the Installation feature and icon.

- Configure folders and folder structure.

  - Configure the ExecuteCatalogPackageTask GAC registration.

  - Configure the ExecuteCatalogPackageTask Tasks deployment folder.

  - Configure the ExecuteCatalogPackageTaskComplexUI GAC registration.

  - Configure the ExecuteCatalogPackageTaskComplexUI Tasks deployment folder.

© Andy Leonard 2021
A. Leonard, *Building Custom Tasks for SQL Server Integration Services*,
https://doi.org/10.1007/978-1-4842-6482-9_22

Installer projects create a file named setup.exe or *<project name>*.msi. A Windows application named MsiExec.exe executes msi files, which installs the desired software. Visual Studio supports extensions that surface installer projects. One extension is Windows Installer XML, WiX. Visit the WiX Toolset page (wixtoolset.org) to download and install the Visual Studio project template we will use to build the ExecuteCatalogPackageTask.msi file.

To follow the demonstrations and samples included in this chapter, the reader *must* visit wixtoolset.org, download the latest version of the software, and follow the WiX Toolset installation instructions found at wixtoolset.org.

This chapter merely lists the XML required to configure an msi installer file for the Execute Catalog Package Task without providing much explanation. The reader is encouraged to learn more about using the WiX Toolset at wixtoolset.org where one may find in-depth documentation and examples at wixtoolset.org/documentation.

Adding the ExecuteCatalogPackageTaskSetup Project

To add an installer project to the ExecuteCatalogPackageTask solution, right-click the solution in Solution Explorer, hover over Add, and then click New Project, as shown in Figure 22-1:

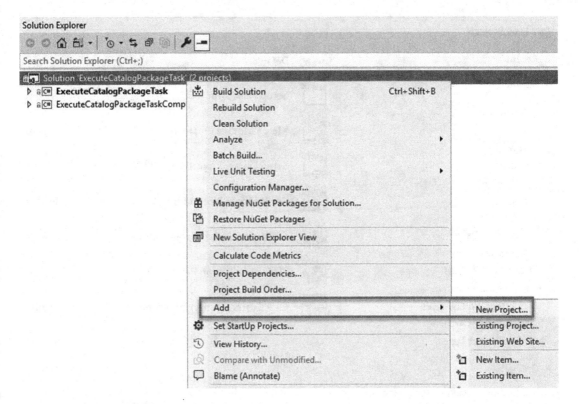

Figure 22-1. *Adding a new setup project*

When the Add New Project dialog displays, navigate to the WiX Toolset template category and select the latest version. Select Setup Project for WiX in the available templates list, and then name the new project "ExecuteCatalogPackageTaskSetup," as shown in Figure 22-2:

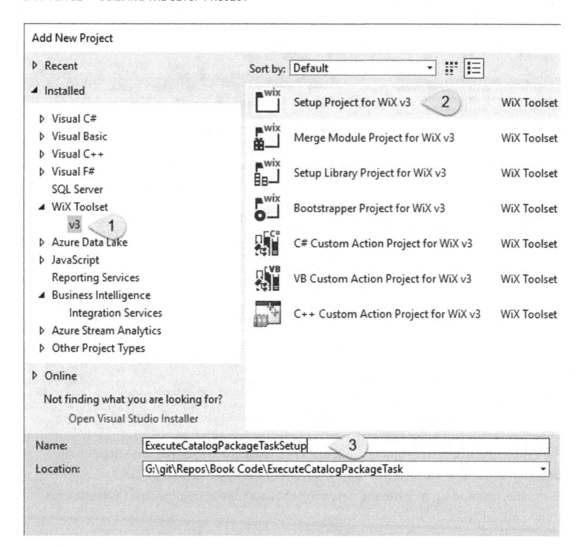

Figure 22-2. *Adding the ExecuteCatalogPackageTaskSetup project*

Once the new project has been added to the ExecuteCatalogPackageTask solution,
Solution Explorer appears as shown in Figure 22-3:

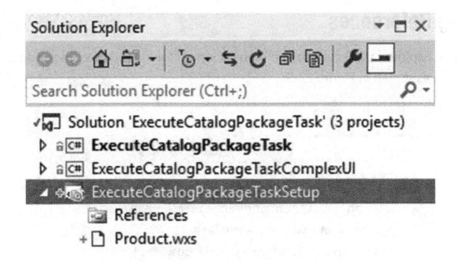

Figure 22-3. *The ExecuteCatalogPackageTaskSetup project*

Rename the ExecuteCatalogPackageTask.wxs file "ExecuteCatalogPackageTask.wxs," as shown in Figure 22-4:

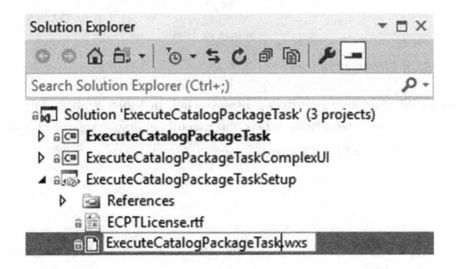

Figure 22-4. *Renaming the ExecuteCatalogPackageTask.wxs file ExecuteCatalogPackageTask.wxs*

The next step is to add references.

Adding References

In Solution Explorer, right-click the References virtual folder and then click Add
References, as shown in Figure 22-5:

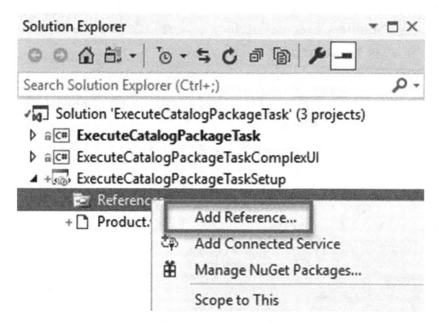

Figure 22-5. *Adding References*

When the WiX Add Reference dialog displays, click the Projects tab, and then select –
and add – the ExecuteCatalogPackageTask and ExecuteCatalogPackageTaskComplexUI
projects, as shown in Figure 22-6:

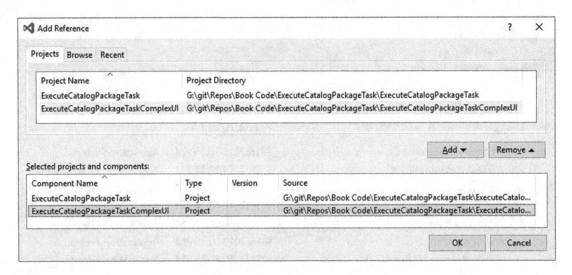

Figure 22-6. *Adding the ExecuteCatalogPackageTask and ExecuteCatalogPackageTaskComplexUI projects*

Click the OK button to add the projects and close the WiX Add Reference dialog.

Next, add references to the WixUIExtension and WixUtilExtension assemblies, which will be located in the WiX Toolset installation directory (on my machine, these files are located in the C:\Program Files (x86)\WiX Toolset v3.11\bin folder), as shown in Figure 22-7:

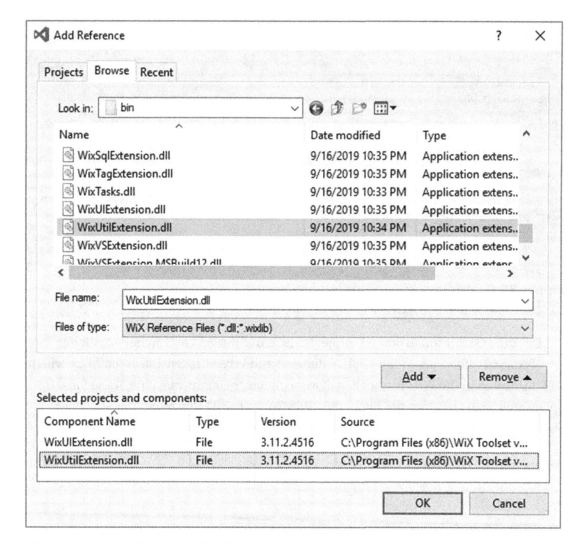

Figure 22-7. *Adding the WixUIExtension and WixUtilExtension assemblies*

The previous two steps are separated for the sake of clarification, but they can be easily combined into a single step where the WiX assemblies *and* projects are added together, as shown in Figure 22-8:

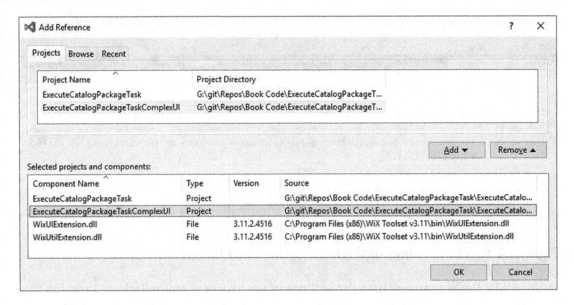

Figure 22-8. *Adding WiX assemblies and Projects in one step*

The next step is to configure the ExecuteCatalogPackageTask.wxs Product tag.

Configuring Tags

In this section, we configure WiX tags to build the installation project to install the
Execute Catalog Package Task on Windows Server 2016 running SQL Server 2017.

Configure the Product tag

In Solution Explorer, double-click the ExecuteCatalogPackageTask.wxs file to open the
file in the Visual Studio editor, as shown in Figure 22-9:

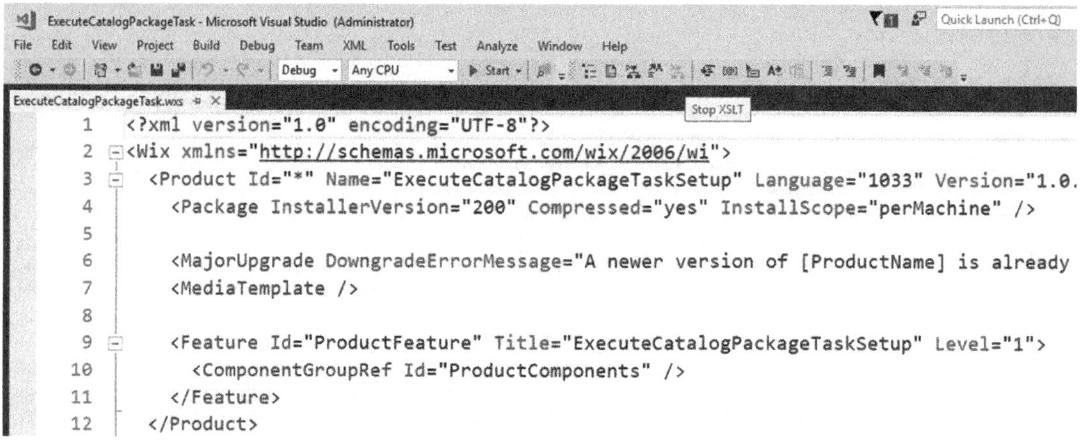

```
 1    <?xml version="1.0" encoding="UTF-8"?>
 2    <Wix xmlns="http://schemas.microsoft.com/wix/2006/wi">
 3      <Product Id="*" Name="ExecuteCatalogPackageTaskSetup" Language="1033" Version="1.0.
 4        <Package InstallerVersion="200" Compressed="yes" InstallScope="perMachine" />
 5
 6        <MajorUpgrade DowngradeErrorMessage="A newer version of [ProductName] is already
 7        <MediaTemplate />
 8
 9        <Feature Id="ProductFeature" Title="ExecuteCatalogPackageTaskSetup" Level="1">
10          <ComponentGroupRef Id="ProductComponents" />
11        </Feature>
12      </Product>
```

Figure 22-9. *The ExecuteCatalogPackageTask.wxs file*

The WiX Toolset process uses the settings in the ExecuteCatalogPackageTask.wxs file to configure the msi installer project and includes a helpful template by default. The next step is to edit the template, where needed, to install the Execute Catalog Package Task.

The ExecuteCatalogPackageTask.wxs file begins with an XML declaration shown in Figure 22-10:

```
<?xml version="1.0" encoding="UTF-8"?>
<Wix xmlns="http://schemas.microsoft.com/wix/2006/wi">
```

Figure 22-10. *The xml tag*

The next tag, the Wix tag, encapsulates the remainder of the ExecuteCatalogPackageTask.wxs file, as shown in Figure 22-11:

```
<Wix xmlns="http://schemas.microsoft.com/wix/2006/wi">
  <Product Id="*" Name="ExecuteCatalogPackageTaskSetup" Language="1033" Version="1.0.0.0" Manufacturer=""
    <Package InstallerVersion="200" Compressed="yes" InstallScope="perMachine" />

    <MajorUpgrade DowngradeErrorMessage="A newer version of [ProductName] is already installed." />
    <MediaTemplate />

    <Feature Id="ProductFeature" Title="ExecuteCatalogPackageTaskSetup" Level="1">
      <ComponentGroupRef Id="ProductComponents" />
    </Feature>
  </Product>

  <Fragment>
    <Directory Id="TARGETDIR" Name="SourceDir">
      <Directory Id="ProgramFilesFolder">
        <Directory Id="INSTALLFOLDER" Name="ExecuteCatalogPackageTaskSetup" />
      </Directory>
    </Directory>
  </Fragment>

  <Fragment>
    <ComponentGroup Id="ProductComponents" Directory="INSTALLFOLDER">
      <!-- TODO: Remove the comments around this Component element and the ComponentRef below in order to
      <!-- <Component Id="ProductComponent"> -->
        <!-- TODO: Insert files, registry keys, and other resources here. -->
      <!-- </Component> -->
    </ComponentGroup>
  </Fragment>
</Wix>
```

Figure 22-11. *The Wix tag*

The next step is to configure the Product tag. Begin by placing Product tag attributes on different lines. The Product Id value is configured to "*" which indicates the value will be automatically generated. Update the Product Name attribute value to "Execute Catalog Package Task," the Product Version attribute value, and the Product Manufacturer attribute value, if desired. I recommend leaving the Product Language and UpgradeCode attribute values set to their default values. Since XML ignores whitespace, feel free to add space to the ExecuteCatalogPackageTask.wxs file, as shown in Figure 22-12:

```
<?xml version="1.0" encoding="UTF-8"?>
<Wix xmlns="http://schemas.microsoft.com/wix/2006/wi">
```

```
<Product Id="*"
         Name="Execute Catalog Package Task"
         Language="1033"
         Version="1.0.0.0"
         Manufacturer="Andy Leonard Training, Inc."
         UpgradeCode="98d780e5-59db-4f86-b709-47db487643f4">
```

Figure 22-12. *Updating the Product tag*

Configure the Package Tag

The installation will require administrative permissions to search the registry, install to the Program Files (x86) path, and register the assemblies in the Global Assembly Cache (GAC) on the target server. Configure the Package tag by adding two attributes – InstallPrivileges and AdminImage – to permit installation as an administrator using the XML in Listing 22-1:

Listing 22-1. Permit Administrator installation

```
InstallPrivileges="elevated"
AdminImage="yes"
```

Once added, the XML appears as shown in Figure 22-13:

```
<Package InstallerVersion="200"
         Compressed="yes"
         InstallScope="perMachine"
         InstallPrivileges="elevated"
         AdminImage="yes" />
```

Figure 22-13. *Package edited to permit administrative installation privileges*

Configure the Installation Path Property Tags

SSIS task assemblies are installed in the *<drive>*:\ Program Files (x86)\Microsoft SQL Server*<version>*\DTS\Tasks folder for use during development. SSIS task assemblies are registered in the Global Assembly Cache or GAC for use during execution.

The next step is to add a property for the SSIS Task Installation Folder using the XML in Listing 22-2:

Listing 22-2. Add the SSIS Task Installation Folder property

```
<!-- Add a property for the custom task installation folder -->
<Property Id="SSISTASKINSTALLFOLDER" Value="SSISINSTALLFOLDER" />
```

When added, the XML appears as shown in Figure 22-14:

```
<!-- Add a property for the custom task installation folder -->
<Property Id="SSISTASKINSTALLFOLDER" Value="SSISINSTALLFOLDER" />
```

Figure 22-14. *Adding the SSIS Task Installation Folder property*

The next step is to add the SSIS Folder property using the XML in Listing 22-3:

Listing 22-3. Add the SSIS Folder property

```
<!-- Add a property for the SQL Server folder -->
<Property Id="SSISFOLDER" Value="C:\Program Files (x86)\Microsoft SQL
Server\140">
```

When added, the XML appears as shown in Figure 22-15:

```
20 <!-- Add a property for the SQL Server folder -->
21 <Property Id="SSISFOLDER" Value="C:\Program Files (x86)\Microsoft SQL Server\140">
```

Figure 22-15. *Adding the SSIS Folder property*

On line 21, the property is configured by setting the Id attribute value and supplying a default Value property value.

The next step is to add the SSIS Folder property. This step poses the highest challenge in configuring the installation project because it relies on the Windows Registry, and the registry for different Windows operating systems and different versions of SQL Server stores values in different locations. How and where you isolate registry values – and whether the values you find are *accurate*, even – may be a matter of trial and error.

For SQL Server 2017 running on Windows Server 2016, configure the registry-search XML using the XML in Listing 22-4:

Listing 22-4. Add the RegistrySearch XML

```
<!-- Search the registry for 32-bit and 64-bit SQL Server folder locations
  -->
  <!-- By far, this is the trickiest part of the WiX configuration,
        trying to find a registry value that is accurate and works.
        The HKEY_LOCAL_MACHINE\SOFTWARE\WOW6432Node\Microsoft\Microsoft SQL
        Server\140\VerSpecificRootDir
        entry works on Windows Server 2016. Yes, it's different for other
        OS's. -->
        <RegistrySearch Id="SSISFOLDER_REG_32"
                        Type="directory"
                        Key="SOFTWARE\WOW6432Node\Microsoft\Microsoft SQL
                        Server\140"
                        Name="VerSpecificRootDir"
                        Root="HKLM" Win64="no" />
</Property>
```

When added, the XML appears as shown in Figure 22-16:

```
20  <!-- Add a property for the SQL Server folder -->
21  <Property Id="SSISFOLDER" Value="C:\Program Files (x86)\Microsoft SQL Server\140">
22    <!-- Search the registry for 32-bit and 64-bit SQL Server folder locations -->
23    <!-- By far, this is the trickiest part of the WiX configuration,
24          trying to find a registry value that is accurate and works.
25          The HKEY_LOCAL_MACHINE\SOFTWARE\WOW6432Node\Microsoft\Microsoft SQL Server\140\VerSpecificRootDir
26          entry works on Windows Server 2016. Yes, it's different for other OS's. -->
27    <RegistrySearch Id="SSISFOLDER_REG_32"
28                    Type="directory"
29                    Key="SOFTWARE\WOW6432Node\Microsoft\Microsoft SQL Server\140"
30                    Name="VerSpecificRootDir"
31                    Root="HKLM" Win64="no" />
32  </Property>
```

Figure 22-16. *Adding the RegistrySearch XML*

On lines 27–31, the `HKEY_LOCAL_MACHINE\SOFTWARE\WOW6432Node\Microsoft\` `Microsoft SQL Server\140\VerSpecificRootDir` registry key is read and used to set the property Value attribute with the key value, which is shown in Figure 22-17:

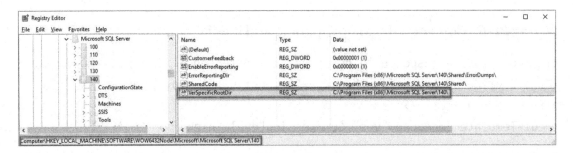

Figure 22-17. *Reading the HKEY_LOCAL_MACHINE\SOFTWARE\ WOW6432Node\Microsoft\Microsoft SQL Server\140\VerSpecificRootDir registry key value*

Please note the Root attribute value on line 27 is "`HKLM.`" `HKLM` is an abbreviation for `HKEY_LOCAL_MACHINE`.

The next step is to set the SSIS installation directory by combining the previous properties to complete the value of the SSISINSTALLFOLDER property value using the XML in Listing 22-5:

Listing 22-5. Complete the SSISINSTALLFOLDER value configuration

```
<!-- Set the SSISINSTALLFOLDER to the WiX UI Install Directory -->
<SetDirectory Id="SSISINSTALLFOLDER" Sequence="first" Value="[SSISFOLDER]\
DTS\Tasks" />
```

When added, the XML appears as shown in Figure 22-18:

```
<!-- Set the SSISINSTALLFOLDER to the WiX UI Install Directory -->
<SetDirectory Id="SSISINSTALLFOLDER" Sequence="first" Value="[SSISFOLDER]\DTS\Tasks" />
```

Figure 22-18. *Completing the SSISINSTALLFOLDER value configuration*

The SSISINSTALLFOLDER value is now configured.

Configure the MajorUpgrade and MediaTemplate Tags

The next step is configuring the MajorUpgrade and MediaTemplate tags using the XML in Listing 22-6:

Listing 22-6. Configure the MajorUpgrade and MediaTemplate tags

```
<!-- Configure a response to newer version detected -->
<MajorUpgrade DowngradeErrorMessage="A newer version of [ProductName] is
already installed." />
<MediaTemplate EmbedCab="yes" CompressionLevel="high" />
```

The MajorUpgrade tag contains a message (found in the DowngradeErrorMessage attribute) to display when a newer version of the Execute Catalog Package Task is already installed. The MediaTemplate tag attributes are EmbedCab and CompressionLevel. EmbedCab controls whether the *cabinet*, or cab, file, which contains the Execute Catalog Package Task installation code, is embedded in the product (msi) file. CompressionLevel sets compression for the cab file.

When added, the XML appears as shown in Figure 22-19:

```
<!-- Configure a response to newer version detected -->
<MajorUpgrade DowngradeErrorMessage="A newer version of [ProductName] is already installed." />
<MediaTemplate EmbedCab="yes" CompressionLevel="high" />
```

Figure 22-19. *Configuring the MajorUpgrade and MediaTemplate tags*

The next step is: Initialize the UIRef and License file tags.

Initialize the UIRef and License File Tags

Initialize the UIRef and License file tags using the XML in Listing 22-7:

Listing 22-7. Initializing the UIRef and License tags

```
<!-- Initialize UI -->
<UIRef Id="WixUI_Minimal"/>
<WixVariable Id="WixUILicenseRtf" Value="ECPTLicense.rtf" />
```

When added, the XML appears as shown in Figure 22-20:

```
<!-- Initialize UI -->
<UIRef Id="WixUI_Minimal"/>
<WixVariable Id="WixUILicenseRtf" Value="ECPTLicense.rtf" />
```

Figure 22-20. *Adding and initializing UIRef and WixUILicenseRtf WixVariable*

Software licensing is above my pay grade, so I used the tools available at creativecommons.org, as shown in Figure 22-21:

Figure 22-21. *Creativecommons.org*

At the time of this writing, the Creative Commons website presents a step-based page named Chooser (currently in beta at chooser-beta.creativecommons.org) where users answer questions and the Chooser suggests a license, as shown in Figure 22-22:

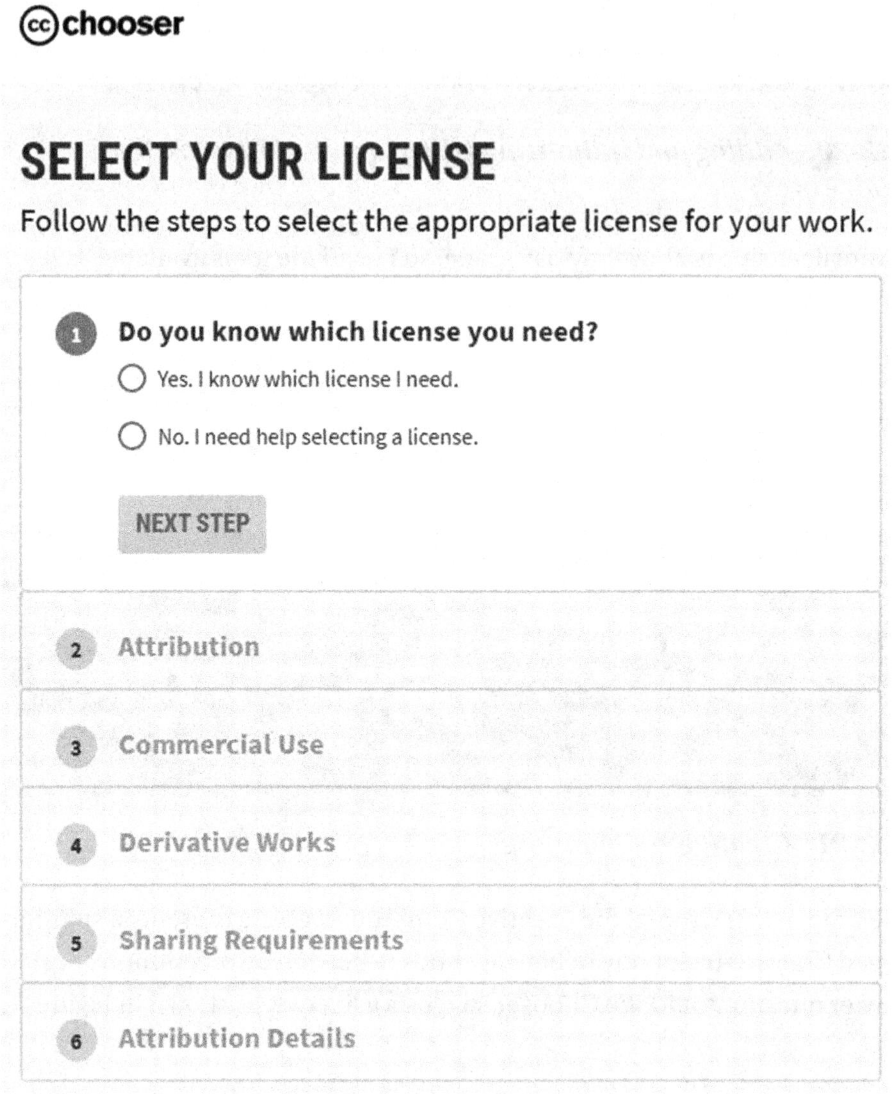

Figure 22-22. *Chooser*

Once the questions are complete, copy the rich text format documentation from the website, as shown in Figure 22-23:

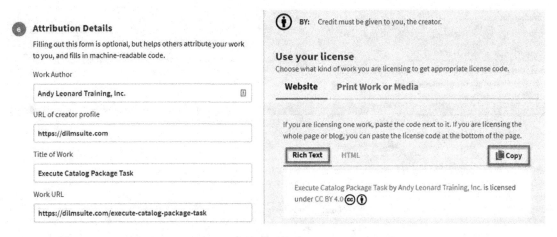

Figure 22-23. *Copying the license rich text format*

Once copied, open WordPad (or another rich text format editor) and paste the contents of the clipboard, as shown in Figure 22-24:

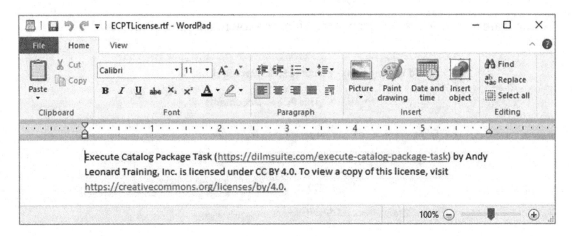

Figure 22-24. *License RTF*

Save the license RTF file and then add it to the setup project by right-clicking the ExecuteCatalogPackageTaskSetup project, hovering over Add, and then clicking Existing Item, as shown in Figure 22-25:

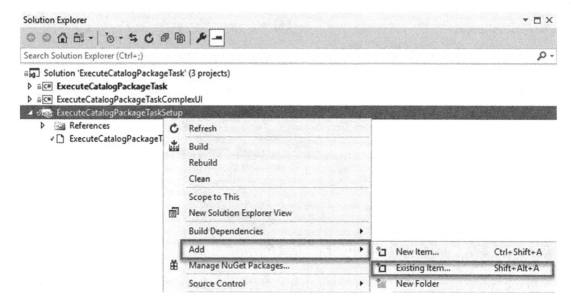

Figure 22-25. *Adding the license file to the setup project*

Navigate to and select the license RTF file, as shown in Figure 22-26:

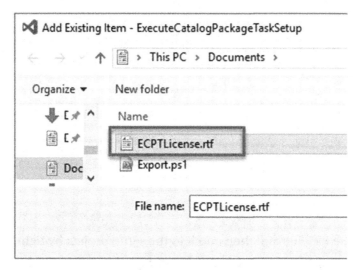

Figure 22-26. *Selecting the license RTF file*

Click the Add button to add the license RTF file to the
ExecuteCatalogPackageTaskSetup project, as shown in Figure 22-27:

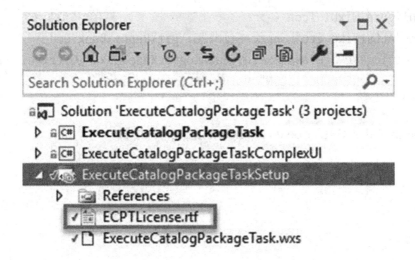

Figure 22-27. *Adding the license RTF file to the ExecuteCatalogPackageTaskSetup project*

The next step is configuring the installation feature and icon.

Configure the Installation Feature and Icon

The Feature tag identifies the ExecuteCatalogPackageTask as the "unit of installation" in the Title attribute.

The icon need not be imported into the WiX project because the SourceFile tag identifies the path to the icon file. The ARPPRODUCTICON property is used to set the icon to the installation file. If you want to use the ALStrike.ico, you may; it's part of the ExecuteCatalogPackageTask Visual Studio project.

Configure the installation Feature and Icon using the XML in Listing 22-8:

Listing 22-8. Configure the installation feature and icon

```
<!-- Configure the unit of installation (feature) -->
<Feature Id="CustomTask" Title="ExecuteCatalogPackageTask" Level="1">
  <ComponentGroupRef Id="CustomSSISTask" />
</Feature>
```

```
<!-- Configure WixUI icon -->
<Icon Id="ALCstrike.ico" SourceFile="G:\git\Repos\Book Code\
ExecuteCatalogPackageTask\ExecuteCatalogPackageTask\ALCStrike.ico" />
<Property Id="ARPPRODUCTICON" Value="ALCstrike.ico" />
</Product>
```

When added, the XML appears as shown in Figure 22-28:

```
<!-- Configure the unit of installation (feature) -->
<Feature Id="CustomTask" Title="ExecuteCatalogPackageTask" Level="1">
  <ComponentGroupRef Id="CustomSSISTask" />
</Feature>

<!-- Configure WixUI icon -->
<Icon Id="ALCstrike.ico" SourceFile="G:\git\Repos\Book Code\ExecuteCatalogPackageTask\ExecuteCatalogPackageTask\ALCStrike.ico" />
<Property Id="ARPPRODUCTICON" Value="ALCstrike.ico" />
</Product>
```

Figure 22-28. *Configuring the installation feature and icon*

Configure Folders and Folder Structure

In this section of the ExecuteCatalogPackageTask.wxs installation file configuration, we configure two paths for each assembly:

- The Tasks folder

- The Global Assembly Cache, or GAC

As stated earlier, Visual Studio uses assemblies deployed to the Tasks folder to populate the SSIS Toolbox for development. The SSIS execution engine uses the assemblies registered with the GAC for execution.

Configure the folders and folder structure fragment using the XML in Listing 22-9:

Listing 22-9. Configure the folders and folder structure fragment

```
<Fragment>
  <Directory Id="TARGETDIR" Name="SourceDir">
    <Directory Id="GAC" Name="GAC" />
    <Directory Id="SSISINSTALLFOLDER" />
  </Directory>
</Fragment>
```

When added, the XML appears as shown in Figure 22-29:

```
51 <!-- Configure folders and folder structure -->
52 <Fragment>
53   <Directory Id="TARGETDIR" Name="SourceDir">
54     <Directory Id="GAC" Name="GAC" />
55     <Directory Id="SSISINSTALLFOLDER" />
56   </Directory>
57 </Fragment>
```

Figure 22-29. *Configuring the folders and folder structure fragment*

In Figure 22-29, the Fragment tag spans lines 51–57. The outermost Directory tag opens on line 53 and closes on line 56. The outermost Directory tag's Id attribute value is TARGETDIR and its Name attribute value is SourceDir. The Directory tag on line 54 contains Id and Name attributes set to GAC is a self-closing Directory tag because the installer recognizes the values for the GAC. On line 55, the SSISINSTALLFOLDER property Id is specified in a Directory tag that defines the SSISINSTALLFOLDER registry-informed path – configured earlier – to the SSIS Tasks folder. On my virtual machine running the Windows Server 2016 operation system, SQL Server 2017 is installed on the E: drive, and my SSISINSTALLFOLDER path resolves to E:\Program Files (x86)\Microsoft SQL Server\140\DTS\Tasks. Once installed on my virtual machine, the ExecuteCatalogPackageTask and ExecuteCatalogPackageTaskComplexUI assemblies will be deployed to E:\Program Files (x86)\Microsoft SQL Server\140\DTS\Tasks, as shown in Figure 22-30:

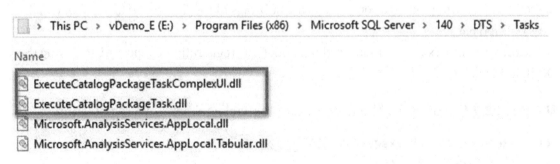

Figure 22-30. *Task assemblies used in SSIS 2017 development*

The ComponentGroup, Folders, and Folder Structure Fragment

The next Fragment tag covers the remainder of the WiX configuration.

Configure opening tags for the ComponentGroup and folders and folder structure Fragment using the XML in Listing 22-10:

Listing 22-10. Open the ComponentGroup fragment tag

```
<Fragment>
  <ComponentGroup Id="CustomSSISTask">
```

When added, the XML appears as shown in Figure 22-31:

```
<Fragment>
    <ComponentGroup Id="CustomSSISTask">
```

Figure 22-31. *Opening the ComponentGroup fragment tag*

Configure the ExecuteCatalogPackageTask GAC Registration

This last Fragment tag in the ExecuteCatalogPackageTask.wxs file configures the deployment of each assembly – ExecuteCatalogPackageTask and ExecuteCatalogPackageTaskComplexUI – in the development folder and the GAC. The Fragment details each deployment target in Component tags that include File and RemoveFile sub-tags. All Component tags are sub-tags of the ComponentGroup tag, which was defined earlier.

Configure the ExecuteCatalogPackageTask GAC registration Component tag using the XML in Listing 22-11:

Listing 22-11. Configure the ExecuteCatalogPackageTask GAC registration

```
<!-- ExecuteCatalogPackageTask [GAC] -->
<Component Id="Tasks_GAC"
          Directory="GAC"
          Guid="F4B72F57-AE0E-4EEE-8B04-10198ABDC523">
```

```
<File Id="Task_GAC"
      Name="$(var.ExecuteCatalogPackageTask.TargetFileName)"
      Source="$(var.ExecuteCatalogPackageTask.TargetPath)"
      Assembly=".net"
      KeyPath="yes"
      Checksum="yes" />
  <RemoveFile Id="Task_GAC"
              On="uninstall"
              Name="$(var.ExecuteCatalogPackageTask.TargetFileName)" />
</Component>
```

When added, the XML appears as shown in Figure 22-32:

```
<!-- ExecuteCatalogPackageTask [GAC] -->
<Component Id="Tasks_GAC"
           Directory="GAC"
           Guid="F4B72F57-AE0E-4EEE-8B04-10198ABDC523">
  <File Id="Task_GAC"
        Name="$(var.ExecuteCatalogPackageTask.TargetFileName)"
        Source="$(var.ExecuteCatalogPackageTask.TargetPath)"
        Assembly=".net"
        KeyPath="yes"
        Checksum="yes" />
  <RemoveFile Id="Task_GAC"
              On="uninstall"
              Name="$(var.ExecuteCatalogPackageTask.TargetFileName)" />
</Component>
```

Figure 22-32. *Configuring the ExecuteCatalogPackageTask GAC registration*

The next step is to configure the Component tag for installing the ExecuteCatalogPackageTask assembly to the development folder.

Configure the ExecuteCatalogPackageTask Tasks Deployment Folder

Configure the ExecuteCatalogPackageTask assembly deployment folder using the XML for the Component tag in Listing 22-12:

Listing 22-12. Configure the ExecuteCatalogPackageTask deployment folder

```
<!-- ExecuteCatalogPackageTask [Tasks] -->
<Component Id="Tasks_SSIS"
          Directory="SSISINSTALLFOLDER"
          Guid="F4B72F57-AE0E-4EEE-8B04-10198ABDC524">
  <File Id="Task_SSIS"
        Name="$(var.ExecuteCatalogPackageTask.TargetFileName)"
        Source="$(var.ExecuteCatalogPackageTask.TargetPath)"
        KeyPath="yes"
        Checksum="yes" />
  <RemoveFile Id="Task_SSIS"
              On="uninstall"
              Name="$(var.ExecuteCatalogPackageTask.TargetFileName)" />
</Component>
```

When added, the XML appears as shown in Figure 22-33:

```
<!-- ExecuteCatalogPackageTask [Tasks] -->
<Component Id="Tasks_SSIS"
          Directory="SSISINSTALLFOLDER"
          Guid="F4B72F57-AE0E-4EEE-8B04-10198ABDC524">
  <File Id="Task_SSIS"
        Name="$(var.ExecuteCatalogPackageTask.TargetFileName)"
        Source="$(var.ExecuteCatalogPackageTask.TargetPath)"
        KeyPath="yes"
        Checksum="yes" />
  <RemoveFile Id="Task_SSIS"
              On="uninstall"
              Name="$(var.ExecuteCatalogPackageTask.TargetFileName)" />
</Component>
```

Figure 22-33. *Configuring the ExecuteCatalogPackageTask deployment folder*

The next steps repeat configuration of the target directory installation locations for the ExecuteCatalogPackageTaskComplexUI assemblies.

Configure the ExecuteCatalogPackageTaskComplexUI GAC Registration

Configure the ExecuteCatalogPackageTaskComplexUI GAC registration fragment using the XML in Listing 22-13:

Listing 22-13. Configure the ExecuteCatalogPackageTaskComplexUI GAC registration

```xml
<!-- ExecuteCatalogPackageTaskComplexUI [GAC] -->
<Component Id="Tasks_UI_GAC"
          Directory="GAC"
          Guid="F4B72F57-AE0E-4EEE-8B04-10198ABDC525">
  <File Id="Task_UI_GAC"
        Name="$(var.ExecuteCatalogPackageTaskComplexUI.TargetFileName)"
        Source="$(var.ExecuteCatalogPackageTaskComplexUI.TargetPath)"
        Assembly=".net"
        KeyPath="yes"
        Checksum="yes" />
    <RemoveFile Id="Task_UI_GAC"
                On="uninstall"
                Name="$(var.ExecuteCatalogPackageTaskComplexUI.
                TargetFileName)" />
</Component>
```

When added, the XML appears as shown in Figure 22-34:

```
<!-- ExecuteCatalogPackageTaskComplexUI [GAC] -->
<Component Id="Tasks_UI_GAC"
          Directory="GAC"
          Guid="F4B72F57-AE0E-4EEE-8B04-10198ABDC525">
  <File Id="Task_UI_GAC"
        Name="$(var.ExecuteCatalogPackageTaskComplexUI.TargetFileName)"
        Source="$(var.ExecuteCatalogPackageTaskComplexUI.TargetPath)"
        Assembly=".net"
        KeyPath="yes"
        Checksum="yes" />
  <RemoveFile Id="Task_UI_GAC"
              On="uninstall"
              Name="$(var.ExecuteCatalogPackageTaskComplexUI.TargetFileName)" />
</Component>
```

Figure 22-34. *Configuring the ExecuteCatalogPackageTaskComplexUI GAC registration*

The next step is to configure the deployment folder for the ExecuteCatalogPackageTaskComplexUI assembly.

Configure the ExecuteCatalogPackageTaskComplexUI Tasks Deployment Folder

Configure the ExecuteCatalogPackageTaskComplexUI Tasks deployment folder using the XML in Listing 22-14:

Listing 22-14. Configure the ExecuteCatalogPackageTaskComplexUI deployment folder

```
<!-- ExecuteCatalogPackageTaskComplexUI [Tasks] -->
<Component Id="Tasks_UI_SSIS"
          Directory="SSISINSTALLFOLDER"
          Guid="F4B72F57-AE0E-4EEE-8B04-10198ABDC526">
  <File Id="Task_UI_SSIS"
        Name="$(var.ExecuteCatalogPackageTaskComplexUI.TargetFileName)"
        Source="$(var.ExecuteCatalogPackageTaskComplexUI.TargetPath)"
        KeyPath="yes"
        Checksum="yes" />
```

```
<RemoveFile Id="Task_UI_SSIS"
            On="uninstall"
            Name="$(var.ExecuteCatalogPackageTaskComplexUI.
TargetFileName)" />
</Component>
```

When added, the XML appears as shown in Figure 22-35:

```
<!-- ExecuteCatalogPackageTaskComplexUI [Tasks] -->
<Component Id="Tasks_UI_SSIS"
           Directory="SSISINSTALLFOLDER"
           Guid="F4B72F57-AE0E-4EEE-8B04-10198ABDC526">
  <File Id="Task_UI_SSIS"
        Name="$(var.ExecuteCatalogPackageTaskComplexUI.TargetFileName)"
        Source="$(var.ExecuteCatalogPackageTaskComplexUI.TargetPath)"
        KeyPath="yes"
        Checksum="yes" />
  <RemoveFile Id="Task_UI_SSIS"
              On="uninstall"
              Name="$(var.ExecuteCatalogPackageTaskComplexUI.TargetFileName)" />
</Component>
```

Figure 22-35. *Configuring the ExecuteCatalogPackageTaskComplexUI deployment folder*

The configurations of deployment directories for installing the ExecuteCatalogPackageTask and ExecuteCatalogPackageTaskComplexUI assemblies into the development directory and the GAC are complete.

Close the ComponentGroup and Folders and Folder Structure Fragment

Configure closing tags for the ComponentGroup and folders and folder structure Fragment using the XML in Listing 22-15:

Listing 22-15. Close the ComponentGroup fragment tags

```
  </ComponentGroup>
</Fragment>
```

When added, the XML appears as shown in Figure 22-36:

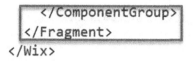

```
    </ComponentGroup>
    </Fragment>
  </Wix>
```

Figure 22-36. *Closing the ComponentGroup and fragment tags*

The folders and folder structure configurations are complete and closed.

Rename the Output

Before we leave this section, right-click the ExecuteCatalogPackageTaskSetup project in Solution Explorer, and then click Properties. When the ExecuteCatalogPackageTaskSetup properties display, click the Installer tab and then change the "Output name" property to "ExecuteCatalogPackageTask," as shown in Figure 22-37:

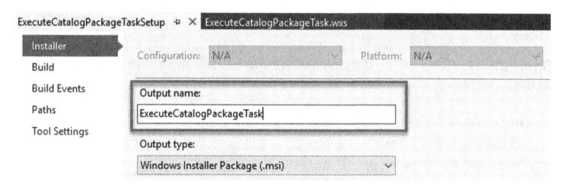

Figure 22-37. *Renaming the output file*

Build and Install

Once the WiX tags are configured, the msi file is generated when we execute a build for the ExecuteCatalogPackageTaskSetup project. If all goes as planned, the building of the ExecuteCatalogPackageTaskSetup project will produce the ExecuteCatalogPackageTask. msi file, which we may use to install the Execute Catalog Package Task on additional servers throughout the enterprise.

In Solution Explorer, right-click the ExecuteCatalogPackageTaskSetup project, and then click Build, as shown in Figure 22-38:

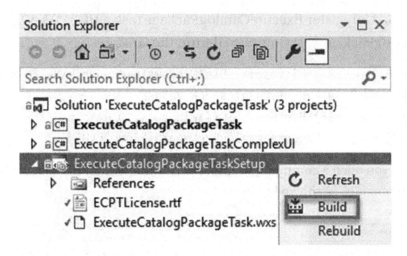

Figure 22-38. *Building the ExecuteCatalogPackageTaskSetup project*

Navigate to the location of your ExecuteCatalogPackageTaskSetup.msi file – which will be located in your ExecuteCatalogPackageTaskSetup Visual Studio project folder – drill into the bin folder, and then drill into the Debug folder, as shown in Figure 22-39:

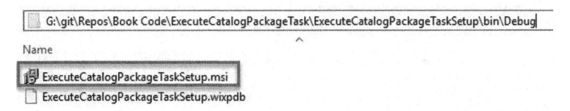

Figure 22-39. *Finding your ExecuteCatalogPackageTaskSetup.msi file*

Please be aware that the state of the Execute Catalog Package Task installed on your test server affects the results of executing your ExecuteCatalogPackageTaskSetup.msi file.

Cleaning Up

To make sure we are starting from the same starting point, unregister the ExecuteCatalogPackageTask and ExecuteCatalogPackageTaskComplexUI assemblies from the GAC using the commands in Listing 22-16:

Listing 22-16. Unregister ExecuteCatalogPackageTask and ExecuteCatalogPackageTaskComplexUI from the GAC

```
"C:\Program Files (x86)\Microsoft SDKs\Windows\v10.0A\bin\NETFX 4.7.2
Tools\gacutil.exe" -u ExecuteCatalogPackageTask
"C:\Program Files (x86)\Microsoft SDKs\Windows\v10.0A\bin\NETFX 4.7.2
Tools\gacutil.exe" -u ExecuteCatalogPackageTaskComplexUI
```

Make sure you open a command prompt as an administrator to execute the GAC unregister commands, as shown in Figure 22-40:

Figure 22-40. *Unregistering ExecuteCatalogPackageTask and ExecuteCatalogPackageTaskComplexUI from the GAC*

In Figure 22-40, my server displays "Number of assemblies uninstalled = 0" which indicates the assemblies are already uninstalled. Your mileage may vary.

Double-check the GAC path and delete any residual files you may discover in that location, as shown in Figure 22-41:

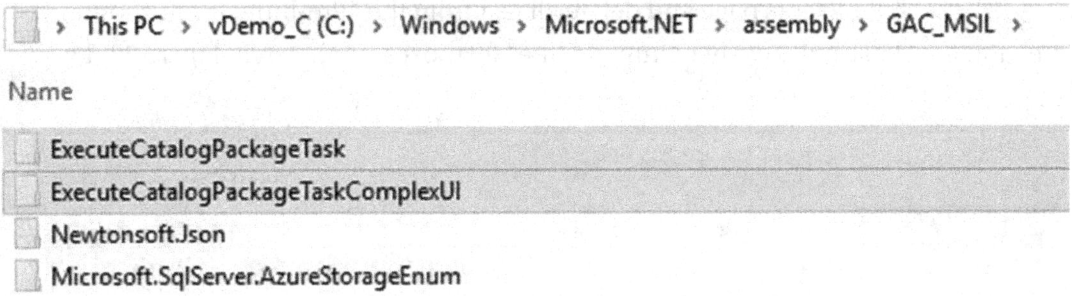

> This PC > vDemo_C (C:) > Windows > Microsoft.NET > assembly > GAC_MSIL >

Name

ExecuteCatalogPackageTask

ExecuteCatalogPackageTaskComplexUI

Newtonsoft.Json

Microsoft.SqlServer.AzureStorageEnum

Figure 22-41. *Cleaning the GAC*

On my virtual machine, the location of the GAC files is C:\Windows\Microsoft.NET\ assembly\GAC_MSIL. The location of your GAC may be a different path.

Next, open the Properties for the ExecuteCatalogPackageTask Visual Studio project by right-clicking the project name in Solution Explorer and then clicking Properties. On the Build page, change the Output path property to "bin\Debug\" as shown in Figure 22-42:

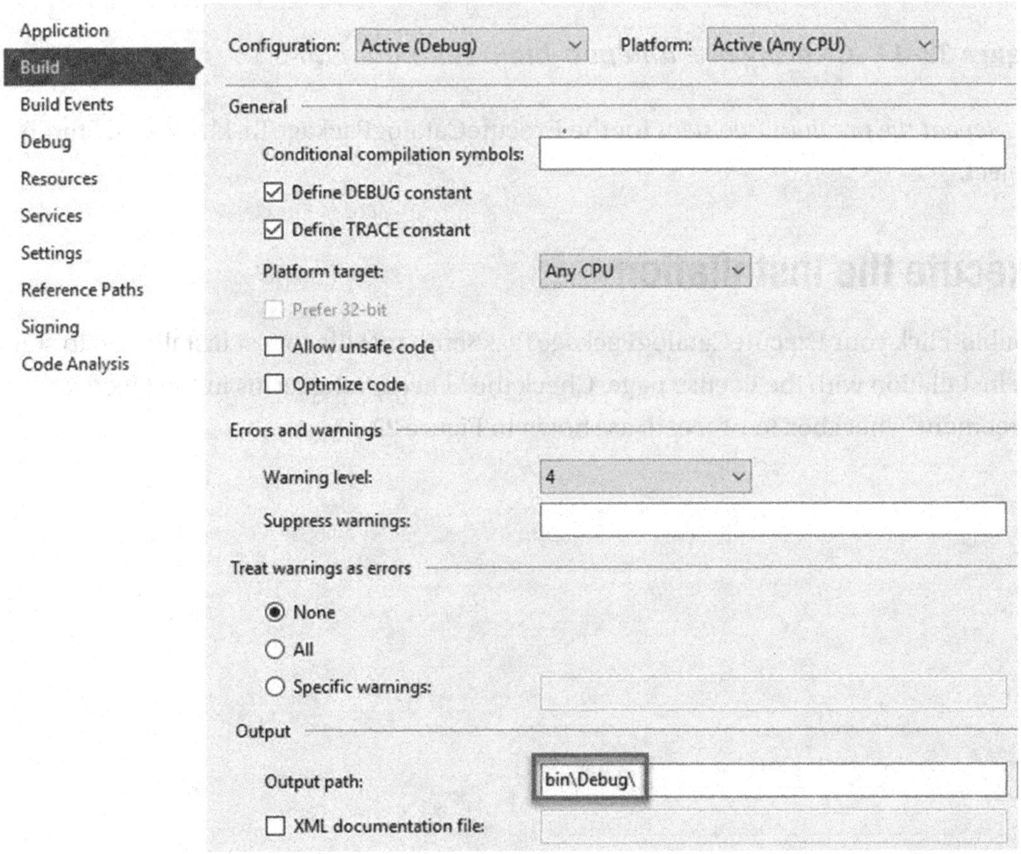

Application	Configuration: Active (Debug) ∨	Platform: Active (Any CPU) ∨
Build		
Build Events	General	
Debug	Conditional compilation symbols:	
Resources	☑ Define DEBUG constant	
Services	☑ Define TRACE constant	
Settings	Platform target: Any CPU ∨	
Reference Paths	☐ Prefer 32-bit	
Signing	☐ Allow unsafe code	
Code Analysis	☐ Optimize code	

Errors and warnings

Warning level: 4

Suppress warnings:

Treat warnings as errors

◉ None

○ All

○ Specific warnings:

Output

Output path: bin\Debug\

☐ XML documentation file:

Figure 22-42. *Editing the Output path property*

Click the Build Events page and delete all text from the "Pre-build event command line" and the "Post-build event command line" textboxes, as shown in Figure 22-43:

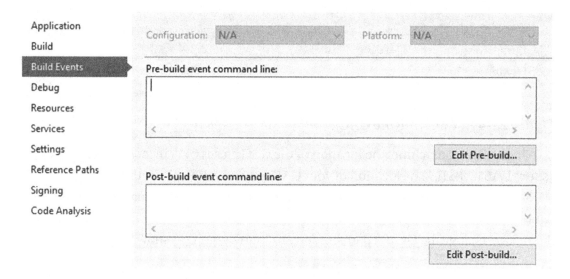

Figure 22-43. *Clearing pre- and post-build command lines*

Repeat the previous two steps for the ExecuteCatalogPackageTaskUI Visual Studio project.

Execute the Installation

Double-click your ExecuteCatalogPackageTaskSetup.msi file to test installation to start the installation with the license page. Check the "I accept the terms in the License Agreement" checkbox to proceed, as shown in Figure 22-44:

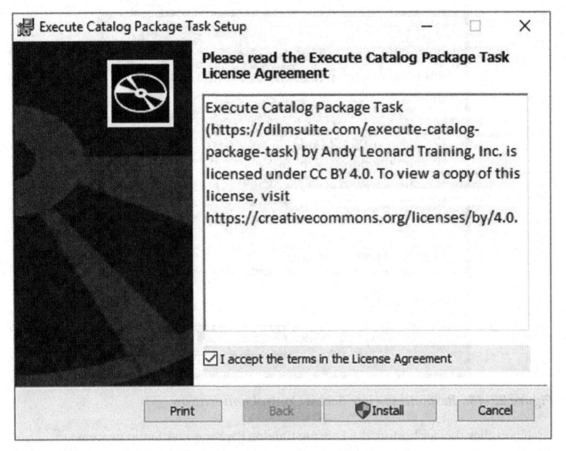

Figure 22-44. *Starting the Execute Catalog Package Task Setup at the license agreement*

The next step is to reply to the User Account Control notification, as shown in Figure 22-45:

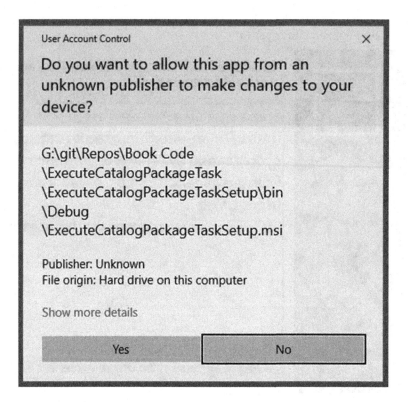

Figure 22-45. *Respond to User Access Control notification*

If you click the Yes button, the Execute Catalog Package Task Setup process completes, as shown in Figure 22-46:

Figure 22-46. *Completing the Execute Catalog Package Task Setup process*

Re-executing the ExecuteCatalogPackageTaskSetup.msi file presents Repair and Remove buttons, which are self-explanatory, as shown in Figure 22-47:

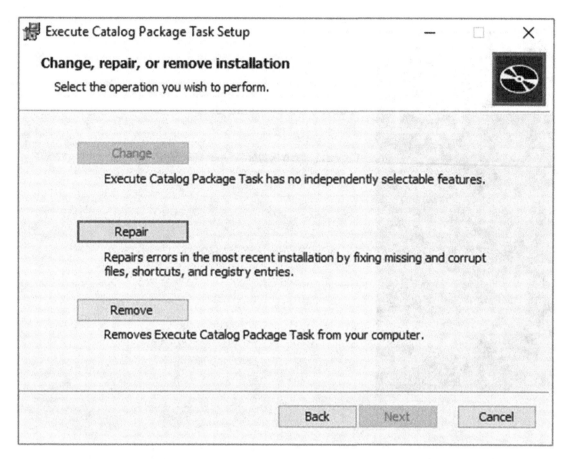

Figure 22-47. *Re-executing the ExecuteCatalogPackageTaskSetup.msi file*

Verify the install file deploys the ExecuteCatalogPackageTask and
ExecuteCatalogPackageTaskComplexUI assemblies (DLL files) to the SSIS Tasks (or
development) folder, as shown in Figure 22-48:

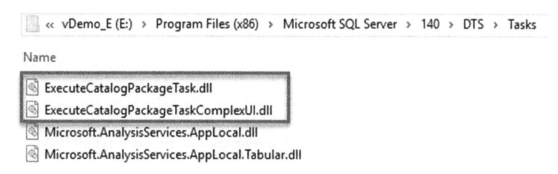

Figure 22-48. *Verifying installation to the SSIS Tasks folder*

On my virtual machine, the path to the SSIS Tasks (or development) folder is E:\
Program Files\Microsoft SQL Server\140\DTS\Tasks.

Verify the install file deploys the ExecuteCatalogPackageTask and
ExecuteCatalogPackageTaskComplexUI assemblies to the GAC, as shown in Figure 22-49:

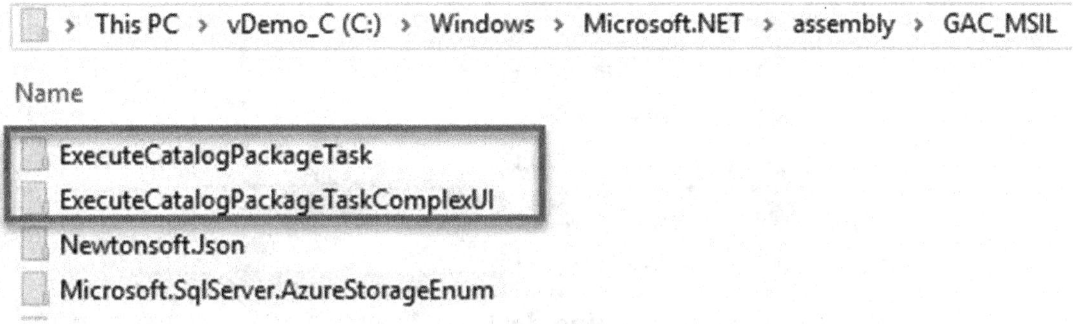

> This PC > vDemo_C (C:) > Windows > Microsoft.NET > assembly > GAC_MSIL

Name

- ExecuteCatalogPackageTask
- ExecuteCatalogPackageTaskComplexUI
- Newtonsoft.Json
- Microsoft.SqlServer.AzureStorageEnum

Figure 22-49. *Verifying installation to the GAC*

The location of the GAC files is C:\Windows\Microsoft.NET\assembly\GAC_MSIL on
my virtual machine, as stated earlier.

Let's Test It!

After executing the ExecuteCatalogPackageTaskSetup.msi installer file, open a test SSIS
project and test SSIS package. Open the SSIS Toolbox and check for the Execute Catalog
Package Task, as shown in Figure 22-50:

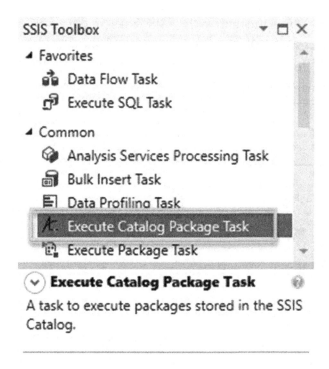

Figure 22-50. *Execute Catalog Package Task, check*

If the Execute Catalog Package Task is available in the SSIS Toolbox, you should be able to configure the task in SSIS on your server.

Troubleshooting the Installation

Building an install file can be tricky. In this section are three helpful tips for troubleshooting.

It is important to remember to install the Execute Catalog Package Task on every server in your enterprise Data Integration Lifecycle. Deploying an SSIS package to a server where the Execute Catalog Package Task has *not* been installed will result an error similar to "`Error loading Package.dtsx: Cannot create a task from XML for task "Execute Catalog Package Task", type "ExecuteCatalogPackageTask. ExecuteCatalogPackageTask, ExecuteCatalogPackageTask, Version=1.0.0.0, Culture=neutral, PublicKeyToken=e86e33313a45419e" due to error 0x80070057 "The parameter is incorrect.".`" When opening an SSIS package on a server where the Execute Catalog Package Task has not been installed, the SSIS project throws errors, and the Execute Catalog Package Task appears as shown in Figure 22-51:

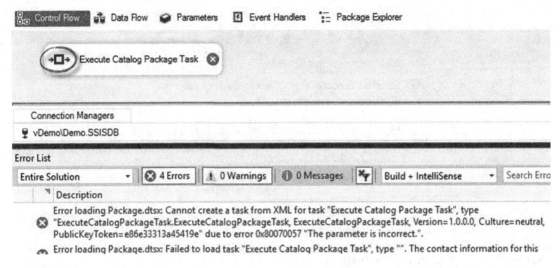

Figure 22-51. *Opening an SSIS package with an Execute Catalog Package Task configured, on a server on which the Execute Catalog Package Task has not been installed*

Note the generic SSIS package task logo, circle in Figure 22-51.

Logged Installation

You may log the installation using a command similar to that shown in Listing 22-17:

Listing 22-17. Logging the msi file execution

```
msiexec /i ExecuteCatalogPackageTask.msi /l*v ECPT_Installation_Log.txt
```

After executing the installation, you may view the contents of the log file.

Cleaning the MSI File

Before each build of the WiX setup project, clean the output by right-clicking the WiX setup project and then clicking Clean, as shown in Figure 22-52:

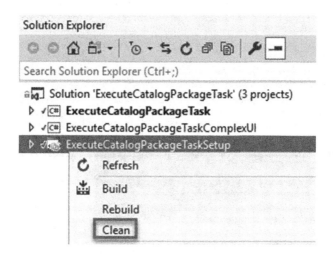

Figure 22-52. *Cleaning the output*

Verify the output is clean by browsing to the output folder, as shown in Figure 22-53:

Figure 22-53. *Verifying a cleaned output folder*

The ExecuteCatalogPackageTask.msi and ExecuteCatalogPackageTask.wixpdb files should be absent from the ExecuteCatalogPackageTaskSetup bin\Debug directory after executing the Clean.

The next step is to build the WiX setup project, as shown in Figure 22-54:

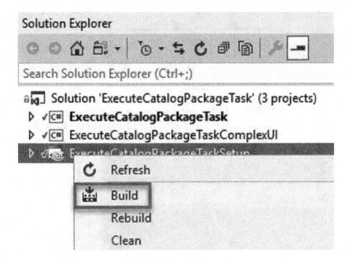

Figure 22-54. *Building the Wix setup project*

Verify a successful build by re-checking the output folder, as shown in Figure 22-55:

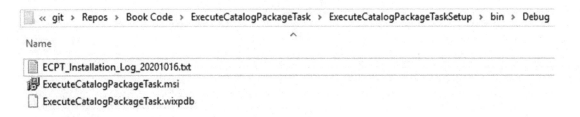

Figure 22-55. *Verifying a successful build*

If all goes as planned, the ExecuteCatalogPackageTask.msi and
ExecuteCatalogPackageTask.wixpdb files should appear in the output folder.

Conclusion

The reader is encouraged to learn more about using the WiX Toolset at wixtoolset.
org where one may find in-depth documentation and examples at wixtoolset.org/
documentation.

The next step is to use the Execute Catalog Package Task in an enterprise data
engineering framework solution.

Now would be an excellent time to check in your code.

CHAPTER 23

Using the Execute Catalog Package Task in an SSIS Framework

In the book titled *SQL Server Data Automation Through Frameworks: Building Metadata-Driven Frameworks with T-SQL, SSIS, and Azure Data Factory* (amazon. com/Server-Data-Automation-Through-Frameworks/dp/1484262123), Kent Bradshaw and I describe and demonstrate data frameworks that execute stored procedures and SSIS packages. Kent shares a metadata-driven stored procedure-based framework that executes other stored procedures and records execution report data. I share an SSIS framework that executes SSIS packages stored in on-premises file systems and a variation that executes SSIS packages stored in Azure file shares. Like Kent's stored procedure-based framework, both SSIS frameworks are metadata-driven and record execution metadata. The on-premises version of the SSIS framework uses an SSIS package as the framework "engine." The Azure-SSIS version is driven by two Azure Data Factory pipelines.

In this chapter, we use the Execute Catalog Package Task to build a metadata-driven SSIS Catalog-based SSIS framework. The framework we will build is similar to the on-premises version of the SSIS framework in the SQL Server Data Automation Through Frameworks book and is also similar to SSIS Framework Community Edition (dilmsuite. com/ssis-framework-community-edition) – a free and open source project that is part of the collection of utilities that make up the Data Integration Lifecycle Management Suite (dilmsuite.com).

The SSIS framework we build in this chapter has additional functionality, however: the ability to start package executions serially *or* start executions in parallel (well, *nearly* in parallel). It's possible to achieve parallelism in the other framework versions; you

© Andy Leonard 2021
A. Leonard, *Building Custom Tasks for SQL Server Integration Services*,
https://doi.org/10.1007/978-1-4842-6482-9_23

just need to build an (additional) SSIS package or ADF pipeline to manage parallel-execution orchestration. The Execute Catalog Package Task surfaces a Synchronized property, which means our framework can store values for the Synchronized property in metadata; no extra SSIS package required. As with all engineering, there is no free lunch. The word "start" in an earlier sentence is carefully chosen; the desired design *may* revolve around the *completions* of SSIS package parallel executions.

We begin with an examination of an SSIS package that revolves around SSIS package parallel execution completions.

The Controller SSIS Design Pattern

Orchestration is a complex topic in data engineering. Workflow management is easy to underestimate. In the introduction to this chapter, we find one such example: The Execute Catalog Package Task supports *starting nearly parallel* SSIS package executions. The emphases in the previous sentence underscore orchestration challenges.

When designing for parallelism, most SSIS developers are more concerned with *virtual steps*. A virtual step is a collection of operations that execute as a block (or step). Most often, the next step starts after *all* operations in the previous step *complete*. Another way to think about this kind of workflow management is: The next step doesn't start until the last operation in the previous step completes. Please note we are not considering the execution status, which multiplies the complexity of any metadata solution.

The Controller SSIS design pattern is one solution for managing workflow.

Begin by adding a new SSIS package to a new SSIS project named ECPTFramework. Rename the new SSIS package "ECPTController.dtsx," as shown in Figure 23-1:

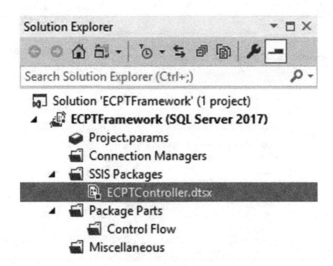

Figure 23-1. *Adding the ECPTController.dtsx SSIS package*

Add two Sequence Containers to the control flow. Name the first "SEQ Step 1" and the second "SEQ Step 2." Add an Execute Catalog Package Task to SEQ Step 1, and rename it "ECPT Execute ReportAndSucceed." Configure ECPT Execute ReportAndSucceed to execute the ReportAndSucceed.dtsx SSIS package synchronously, as shown in Figure 23-2:

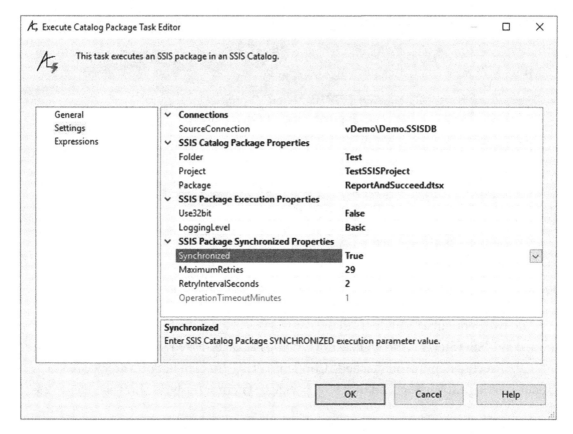

Figure 23-2. *Configuring ReportAndSucceed execution*

Add another Execute Catalog Package Task to SEQ Step 1 and rename it "ECPT Execute RunForSomeTime." Configure ECPT Execute RunForSomeTime to execute the ECPT Execute RunForSomeTime.dtsx SSIS package synchronously, as shown in Figure 23-3:

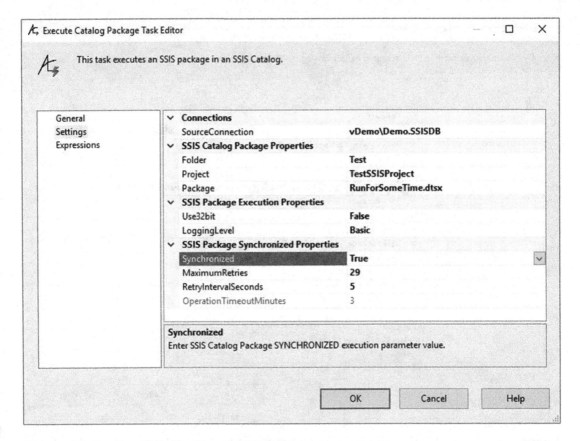

Figure 23-3. *Configuring RunForSomeTime execution*

Add an Execute Catalog Package Task to SEQ Step 2 and rename it "ECPT Execute *<Some other package>*." Configure ECPT Execute *<Some other package>* to execute any SSIS package asynchronously, as shown in Figure 23-4:

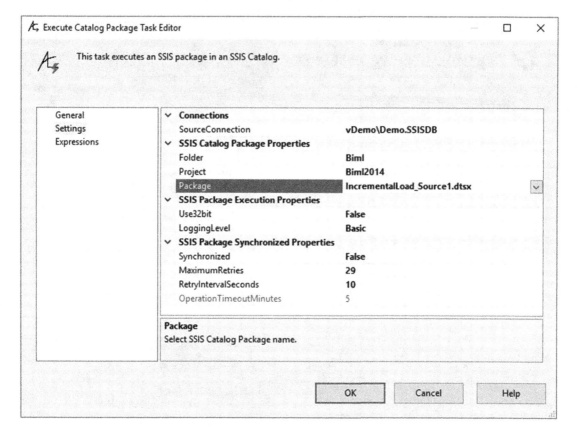

Figure 23-4. *Configuring any other SSIS package for execution*

Use a precedence constraint to connect SEQ Step 1 to SEQ Step 2, as shown in Figure 23-5:

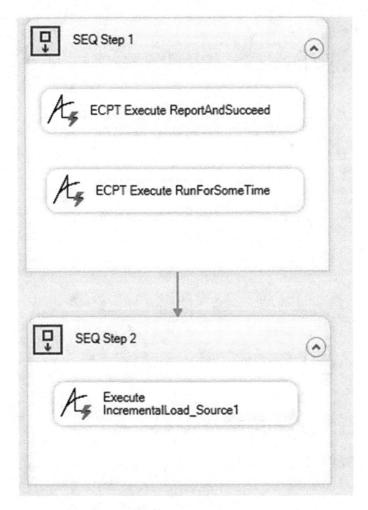

Figure 23-5. *The Controller, configured*

Execute the Controller SSIS package and note the (virtual) steps of execution. The first step is ECPT Execute ReportAndSucceed and ECPT Execute RunForSomeTime starting in parallel in SEQ Step 1, as shown in Figure 23-6:

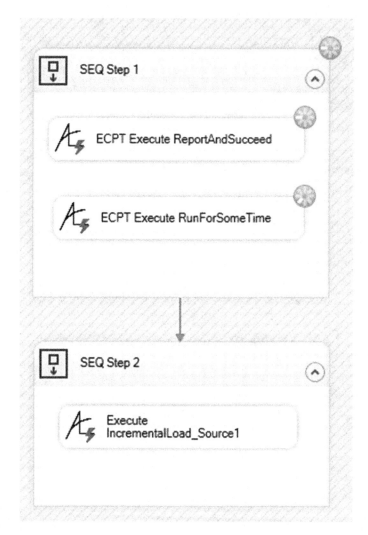

Figure 23-6. *Virtual step 1*

When ECPT Execute ReportAndSucceed completes and succeeds, ECPT Execute RunForSomeTime continues executing, as shown in Figure 23-7:

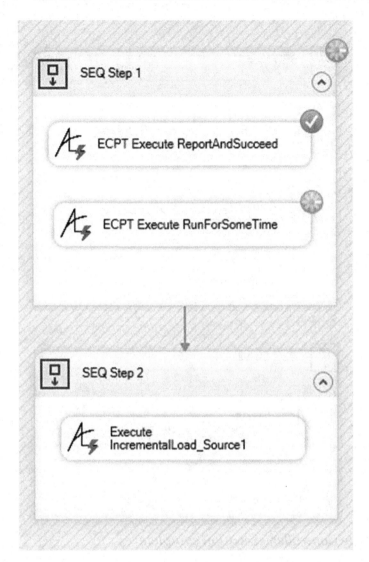

Figure 23-7. *Virtual step 2*

The execution of the ECPT Execute Child1 Execute Catalog Package Task – nestled inside SEQ Step 2 in my example – does not *start* executing until *all* tasks in SEQ Step 1 *complete,* as shown in Figure 23-8:

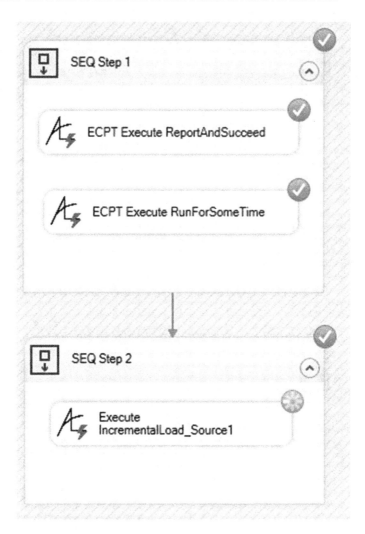

Figure 23-8. *The Controller, execution complete*

When SSIS developers consider executing SSIS packages in parallel, they most often imagine Controller functionality; starting the next virtual step after the previous virtual step has completed execution.

A Metadata-Driven SSIS Execution Framework

An SSIS framework has three functions:

1. Configuration

2. Execution

3. Logging

By this definition, the SSIS Catalog is an SSIS framework.

Why use a framework? As stated in the *SQL Server Data Automation Through Frameworks* book:

"Executing a few dozen SSIS packages is different – really different – from managing the execution of thousands of SSIS packages. Don't take my word for it, ask any data engineer managing a larger enterprise." If your enterprise uses only a few SSIS packages, a framework is most likely unnecessary overhead. If, however, your enterprise executes hundreds or thousands of SSIS packages per day, an SSIS framework is a *necessity*.

This framework focuses on execution, but you could add logging using the framework Kent and I describe in the book titled *SQL Server Data Automation Through Frameworks: Building Metadata-Driven Frameworks with T-SQL, SSIS, and Azure Data Factory* (amazon.com/Server-Data-Automation-Through-Frameworks/dp/1484262123).

We begin by defining an *SSIS application* as a collection of SSIS packages that execute as a group. In order to execute a group of SSIS packages, the framework requires SSIS package location metadata. The cardinality between applications and packages appears simple – one-to-one – until we consider use cases such as a package that archives flat files after their data is loaded.

In SSIS projects designed for the SSIS Catalog, developers may use the Execute Package Task to call additional SSIS packages, but there's a catch: The child package called by the Execute Package Task must reside in the same SSIS project as the (parent) package *calling* the child package. Applied to a package designed to archive files, this constraint means the same SSIS package – "ArchiveFile.dtsx," for example – must be imported into every SSIS project that will call ArchiveFile.dtsx. Copying the same code over and over is not prudent. A better solution is to build one version of the ArchiveFile.dtsx package and deploy it to the SSIS Catalog and then execute ArchiveFile.dtsx from that single location whenever it is time to archive a file. If there are multiple copies of ArchiveFile.dtsx spread around the enterprise (or even a single SSIS Catalog), how do developers add functionality? Or fix a bug? It can be done, but it's messy and horribly inefficient.

Because SSIS packages like ArchiveFile.dtsx exist, the SSIS application-to-SSIS package cardinality is many-to-many. Our framework solution is 3rd normal form, so it requires a bridge (or resolver) table. Our bridge table is *application packages*.

Adding Metadata Database Objects

To start building this SSIS framework, connect to a SQL Server instance with an SSIS Catalog configured. Add a schema named fw to the SSISDB database using the T-SQL in Listing 23-1:

Listing 23-1. Adding the fw schema

```
Use SSISDB
Go

print 'Fw schema'
If Not Exists(Select s.[name]
                     From [sys].[schemas] s
                     Where s.[name] = N'fw')
 begin
  print ' - Create fw schema'
  declare @sql varchar(30) = 'Create schema fw'
  exec(@sql)
  print ' - Fw schema created'
 end
Else
 begin
  print ' - Fw schema already exists.'
 end
go
```

When executed (the first time), the Messages tab displays as shown in Figure 23-9:

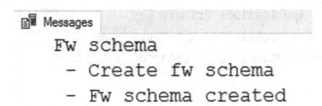

Figure 23-9. *Creating the fw schema*

The T-SQL is idempotent, meaning the script may be executed multiple times and return the same result. Re-executing the T-SQL, the Messages tab displays as shown in Figure 23-10:

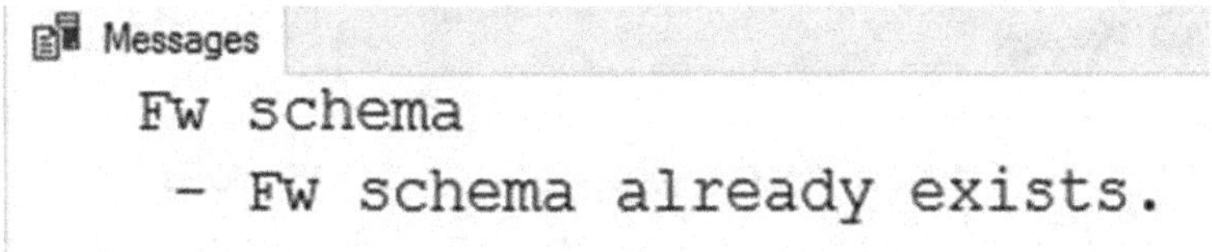

Figure 23-10. *Verifying the fw schema exists*

Many T-SQL scripts in this chapter are idempotent.

Next, build the Applications table in the fw schema using the T-SQL in Listing 23-2:

Listing 23-2. Adding the fw.Applications table

```
Use SSISDB
go

print 'Fw.Applications table'
If Not Exists(Select s.[name] + '.' + t.[name]
                From [sys].[tables] t
                Join [sys].[schemas] s
                  On s.[schema_id] = t.[schema_id]
                Where s.[name] = N'fw'
                And t.[name] = N'Applications')
  begin
   print ' - Create fw.Applications table'
   Create Table fw.Applications
   (ApplicationId int identity(1, 1)
```

```
    Constraint PK_Applications Primary Key
  ,ApplicationName nvarchar(130) Not NULL)
  print ' - Fw.Applications table created'
 end
Else
 begin
  print ' - Fw.Applications table already exists.'
 end
go
```

When executed (the first time), the Messages tab displays as shown in Figure 23-11:

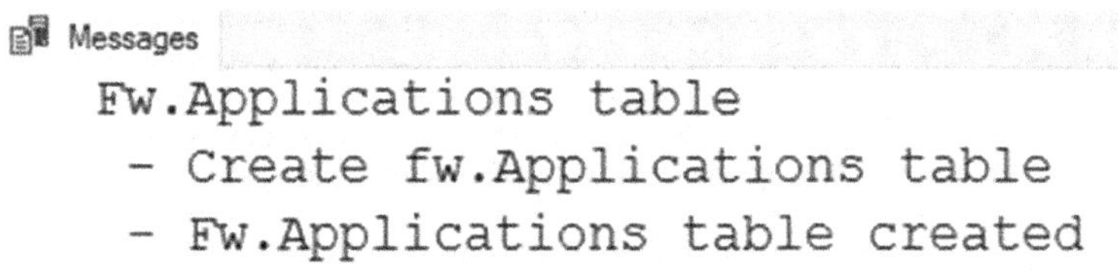

Figure 23-11. *Creating the fw.Applications table*

Add the Packages table using the T-SQL in Listing 23-3:

Listing 23-3. Adding the Packages table

```
Use SSISDB
go

print 'Fw.Packages table'
If Not Exists(Select s.[name] + '.' + t.[name]
                    From [sys].[tables] t
                    Join [sys].[schemas] s
                      On s.[schema_id] = t.[schema_id]
                    Where s.[name] = N'fw'
                      And t.[name] = N'Packages')
 begin
  print ' - Create fw.Packages table'
  Create Table fw.Packages
  (PackageId int identity(1, 1)
```

```
   Constraint PK_Packages Primary Key
  ,FolderName nvarchar(130) Not NULL
  ,ProjectName nvarchar(130) Not NULL
  ,PackageName nvarchar(260) Not NULL)
  print ' - Fw.Packages table created'
 end
Else
 begin
  print ' - Fw.Packages table already exists.'
 end
go
```

When executed (the first time), the Messages tab displays as shown in Figure 23-12:

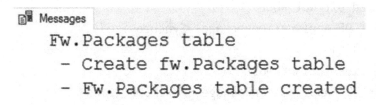

Figure 23-12. *Creating the fw.Packages table*

Resolve the many-to-many cardinality between Applications and Packages by adding the ApplicationPackages table using the T-SQL in Listing 23-4:

Listing 23-4. Adding the ApplicationPackages table

```
Use SSISDB
go

print 'Fw.ApplicationPackages table'
If Not Exists(Select s.[name] + '.' + t.[name]
                   From [sys].[tables] t
                   Join [sys].[schemas] s
                     On s.[schema_id] = t.[schema_id]
                   Where s.[name] = N'fw'
                     And t.[name] = N'ApplicationPackages')
  begin
```

```
  print ' - Create fw.ApplicationPackages table'
  Create Table fw.ApplicationPackages
  (ApplicationPackageId int identity(1, 1)
    Constraint PK_ApplicationPackages Primary Key
  ,ApplicationId int Not NULL
    Constraint FK_ApplicationPackages_Applications
        Foreign Key References fw.Applications(ApplicationId)
  ,PackageId int Not NULL
    Constraint FK_ApplicationPackages_Packages
        Foreign Key References fw.Packages(PackageId)
  ,ExecutionOrder int Not NULL
    Constraint DF_ApplicationPackages_ExecutionOrder
        Default(10)
  ,Synchronized bit Not NULL
    Constraint DF_ApplicationPackages_Synchronized
        Default(1)
  ,MaximumRetries int Not NULL
    Constraint DF_ApplicationPackages_MaximumRetries
        Default(100)
  ,RetryIntervalSeconds int Not NULL
    Constraint DF_ApplicationPackages_RetryIntervalSeconds
        Default(10)
  ,Use32bit int Not NULL
    Constraint DF_ApplicationPackages_Use32bit
        Default(0)
  ,LoggingLevel nvarchar(25) Not NULL
    Constraint DF_ApplicationPackages_LoggingLevel
        Default('Basic')
)
  print ' - Fw.ApplicationPackages table created'
 end
Else
 begin
  print ' - Fw.ApplicationPackages table already exists.'
 end
go
```

When executed (the first time), the Messages tab displays as shown in Figure 23-13:

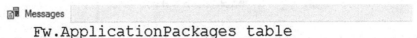

```
Messages
        Fw.ApplicationPackages table
         - Create fw.ApplicationPackages table
         - Fw.ApplicationPackages table created
```

Figure 23-13. *Creating the fw.ApplicationPackages table*

The ApplicationPackages table contains several SSIS package execution settings available in the Execute Catalog Package Task. Why not add these attributes to the Packages table? Recall the same package may be used in multiple applications. It's possible we may desire to execute ArchiveFile.dtsx, for example, synchronously in one application and asynchronously in another application. The same applies to the other attributes.

Add the Execution Engine

The execution engine for our framework is an SSIS package that uses our Execute Catalog Package Task. Click the Parameters tab and add a new String type package parameter named ApplicationName, as shown in Figure 23-14:

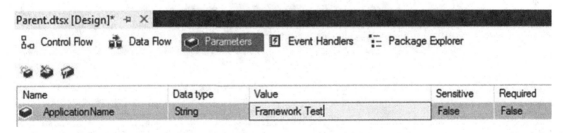

Figure 23-14. *Adding the ApplicationName package parameter*

Add a new SSIS package-scoped ADO.Net Connection Manager named "Framework SSIS Catalog" to the Parent.dtsx SSIS package, connected to the SQL Server instance that hosts the framework SSIS Catalog, as shown in Figure 23-15:

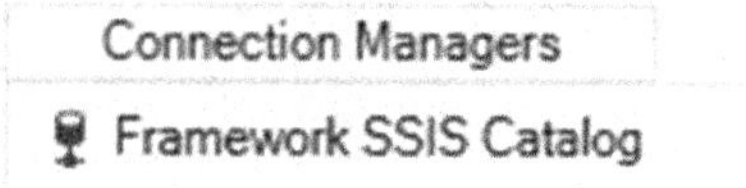

Connection Managers

🍷 Framework SSIS Catalog

Figure 23-15. *Adding the Framework SSIS Catalog connection manager*

Add a new SSIS package named Parent.dtsx to the ECPTFramework SSIS project. Add an Execute SQL Task to the Parent.dtsx Control Flow, and rename the Execute SQL Task "SQL Get Application Packages," as shown in Figure 23-16:

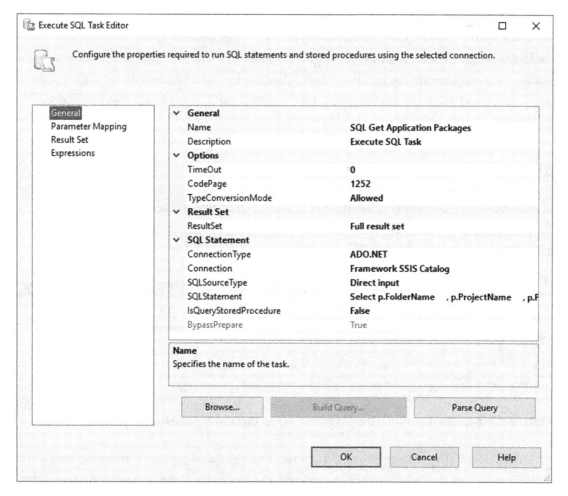

Figure 23-16. *SQL Get Application Packages General view*

Set the ConnectionType property to ADO.NET and the Connection property to the Framework SSIS Catalog connection manager. In the SQLStatement property, enter the T-SQL in Listing 23-5:

Listing 23-5. T-SQL to get application packages

```
Select p.FolderName
     , p.ProjectName
     , p.PackageName
     , ap.Synchronized
     , ap.MaximumRetries
     , ap.RetryIntervalSeconds
     , ap.Use32bit
     , ap.LoggingLevel
From fw.ApplicationPackages ap
Join fw.Applications a
  On a.ApplicationId = ap.ApplicationId
Join fw.Packages p
  On p.PackageId = ap.PackageId
Where a.ApplicationName = @ApplicationName
Order By ap.ExecutionOrder
```

Once added to the SQLStatement property, the T-SQL appears as shown in Figure 23-17:

Figure 23-17. *T-SQL for the SQL Statement property*

Configure the ResultSet property to "Full result set." Click the Parameter Mapping page and click the Add button. Set the Variable Name to $Package::ApplicationName, Data Type to String, and the Parameter Name to ApplicationName, as shown in Figure 23-18:

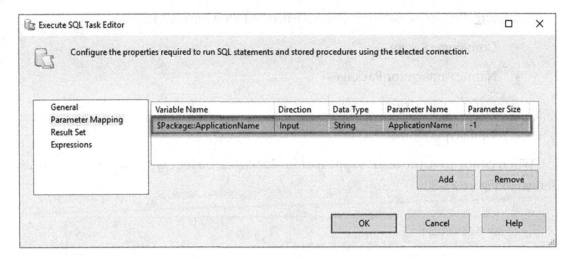

Figure 23-18. *Configuring the Parameter Mapping*

On the Result Set page, click the Add button and rename the Result Name "0." Click the Variable Name dropdown and select "<New variable...>," as shown in Figure 23-19:

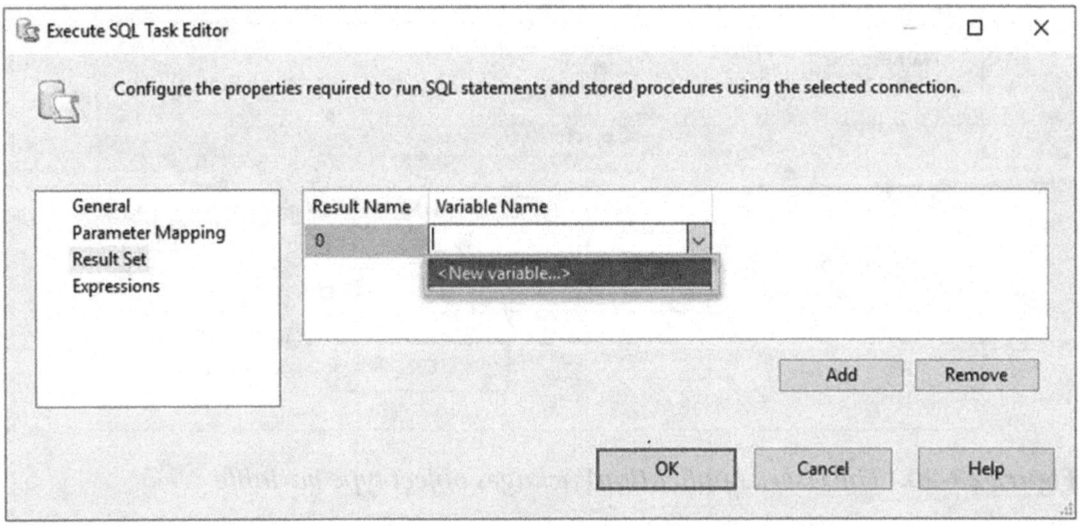

Figure 23-19. *Creating a new variable for the result set*

Configure the new variable properties with the following settings:

- Container: Parent

- Name: ApplicationPackages

- Namespace: User

- Value type: Object

When configured, the User::ApplicationPackages Object type variable appears as shown in Figure 23-20:

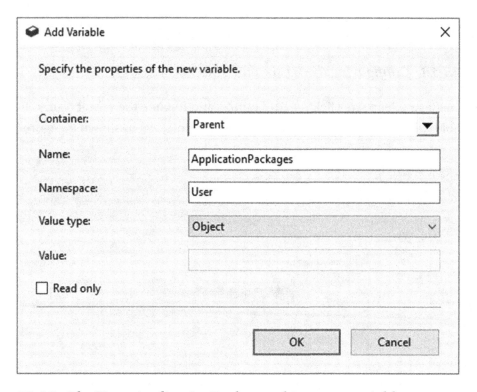

Figure 23-20.   *The User::ApplicationPackages object type variable*

Click the OK button to close the Add Variable dialog. The Result Set page appears as shown in Figure 23-21:

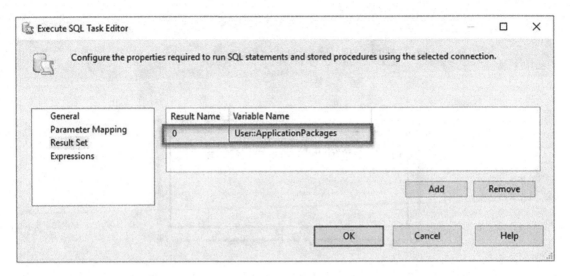

Figure 23-21. *Configuring the Result Set*

Click the OK button to close the Execute SQL Task Editor. The Parent.dtsx control flow appears as shown in Figure 23-22:

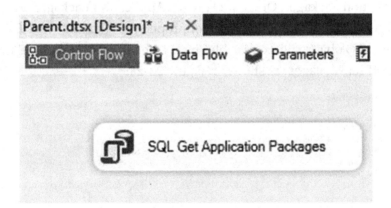

Figure 23-22. *SQL Get Application Packages configured*

Drag a Foreach Loop Container onto the Parent.dtsx control flow, and rename the Foreach Loop Container "Foreach Application Package," as shown in Figure 23-23:

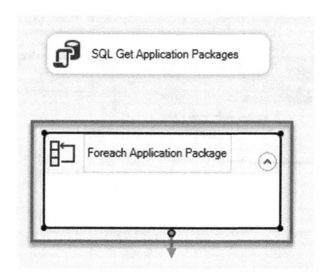

Figure 23-23. *Adding the "Foreach Application Packages" Foreach Loop Container*

Connect a Success precedence constraint from SQL Get Application Packages to Foreach Application Packages. Open the Foreach Application Packages Editor, click the Collection page, and then set the Enumerator property to "Foreach ADO Enumerator." Configure the "ADO object source variable" by clicking the dropdown and then selecting User::ApplicationPackages, as shown in Figure 23-24:

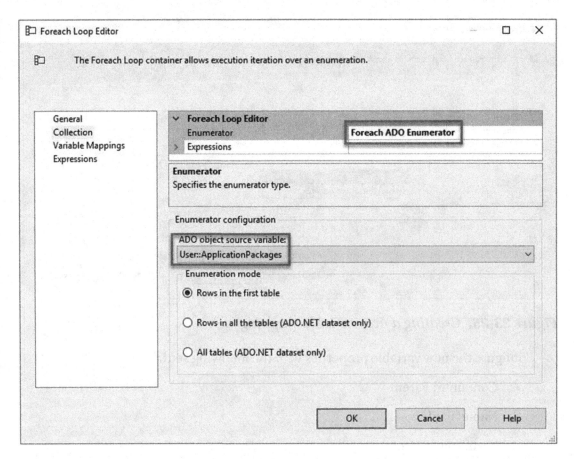

Figure 23-24. *Configuring the Foreach ADO Enumerator*

Click the Variable Mappings page. Click the Variable dropdown and select "<New variable...>," as shown in Figure 23-25:

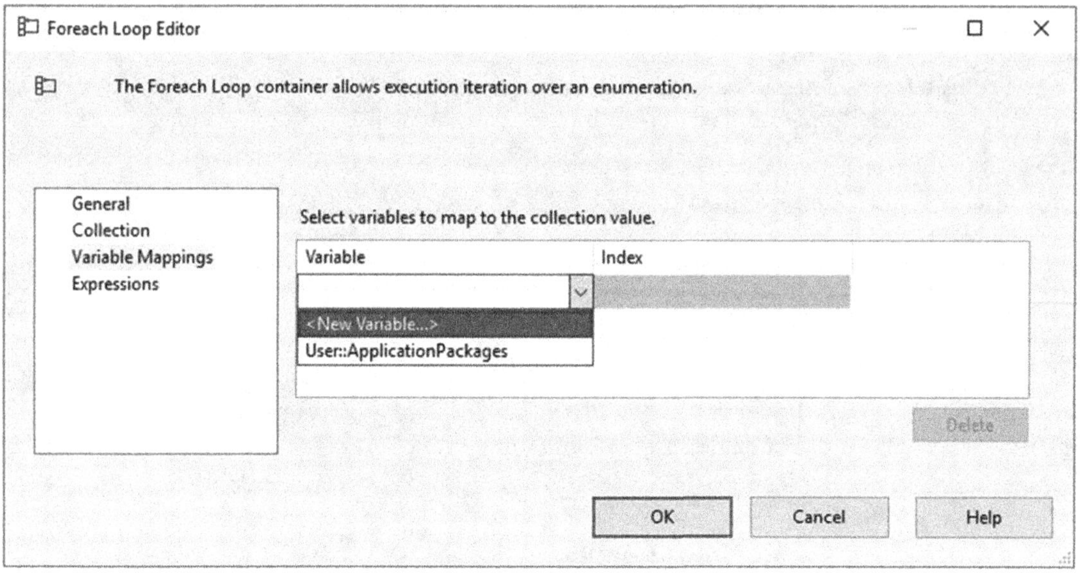

Figure 23-25. *Creating a new variable mapping*

Configure the new variable properties with the following settings:

- Container: Parent

- Name: Folder

- Namespace: User

- Value type: String

- Value: *<insert the name of an SSIS Catalog folder>*

When configured, the User::Folder String type variable appears as shown in
Figure 23-26:

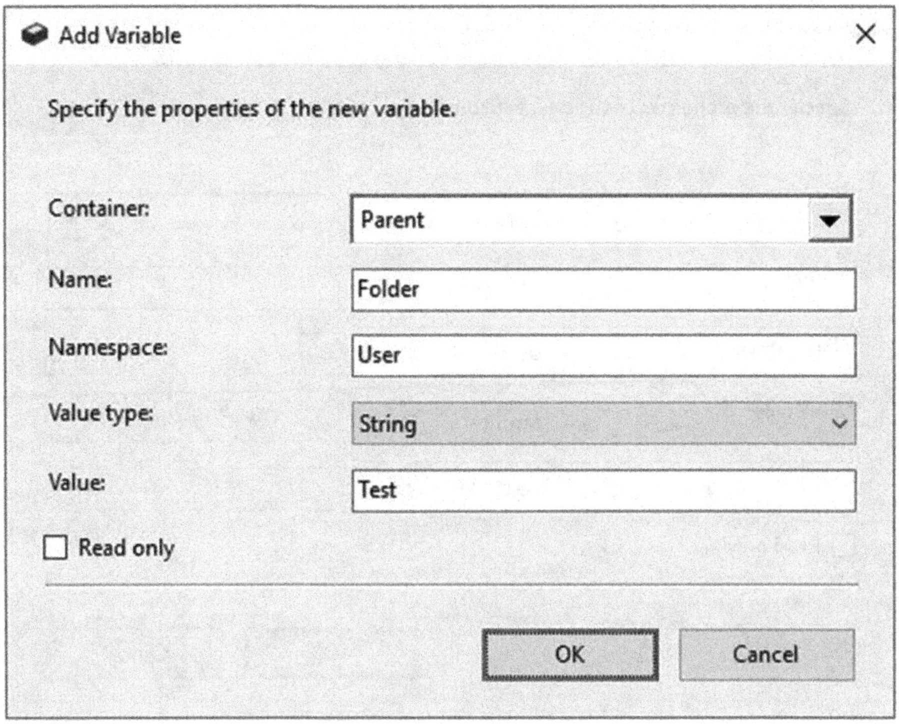

Figure 23-26. *Creating the User::Folder variable*

Create another new variable and configure the properties with the following settings:

- Container: Parent

- Name: Project

- Namespace: User

- Value type: String

- Value: <*insert the name of an SSIS Catalog project*>

When configured, the User::Project String type variable appears as shown in Figure 23-27:

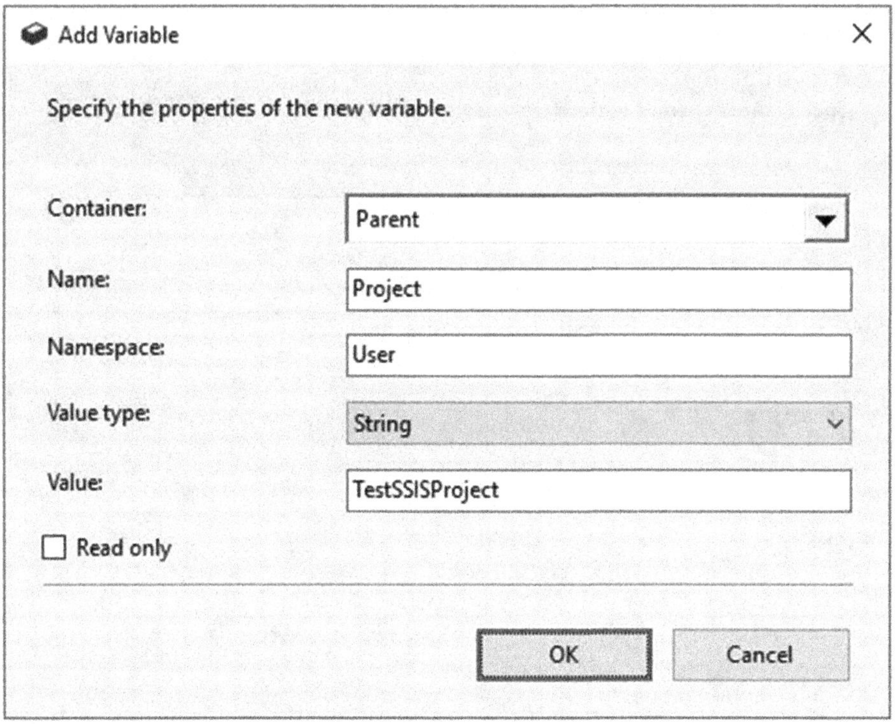

Figure 23-27. *Creating the User::Project variable*

Create another new variable and configure the properties with the following settings:

- Container: Parent

- Name: Package

- Namespace: User

- Value type: String

- Value: <*insert the name of an SSIS Catalog package*>

When configured, the User::Package String type variable appears as shown in Figure 23-28:

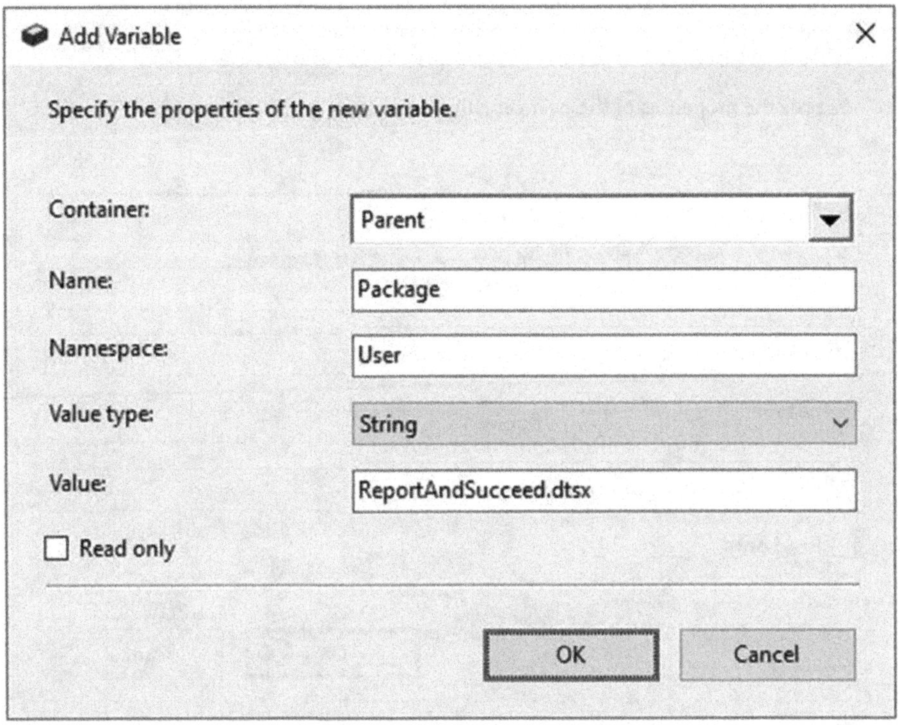

Figure 23-28. *Creating the User::Package variable*

Create yet another new variable and configure the properties with the following settings:

- Container: Parent
- Name: Synchronized
- Namespace: User
- Value type: Boolean
- Value: true

When configured, the User::Synchronized Boolean type variable appears as shown in Figure 23-29:

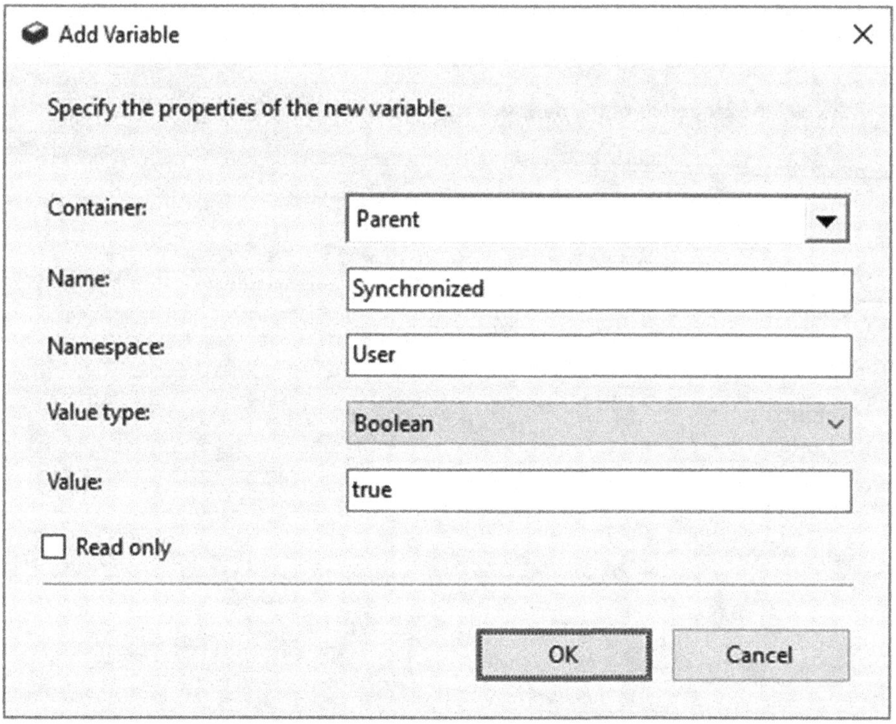

Figure 23-29. *Creating the User::Synchronized variable*

Create yet another new variable and configure the properties with the following settings:

- Container: Parent

- Name: MaximumRetries

- Namespace: User

- Value type: Int32

- Value: 29

When configured, the User::MaximumRetries Int32 type variable appears as shown in Figure 23-30:

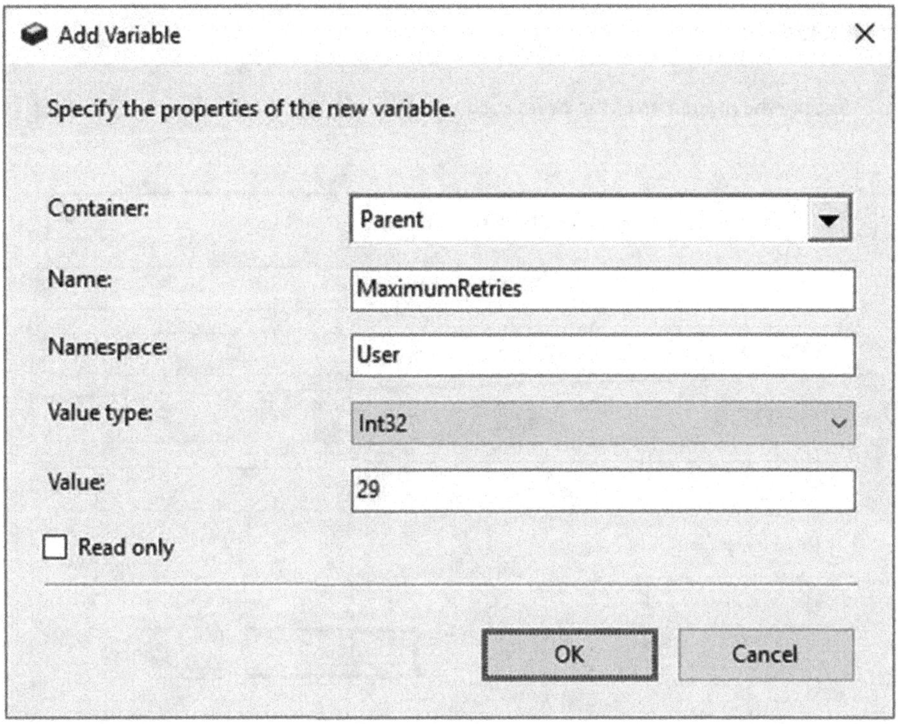

Figure 23-30. *Creating the User::MaximumRetries variable*

Create a new variable and configure the properties with the following settings:

- Container: Parent

- Name: RetryIntervalSeconds

- Namespace: User

- Value type: Int32

- Value: 10

When configured, the User::RetryIntervalSeconds Int32 type variable appears as shown in Figure 23-31:

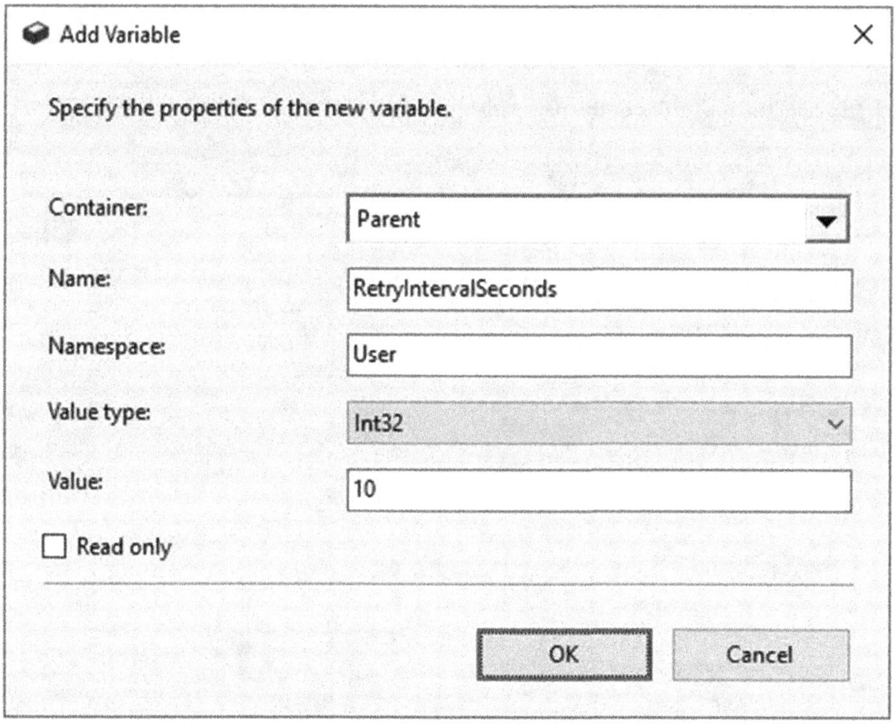

Figure 23-31. *Creating the User::RetryIntervalSeconds variable*

Create a new variable and configure the properties with the following settings:

- Container: Parent

- Name: Use32bit

- Namespace: User

- Value type: Boolean

- Value: false

When configured, the User::Use32bit Boolean type variable appears as shown in
Figure 23-32:

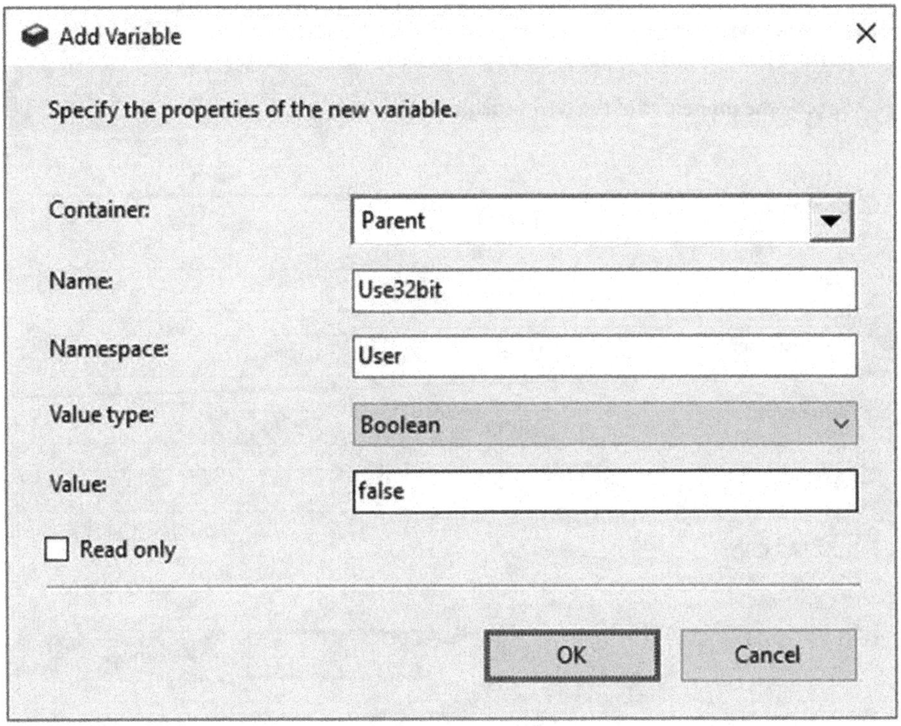

Figure 23-32. *Creating the User::Use32bit variable*

Create one last Foreach Application Packages variable and configure the properties with the following settings:

- Container: Parent

- Name: LoggingLevel

- Namespace: User

- Value type: String

- Value: Basic

When configured, the User::LoggingLevel Int32 type variable appears as shown in Figure 23-33:

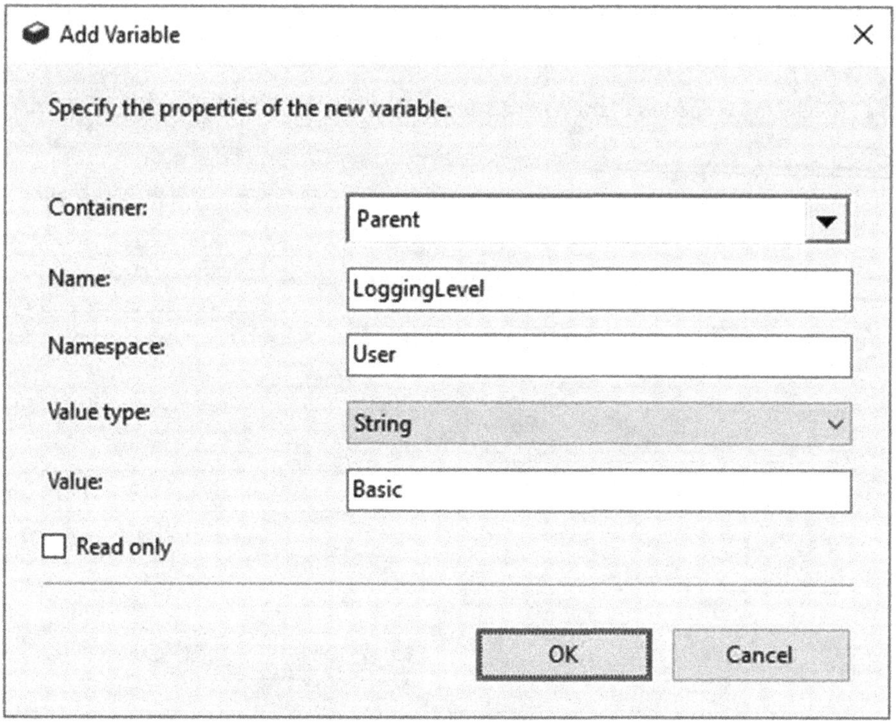

Figure 23-33. *Creating the User::LoggingLevel variable*

After these variables have been created and mapped, the Foreach Application
Packages Variable Mappings page appears as shown in Figure 23-34:

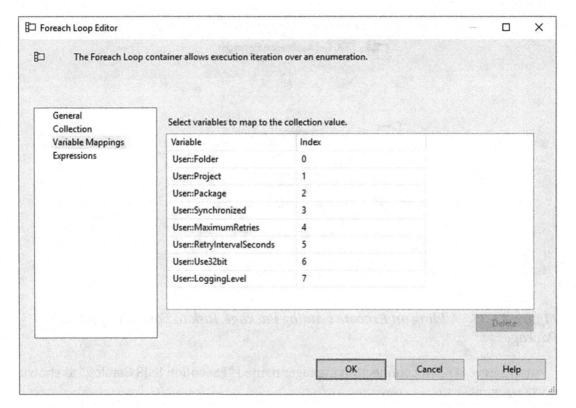

Figure 23-34. *The Foreach Application Packages Variable Mappings page, configured*

Click the OK button to close the Foreach Application Packages Foreach loop container editor.

The next step is to add an Execute Catalog Package Task to the Foreach Application Packages Foreach loop container, as shown in Figure 23-35:

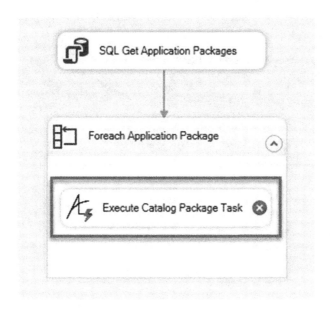

Figure 23-35. *Adding an Execute Catalog Package Task to Foreach Application Packages*

Add a new ADO.Net connection manager named "Execution SSIS Catalog," as shown in Figure 23-36:

Figure 23-36. *The Execution SSIS Catalog connection manager*

Open the Execute Catalog Package Task Editor and rename it "Execute Application Package" on the General page. On the Settings page, click the SourceConnection dropdown and select "Execute SSIS Catalog," as shown in Figure 23-37:

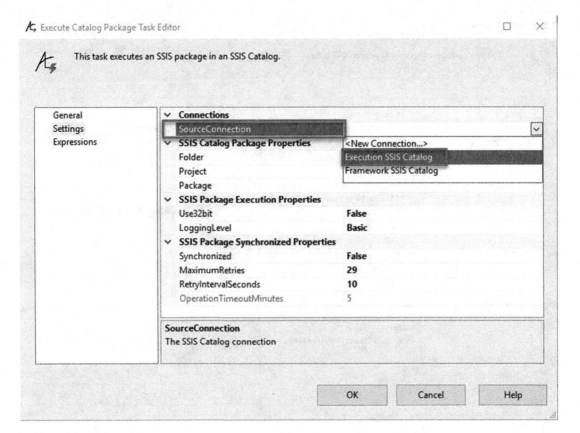

Figure 23-37. *Setting SourceConnection*

Continue configuring the Execute Catalog Package Task by selecting a folder, as shown in Figure 23-38:

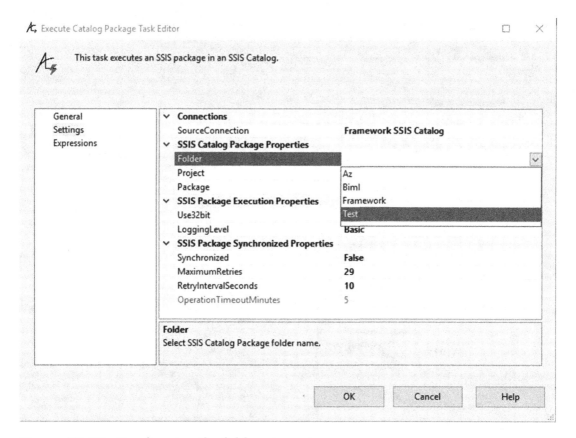

Figure 23-38. Configuring the folder property

Continue configuring the Execute Catalog Package Task by selecting a project, as shown in Figure 23-39:

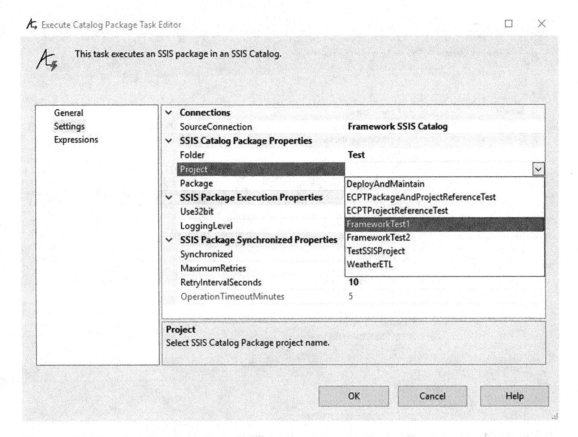

Figure 23-39. *Configuring the project property*

Continue configuring the Execute Catalog Package Task by selecting a package, as shown in Figure 23-40:

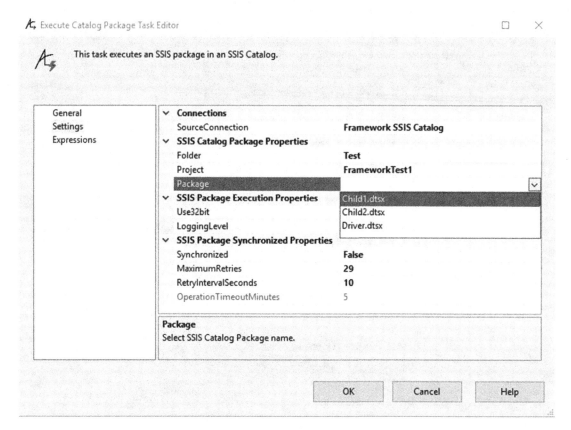

Figure 23-40. *Configuring the package property*

Once configured, the Execute Catalog Package Task settings should appear as shown in Figure 23-41:

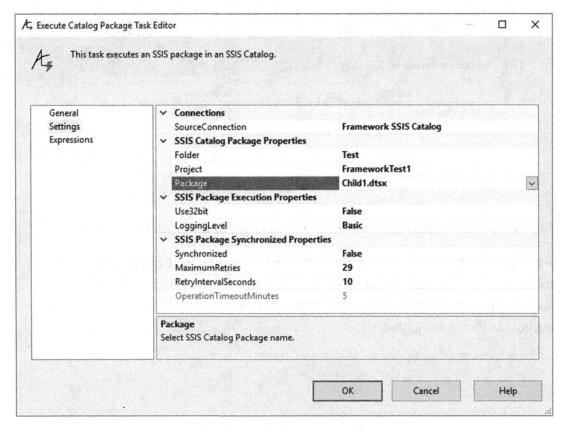

Figure 23-41. *Execute Catalog Package Task, configured*

The last step for constructing the execution engine for this version of an SSIS framework is configuring Property Expressions for the Execute Catalog Package Task. Click the Expressions page, click the ellipsis, and map Execute Catalog Package Task properties to the variables we created when configuring the Foreach Application Packages Variable Mappings page. Earlier in the book, we configured Execute Catalog Package Task Expressions (twice, even).

Map Execute Catalog Package Task the `PackageFolder` property to the `User::Folder` variable. Begin by selecting the PackageFolder property in the Property Expressions Editor, as shown in Figure 23-42:

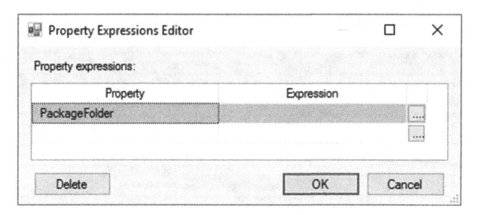

Figure 23-42. *Preparing to override the PackageFolder property*

Click the ellipsis beside the Expression textbox to open the Expression Builder. Expand the Variables and Parameters node, and then User::Folder into the Expression textbox. Click the Evaluate Expression button to view the value in the Evaluated value textbox, as shown in Figure 23-43:

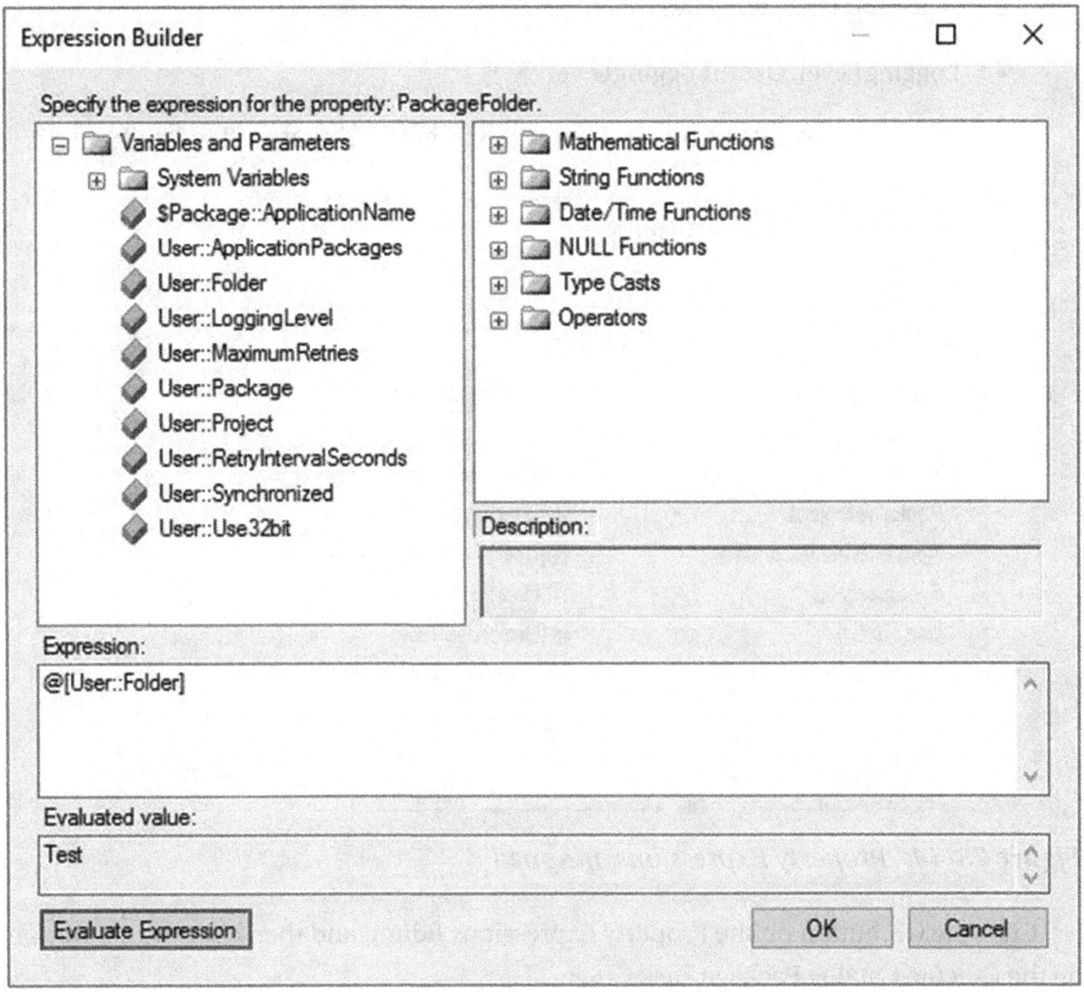

Figure 23-43. *Mapping the User::Folder variable to the PackageFolder property*

Repeat the process described above for mapping the following properties:

- PackageFolder: User::Folder

- PackageProject: User::Project

- PackageName: User::Package

- Synchronized: User::Synchronized

- MaximumRetries: User::MaximumRetries

- RetryIntervalSeconds: User::RetryIntervalSeconds

- Use32bit: User::Use32bit

- LoggingLevel: User::LoggingLevel

When complete, the Property Expressions Editor appears as shown in Figure 23-44:

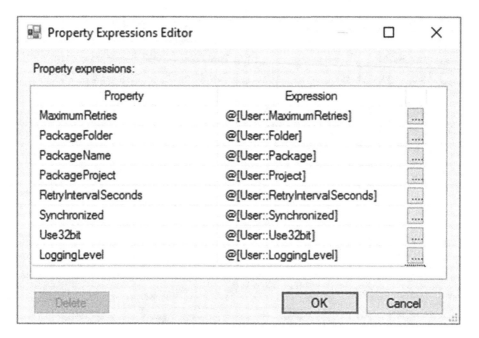

Figure 23-44. *Property Expressions, mapped*

Click the OK button on the Property Expressions Editor, and then click the OK button on the Execute Catalog Package Task.

Just Add Metadata

The next step is to add Applications, Packages, and ApplicationPackages metadata to the framework tables. Add Applications metadata using the T-SQL in Listing 23-6:

Listing 23-6. Adding Applications metadata

```
Insert Into fw.Applications
(ApplicationName)
Values('Framework Test')
go

Select * From fw.Applications
go
```

When executed, the T-SQL results appear as shown in Figure 23-45:

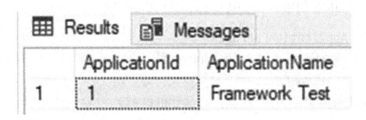

Figure 23-45. *Adding an SSIS framework application*

Add Packages metadata using the T-SQL in Listing 23-7:

Listing 23-7. Adding Packages metadata

```
Insert Into fw.Packages
(FolderName, ProjectName, PackageName)
Values
  ('Test', 'TestSSISProject', 'ReportAndSucceed.dtsx')
, ('Test', 'TestSSISProject', 'ReportParameterAndSucceed.dtsx')
, ('Test', 'TestSSISProject', 'RunForSomeTime.dtsx')
go

Select * From fw.Packages
go
```

When executed, the T-SQL results appear as shown in Figure 23-46:

	PackageId	FolderName	ProjectName	PackageName
1	1	Test	TestSSISProject	ReportAndSucceed.dtsx
2	2	Test	TestSSISProject	ReportParameterAndSucceed.dtsx
3	3	Test	TestSSISProject	RunForSomeTime.dtsx

Figure 23-46. *Adding SSIS framework packages*

Add ApplicationPackages metadata using the T-SQL in Listing 23-8:

Listing 23-8. Adding ApplicationPackages metadata

```
Insert Into fw.ApplicationPackages
(ApplicationId, PackageId, ExecutionOrder
, Synchronized, MaximumRetries
, RetryIntervalSeconds, Use32bit, LoggingLevel)
Values
  (1, 1, 10, 1, 10, 2, 0, 'Basic')
, (1, 2, 20, 0, 10, 2, 1, 'Performance')
, (1, 3, 30, 1, 30, 2, 1, 'Verbose')
go

Select * From fw.ApplicationPackages
go
```

Be sure the ApplicationId and PackageId values match corresponding values auto-generated by identity values in the fw.Applications and fw.Packages tables, respectively.

When executed, the T-SQL results appear as shown in Figure 23-47:

	ApplicationPackageId	ApplicationId	PackageId	ExecutionOrder	Synchronized	MaximumRetries	RetryIntervalSeconds	Use32bit	LoggingLevel
1	1	1	1	10	1	10	2	0	Basic
2	2	1	2	20	0	10	2	1	Performance
3	3	1	3	30	1	30	2	1	Verbose

Figure 23-47. *Adding SSIS framework application packages*

Let's Test It!

If all goes as planned, a test execution of the Parent.dtsx SSIS package execution succeeds. As shown in Figure 23-48:

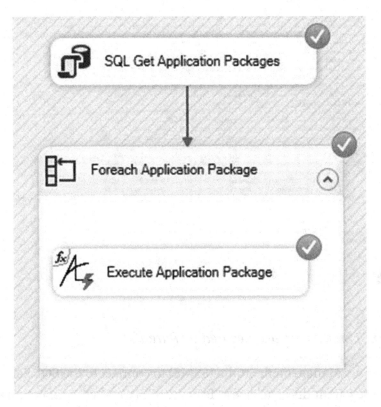

Figure 23-48. *A successful test execution*

The Progress/Execution Results tab appears as shown in Figure 23-49:

```
→ Parent
  ʔᴑ Validation has started
⊟ → Foreach Application Package
     ʔᴑ Validation has started
  ⊟ → Task Execute Application Package
       ʔᴑ Validation has started (4)
       ᴑ Validation is completed (4)
       ⊙ Start (3)
       ⓘ [Execute Application Package] Information: Starting \SSISDB\Test\TestSSISProject\ReportAndSucceed.dtsx on vDemo17\Demo.
       ⓘ [Execute Application Package.CheckStatus] Information: Asynchronous Execution Retry Count: 1 (Maximum Retry Count: 10)
       ⓘ [Execute Application Package.CheckStatus] Information: Asynchronous Execution Retry Count: 2 (Maximum Retry Count: 10)
       ⓘ [Execute Application Package] Information: \SSISDB\Test\TestSSISProject\ReportAndSucceed.dtsx on vDemo17\Demo succeeded. Package Execution Time: 00:00:02.072
       ⓘ [Execute Application Package] Information: Starting \SSISDB\Test\TestSSISProject\ReportParameterAndSucceed.dtsx on vDemo17\Demo.
       ⚠ [Execute Application Package] Warning: \SSISDB\Test\TestSSISProject\ReportParameterAndSucceed.dtsx on vDemo17\Demo started. Check SSIS Catalog Reports for package execution results.
       ⓘ [Execute Application Package] Information: Starting \SSISDB\Test\TestSSISProject\RunForSomeTime.dtsx on vDemo17\Demo.
       ⓘ [Execute Application Package.CheckStatus] Information: Asynchronous Execution Retry Count: 1 (Maximum Retry Count: 30)
       ⓘ [Execute Application Package.CheckStatus] Information: Asynchronous Execution Retry Count: 2 (Maximum Retry Count: 30)
       ⓘ [Execute Application Package.CheckStatus] Information: Asynchronous Execution Retry Count: 3 (Maximum Retry Count: 30)
       ⓘ [Execute Application Package.CheckStatus] Information: Asynchronous Execution Retry Count: 4 (Maximum Retry Count: 30)
       ⓘ [Execute Application Package.CheckStatus] Information: Asynchronous Execution Retry Count: 5 (Maximum Retry Count: 30)
       ⓘ [Execute Application Package.CheckStatus] Information: Asynchronous Execution Retry Count: 6 (Maximum Retry Count: 30)
       ⓘ [Execute Application Package.CheckStatus] Information: Asynchronous Execution Retry Count: 7 (Maximum Retry Count: 30)
       ⓘ [Execute Application Package.CheckStatus] Information: Asynchronous Execution Retry Count: 8 (Maximum Retry Count: 30)
       ⓘ [Execute Application Package.CheckStatus] Information: Asynchronous Execution Retry Count: 9 (Maximum Retry Count: 30)
       ⓘ [Execute Application Package.CheckStatus] Information: Asynchronous Execution Retry Count: 10 (Maximum Retry Count: 30)
       ⓘ [Execute Application Package.CheckStatus] Information: Asynchronous Execution Retry Count: 11 (Maximum Retry Count: 30)
       ⓘ [Execute Application Package.CheckStatus] Information: Asynchronous Execution Retry Count: 12 (Maximum Retry Count: 30)
       ⓘ [Execute Application Package.CheckStatus] Information: Asynchronous Execution Retry Count: 13 (Maximum Retry Count: 30)
       ⓘ [Execute Application Package.CheckStatus] Information: Asynchronous Execution Retry Count: 14 (Maximum Retry Count: 30)
       ⓘ [Execute Application Package.CheckStatus] Information: Asynchronous Execution Retry Count: 15 (Maximum Retry Count: 30)
       ⓘ [Execute Application Package.CheckStatus] Information: Asynchronous Execution Retry Count: 16 (Maximum Retry Count: 30)
       ⓘ [Execute Application Package.CheckStatus] Information: Asynchronous Execution Retry Count: 17 (Maximum Retry Count: 30)
       ⓘ [Execute Application Package] Information: \SSISDB\Test\TestSSISProject\RunForSomeTime.dtsx on vDemo17\Demo succeeded. Package Execution Time: 00:00:32.067
       ⊙ Stop (3)
     ᴑ Validation is completed
     ⊙ Start, 12:52:49 PM
     ⊙ Finished, 12:53:23 PM, Elapsed time: 00:00:34.516
  ⊟ → Task SQL Get Application Packages
       ʔᴑ Validation has started (2)
       ᴑ Validation is completed (2)
       ⊙ Start, 12:52:49 PM
       → Progress: Executing query "Select p.FolderName    , p.ProjectName    , p....". - 100 percent complete
       ⊙ Finished, 12:52:49 PM, Elapsed time: 00:00:00.093
  ᴑ Validation is completed
  ⊙ Start, 12:52:49 PM
  ⊙ Finished, 12:53:23 PM, Elapsed time: 00:00:34.688
```

Figure 23-49. *Three packages executed by Parent.dtsx*

Use SQL Server Management Studio (SSMS) to connect to the SQL Server instance configured in the Parent.dtsx package's "Execute SSIS Catalog" connection manager, and view the SSIS Catalog All Executions report, as shown in Figure 23-50:

All Executions

ID	Status	Report			Folder Name	Project Name	Package Name
4	Succeeded	Overview	All Messages	Execution Performance	Test	TestSSISProject	RunForSomeTime.dtsx
3	Succeeded	Overview	All Messages	Execution Performance	Test	TestSSISProject	ReportParameterAndSucce ed.dtsx
2	Succeeded	Overview	All Messages	Execution Performance	Test	TestSSISProject	ReportAndSucceed.dtsx

Figure 23-50. *Viewing the All Executions report*

The All Executions report displays the three SSIS packages executed according to the metadata we configured.

Caveats

The demo in this chapter makes a number of assumptions, and as a result, there are many caveats. Suffice it to say the author is aware of many, but not all, of the assumptions and caveats and is intrigued to see how readers adapt and change and improve the ideas presented herein.

Conclusion

In this chapter, we leveraged the Execute Catalog Package Task to build a metadata-driven SSIS Catalog-based SSIS framework. The metadata-driven framework was similar to the on-premises version of the SSIS framework in the *SQL Server Data Automation Through Frameworks* book and SSIS Framework Community Edition (dilmsuite.com/ssis-framework-community-edition) – a free and open source project that is part of the collection of utilities that make up the Data Integration Lifecycle Management Suite (dilmsuite.com).

The framework in this chapter does not exhaust the capabilities of the Execute Catalog Package Task. You may configure the Expressions view to override *any* property expression, as shown in Figure 23-51:

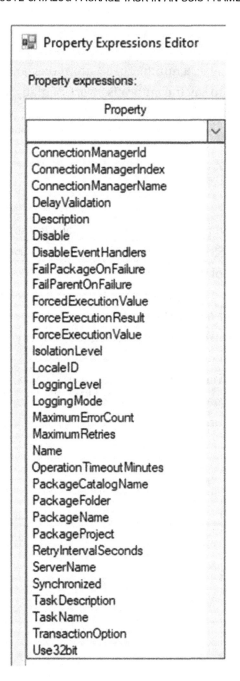

Figure 23-51. *Execute Catalog Package Task Property Expressions*

Now would be an excellent time to check in your code.

CHAPTER 24

Deploying to Azure-SSIS

In the previous chapter, we built an SSIS framework to execute metadata-driven collections of SSIS packages using the Execute Catalog Package Task. In this chapter, we build an instance of the Azure-SSIS integration runtime that installs the Execute Catalog Package Task, and then we migrate the metadata-drive framework from the previous chapter to Azure. To accomplish this goal, we will

- Provision an Azure SQL Database instance to host the SSISDB database and SSIS Catalog

- Provision an Azure Data Factory

- Create and configure the Deployment Container

- Provision an Azure-SSIS Integration Runtime (IR) configured to install the Execute Catalog Package Task's msi file

Before moving forward, let's take a look at SSIS package location options surfaced by the Azure Data Factory Execute SSIS Package activity.

Examining Package Location Options

SSIS packages may be executed in Azure Data Factory using the Execute SSIS Package Activity. At the time of this writing, the Package Location property lists five options for SSIS package sources, as shown in Figure 24-1:

© Andy Leonard 2021
A. Leonard, *Building Custom Tasks for SQL Server Integration Services*,
https://doi.org/10.1007/978-1-4842-6482-9_24

Figure 24-1. *Package Location options for Execute SSIS Package Activity*

SSISDB is the SSIS Catalog, which we will use in this chapter. File System (Package) refers to individual SSIS package dtsx files stored in an Azure File Share. File System (Project) refers to ispac files, which are SSIS project deployment files that contain individual SSIS package dtsx files for SSIS packages included in the SSIS project, stored in an Azure File Share. Embedded Package allows developers to upload an individual SSIS package dtsx file. Package store is similar to the legacy SSIS package store. See Microsoft's SSIS package store documentation (docs.microsoft.com/en-us/azure/data-factory/azure-ssis-integration-runtime-package-store [as of 28 Oct 2020]) for more information.

In sum, an Azure-SSIS IR supports

- Running packages deployed into SSIS catalog (SSISDB) hosted by Azure SQL Database server/Managed Instance (Project Deployment Model)

- Running packages deployed into file system, Azure Files, or SQL Server database (MSDB) hosted by Azure SQL Managed Instance (Package Deployment Model)

Package Deployment Modelsupports provisioning an Azure-SSIS IR with *package stores*. Package stores surface a package management layer on top of file system, Azure Files, or MSDB hosted in an Azure SQL Managed Instance. Azure-SSIS IR package store allows developers to import, export, delete, and run packages, as well as monitor and stop running packages via SQL Server Management Studio (SSMS) – similar to the legacy SSIS package store.

The first step is to provision an Azure SQL DB.

Provisioning an Azure SQL Database

Azure SQL Database – or Azure SQL DB – is a flexible and scalable Platform-as-a-Service (PaaS) cloud database offering from Azure. Azure SQL DB sizes (and costs) range from small to very large.

Connect to Azure and click New Resource to open the New blade, as shown in Figure 24-2:

Figure 24-2. Preparing to provision a new Azure SQL database

The SQL Database link on the New blade opens the Create SQL Database blade. When provisioning a new "work area" in Azure, start by creating a new Resource group, as shown in Figure 24-3:

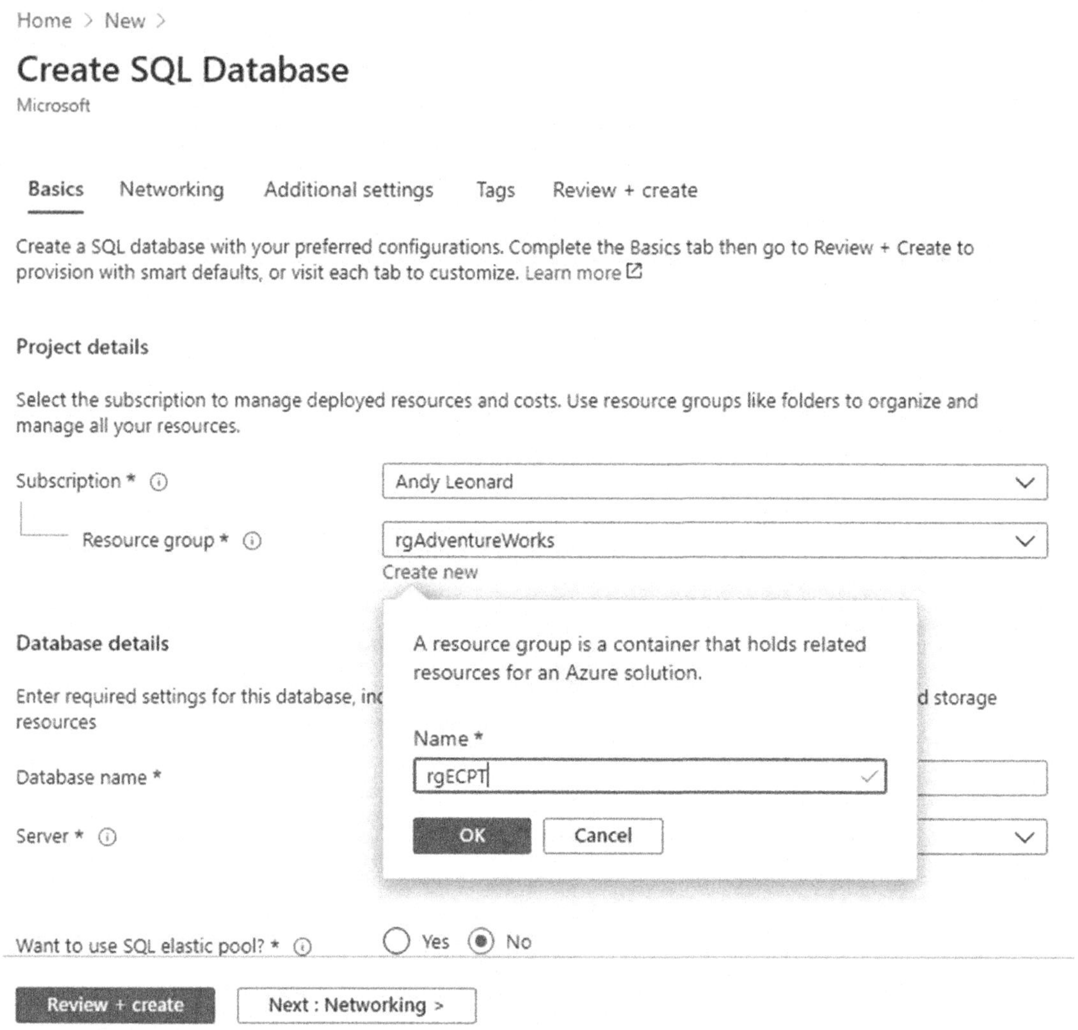

Home > New >

Create SQL Database
Microsoft

Basics   Networking   Additional settings   Tags   Review + create

Create a SQL database with your preferred configurations. Complete the Basics tab then go to Review + Create to provision with smart defaults, or visit each tab to customize. Learn more 🔗

Project details

Select the subscription to manage deployed resources and costs. Use resource groups like folders to organize and manage all your resources.

Subscription * ⓘ   Andy Leonard   ⌄

Resource group * ⓘ   rgAdventureWorks   ⌄

Create new

A resource group is a container that holds related resources for an Azure solution.

Database details

Enter required settings for this database, in   d storage resources

Name *

Database name *   rgECPT ✓

Server * ⓘ

     OK   Cancel

Want to use SQL elastic pool? * ⓘ   ◯ Yes   ◉ No

Review + create   Next : Networking >

Figure 24-3. *Creating the rgECPT resource group while provisioning an Azure SQL database*

The next step is to enter the database name. In the last chapter, we re-used the SSISDB database. Since we are not enforcing referential integrity (foreign keys) or using SSISDB's encryption in this framework, we may provision a different database to host framework metadata, as shown in Figure 24-4:

Project details

Select the subscription to manage deployed resources and costs. Use resource groups like folders to organize and manage all your resources.

Subscription * ⓘ	Andy Leonard ⌄
└─── Resource group * ⓘ	(New) rgECPT ⌄
	Create new

Database details

Enter required settings for this database, including picking a logical server and configuring the compute and storage resources

Database name *	SSISFramework ✓

Figure 24-4. *Provisioning the SSISFramework database*

The next step is to select or create a new SQL Server. Figure 24-5 shows the New Server blade displaying after the "Create new" link beneath the Server dropdown was clicked:

Project details

Select the subscription to manage deployed resources and costs. Use resource groups like folders to organize and manage all your resources.

Subscription * ⓘ	Andy Leonard ⌄
└─── Resource group * ⓘ	(New) rgECPT ⌄
	Create new

Database details

Enter required settings for this database, including picking a logical server and configuring the compute and storage resources

Database name *	SSISFramework ✓
Server * ⓘ	Select a server ⌄
	Create new

New server   ✕

Microsoft

Server name *

svecpt	🔏

.database.windows.net

Server admin login *

administrator_1	✓

Password *

••••••••	👁

Confirm password *

••••••••	👁

Location *

(US) East US	⌄

Figure 24-5. *Provisioning a new SQL server*

Leave the "Want to use SQL elastic pool" property set to "No." The General Purpose server with Gen5, 2 vCores, and 32 GB storage is a bit more than we need, so click the "Configure database" link for the "Compute + storage" property, as shown in Figure 24-6:

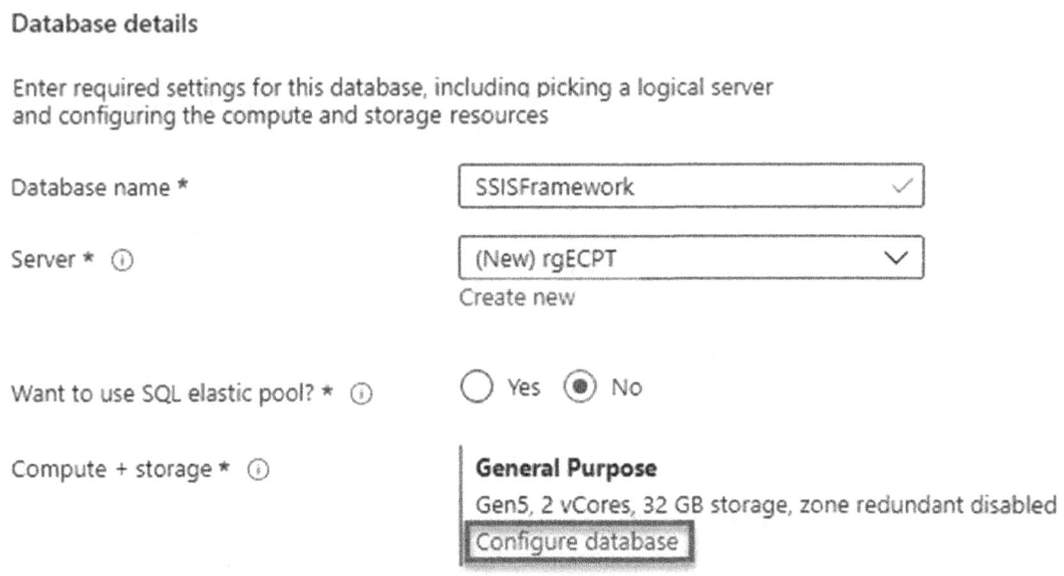

Database details

Enter required settings for this database, including picking a logical server and configuring the compute and storage resources

Database name *	SSISFramework ✓
Server * ⓘ	(New) rgECPT ▾
	Create new
Want to use SQL elastic pool? * ⓘ	◯ Yes ◉ No
Compute + storage * ⓘ	**General Purpose** Gen5, 2 vCores, 32 GB storage, zone redundant disabled [Configure database]

Figure 24-6. Preparing to configure the SQL server

Configure the SQL Server by selecting the Basic configuration, as shown in Figure 24-7:

Configure

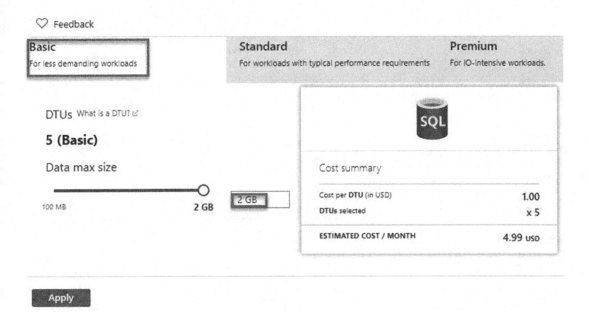

Figure 24-7. Selecting the Basic configuration

Click the Apply button to return to the Create SQL Database blade, which appears as shown in Figure 24-8:

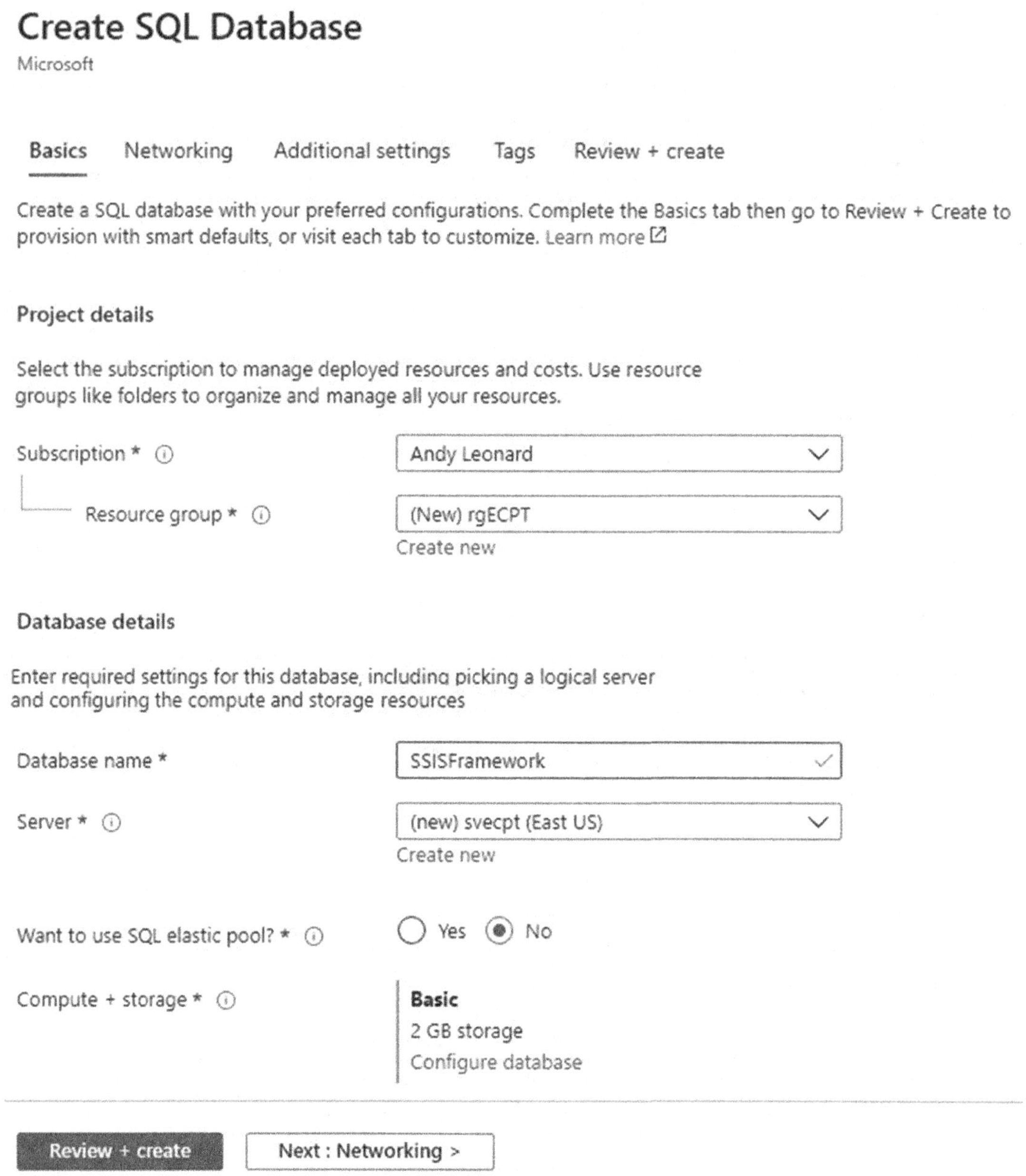

Create SQL Database

Microsoft

Basics   Networking   Additional settings   Tags   Review + create

Create a SQL database with your preferred configurations. Complete the Basics tab then go to Review + Create to provision with smart defaults, or visit each tab to customize. Learn more ⬚

Project details

Select the subscription to manage deployed resources and costs. Use resource groups like folders to organize and manage all your resources.

Subscription * ⓘ
| Andy Leonard ∨ |

Resource group * ⓘ
| (New) rgECPT ∨ |
Create new

Database details

Enter required settings for this database, including picking a logical server and configuring the compute and storage resources

Database name *
| SSISFramework ✓ |

Server * ⓘ
| (new) svecpt (East US) ∨ |
Create new

Want to use SQL elastic pool? * ⓘ   ◯ Yes ⦿ No

Compute + storage * ⓘ   **Basic**
2 GB storage
Configure database

Review + create   Next : Networking >

Figure 24-8. *Ready to create the database*

The next step is to click the "Review + create" button at the bottom of the blade which displays the Review blade shown in Figure 24-9:

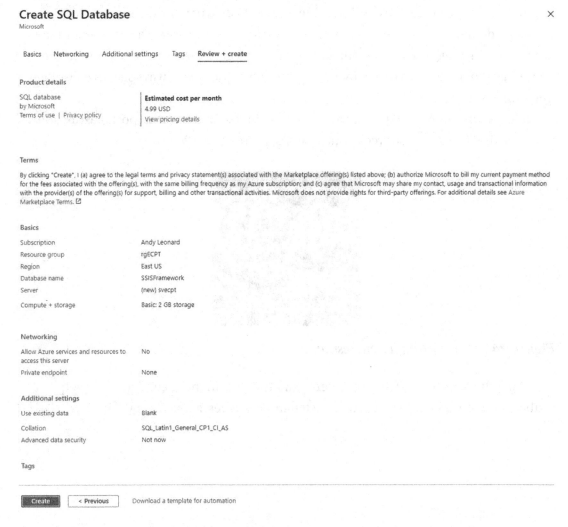

Figure 24-9. *Reviewing the SQL database and server configuration*

Click the Create button at the bottom of the blade to complete provisioning the Azure SQL Database.

The next step is to provision an Azure Data Factory.

Provisioning an Azure Data Factory

Azure Data Factory (ADF) is a data integration PaaS (Platform-as-a-Service) offering on Microsoft Azure. At the time of this writing, ADFv2 is the current version.

If you do not have an Azure account, visit azure.com and create an account. At the time of this writing, you may sign up for free and you get 12 months of free services. Azure sign-up offers have varied over time, but the author has always seen Azure offer free stuff at sign-up.

To provision an Azure Data Factory, connect to the Azure Portal (portal.azure.com) and click the "Create a resource" option, as shown in Figure 24-10:

Figure 24-10. *Creating a new resource*

When the New blade displays, enter "Data Factory" in the "Search the Marketplace" textbox, and then click "Data Factory" listed in the suggestions, as shown in Figure 24-11:

New

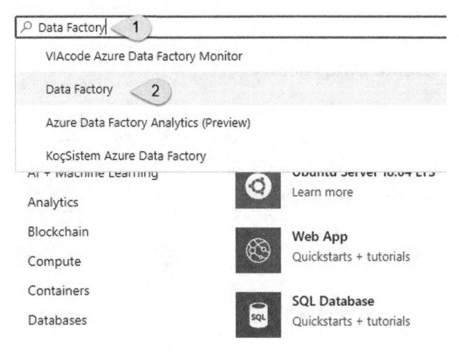

Figure 24-11. Selecting Data Factory

Clicking "Data Factory" opens the Data Factory overview blade, as shown in Figure 24-12:

Figure 24-12. Preparing to create the Data Factory

Click the Create button to open the Create Data Factory blade. Configure the Resource group, Region, Name, and Version properties, and then click the "Git configuration" tab, as shown in Figure 24-13:

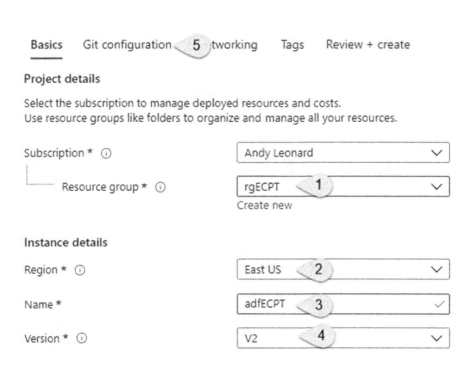

Home > New > Data Factory >

Create Data Factory

Basics   Git configuration   5 tworking   Tags   Review + create

Project details

Select the subscription to manage deployed resources and costs.
Use resource groups like folders to organize and manage all your resources.

Subscription * ⓘ

Andy Leonard

Resource group * ⓘ

rgECPT   1

Create new

Instance details

Region * ⓘ

East US   2

Name *

adfECPT   3

Version * ⓘ

V2   4

Figure 24-13. *Configuring the Data Factory*

Check the "Configure Git later" checkbox, and then click the "Review + create" button, as shown in Figure 24-14:

Figure 24-14. *Configuring the Git configuration tab*

Azure validates the Azure Data Factory configuration and notifies you if the validation passes or if an issue is discovered. Once validation passes, review the settings and – if acceptable – click the Create button, as shown in Figure 24-15:

Home > New > Data Factory >

Create Data Factory

Validation Passed

| Basics | Git configuration | Networking | Tags | Review + create |

TERMS

By clicking "Create", I (a) agree to the legal terms and privacy statement(s) associated with the Marketplace offering(s) listed above; (b) authorize Microsoft to bill my current payment method for the fees associated with the offering(s), with the same billing frequency as my Azure subscription; and (c) agree that Microsoft may share my contact, usage and transactional information with the provider(s) of the offering(s) for support, billing and other transactional activities. Microsoft does not provide rights for third-party offerings. See the Azure Marketplace Terms for additional details.

Basics

Subscription	Andy Leonard
Resource group	rgECPT
Region	East US
Name	adfECPT
Version	V2

Networking

Managed Virtual Network (Preview)	Disabled
Connectivity method	Public endpoint

Create   < Previous   Next   Download a template for automation

Figure 24-15. *Reviewing the settings*

If all goes as planned, deployment succeeds and the Overview blade displays, as shown in Figure 24-16:

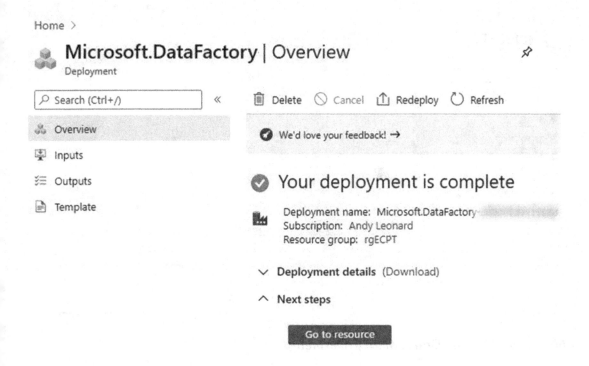

Figure 24-16. *Deployment success*

Click the "Go to resource" button to open the Data Factory Overview, as shown in Figure 24-17:

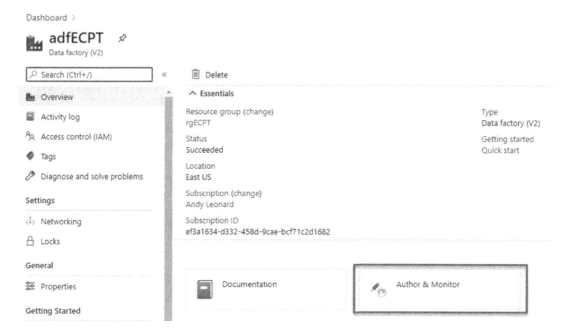

Figure 24-17. *The Data Factory overview*

To configure Azure Data Factory artifacts, click the "Author & Monitor" button. The Data Factory author and monitor overview page displays, as shown in Figure 24-18:

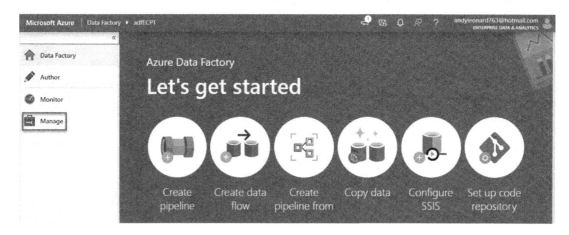

Figure 24-18. *The Data Factory author and monitor overview page*

The Azure Data Factory is provisioned. The next step is to create and configure the deployment container.

Creating and Configuring the Deployment Container

Azure Blob Storage serves as the Azure file system. In this section, we create an Azure Storage account. Azure storage accounts allow developers to create containers, which store documents in Azure for distributed access. To learn more, visit docs.microsoft.com/en-us/azure/storage/blobs/storage-blobs-introduction.

We follow these steps to create and configure a deployment container:

- Provision an Azure Storage account.

- Create the deployment container.

- Upload the ExecuteCatalogPackageTask.msi file.

- Create and upload the main.cmd file.

Provision an Azure Storage Account

The steps required to create and configure a deployment container begin with provisioning an Azure storage account. To provision an Azure storage account, connect to the portal, and then click "Create a resource" from the menu. If "Storage account" does not display on the "New" blade's default screen, search for "Storage account" using the "Search the marketplace" functionality, as shown in Figure 24-19:

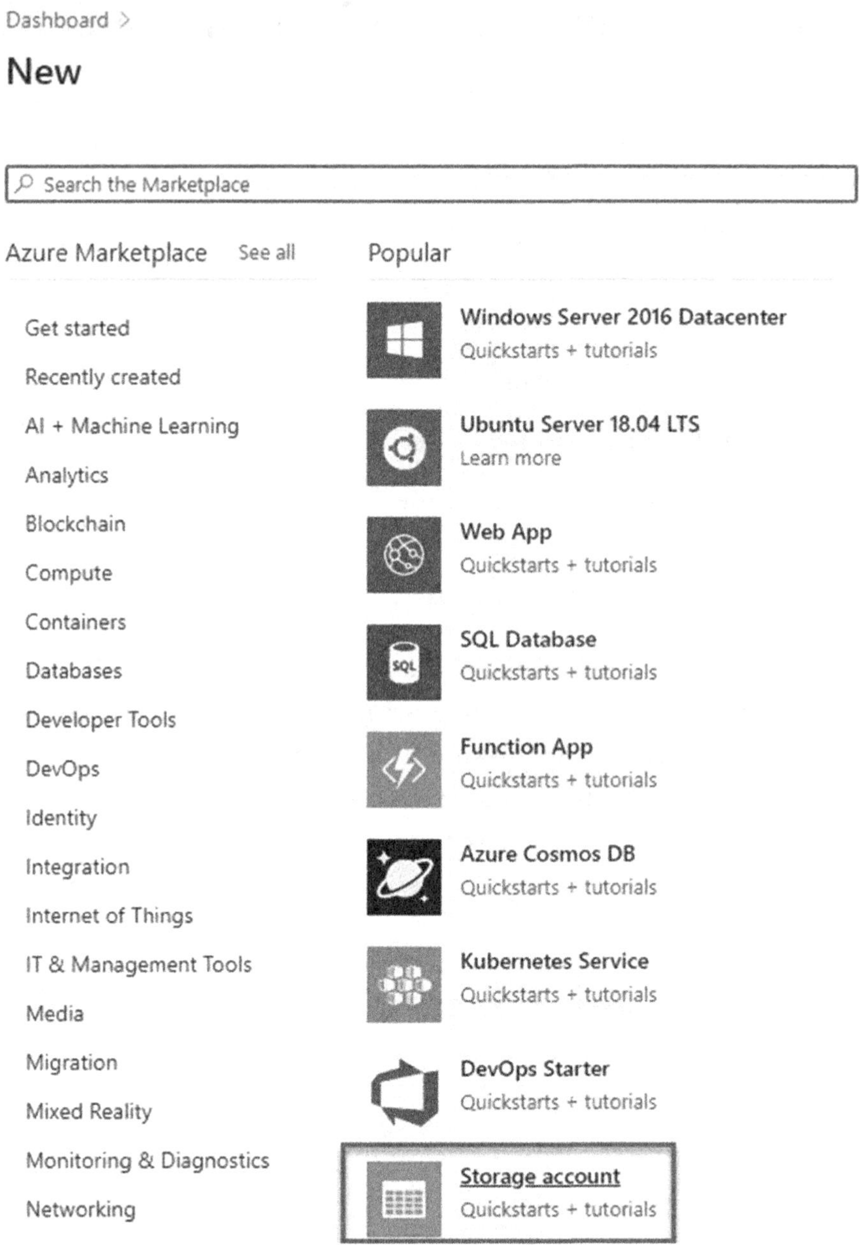

Dashboard >

New

🔍 Search the Marketplace

Azure Marketplace   See all   Popular

Get started

Recently created

AI + Machine Learning

Analytics

Blockchain

Compute

Containers

Databases

Developer Tools

DevOps

Identity

Integration

Internet of Things

IT & Management Tools

Media

Migration

Mixed Reality

Monitoring & Diagnostics

Networking

Windows Server 2016 Datacenter
Quickstarts + tutorials

Ubuntu Server 18.04 LTS
Learn more

Web App
Quickstarts + tutorials

SQL Database
Quickstarts + tutorials

Function App
Quickstarts + tutorials

Azure Cosmos DB
Quickstarts + tutorials

Kubernetes Service
Quickstarts + tutorials

DevOps Starter
Quickstarts + tutorials

Storage account
Quickstarts + tutorials

Figure 24-19. Preparing to add a storage account

Configure the new storage account by selecting the resource group, entering a storage account name, and selecting location, performance, account kind, and replication properties, as shown in Figure 24-20:

Dashboard > New >

Create storage account

Basics   Networking   Data protection   Advanced   Tags   Review + create

Azure Storage is a Microsoft-managed service providing cloud storage that is highly available, secure, durable, scalable, and redundant. Azure Storage includes Azure Blobs (objects), Azure Data Lake Storage Gen2, Azure Files, Azure Queues, and Azure Tables. The cost of your storage account depends on the usage and the options you choose below.
Learn more about Azure storage accounts ⊡

Project details

Select the subscription to manage deployed resources and costs. Use resource groups like folders to organize and manage all your resources.

Subscription *	Andy Leonard	⌄
└─── Resource group *	rgECPT	⌄
	Create new	

Instance details

The default deployment model is Resource Manager, which supports the latest Azure features. You may choose to deploy using the classic deployment model instead. Choose classic deployment model

Storage account name * ⓘ	stframework	✓
Location *	(US) East US	⌄
Performance ⓘ	⦿ Standard ◯ Premium	
Account kind ⓘ	StorageV2 (general purpose v2)	⌄
Replication ⓘ	Locally-redundant storage (LRS)	⌄

Review + create   < Previous   Next : Networking >

***Figure 24-20.** Configuring the storage account properties*

Click the "Review + create" button to proceed to the review blade, as shown in Figure 24-21:

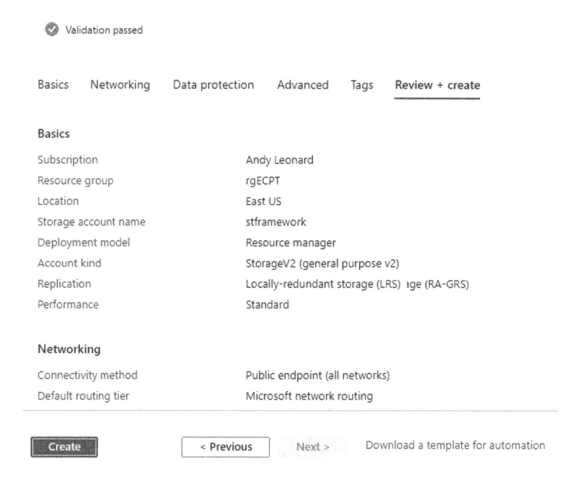

Dashboard > New >

Create storage account

✅ Validation passed

Basics   Networking   Data protection   Advanced   Tags   **Review + create**

Basics

Subscription	Andy Leonard
Resource group	rgECPT
Location	East US
Storage account name	stframework
Deployment model	Resource manager
Account kind	StorageV2 (general purpose v2)
Replication	Locally-redundant storage (LRS) ige (RA-GRS)
Performance	Standard

Networking

Connectivity method	Public endpoint (all networks)
Default routing tier	Microsoft network routing

Create   < Previous   Next >   Download a template for automation

Figure 24-21. *Review storage account configuration*

Click the Create button to create the storage account.

The next step is to create the deployment container.

Create the Deployment Container

The deployment container will initially host two files: main.cmd and ExecuteCatalogPackageTask.msi. Main.cmd contains instructions for installing the Execute Catalog Package Task on Azure-SSIS nodes. Later, the container will also host log files containing details of each installation of the ExecuteCatalogPackageTask.msi installer file.

Before we begin, browse to storageexplorer.com and download Microsoft Azure Storage Explorer, as shown in Figure 24-22:

Figure 24-22. *Downloading Storage Explorer*

Once downloaded, install Microsoft Azure Storage Explorer. Once installed, open Storage Explorer and configure your Azure account. After your Azure account has been configured, Storage Explorer should display the storage account you configured earlier, as shown in Figure 24-23:

611

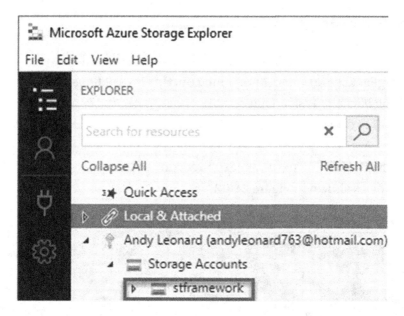

Figure 24-23. *Storage account in Storage Explorer*

The next step is to create the container. Right-click the storage account and then click Create Blob Container, as shown in Figure 24-24:

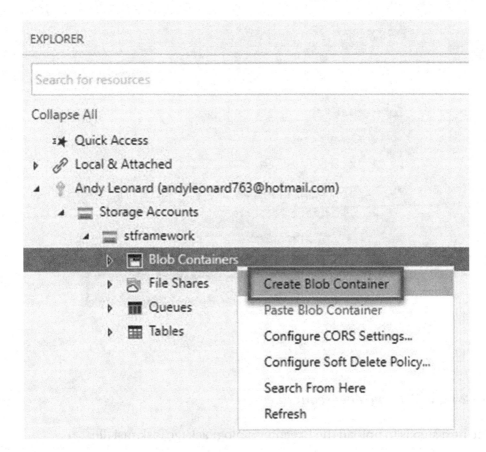

Figure 24-24. *Creating a new container*

When the new and unnamed container is added to the "Blob Containers" node in the storage account, enter the name of your new container, as shown in Figure 24-25:

Figure 24-25. *Adding a new container*

The next step is to upload the ExecuteCatalogPackageTask.msi file.

Upload the ExecuteCatalogPackageTask.msi File

Press the Enter key when finished entering the name of the new container. Storage explorer selects the new container and displays "No data available in this blob container". Click the Upload button, and then select "Upload Files…" from the dropdown, as shown in Figure 24-26:

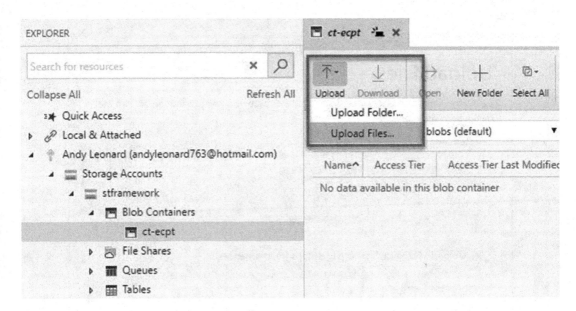

Figure 24-26. *Preparing to upload files*

When the Upload Files dialog displays, click the ellipsis to the right of the "Selected files" property textbox, highlighted in Figure 24-27:

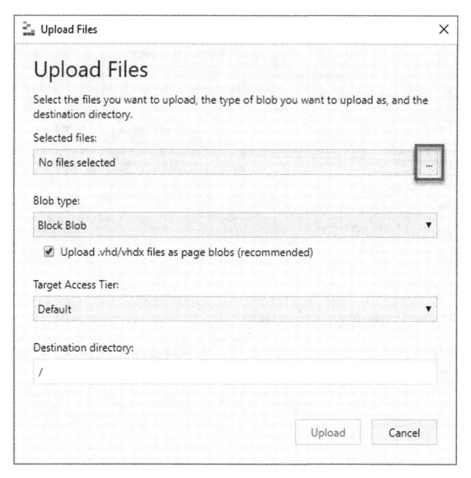

Figure 24-27.   *Preparing to select the msi file*

When the "Choose files to upload" dialog displays, navigate to – and select – the
ExecuteCatalogPackageTask.msi file, as shown in Figure 24-28:

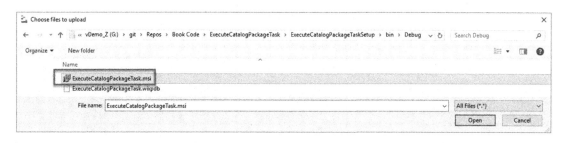

Figure 24-28.   *Selecting the msi file*

Click the Open button to return to the Upload Files dialog, as shown in Figure 24-29:

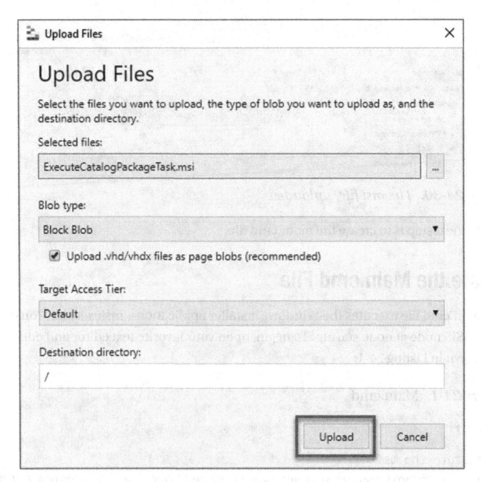

Figure 24-29. Preparing to upload the msi file

Click the Upload button to upload the ExecuteCatalogPackageTask.msi file to the blob container, as shown in Figure 24-30:

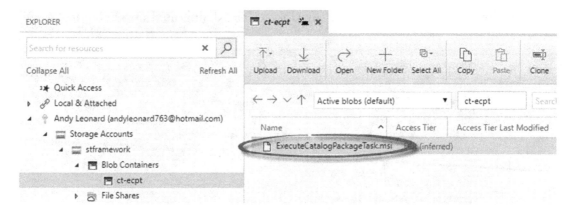

Figure 24-30. *The msi file, uploaded*

The next step is to create the main.cmd file.

Create the Main.cmd File

The main.cmd file executes the Windows installer application – msiexec.exe – on each Azure-SSIS node at node startup. To begin, open your favorite text editor and enter the text shown in Listing 24-1:

Listing 24-1. Main.cmd

```
@echo off

rem execute the msi
msiexec /i %~dp0\ExecuteCatalogPackageTask.msi /passive /l %CUSTOM_SETUP_
SCRIPT_LOG_DIR%\ExecuteCatalogPackageTaskInstall.log
echo
echo Execute Catalog Package Task installed.
```

Save the file as main.cmd, and then upload main.cmd to the Azure Blob container, as shown in Figure 24-31:

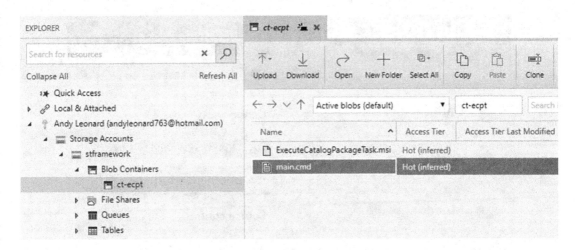

Figure 24-31. *The main.cmd file, uploaded*

You may learn more about customizing Azure-SSIS Integration Runtimes at docs. microsoft.com/en-us/azure/data-factory/how-to-configure-azure-ssis-ir-custom-setup.

You may learn more about the msiexec application at docs.microsoft.com/en-us/ windows-server/administration/windows-commands/msiexec.

The next step is to provision an Azure-SSIS Integration Runtime.

Provisioning an Azure-SSIS Integration Runtime

To open the Azure Data Factory Management page, click the Manage link in the Azure Data Factory page, as shown in Figure 24-32:

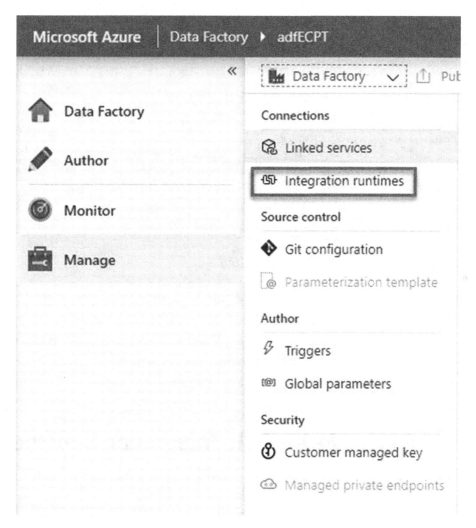

Figure 24-32. *The Azure Data Factory Management page*

To view Azure Data Factory Integration runtimes, click the "Connections ➤ Integration runtimes" link in the left-side list, as shown in Figure 24-33:

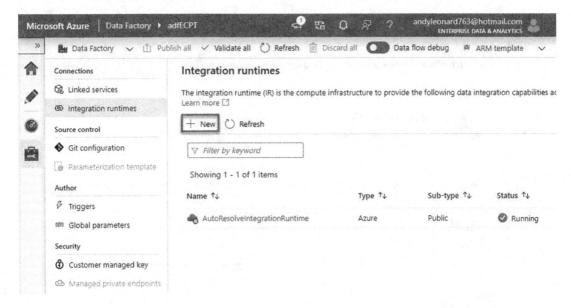

Figure 24-33. *Viewing Azure Data Factory Integration runtimes*

Whenever one provisions an Azure Data Factory, an Azure integration runtime named AutoResolveIntegrationRuntime is provisioned. Integration Runtimes, or IRs, are used to dispatch ADF pipeline activity execution, connecting internal activity functionality to external resources via ADF Linked Services. To learn more about the AutoResolveIntegrationRuntime, please visit docs.microsoft.com/en-us/azure/data-factory/concepts-integration-runtime.

Click the "+ New" link to create a new Integration Runtime. When the "Integration runtime setup" blade displays, select the "Azure-SSIS" integration runtime, as shown in Figure 24-34:

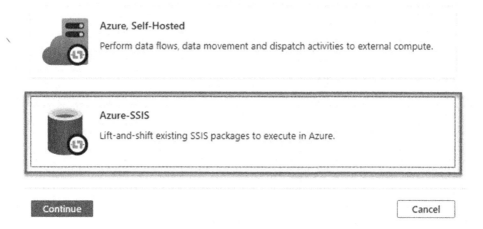

Integration runtime setup

Integration Runtime is the native compute used to execute or dispatch activities. Choose what integration runtime to create based on required capabilities. Learn more

Azure, Self-Hosted

Perform data flows, data movement and dispatch activities to external compute.

Azure-SSIS

Lift-and-shift existing SSIS packages to execute in Azure.

Continue   Cancel

Figure 24-34. *Selecting the Azure-SSIS integration runtime*

Click the Continue button to continue Azure-SSIS IR configuration. Enter a name and optional description for the Azure-SSIS integration runtime, and then configure Location, Node Size, Node Number, and Edition properties, as shown in Figure 24-35:

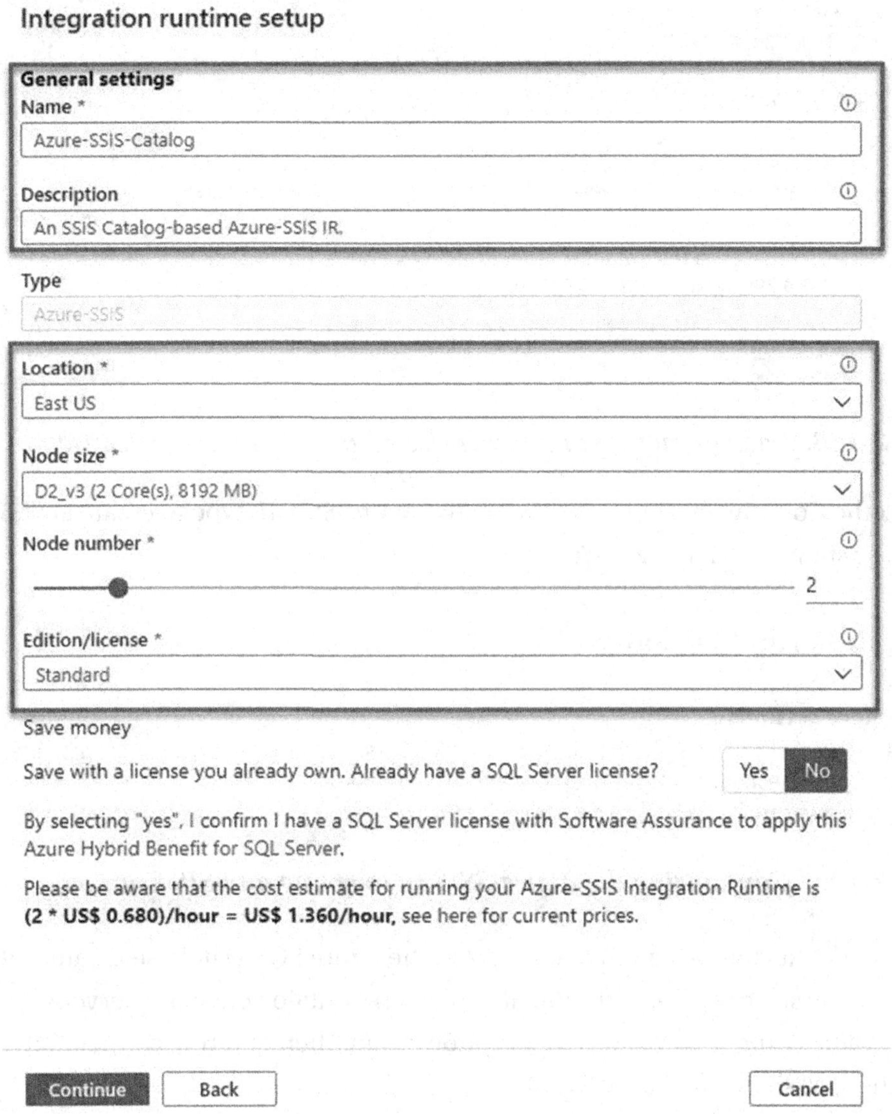

Integration runtime setup

General settings

Name *   ⓘ

Azure-SSIS-Catalog

Description   ⓘ

An SSIS Catalog-based Azure-SSIS IR.

Type

Azure-SSIS

Location *   ⓘ

East US   ∨

Node size *   ⓘ

D2_v3 (2 Core(s), 8192 MB)   ∨

Node number *   ⓘ

●── 2

Edition/license *   ⓘ

Standard   ∨

Save money

Save with a license you already own. Already have a SQL Server license?   Yes   **No**

By selecting "yes", I confirm I have a SQL Server license with Software Assurance to apply this Azure Hybrid Benefit for SQL Server.

Please be aware that the cost estimate for running your Azure-SSIS Integration Runtime is **(2 * US$ 0.680)/hour = US$ 1.360/hour,** see here for current prices.

Continue   Back   Cancel

Figure 24-35. *Configuring the Azure-SSIS integration runtime*

Please note you can save money if your enterprise already owns a SQL Server license, as shown in Figure 24-36:

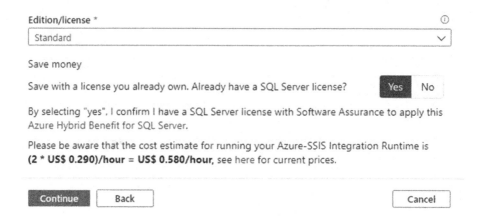

Figure 24-36. Save money if your enterprise owns a SQL Server license

Click the Continue button to configure the Azure-SSIS IR type to create an SSIS Catalog, as shown in Figure 24-37:

Integration runtime setup

Deployment settings

Figure 24-37. Configuring the Azure-SSIS IR to create an SSIS Catalog

Configure the Azure-SSIS IR to connect to the Azure SQL Database created earlier in this chapter by selecting Subscription, location, and Catalog database server endpoint property values from their respective dropdowns and then entering connection information, as shown in Figure 24-38:

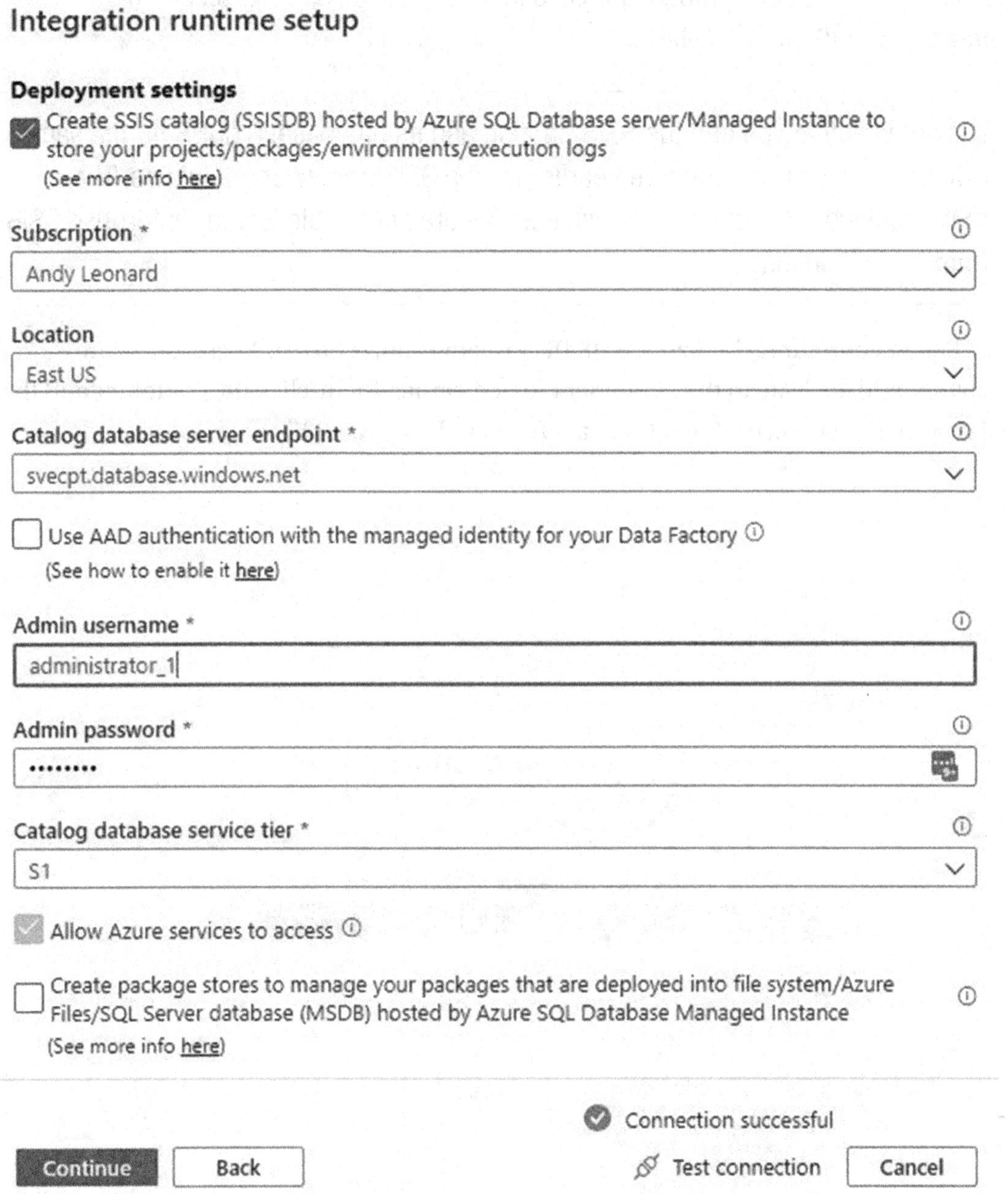

Integration runtime setup

Deployment settings

☑ Create SSIS catalog (SSISDB) hosted by Azure SQL Database server/Managed Instance to ⓘ
store your projects/packages/environments/execution logs
(See more info here)

Subscription * ⓘ

| Andy Leonard | ∨ |

Location ⓘ

| East US | ∨ |

Catalog database server endpoint * ⓘ

| svecpt.database.windows.net | ∨ |

☐ Use AAD authentication with the managed identity for your Data Factory ⓘ
(See how to enable it here)

Admin username * ⓘ

| administrator_1 |

Admin password * ⓘ

| •••••••• | |

Catalog database service tier * ⓘ

| S1 | ∨ |

☑ Allow Azure services to access ⓘ

☐ Create package stores to manage your packages that are deployed into file system/Azure ⓘ
Files/SQL Server database (MSDB) hosted by Azure SQL Database Managed Instance
(See more info here)

✔ Connection successful

[Continue] [Back]   ⌀ Test connection   [Cancel]

Figure 24-38. *Configuring Azure-SSIS properties for the SSIS Catalog*

Click the Continue button to proceed to the Advanced Settings section of the Integration runtime setup blade.

It is not vital that you add the SSIS Catalog and its database, SSISDB, to the same SQL Server instance configured earlier for the SSISFramework database. The SSISFramework database may reside anywhere accessible to your enterprise SSIS framework solution.

Before continuing the Azure-SSIS IR configuration, return to Microsoft Azure Storage Explorer and navigate to the container created earlier. Right-click the container and then click "Get Shared Access Signature," as shown in Figure 24-39:

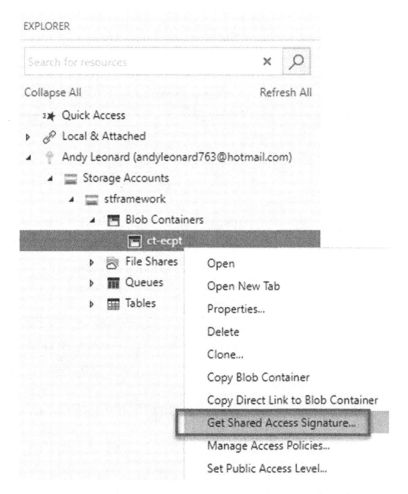

Figure 24-39. *Preparing to get a Shared Access Signature (SAS)*

Set the Expiry time to date-time well into the future because each time Azure-SSIS nodes are started, this folder is accessed. In addition to the default (Read and List) permissions, check the Add, Create, and Write permission checkboxes, as shown in Figure 24-40:

Figure 24-40. *Configuring the SAS*

Click the Create button to create the Shared Access Signature Uniform Resource Identifier (URI) and Query string, as shown in Figure 24-41:

Figure 24-41. *The Shared Access Signature Uniform Resource Identifier (URI) and Query string*

Click the Copy button beside the SAS URI textbox.

Return to the Azure-SSIS Integration runtime setup blade, check the "Customize your Azure-SSIS Integration Runtime with additional system configurations/component installations" checkbox, and then paste the SAS URI into the "Custom setup container SAS URI" textbox, as shown in Figure 24-42:

Integration runtime setup

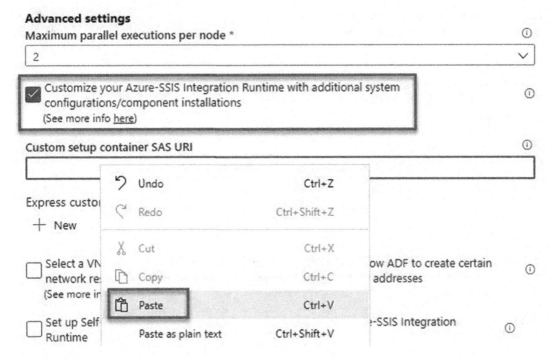

Advanced settings

Maximum parallel executions per node *   ⓘ

| 2 | ⌄ |

☑ Customize your Azure-SSIS Integration Runtime with additional system   ⓘ
configurations/component installations
(See more info here)

Custom setup container SAS URI   ⓘ

Express custo┆

+ New

☐ Select a VN┆   ow ADF to create certain   ⓘ
network re┆   addresses
(See more ir┆

☐ Set up Self┆   e-SSIS Integration   ⓘ
Runtime

↺ Undo	Ctrl+Z
↻ Redo	Ctrl+Shift+Z
✂ Cut	Ctrl+X
▭ Copy	Ctrl+C
▭ Paste	Ctrl+V
Paste as plain text	Ctrl+Shift+V

Figure 24-42. *Customizing the Azure-SSIS IR to install the custom task*

Once pasted, the SAS URI appears similar to the SAS URI (your values will likely be different) shown in Figure 24-43:

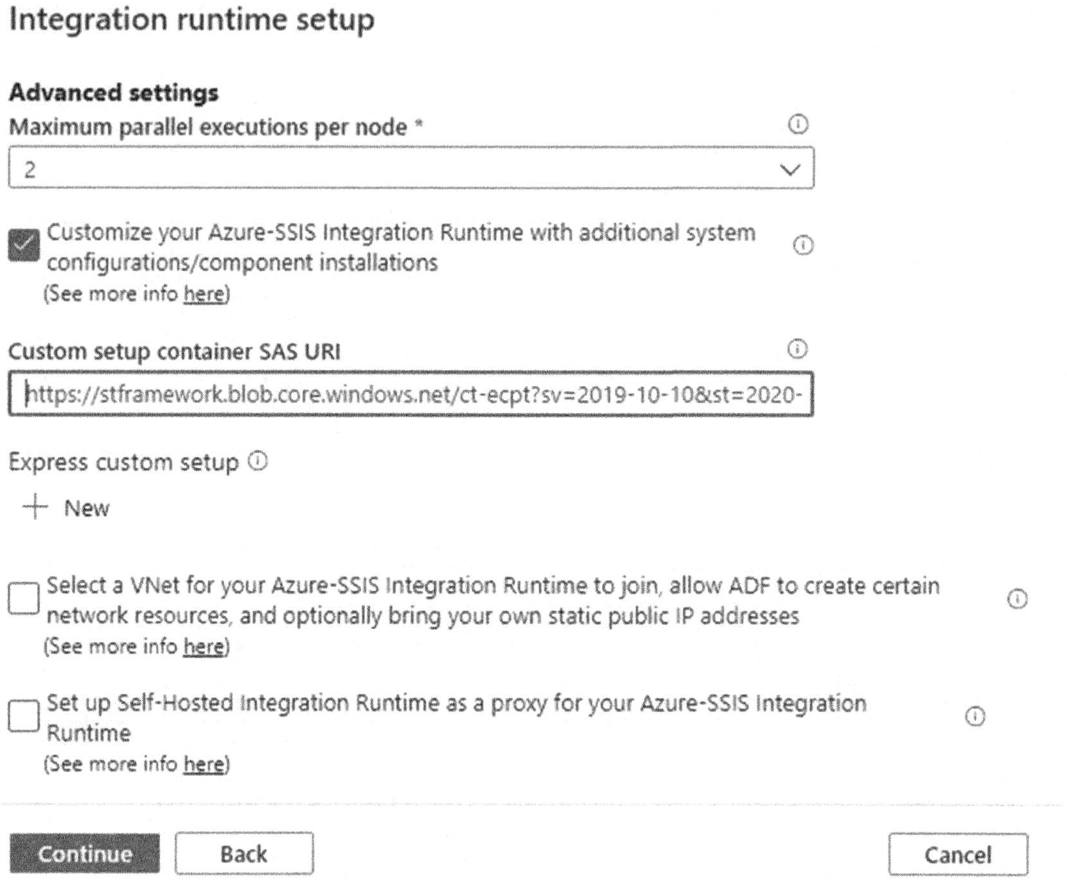

Integration runtime setup

Advanced settings

Maximum parallel executions per node *   ⓘ

| 2 | ∨ |

☑ Customize your Azure-SSIS Integration Runtime with additional system   ⓘ
  configurations/component installations
  (See more info here)

Custom setup container SAS URI   ⓘ

| https://stframework.blob.core.windows.net/ct-ecpt?sv=2019-10-10&st=2020- |

Express custom setup ⓘ

  ＋ New

☐ Select a VNet for your Azure-SSIS Integration Runtime to join, allow ADF to create certain   ⓘ
  network resources, and optionally bring your own static public IP addresses
  (See more info here)

☐ Set up Self-Hosted Integration Runtime as a proxy for your Azure-SSIS Integration   ⓘ
  Runtime
  (See more info here)

| Continue | Back | | Cancel |

Figure 24-43. *The SAS URI, pasted*

Click the Continue button to review the Summary of the Azure-SSIS IR configuration, as shown in Figure 24-44:

Integration runtime setup

Summary
Your Azure-SSIS Integration Runtime (IR) is created with the following settings:

Azure Data Factory Settings
- **Subscription:** ef3a1634-d332-458d-9cae-bcf71c2d1682
- **Resource group:** rgECPT
- **Name:** adfECPT
- **Location:** eastus

General settings
- **Name:** Azure-SSIS-Catalog
- **Description:** An SSIS Catalog-based Azure-SSIS IR.
- **Location:** East US
- **Node size:** Standard_D2_v3
- **Node number:** 2
- **Edition:** Standard
- **Azure Hybrid Benefit:** BasePrice

Deployment settings
- **Catalog database server endpoint:** svadventureworks.database.windows.net
- **Catalog database server location:** East US
- **Catalog database service tier:** S1

Advanced settings
- **Maximum parallel executions per node:** 2
- **Custom setup container SAS URI:** https://stframework.blob.core.windows.net/ct-ecpt?
  sv=2019-10-10&st=2020-10-30T19%3A53%3A05Z&se=2021-12-
  31T20%3A53%3A00Z&sr=c&sp=racwl&sig=SaxABkVWBJ%2Bot1abgNTQalGNsLiM3Ab7d
  no6HRcjrLw%3D
- If you need to access data on premises, click **Previous** to do any of the followings:
    ○ Join your Azure-SSIS IR to a VNet connected to your on-premises network OR
    ○ Set up Self-Hosted Integration Runtime as a proxy for your Azure-SSIS Integration
      Runtime

If you want to change any of the above settings, click **Previous** to do so.

Once your Azure-SSIS IR is running, you can execute your packages on it after deploying
them into your file system/Azure Files/SSISDB hosted by
svadventureworks.database.windows.net.

Please be aware that the cost estimate for running your Azure-SSIS Integration Runtime is
(2 * US$ 0.290)/hour = US$ 0.580/hour, see here for current prices.

To manage the running cost of your Azure-SSIS IR, you can stop & restart it whenever
convenient or schedule it just in time.

| Create | Previous | | Cancel |

Figure 24-44. *Summary of the Azure-SSIS configuration*

Click the Create button to start creating the Azure-SSIS integration runtime, as shown in Figure 24-45:

Figure 24-45. *Starting the Azure-SSIS integration runtime*

Once the Azure-SSIS integration runtime has started, the Manage ➤ Integration runtimes page appears as shown in Figure 24-46:

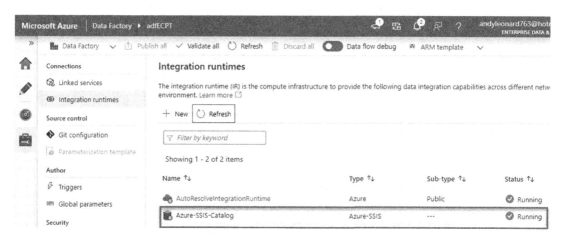

Figure 24-46. *The Azure-SSIS integration runtime, started*

The Azure-SSIS integration runtime displays the status "Running." This is a very good sign.

Reviewing the Installation Log

Before we move on, return to Storage Explorer and refresh the container. Note a new folder named "main.cmd.log" is displayed in the container, as shown in Figure 24-47:

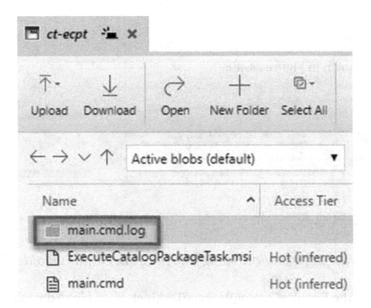

Figure 24-47. *The main.cmd.log folder*

Double-click the main.cmd.log folder to view the installation folder, as shown in Figure 24-48:

Figure 24-48. *Viewing the installation folder*

Double-click the installation folder to view the four files contained therein:

- ExecuteCatalogPackageTaskInstall.log

- InstallationSummary.log

- stderr.log

- stdout.log

All files are shown in Figure 24-49:

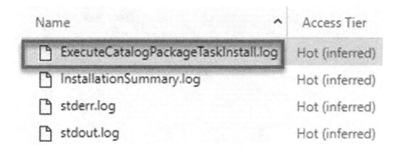

Figure 24-49. *Viewing installation log files in the installation folder*

Double-click the ExecuteCatalogPackageTaskInstall.log file to download the file and view it, as shown in Figure 24-50:

```
ExecuteCatalogPackageTaskInstall.log - Notepad
File  Edit  Format  View  Help
Action start 20:21:54: PublishProduct.
Action ended 20:21:54: PublishProduct. Return value 1.
Action start 20:21:54: InstallFinalize.
Action ended 20:21:55: InstallFinalize. Return value 1.
Action ended 20:21:55: INSTALL. Return value 1.
MSI (s) (24:38) [20:21:55:013]: Product: Execute Catalog Package Task -- Installation completed successfully.

MSI (s) (24:38) [20:21:55:013]: Windows Installer installed the product. Product Name: Execute Catalog Package Task.
 Product Version: 1.0.0.0. Product Language: 1033. Manufacturer: Andy Leonard Training, Inc..
 Installation success or error status: 0.

=== Logging stopped: 10/30/2020  20:21:55 ===
```

Figure 24-50. *Viewing the ExecuteCatalogPackageTaskInstall.log file*

The highlighted section appears on a single line. The author has added two line breaks for aesthetic purposes. The most important text is `Installation success or error status: 0`.

"Installation success or error status: 0." indicates the ExecuteCatalogPackageTask. msi installation occurred without error.

Conclusion

In this chapter, we built an instance of the Azure-SSIS integration runtime that included installation instructions for the Execute Catalog Package Task by implementing the following steps:

- Provisioning an Azure SQL Database instance to host the SSISDB database and SSIS Catalog

- Provisioning an Azure Data Factory

- Creating and configuring a Deployment Container

- Provisioning an Azure-SSIS Integration Runtime (IR) configured to install the Execute Catalog Package Task's msi file

The next step is to test the Execute Catalog Package Task's installation in the Azure-SSIS nodes.

CHAPTER 25

Test the Task in Azure Data Factory

In the previous chapter, we provisioned an Azure SQL Database, an Azure Data Factory, a storage account and deployment container, and an Azure-SSIS integration runtime. In this chapter, we test Execute Catalog Package Task functionality in Azure Data Factory by

- Deploying TestSSISProject to the SSIS Catalog hosted on the Azure SQL DB provisioned in the previous chapter

- Deploying the ECPTFramework SSIS project

- Lifting and shifting framework metadata to an Azure SQL DB (not SSISDB)

- Deploying the ECPTFramework SSIS project

- Testing

Deploying TestSSISProject

Open a test SSIS project (mine is named "TestSSISProject") in Visual Studio. Open Solution Explorer, right-click the project name, and then click "Deploy," as shown in Figure 25-1:

© Andy Leonard 2021
A. Leonard, *Building Custom Tasks for SQL Server Integration Services*,
https://doi.org/10.1007/978-1-4842-6482-9_25

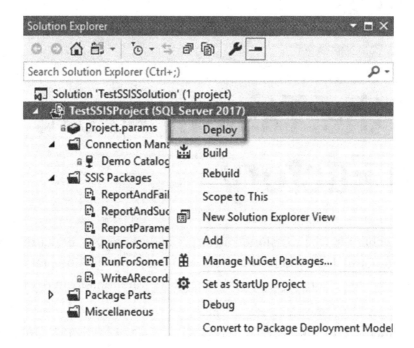

Figure 25-1. *Preparing to deploy TestSSISProject*

When the Integration Services Deployment Wizard displays, click the Next button to proceed, as shown in Figure 25-2:

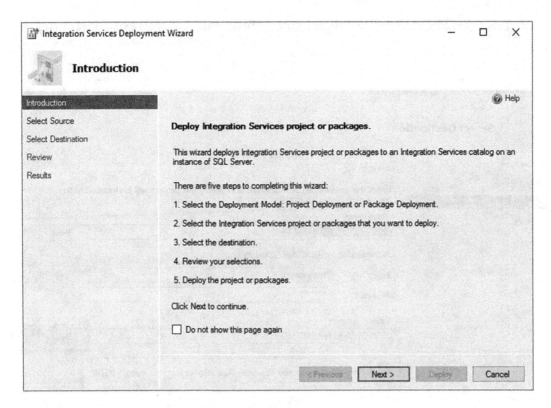

Figure 25-2. *The Integration Services Deployment Wizard*

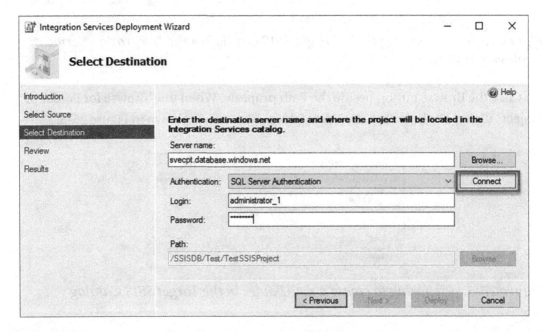

Figure 25-3. *Selecting the Destination in the Integration Services Deployment Wizard*

In this new SSIS Catalog, the folder named "Test" does not (yet) exist, as shown in Figure 25-4:

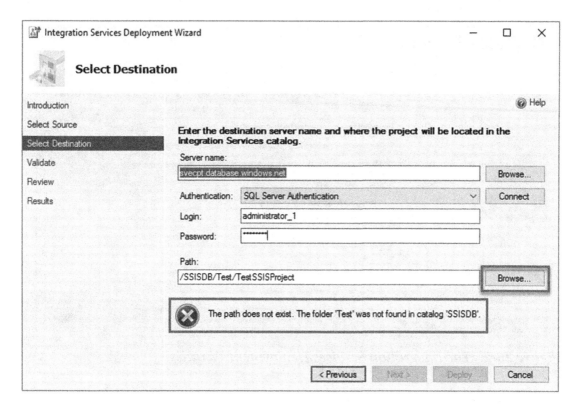

Figure 25-4. *Connecting to the Target SSIS Catalog in the Integration Services Deployment Wizard*

Click the Browse button beside the Path property. When the "Browse for Folder or Project" dialog displays, click the "New folder..." button, as shown in Figure 25-5:

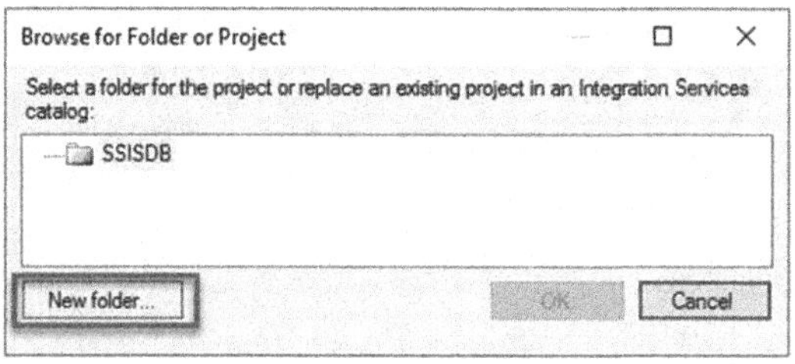

Figure 25-5. *Preparing to create a new Folder in the Target SSIS Catalog*

When the "Create New Folder" dialog displays, enter "Test" as the name of the new folder, and then click the Ok button to close the "Create New Folder" dialog, as shown in Figure 25-6:

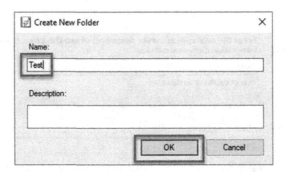

Figure 25-6. *Creating a new Folder in the Target SSIS Catalog*

Click the OK button to close the "Create New Folder" dialog, as shown in Figure 25-7:

Figure 25-7. *Selecting the new Folder in the Target SSIS Catalog*

Click the OK button to close the "Browse for Folder or Project" dialog, as shown in Figure 25-8:

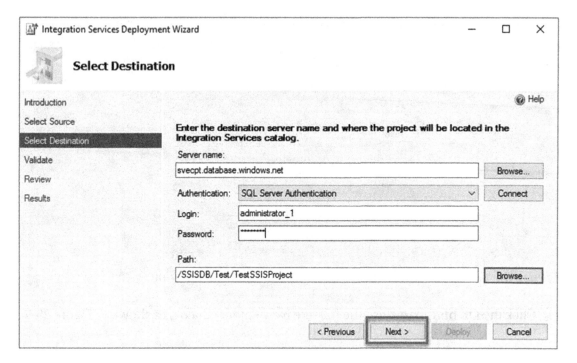

Figure 25-8. *Integration Services Deployment Wizard Destination, configured*

Click the Next button to open the Validate page, which tests connection manager connection strings for local configurations, as shown in Figure 25-9:

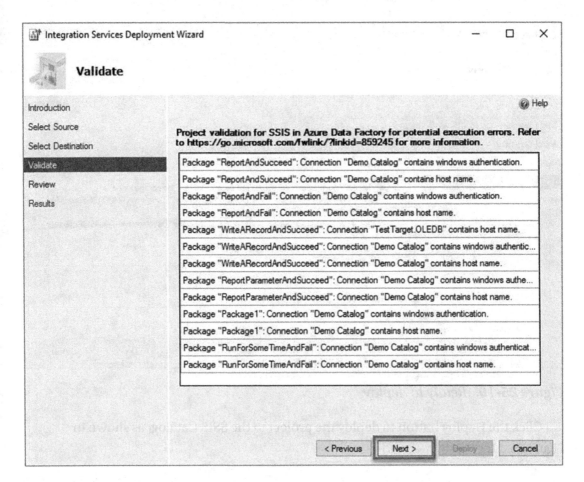

Figure 25-9. *Validating the Project and Package Connection Managers*

Review settings on the Review page, as shown in Figure 25-10:

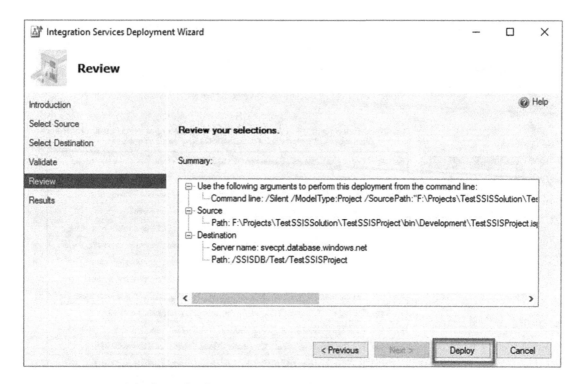

Figure 25-10. Ready to deploy

Click the Deploy button to deploy the project to the SSIS Catalog, as shown in
Figure 25-11:

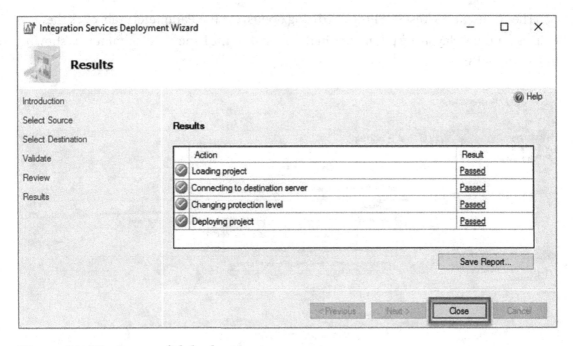

Figure 25-11. *Successful deployment*

The next step is to configure the SSIS Catalog project.

Configuring TestSSISProject

Use SSMS to connect to the Azure SQL database instance that hosts the SSIS Catalog for your Azure-SSIS integration runtime. To open the Configure dialog, right-click TestSSISProject, and then click "Configure," as shown in Figure 25-12:

Figure 25-12. *Opening the TestSSISProject Configure dialog*

The "Configure – TestSSISProject" dialog opens. On the Parameters tab, click the ellipsis for the DelayString parameter in the RunForSomeTime.dtsx container, as shown in Figure 25-13:

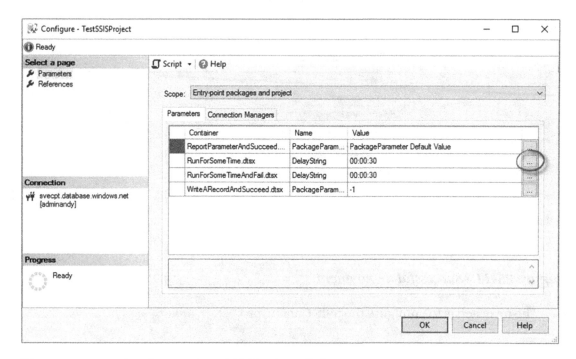

Figure 25-13. *Configure – TestSSISProject dialog*

When the Set Parameter Value for the "[RunForSomeTime.dtsx].[DelayString]" parameter opens, select the "edit value" option and enter "00:00:35" in the corresponding textbox (which adds a Configuration Literal Value), and then click the OK button, as shown in Figure 25-14:

Figure 25-14. *Overriding the DelayString parameter value with a Configuration Literal value*

Configuration Literal values display in **bold** text decoration, as shown in Figure 25-15:

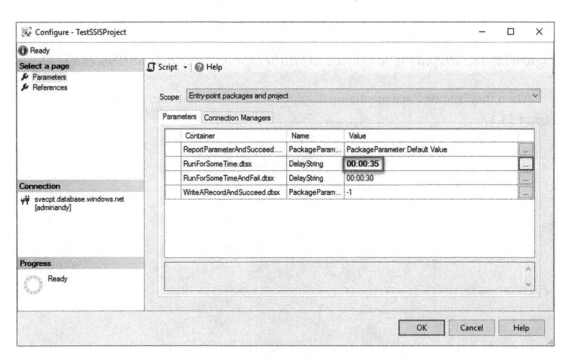

Figure 25-15. *Configuration Literal values display in bold*

Let's test it!

Testing the Configuration

To test the configuration changes, use SQL Server Management Studio (SSMS) to connect to the instance of Azure SQL DB that hosts the SSIS Catalog used by your Azure-SSIS integration runtime. Navigate to the TestSSISProject packages virtual folder, right-click the RunForSomeTime.dtsx SSIS package, and then click "Execute…," as shown in Figure 25-16:

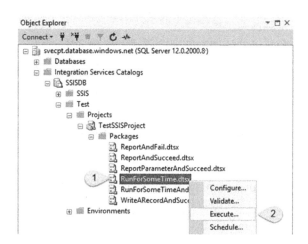

Figure 25-16. *Preparing to execute the RunForSomeTime.dtsx SSIS package*

When the Execute Package dialog displays, click the OK button, as shown in Figure 25-17:

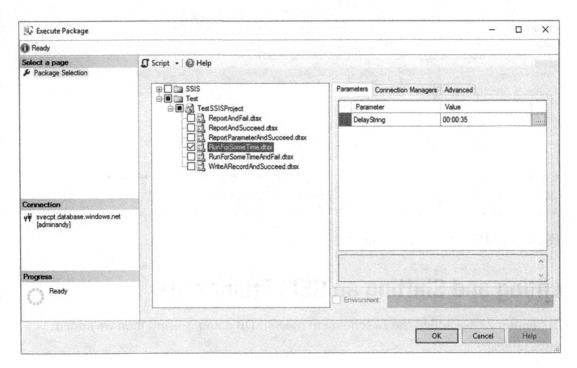

Figure 25-17. *Executing the RunForSomeTime.dtsx SSIS package*

When prompted to display the Execution Report, click the Yes button, as shown in Figure 25-18:

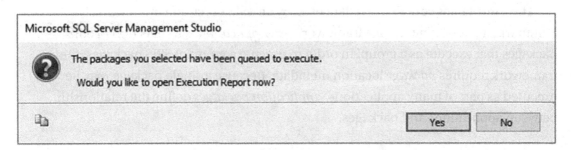

Figure 25-18. *Clicking the Yes button to open the Execution Report*

The SSIS Catalog All Executions report displays and, after some time, reports the RunForSomeTime.dtsx SSIS package completes and succeeds, as shown in Figure 25-19:

Figure 25-19. *Execution success!*

Lifting and Shifting an SSIS Framework

In Chapter 23, we added the fw schema to the SSISDB database, and then we added
three tables:

1. fw.Applications

2. fw.Packages

3. fw.ApplicationPackages

The three tables contain metadata used by an SSIS execution framework.
Summarizing the definition of a framework: An *application* is a collection of SSIS
packages that execute as a group. In order to execute a group of SSIS packages, the
framework requires *package* location metadata. Because a single package may be
executed as part of many applications, *application packages* define the relationship
between applications and packages.

Lifting and Shifting Framework Metadata Tables

When engineers migrate data from on-premises to the cloud, the operation is often
described as *lifting and shifting*. In this section, we lift and shift the framework metadata
artifacts and data using the same T-SQL used in Chapter 23, but with a different database
target. This time, the target is the Azure SQL database named SSISFramework, the
database we provisioned in Chapter 24.

If the following looks like it was copied from Chapter 23, pasted here, and then edited ever so slightly, that's because the following was copied from Chapter 23, pasted here, and then edited ever so slightly.

To begin, open SQL Server Management Studio (SSMS) and connect to the Azure SQL Server instance that hosts the SSIS Catalog database (SSISDB) used by your Azure-SSIS integration runtime. The next few T-SQL scripts are almost identical to the T-SQL scripts in Chapter 23. The difference is: no Use directives. At the time of this writing, Azure SQL DB does not support the Use directive. Work around this limitation by clicking the Working Database dropdown in SSMS and selecting the SSISFramework database, as shown in Figure 25-20:

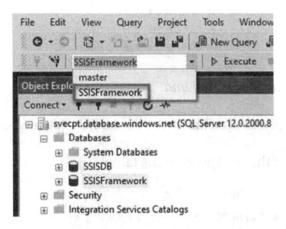

Figure 25-20. *Selecting the SSISFramework working database*

Open a new query window in SSMS. Add a schema named fw to the SSISDB database using the T-SQL in Listing 25-1:

Listing 25-1. Adding the fw schema

```
print 'Fw schema'
If Not Exists(Select s.[name]
                 From [sys].[schemas] s
                 Where s.[name] = N'fw')
 begin
  print ' - Create fw schema'
```

```
  declare @sql varchar(30) = 'Create schema fw'
  exec(@sql)
  print ' - Fw schema created'
 end
Else
 begin
  print ' - Fw schema already exists.'
 end
go
```

When executed (the first time), the Messages tab displays as shown in Figure 25-21:

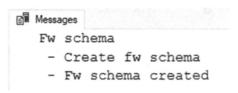

Figure 25-21. *Creating the fw schema*

Next, build the Applications table in the fw schema using the T-SQL in Listing 25-2:

Listing 25-2. Adding the fw.Applications table

```
print 'Fw.Applications table'
If Not Exists(Select s.[name] + '.' + t.[name]
                     From [sys].[tables] t
                     Join [sys].[schemas] s
                       On s.[schema_id] = t.[schema_id]
                     Where s.[name] = N'fw'
                       And t.[name] = N'Applications')
 begin
  print ' - Create fw.Applications table'
  Create Table fw.Applications
  (ApplicationId int identity(1, 1)
    Constraint PK_Applications Primary Key
  ,ApplicationName nvarchar(130) Not NULL)
  print ' - Fw.Applications table created'
 end
```

```
Else
 begin
  print ' - Fw.Applications table already exists.'
 end
go
```

When executed (the first time), the Messages tab displays as shown in Figure 25-22:

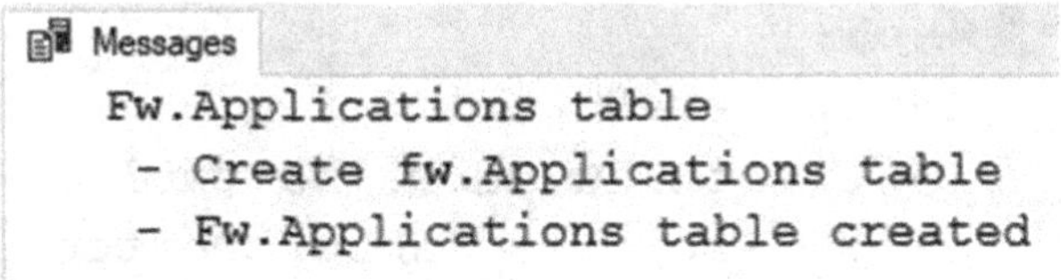

Figure 25-22. *Creating the fw.Applications table*

Add the Packages table using the T-SQL in Listing 25-3:

Listing 25-3. Adding the Packages table

```
print 'Fw.Packages table'
If Not Exists(Select s.[name] + '.' + t.[name]
                     From [sys].[tables] t
                     Join [sys].[schemas] s
                       On s.[schema_id] = t.[schema_id]
                     Where s.[name] = N'fw'
                       And t.[name] = N'Packages')
 begin
  print ' - Create fw.Packages table'
  Create Table fw.Packages
  (PackageId int identity(1, 1)
    Constraint PK_Packages Primary Key
  ,FolderName nvarchar(130) Not NULL
  ,ProjectName nvarchar(130) Not NULL
  ,PackageName nvarchar(260) Not NULL)
  print ' - Fw.Packages table created'
 end
```

```
Else
 begin
  print ' - Fw.Packages table already exists.'
 end
go
```

When executed (the first time), the Messages tab displays as shown in Figure 25-23:

```
Messages
        Fw.Packages table
          - Create fw.Packages table
          - Fw.Packages table created
```

Figure 25-23. *Creating the fw.Packages table*

Resolve the many-to-many cardinality between Applications and Packages by adding the ApplicationPackages table using the T-SQL in Listing 25-4:

Listing 25-4. Adding the ApplicationPackages table

```
print 'Fw.ApplicationPackages table'
If Not Exists(Select s.[name] + '.' + t.[name]
                     From [sys].[tables] t
                     Join [sys].[schemas] s
                       On s.[schema_id] = t.[schema_id]
                     Where s.[name] = N'fw'
                       And t.[name] = N'ApplicationPackages')
 begin
  print ' - Create fw.ApplicationPackages table'
  Create Table fw.ApplicationPackages
  (ApplicationPackageId int identity(1, 1)
    Constraint PK_ApplicationPackages Primary Key
  ,ApplicationId int Not NULL
    Constraint FK_ApplicationPackages_Applications
        Foreign Key References fw.Applications(ApplicationId)
  ,PackageId int Not NULL
    Constraint FK_ApplicationPackages_Packages
        Foreign Key References fw.Packages(PackageId)
```

```
  ,ExecutionOrder int Not NULL
    Constraint DF_ApplicationPackages_ExecutionOrder
        Default(10)
  ,Synchronized bit Not NULL
    Constraint DF_ApplicationPackages_Synchronized
        Default(1)
  ,MaximumRetries int Not NULL
    Constraint DF_ApplicationPackages_MaximumRetries
        Default(100)
  ,RetryIntervalSeconds int Not NULL
    Constraint DF_ApplicationPackages_RetryIntervalSeconds
        Default(10)
  ,Use32bit int Not NULL
    Constraint DF_ApplicationPackages_Use32bit
        Default(0)
  ,LoggingLevel nvarchar(25) Not NULL
    Constraint DF_ApplicationPackages_LoggingLevel
        Default('Basic')
)
  print ' - Fw.ApplicationPackages table created'
 end
Else
 begin
  print ' - Fw.ApplicationPackages table already exists.'
 end
go
```

When executed (the first time), the Messages tab displays as shown in Figure 25-24:

```
Messages
        Fw.ApplicationPackages table
          - Create fw.ApplicationPackages table
          - Fw.ApplicationPackages table created
```

Figure 25-24. *Creating the fw.ApplicationPackages table*

The next step is to add Applications, Packages, and ApplicationPackages metadata to the framework tables.

Lifting and Shifting Framework Metadata

Add Applications metadata using the T-SQL in Listing 25-5:

Listing 25-5. Adding Applications metadata

```
Insert Into fw.Applications
(ApplicationName)
Values('Framework Test')
go

Select * From fw.Applications
go
```

When executed, the T-SQL results appear as shown in Figure 25-25:

Figure 25-25. *Adding an SSIS framework application*

Add Packages metadata using the T-SQL in Listing 25-6:

Listing 25-6. Adding Packages metadata

```
Insert Into fw.Packages
(FolderName, ProjectName, PackageName)
Values
  ('Test', 'TestSSISProject', 'ReportAndSucceed.dtsx')
, ('Test', 'TestSSISProject', 'ReportParameterAndSucceed.dtsx')
, ('Test', 'TestSSISProject', 'RunForSomeTime.dtsx')
go

Select * From  fw.Packages
go
```

When executed, the T-SQL results appear as shown in Figure 25-26:

Results | Messages

	PackageId	FolderName	ProjectName	PackageName
1	1	Test	TestSSISProject	ReportAndSucceed.dtsx
2	2	Test	TestSSISProject	ReportParameterAndSucceed.dtsx
3	3	Test	TestSSISProject	RunForSomeTime.dtsx

Figure 25-26. *Adding SSIS framework packages*

Add ApplicationPackages metadata using the T-SQL in Listing 25-7:

Listing 25-7. Adding ApplicationPackages metadata

```
Insert Into fw.ApplicationPackages
(ApplicationId, PackageId, ExecutionOrder
, Synchronized, MaximumRetries
, RetryIntervalSeconds, Use32bit, LoggingLevel)
Values
  (1, 1, 10, 1, 10, 2, 0, 'Basic')
, (1, 2, 20, 0, 10, 2, 1, 'Performance')
, (1, 3, 30, 1, 30, 2, 1, 'Verbose')
go

Select * From fw.ApplicationPackages
go
```

Be sure the ApplicationId and PackageId values match corresponding values auto-generated by identity values in the fw.Applications and fw.Packages tables, respectively.

When executed, the T-SQL results appear as shown in Figure 25-27:

Results | Messages

	ApplicationPackageId	ApplicationId	PackageId	ExecutionOrder	Synchronized	MaximumRetries	RetryIntervalSeconds	Use32bit	LoggingLevel
1	1	1	1	10	1	10	2	0	Basic
2	2	1	2	20	0	10	2	1	Performance
3	3	1	3	30	1	30	2	1	Verbose

Figure 25-27. *Adding SSIS framework application packages*

The next step is to deploy to Azure-SSIS the ECPTFramework SSIS project that we developed in the previous chapter.

Deploying ECPTFramework SSIS Project

Open the ECPTFramework test SSIS project – the project developed in Chapter 23 – in Visual Studio. Open Solution Explorer, right-click the project name, and then click "Deploy," as shown in Figure 25-28:

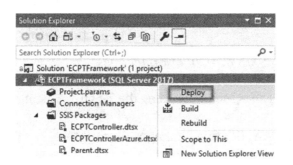

Figure 25-28. *Deploying ECPTFramework*

When the Integration Services Deployment Wizard displays, follow the steps outlined in the "Deploy TestSSISProject" section earlier in this chapter to deploy the "ECPTFramework" SSIS project to the Azure SQL database hosting the SSISDB database you selected when provisioning your Azure-SSIS integration runtime. In this demo, I created a new SSIS Catalog folder named "SSIS" and deployed the "ECPTFramework" SSIS project the SSIS folder.

Configure the ECPTFramework SSIS Project

Once the "ECPTFramework" SSIS project is deployed, open SQL Server Management Studio, and navigate to the "ECPTFramework" SSIS project in the Integration Services Catalogs node. Right-click the "ECPTFramework" SSIS project and then click Configure, as shown in Figure 25-29:

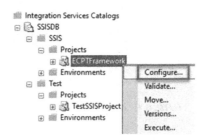

Figure 25-29. *Preparing to configure the ECPTFramework project*

To begin configuring the ECPTFramework, select the Framework SSIS Catalog Connection, and then select the ConnectionString property. Click the ellipsis beside the Value column, as shown in Figure 25-30:

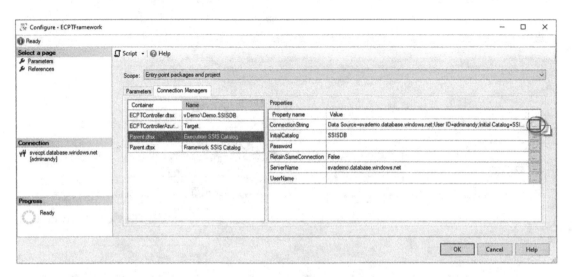

Figure 25-30. *Preparing to configure a literal for the Framework SSIS Catalog ConnectionString property*

The Framework SSIS Catalog connection manager should point to the SQL Server instance – and database – that holds the Framework metadata. Remember, we are making a slight change to this version of the framework; we store metadata in a different database named SSISFramework. The connection string is updated and shown in Figure 25-31:

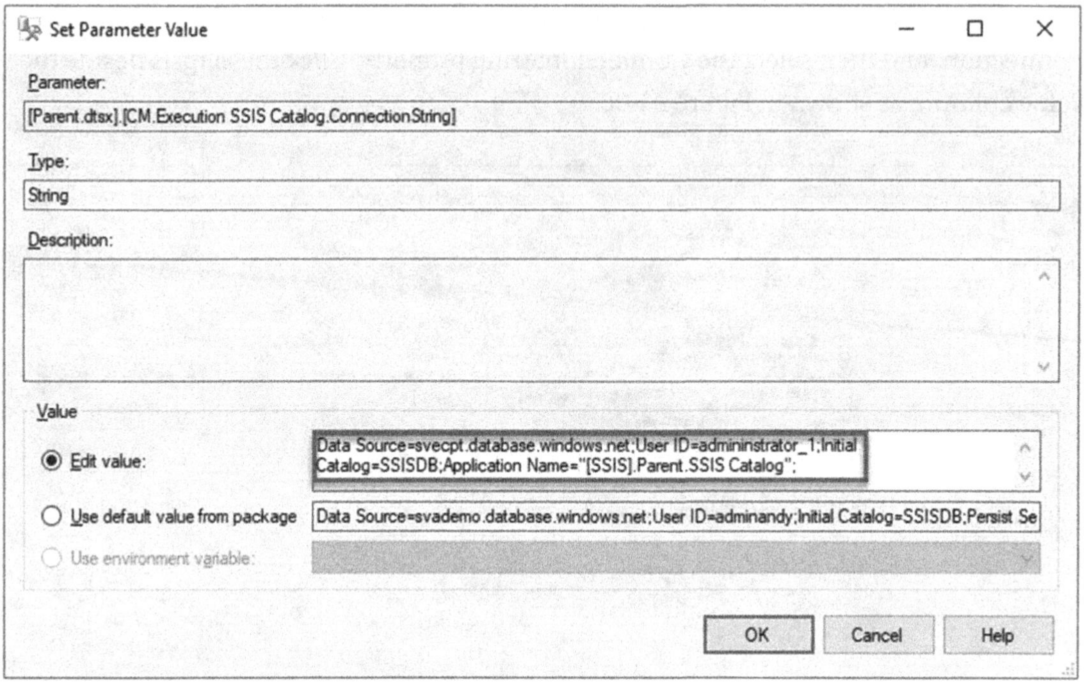

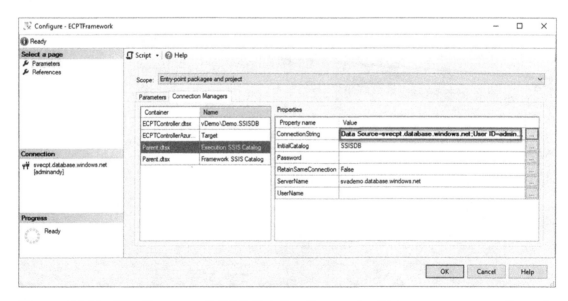

Figure 25-31. *Configuring a literal for the Framework SSIS Catalog ConnectionString property*

When configured, the literal for the Execution SSIS Catalog ConnectionString property appears as shown in Figure 25-32:

Figure 25-32. *The Framework SSIS Catalog ConnectionString property, configured*

Repeat the process for the Framework SSIS Catalog Password property.

When configured, the literal values for the Framework SSIS Catalog ConnectionString and Password properties appear as shown in Figure 25-33:

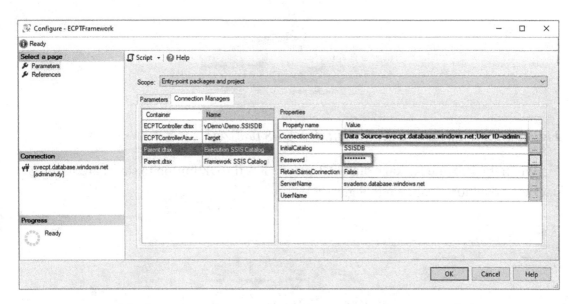

Figure 25-33. *The Framework SSIS Catalog ConnectionString and Password properties, configured*

The Execute SSIS Catalog and Framework SSIS Catalog connection managers have been configured.

The next step is a test execution of the Parent.dtsx SSIS package.

Let's Test It!

In the SQL Server Management Studio's Object Explorer, expand the Integration Services Catalogs node and navigate to the SSIS folder > ECPTFramework project > Parent.dtsx package. Right-click the Parent.dtsx SSIS package and then click "Execute...," as shown in Figure 25-34:

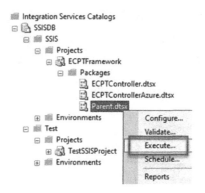

Figure 25-34. *Executing the Parent.dtsx SSIS package*

When the Execute Package dialog displays, click the OK button to start Parent.dtsx package execution, as shown in Figure 25-35:

Figure 25-35. *Starting Parent.dtsx execution*

Open the SSIS Catalog All Executions report to view the resulting executions, as shown in Figure 25-36:

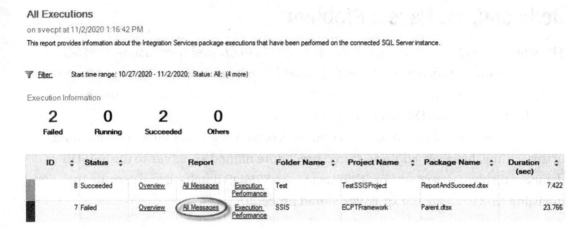

Figure 25-36. *Parent.dtsx fails*

The Parent.dtsx SSIS package fails. The execution of Parent.dtsx results in the execution of the TestSSISProject\ReportAndSucceed.dtsx SSIS package. We need more information to troubleshoot this error. Click on the "All Messages" link in the Parent.dtsx report row to open the Messages report, as shown in Figure 25-37:

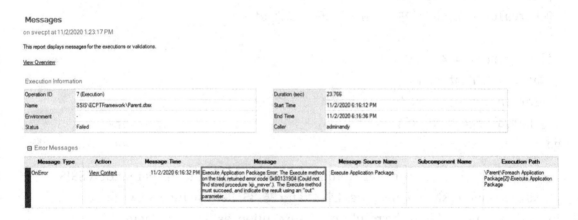

Figure 25-37. *Viewing the error message*

The error message reads: "Execute Application Package:Error: The Execute method on the task returned error code 0x80131904 (Could not find stored procedure 'xp_msver'). The Execute method must succeed, and indicate the result using an "out" parameter." [sic]

Redmond, We Have a Problem

The stored procedure named xp_msver is available in on-premises instances of SQL Server. The stored procedure named xp_msver is available in Azure Managed Instances of SQL Server. At the time of this writing, the stored procedure named xp_msver is *not* available in Azure SQL DB instances of SQL Server.

The author engineered a solution that may, or may not, work for you. At the time of this writing, however, adding a stored procedure named xp_msver to the SSISDB database resolves this condition. Connect to the SSISDB database and execute the code in Listing 25-8 to create the xp_msver stored procedure:

Listing 25-8. Add the xp_msver stored procedure to the SSISDB database

```
Create or Alter Procedure xp_msver
 @arg sql_variant = N'Platform'
,@index int = 4 output
,@name nvarchar(25) = N'Platform' output
,@internalvalue int = NULL output
,@charvalue nvarchar(25) = N'NT x64' output
As
Select @index = 4
, @name = N'Platform'
, @internalvalue = NULL
, @charvalue = N'NT x64'
go
```

After deploying the xp_msver stored procedure, re-execute the Parent.dtsx SSIS package as before, shown in Figures 25-34 and 25-35. Refresh the SSIS Catalog All Executions report to view the results of this execution, as shown in Figure 25-38:

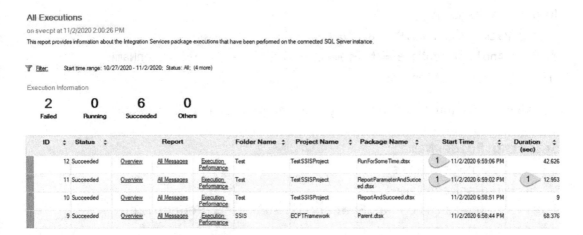

Figure 25-38. *Framework application execution success*

The next step is analysis of our test results.

Analyzing the Results

Comparing the metadata configuration will let us know if the test really succeeded.
The metadata configuration may be gleaned by executing the query in the Parent.dtsx
package's "SQL Get Application Packages" and is shown – slightly modified to supply the
ApplicationName parameter value – in Listing 25-9:

Listing 25-9. SSISFramework metadata

```
Select p.FolderName
    , p.ProjectName
    , p.PackageName
        , Convert(bit, ap.Synchronized) As Synchronized
        , ap.MaximumRetries
        , ap.RetryIntervalSeconds
        , Convert(bit, ap.Use32bit) As Use32bit
        , ap.LoggingLevel
From fw.ApplicationPackages ap
Join fw.Applications a
  On a.ApplicationId = ap.ApplicationId
```

```
Join fw.Packages p
  On p.PackageId = ap.PackageId
Where a.ApplicationName = N'Framework Test' -- @ApplicationName
Order By ap.ExecutionOrder
```

When pasted into SSMS, the query appears as shown in Figure 25-39:

```
Select p.FolderName
     , p.ProjectName
     , p.PackageName
     , Convert(bit, ap.Synchronized) As Synchronized
     , ap.MaximumRetries
     , ap.RetryIntervalSeconds
     , Convert(bit, ap.Use32bit) As Use32bit
     , ap.LoggingLevel
From fw.ApplicationPackages ap
Join fw.Applications a
  On a.ApplicationId = ap.ApplicationId
Join fw.Packages p
  On p.PackageId = ap.PackageId
Where a.ApplicationName = N'Framework Test' -- @ApplicationName
Order By ap.ExecutionOrder
```

Figure 25-39. *Framework metadata from the SSISFramework database*

When executed, the query results appear as shown in Figure 25-40:

	FolderName	ProjectName	PackageName	Synchronized	MaximumRetries	RetryIntervalSeconds	Use32bit	LoggingLevel
1	Test	TestSSISProject	ReportAndSucceed.dtsx	1	10	2	0	Basic
2	Test	TestSSISProject	ReportParameterAndSucceed.dtsx	0 1	10	2	1	Performance
3	Test	TestSSISProject	RunForSomeTime.dtsx	1 1	30	2	1	Verbose

Figure 25-40. *Metadata query results*

Comparing the items labeled "1" in Figures 25-38 and 25-40, we note the Synchronized is configured to 0 – or false – for the execution of the second SSIS package (ReportParameterAndSucceed.dtsx). Since the first SSIS package – ReportAndSucceed. dtsx – is configured to run synchronously, the second SSIS package and third SSIS package (RunForSomeTime.dtsx) should start as quickly as the Execute Catalog Package Task can start them. And this is what we find in Figure 25-38; RunForSomeTime.dtsx starts 4 seconds after ReportParameterAndSucceed.dtsx begins executing.

You can also see the execution of RunForSomeTime.dtsx did *not* wait for the completion of the execution of ReportParameterAndSucceed.dtsx. ReportParameterAndSucceed.dtsx executed for almost 13 seconds (see the Duration column).

We next turn our analysis to the Use32bit metadata – denoted in the green box in Figure 25-40. The SSIS Catalog reports built into SQL Server Management Studio are awesome. There are additional ways to view the data. Use the T-SQL in Listing 25-10 to view usage of the Use32bit metadata.

Listing 25-10. View Use32bit execution settings

```
Select execution_id
     , folder_name
     , project_name
     , package_name
     , use32bitruntime
From [catalog].executions
Where execution_id >= 10 /* ReportAndSucceed.dtsx execution_id */
Order By execution_id Desc
```

The query results match our metadata configuration precisely, as shown in Figure 25-41:

	execution_id	folder_name	project_name	package_name	use32bitruntime
1	12	Test	TestSSISProject	RunForSomeTime.dtsx	1
2	11	Test	TestSSISProject	ReportParameterAndSucceed.dtsx	1
3	10	Test	TestSSISProject	ReportAndSucceed.dtsx	0

Figure 25-41. *Use32bit metadata in action*

Finally, analyze the application of Logging Level metadata – denoted in the blue box in Figure 25-40. Click on each execution's Overview report to view the Parameters Used tablix. The author edited the image for Figure 25-42 to get some of the Execution Information legible and in the same screenshot as the Parameters Used tablix:

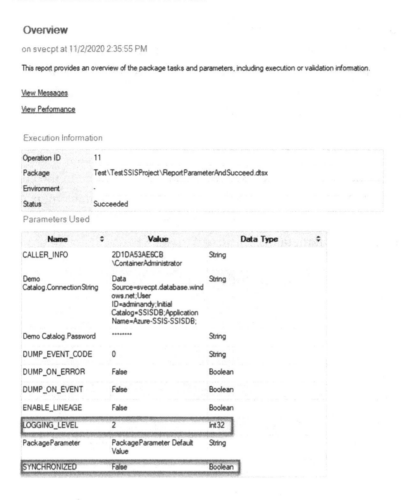

Figure 25-42. *View Parameters Used on the overview report*

Note the LOGGING_LEVEL execution parameter was set to 2 for this execution of the ReportParameterAndSucceed.dtsx SSIS package. SSIS Catalog Logging Levels are an enumeration:

- 0: None
- 1: Basic
- 2: Performance
- 3: Verbose
- 4: RuntimeLineage

SSIS Catalog users may also create custom logging levels, provided they have the proper SSIS Catalog permissions.

Note also that one can view the SYNCHRONIZED execution parameter value for this execution of the ReportParameterAndSucceed.dtsx SSIS package, shown in Figure 25-42. Both execution parameters match the metadata configuration in Figure 25-40.

This analysis, cursory though it may be, reveals our framework is working as designed.

Conclusion

In this chapter, we tested Execute Catalog Package Task functionality in an Azure Data Factory Azure-SSIS integration runtime by

- Deploying TestSSISProject to the SSIS Catalog hosted on the Azure SQL DB provisioned in the previous chapter

- Deploying the ECPTFramework SSIS project

- Lifting and shifting framework metadata to an Azure SQL DB other than SSISDB

- Deploying the ECPTFramework SSIS project

- Testing execution of the SSIS framework's Parent.dtsx package

If all went as planned, we achieved the results recorded in this chapter.

Next, the author examines some lessons learned during the development of the Execute Catalog Package Task.

CHAPTER 26

Notes from My Experience

While learning to build a custom SSIS task, I encountered elementary errors that I believe experienced .Net developers avoid. When I searched for solutions, I found very little help. The reason? I believe the issues I encountered are not typical for developers building solutions targeted at the Global Assembly Cache (GAC). When one begins developing in the controls space, one is expected to *Just Know* certain things about .Net development.

I did not know some of those things.

What problems did I encounter, and what practices did I learn that should be done? The following sections highlight some of my learnings.

Start Visual Studio as an Administrator

You want to be able to build to system folders. To build to system folders, you need to start Visual Studio as an administrator. When you open Visual Studio, right-click the Visual Studio tile, and then click the "Run as administrator" as shown in Figure 26-1:

© Andy Leonard 2021
A. Leonard, *Building Custom Tasks for SQL Server Integration Services*,
https://doi.org/10.1007/978-1-4842-6482-9_26

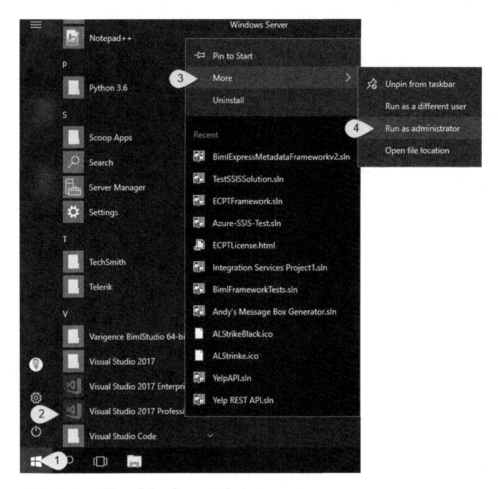

Figure 26-1. *Run Visual Studio as Administrator*

When you click Run Visual Studio as Administrator, you will be prompted to confirm you wish to run Visual Studio as shown in Figure 26-2:

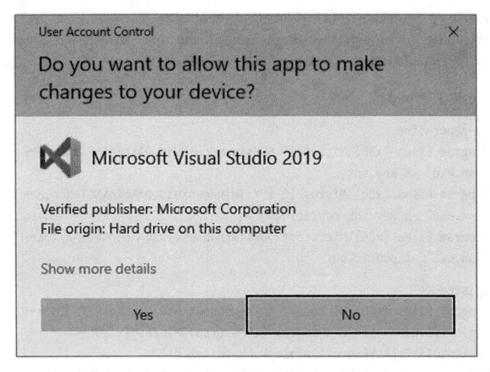

Figure 26-2. *Confirm you really want to run Visual Studio as Administrator*

The reason to run Visual Studio as Administrator is to save the additional step of copying the DLL assemblies from the bin\Debug folder to the ...DTS\Tasks folder. You need the DLLs in the Tasks folder so SQL Server Data Tools can locate (and load) them for SSIS development. You need the DLLs in the GAC so SSIS can utilize them at runtime.

Learn How to Recover

Backups are useless. Recoveries are priceless. Start with a recovery strategy. Ask yourself, "Self, if something tragic happens, how will I get back to Square One?" Answer that question early. You'll be glad you did.

Build a Notes File

You can configure post-build events in Visual Studio Community Edition when building Visual Basic or C# applications. Building a Notes file helped make us familiar with the Tools, though. I'm glad we took this approach. My Notes file holds commands to unregister and register my DLLs in the GAC, along with key-generation commands for building public/private key pairs using the Strong Name utility. As of the end of this project, my Notes file appears as shown in Listing 26-1:

Listing 26-1. Notes

```
-- key generation
"C:\Program Files (x86)\Microsoft SDKs\Windows\v10.0A\bin\NETFX 4.8↪
Tools\sn.exe" -k key.snk
"C:\Program Files (x86)\Microsoft SDKs\Windows\v10.0A\bin\NETFX 4.8↪
Tools\sn.exe" -p key.snk public.out
"C:\Program Files (x86)\Microsoft SDKs\Windows\v10.0A\bin\NETFX 4.8↪
Tools\sn.exe" -t public.out

-- register
"C:\Program Files (x86)\Microsoft SDKs\Windows\v10.0A\bin\NETFX 4.8↪
Tools\gacutil.exe" -if "E:\Program Files (x86)\Microsoft SQL↪
Server\150\DTS\Tasks\ExecuteCatalogPackageTask.dll"
"C:\Program Files (x86)\Microsoft SDKs\Windows\v10.0A\bin\NETFX 4.8↪
Tools\gacutil.exe" -if "E:\Program Files (x86)\Microsoft SQL↪
Server\150\DTS\Tasks\ExecuteCatalogPackageTaskUI.dll"
-- unregister
"C:\Program Files (x86)\Microsoft SDKs\Windows\v10.0A\bin\NETFX 4.8↪
Tools\gacutil.exe" -u ExecuteCatalogPackageTask
"C:\Program Files (x86)\Microsoft SDKs\Windows\v10.0A\bin\NETFX 4.8↪
Tools\gacutil.exe" -u ExecuteCatalogPackageTaskUI
```

Cleaning the Solution

Cleaning the solution is the other step in my four-step recovery process outlined in the following synopsis. When something goes wrong

1. Unregister the assemblies from the GAC.

2. Clean the solution.

3. Correct the issue in the code and Build the solution.

4. Register the assemblies in the GAC.

We configure the Build properties of our assemblies to output our DLLs to the DTS\ Tasks system folder. We configured build events in our project properties to manage unregistering and registering our build output files in the GAC. We were able to accomplish all this because we chose C# and not Visual Basic for our development language.

Change the Icon File's Build Action Property

This particular issue stumped me for ____ (I am embarrassed to say how long, but it was *too* long). You will want to change your icon file's Build Action property to be Embedded Resource. Only after this update will your task icon display the SSIS Toolbox.

By default, the file's Build Action property will be Content. Change it to Embedded Resource as shown in Figure 26-3:

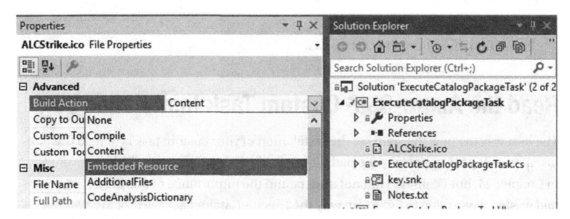

Figure 26-3. *Changing the icon file Build Action*

This is important. If you do not change the Build Action property of the icon file from Content to Embedded Resource, the icon will *not* show up on your task.

Engineering a Solution for the PackageInfo.Execute Timeout

I was nearing the end of ExecuteCatalogPackageTask development when I encountered a "feature" of the Microsoft.SqlServer.Management.IntegrationServices. PackageInfo's Execute method: It times out at 30 seconds. At the time of this writing, I remain uncertain why the timeout exists. I suspect there may be a very good reason, of which (again) I am simply unaware.

A chapter in this book is dedicated to working around the timeout logic using the threading functionality developed to build threadsafe multi-threading applications.

Engineering a Solution for the Missing xp_msver in Azure SQL DB

I was building the last demo of the last coding chapter for ExecuteCatalogPackageTask development when I discovered

1. xp_msver is missing from Azure SQL DB.

2. xp_msver is called by the `Microsoft.SqlServer.Management.IntegrationServices.PackageInfo`'s `Execute` method after the package execution completes.

Please find the solution in Chapter 25.

Read the Azure-SSIS Custom Task Installation Log

The best way to know the status of the installation of your custom task is to read the installation log file, especially the path you provide the main.cmd file. This is covered in Chapter 24, but I confess I did not understand the importance of this file until I had wasted days trying to figure out why the ExecuteCatalogPackageTask msi was not properly installing.

The line you want to read is near the bottom. It's a long line and you want the last sentence to read, "Installation success or error status: 0."

Learn more in Chapter 24.

There Are Bugs in the Code

Every effort was made to ensure all the bugs were found and addressed, and these efforts were mostly successful. Please send bug reports to andy.leonard@entdna.com.

Azure Will Change

During the writing of this book, Azure-SSIS changed, and some of those changes impacted the Execute Catalog Package Task code.

Azure-SSIS will continue to change.

Some of those changes will impact the efficacy of the code in this book. From years of personal experience, I can assure you Azure will never change back. Instead, *you* will have to change any code you write that runs against Azure.

Obtain Source Code

The source code for this book may be obtained at Apress.com by following the link from the book's catalog page on that sight. You may also find the example code at my GitHub site at github.com/aleonard763/ExecuteCatalogPackageTask.

Final Thoughts

As discussed at the outset of this book, I am not a C# developer. I am certain many readers who made it this far in the book have taken a look at the code and thought, "There's a better way to write that." I did not set out to inspire cringes. I set out to share one way to build a custom SSIS task using C#, and my target audience was SSIS developers.

I welcome feedback and suggestions. You may reach me at andy.leonard@EntDNA.com.

Index

A

ADONetConnections TypeConverter
  class documentation, 221
  getADONetConnections, 225, 226
  overridable methods, 222
  SettingsView.cs file, 222
  source code, 223, 224
  SourceConnection property, 227, 228
  StringConverter class, 222
  testing project, 228, 229
  TypeConverter methods, 223
Assembly project, 15
  references
    file system, 23
    folder creation, 23
    manager window, 22
    solution explorer, 20, 21
    virtual folder, 21
  Visual Studio
    administrator, 15
    configuring and naming project, 18
    ExecuteCatalogPackageTask, 19
    local repo, 19
    project type, 17
    references, 20
    startup screen displays, 17
    user account control, 16
Azure Data Factory (ADF)
  author and monitor overview page, 606
  configuration, 602

deployment, 605
ExecuteCatalogPackageTaskInstall.log
    file, 634
git configuration tab, 603
installation folder, 633, 634
integration runtime
  button creation, 632
  configuration, 623
  main.cmd.log folder, 633
  management page, 619
  properties, 625
  selection, 622
  shared access
    signature, 626–632
  SQL Server license, 624
  SSIS catalog creation, 624
  view option, 621
overview blade, 601
overview file, 606
resource option, 600
reviewing option, 604
selection, 601
Azure SQL Database (Azure SQL DB)
  configuration, 596, 597
  database creation, 597, 598
  resources, 593
  review option, 599
  rgECPT resource, 594
  server blade display, 595
  SSISFramework database, 595

© Andy Leonard 2021
A. Leonard, *Building Custom Tasks for SQL Server Integration Services*,
https://doi.org/10.1007/978-1-4842-6482-9

B

X, Y, Z

Printed in the United States
by Baker & Taylor Publisher Services